String Of Beginnings

String Of Beginnings

Intermittent Memoirs
1924 ~ 1954

Michael Hamburger

SKOOB BOOKS PUBLISHING
LONDON

First published in 1973 by Carcanet Press Ltd.

Sections of this book were originally published in *Herbert Read: A Memorial Symposium* (ed. Robin Skelton) Methuen 1969; *Vernon Watkins 1906-1967* (ed. Leslie Norris) Faber 1973.

Published by
SKOOB BOOKS PUBLISHING LTD.
11a–15 Sicilian Avenue
Southampton Row
Holborn
London WC1A 2QH

ISBN 1 871438 66 7 Paperback

Typeset by Shades & Characters Ltd.
Printed by Hillman Printers (Frome) Ltd.

String of beginnings, a lifetime long,
So thin, so strong, it's outlasted the bulk it bound,
Whenever light out of haze lifted
Scarred masonry, marred wood
As a mother her child from the cot,
To strip, to wash, to dress again,
And the cities even were innocent...

Michael Hamburger: *Mornings*

One

On August 1st 1914, before leaving Berlin for the Eastern front, my father wrote a letter to his parents, brothers and sister, intended as a testament in case of his death in action. After apologizing for early laziness at school and occasional 'impetuosity, unfairness and lack of understanding, all-too-human outbursts of emotion' in later years, he continued: 'To take leave of life is not hard for me, only the separation from you, and the thought of no longer being able to help and please you. My disposition, deep down, was too inward, too much fixed on certain relations to the natural and beautiful, to derive pleasure from what is usually called life. My character is too primitive and pure not to have suffered by the compromises it imposes. I made such great demands on myself that I could never be satisfied; and so I was rarely happy. I always felt a peculiar urge towards the natural, the pure and the noble, and my aim was to work for the improvement and true cultivation of the human race. This gave rise to inner conflicts that did not allow me to be quite happy. If I can write about this without self-consciousness and with frankness, it is because this conception of life existed in me quite independently of my physical being, involuntarily, and ruled me completely, so that I could observe this mainspring of my life quite impartially, as though in an experiment.' He asked them to apply themselves to an enlightenment that would make 'later generations exempt from the barbarism of war', and went on to express hopes or wishes for the future of his brothers and sister individually. He begged his brother Freddy 'to steel his will and learn to work in a more purposeful and fruitful way'. His sister Katy, when she was older and wiser, would 'remember our family tradition' and act accordingly. As for his twin brothers Ernest and Paul, he thought that they were on the right path and would go on to even better things.

At the age of not quite thirty, and in his father's lifetime, my father felt morally responsible for the conduct and welfare of his family; but his wishes were not to be fulfilled. Ten years later, his brother Alfred was still an inveterate bohemian never capable for long of earning his living and partly dependent on my father's charity, as he remained until my father could no longer subsidize him, so that he gave up being a violinist, painter and generally 'artistic' drifter and settled for a mere craft at which he was more than competent, bookbinding. His sister Kate had been married and divorced, as she was to be a second time, without ever becoming a mother of that happier and better generation to which the testament looks forward. Worst of all, his father was bankrupt and heart-broken because the promising twins had run off to America with funds held in trust for their father's clients. A major scandal and legal prosecution were avoided only with the help of my other grandfather, but my father's father never recovered from the blow to his honour and affections, fell into a brooding melancholia and died soon after.

He had been born in Upper Silesia, where his father was a schoolteacher in the small town Myslowitz. In early life he had been a journalist, a correspondent in Paris, then in Poland, for German literary reviews. Though Myslowitz was part of Prussia, the Polish connection was close, and it was in Poland that my grandfather Leopold met and married his wife, Antonina, and that my father was born. Since all my grandfather's effects were lost when she was transported to an extermination camp from her flat in Berlin, most probably dying in her native country, the only record I have of my grandfather's literary career are notes to him from Emile Zola and Alphonse Daudet and a long letter from the German novelist Friedrich Spielhagen, kept by my father. From these it appears that my grandfather was trying to introduce French Naturalism to German readers about a decade before it established itself in Germany as a literary movement. In notes dated 1878 and 1880, Daudet apologized for being unable to write the requested study of Zola but offered three 'portraits contemporains' instead, one of them on Rochefort, and asked my grandfather to translate them 'without changing anything'. Zola's undated note asked him to call at the office of the periodical *Voltaire* to collect a copy of an article on Victor Hugo. It is to the editors of Zola's letters that I owe a little more information about my grandfather's brief literary career: they discovered that between 1878 and 1886 he published articles on French writers and their works, sometimes under the pseudonym or anagram L. Burghammer. I assume that it was in 1886, shortly after my father's birth, that my grandfather settled in Berlin and was forced to go into business as a merchant banker, with little inclination or success even before the disaster.

My father, too, was drawn to the arts and would have liked best to be a musician, but he studied medicine at Rostock and Berlin. Together with his Polish cousin Casimir Funk — the inventor of the word 'vitamin' and an eminent scientist at one time — he did research on the dietary causes of rickets. I know this because, as a child, I came across the manuscript of their paper on the subject, which included photographs of dogs whose rickety legs made them look like dachshunds, though they were not, but had been reduced to that state by dietary experiments. The shock of seeing those photographs made them unforgettable. After his war service in the German medical corps, my father worked in Berlin as a paediatrician, both in private practice and at the Charité, where he was a consultant and teacher. It was there, in 1919, that he met my mother, who was a ward sister. She had taken up nursing during the war as a volunteer and found the work more satisfying than the pastimes of her pre-war years: the tennis club for which she played in tournaments, winning several trophies, her accomplished piano playing and the social round of parties and excursions. Unlike my father's family, hers was well-off, if not rich. Her father, Bertrand Hamburg, also a merchant banker, had moved from Mainz to Frankfurt, where my mother was born, then settled in Berlin. This grandfather's forenames, Louis Bertrand, must go back to the francophilia among German Jews since the Napoleonic era, because it was to the *Code Napoléon* that they owed their emancipation from the ghetto. For related reasons, perhaps to do with the Dreyfus affair, this grandfather, too, was a reader of Zola's novels, several of which, in their crumbling paper bindings or rebound, were among the few possessions he kept by him when he emigrated to England in his old age. My mother's mother, Regina (née Münzesheimer) was born in the village of Rohrbach near Sinsheim in Baden-Württemberg. My mother first saw my father standing by a window at the hospital with a newborn baby laid across one outstretched hand — a procedure peculiar to him that must have impressed her, since she recalled it half a century later. When she married my father, after a brief engagement, she gave up hospital work.

My father's cello had to be put aside for decades, until his last years in London, when we had chamber music sessions in our house; but he could also extemporize on the piano or harmonium — as I did after him and my son did after me — at any odd moment snatched from his professional life. I remember seeing him do so with tears in his eyes when he had heard of the death of a close friend, and slipping out as quickly and quietly as I could after that intrusion. The disposition of which he wrote in the testament made it difficult for him to relax. Even when he was on holiday from Berlin, in Scandinavia, Switzerland or Austria, he would treat any case that came his way, and I recall various peasant artefacts given to him by the grateful parents of such patients. On one occasion someone from a circus came to see him in Berlin with a sick chimpanzee, and this chimpanzee, too, was accepted as a patient, though the animal died. On another occasion he was summoned to a Junker estate in Pomerania and asked to treat not only the son and heir of the family but the pigs — whether only the piglets and sucklings, because he was a paediatrician, I am not sure. A difficult case would worry and upset him to a degree hardly conceivable now that medicine tends to be practised rather like a motor mechanic's skill. Most of the families of my father's patients became personal friends, and so did many of the young doctors who were his students at the hospital, including several from Japan, who would turn up at our flat with gifts that could be woodcuts or exotic sweetmeats which we children found more interesting than palatable. There was no end to my father's professional involvements. Though he had been a good oarsman, horseman and swimmer — twice winning medals for saving people from drowning — he had no time to keep up any sport. Even when he had become a professor and his practice was flourishing — before our emigration — money pressures were often acute, with four children and a widowed mother to support, not to mention his brother Alfred, or other beneficiaries of whom we had no knowledge. Up to his early death my father remained hard on himself, while growing less hard on those who did not or could not live up to his expectations of them. Yet the effects his purism had had on some of those closest to him could not be undone — and he knew it before the end.

A life doesn't begin with birth, and I have sketched in a few antecedents, mainly on my father's side, because I inherited not only my father's pocket watch, which kept me more than punctual for some thirty years after his death, but his intransigent super-ego. About this part of my inheritance I can be sure, knowing it by the damage it has done. What is more, when I came to look at some of my father's letters and manuscripts, and used a magnifying glass because his script was so minute, I suddenly noticed that, magnified, his handwriting was almost indistinguishable from mine. Having dabbled in graphology at times, I could no longer doubt that essentially I was very much a chip off the old block, for all the differences between our outward lives and occupations. If nature and beauty — in my father's Schillerian and idealistic German they are one and the same, 'das Natürlich-Schöne' — have more to do with Groddeck's 'It' than with the humanitarian ideals to which my father wanted to couple them, that contradiction, too, is significant. In art and science perhaps, his kind of super-ego can be harnessed to the unknowable ends of the It. In social life it cannot, since the society in which my grandfather, father or I functioned or failed to function demands those compromises which the super-ego refuses, preferring death to compromise. A super-ego that is socially conditioned makes for conformism, renouncing its 'purity' and 'primitiveness', its commitment to the It. This was my father's dilemma, and it came to be mine. Most probably it was my paternal grandfather's too, judging by what seems to have been his total renunciation of literature in later life; but I have been unable to discover more about him than the few bare facts I have recorded.

All the same, I was born; and what is more, with alacrity — so I am told — in the small hours, at the crack of spring, and impatient for it. Impatience, Kafka said, is the primal sin. I was guilty of it, in early years at least. It was the month of the year when Kafka left Berlin to die. It was the day, March 22nd, of Goethe's death and his cry for more light. The year, 1924, was one of relative stabilization after the failure of a Hitler-Ludendorff 'putsch' and the success of Schacht's measures against an inflation so extreme that it had turned most Germans into undernourished millionaires.

The place was Berlin, Charlottenburg, Lietzenburgerstrasse 8A, not far from the Kurfürstendamm, to which the street runs parallel. The block of flats, astonishingly enough, is still there, after the bombing, like all the buildings connected with my family in early childhood years. Kafka's few publications were not among the books in the heavy glass-fronted mahogany cases, which also outlasted all the upheavals, removals and disasters. Goethe's copious works were there, leather-bound and uniform, with duplications and supplements in other shapes and sizes, cheap Reclam paperbacks dating from my father's youth — though his favourite German poet was Schiller — *de luxe* editions from my mother's library, volumes of letters, biographies, even scholarly yearbooks of the Goethe Society, to which my mother had subscribed for a time. Not that I suffer from total recall where books are concerned, or started to read the moment I was born; but most of those books, including the eighteenth century edition of Klopstock's works 'borrowed' by my mother in girl-hood from a grandmother she disliked, were reassembled in London, in the same glass-covered cases. Not the old Bechstein grand, though, which was left behind like the gilt rococo chairs in the best room and the austere Biedermeier portraits of great-grandparents on my mother's side.

Of the three or four reception rooms in our gloomy, but fairly spacious flat, the one I liked best was the one used as a waiting-room for my father's patients, because it contained a tank of tropical fish — one of the earliest points of convergence between my father's interests and mine. More than a decade later he and I would meet in South Molton Street, when I had finished school and he had finished work at his Upper Wimpole Street consulting room, to choose tropical fish at a shop there and take them home. I can still see and smell the two little tubular tins of fish-food that provided a varied diet for those first ones. Somewhere, I think in the dining room, there was a canary, too, in a cage covered at night with an embroidered cloth.

A dark passage led to our bedroom and nursery, perhaps also to the kitchen and servants' room shared by the cook and the housemaid, just as the four of us had to share a room. From time to time we would creep along that passage at night when our parents were entertaining, to catch a whiff or snatch of the incredible freedoms of the adult world, at the risk of being intercepted. Once or twice the cook would connive by giving us a taste of the splendid fare she had prepared for such feasts — grave offence though that was against the discipline imposed on us by our East Prussian governess. Our diet was more strictly regulated than that of the fish, with daily doses of molasses and cod liver oil. Coffee and tea were forbidden. Instead we drank an innocuous substitute called 'malt coffee'. Theatre and cinema were forbidden. Instead we were taken to the planetarium, which was educational and so utterly tedious to me at the time that it left me with a life-long indifference to stars and astronomy.

When decades — ages — later I revisited that block of flats amid the ruins of Berlin, with its marble and stucco that had grown more pathetic than pretentious in the meantime, I thought I recognised the very spot where my perambulator had been parked in the entrance hall. It transmitted wave after wave of tedium, greyness, frustration —

the wages of the sin of impatience, of boyish impulses systematically suppressed and repressed. Of Berlin itself memory has made a perpetual winter. It can't be only that part of the first summers were spent in Mecklenburg and Pomerania, most of them at a seaside resort on the Baltic, Heringsdorf, the later ones by the river Havel, at my maternal grandparents' villa. At one time my family rented a tiny city garden that must have registered spring, summer and autumn, since there was a tree to be climbed. At times we were even taken there by our parents or by my father's mother, whom I adored, because she was childlike and did not care about rules and prohibitions. When she took us out she bought us ice-cream, against the rules, I am sure, and gave us sweets from a small silver box she carried in her handbag, secretly, because she was diabetic and had been forbidden to eat them. For once it was we children who had to promise not to give a grown-up away. In her tiny flat in the Kanststrasse she kept an urn containing the ashes of my grandfather Leopold, and a stuffed French bull-dog, a pet of hers that had been run over, but she seemed to live happily enough with those relics, because she was truly primitive. My father told me that she had reared her five children on the general principle that if they were too ill to get out of bed, they were too ill to eat, and that this had led to miraculous recoveries. We were less fond of her tiny lapdogs, which were spoilt, possessive, and inclined to snap at us if we competed with them. She also kept a bowl of goldfish, one of which was hump-backed, and took them out each day to wash them under the kitchen tap. Like her children, they flourished because or in spite of such treatment. Among the entertainments she offered us in her flat was a crystal set with earphones — a magical toy to us, when our parents kept no wireless of any sort.

Exercise was part of our regimen. There were afternoon walks to one of the three little squares or parks in Charlottenburg or Wilmersdorf where we played, always under the supervision of our governess, though contact with other children could not be wholly avoided. Marbles and hide-and-seek and hoops are some of the games I remember. In winter we learned to skate on the lakes or on the tennis courts converted to ice-rinks in hard frosts — one way of avoiding constant supervision, if only in the shed where skates were screwed on and off and one warmed one's hands against a barrack-room stove. Fresh air was obligatory, too, for our after-lunch siestas on the balcony, where we could be watched through a window and ordered to sleep if we moved, talked or so much as opened our eyes. The sound of traffic and motor horns, like other noises drifting up from the street, was inexhaustibly mysterious to me. I longed to know what it was all about, what the city was for, where everyone was going in such a hurry, and why. No one told us anything about it. We were marched to this place and that, for our health; and we did indoor exercises, too, involving a ladder that was supposed to prevent flat feet.

For educational, hygienic and administrative purposes we were treated as a unit — my two older sisters, myself and my younger brother. Our clothes were made for us by the governess, poor woman, and those I remember — more from photographs than from life — were uniform, except that the girls' frocks were shortened to boys' tunics and their knickers lengthened to boys' mini-shorts. Those were the ceremonial outfit, wholly unfunctional, to be kept as spotless as a soldier's ceremonial dress. If we had rougher clothes, not of embroidered silk, for everyday use before we went to school, these were unfit to be recorded on the early group photographs. As for modifications when we went to school, I recall only the acute shame of having to wear long stockings in winter — winter again! — clipped to a sort of undergarment called combinations. Long trousers were ruled out as the prerogative of men.

We were pampered and deprived. Pampered for the sake of hygiene and decorum, deprived of individual attention, simply because my parents were too busy and had not yet begun to question the conventions that relegated middle-class children to a separate world. Our governess, Maria Baensch, was an upright, efficient, hard-working person who did what she thought it was her duty to do. She was a devout Roman Catholic, and ended her life in an old people's home run by nuns. She never lost her temper with us, never broke down under the strain of her self-denial. If she felt anything about us — and I believe she did, because she kept in touch with my mother for decades after she had left us — felt anything for us or against us as individuals, we never knew it. I remember seeing my mother wince when she uttered some sudden command or reprimand at table; but that was her function, and she performed it with the dedicated austerity of a nun. When, around 1931, she left us for friends of my parents with only one daughter, her successor gave us cause to appreciate her reliability and impartial fairness.

Claustrophobia is what has stuck, making it difficult for me to enjoy any large city, live in a flat, or endure the kind of temperature our central heating provided. (There was a hot water pipe behind the wallpaper of the corner in which I had to stand as a punishment.) Of breaks, treats, remissions I remember little, other than Christmas and birthdays, when the routine was suspended, and at least one illness serious enough to turn me into a person in my own right, fussed over by my mother and father. Eva, the younger of my two sisters and I did have a special place for rougher games which we called the 'romping carpet'. There were children's parties in similar flats with bookcases, antique furniture and grand pianos, the flats of our parents' friends, but our attendance there was also rigorously supervised and timed. Another kind of excursion involved only my mother and myself — perhaps because it belongs to a period when my sisters had started school and my brother was too young. This was shopping, at an outdoor market, one of the large department stores, or in smaller shops to one of which — a hardware shop and laundry — I responded with a loathing close to nausea. To this day I recall its barrels of soft soap and some kind of incomprehensible wooden machine in perpetual motion whose creaking evoked a peculiar horror. All the dreariness of domesticity seemed to be concentrated in that place. Since my grandfather Bertrand would send his Buick limousine for some of these outings, they were also a rare opportunity for relaxed and intimate conversation with my mother. It was in the car that I asked her why my aunt Kate, who was married and beautiful, had no children, and received the puzzling reply that people have children only if they love each other. (I knew far too little about Aunt Kate at the time to do so much as guess what might lie behind that answer. She was one of the family's black sheep — a loose woman, always surrounded by admirers in and out of her marriages; and remained so even in her old age.) Other positive pleasures came from those department stores, like a free drinking fountain of lemonade, and the danger of getting lost in the crowd, as I did at least once.

In Berlin, in the late 'twenties, in a family like mine, any separation of a child from his escorts was feared as an acute danger, one of many that turned our flat into a fortress, hence into a prison. The front door was not only bolted, chained and locked in a variety of ways, but metal-plated on the inside. The criminal underworld whose threat was felt to demand such measures began in the building itself, in the back-building flats on the other side of the bare, forbidding and forbidden courtyard. (In fact it began even nearer home, with skeletons in the family cupboard like our absconded uncles or Aunt Kate's love life, but we had no knowledge of those until much later.) If we heard screams or shrieks through the hygienically open windows at night, they were attributed to the tenants of those unhygienic parts of the building, drunken lesbians, sadistic pimps and the like. These invisible bogies got mixed up in our imaginations with real people we met on our walks, innocuous eccentrics who wanted to talk to us, like the lady we called 'the man-woman', because she was large and gruff and wore a man's hat, or another we called 'die Frau mit dem Wauwau', 'the woman with the woof-woof.' There was no end to the scares about kidnappers, confidence tricksters, thieves, perverts and murderers. A few knick-knacks were stolen from the waiting-room by someone who got in as a patient or parent of patients, and the rings of anxiety spread as far as our nursery. Not that there wasn't plenty of crime in Berlin in those days. When, a few years before we left, my father learned to drive and bought a small Mercedes, the car was stolen or stripped so many times within months that it had to be fitted with an elaborate alarm. I remember hearing it go off.

That, at least, was an event and a thrill for us, unlike the anxiety that made us feel embattled, threatened and walled in, because everything beyond the front door was felt to be dangerous and hostile. Even if it was, it would have been better for us to know more about it, before the really traumatic experiences hit us. Very early on I had seen a runaway cab horse clatter down the street and a man stop it by stepping in front of it with outstretched arms. From the window I had seen a man with a dancing bear on a chain, and heard the music of barrel organs, a sound that affected me strangely when I heard it again some forty years later in the same and utterly different city, on a lecture tour. Because I never went out alone in Berlin — at least before the age of eight or nine, and then only to go to school and back — I have no recollection of the city as such or of any district of it as a whole; and developed no sense of direction or topography, because we were always taken wherever we went. When I came to revisit the city after the war, my explorations had to be guided by something altogether different, altogether less conscious than topography, a sort of somnambulism that led me to one or two rediscoveries of places and landmarks of which I had no conscious memory at all. What I never found again was the second and last school I attended there, wholly erased even from my unconscious memory, probably because it was there that the traumatic blows were struck.

In the country I hardly ever lose my way; and I think the reason is that outside Berlin we were allowed to walk about on our own, so that my sense of direction and habit of observation did develop there, though they still don't function very well in cities. In the late 'sixties I was staying with friends in New Jersey. I went on a long exploratory ramble through fields and woods without paths, in a part of the country completely unknown to me and completely wild, because the small farmers who had cultivated it had been forced to abandon their land by the industrialization and commercialization of agriculture. When I was almost back at the house I noticed that I'd lost my wallet, containing all my money, air tickets and other indispensable documents. I worked out that it was most likely to have dropped from my jacket, which I was carrying, when I jumped over a stream; but miles away, somewhere in the undergrowth lining the length of that woodland stream. Though, as usual, I had paid more attention to details of flora and fauna than to the lie of the land, I not only found the stream again but the exact place of my crossing — and the wallet. In a city I should have panicked and taken a wrong turning, thanks to my childhood in Berlin.

What I recognized on later walks through the city was the landmarks of my dreams and nightmares — the blank, windowless walls of tenant blocks known in Berlin as 'fire-walls'. The heaviness of those late nineteenth century facades with their muscular caryatids and lions' heads — as though a Prussian's house must be his ministry; a heaviness carried over into the interior, too, in my childhood, into the mahogany furniture, like the massive desk I inherited from my father and still use to store documents, though no longer to work at, and reception rooms kept more like museums than as living-rooms. Some of the apartments, like my maternal grandfather's (the address of which, in Bleibtreustrasse, found its way into Joyce's *Ulysses*, because Joyce must have picked up the address from a bizarre newspaper advertisement put out by my grandfather) seemed endless to a child, as awe-inspiring as the suites and passages that we saw in the palace of Sanssouci at Potsdam. Most probably we were never allowed to see the whole of that extensive flat. That made the palace more comprehensible, for one could get an idea of its structure from the outside, from the park, and that made it finite at least, less sealed off from the light of day and the weather.

By drifting with a current deeper than conscious memory I could find some traces of my childhood even among the ruins of Berlin when

I first returned there in 1947, but might not have recognized the building I was born in or the one in which my grandparents lived without the guidance of my surviving relations, two great-uncles who had stayed behind in Germany. Recognition took time, because memory had been overlaid with so much disparate experience and the discontinuity had been so abrupt, that my childhood seemed that of a person who could only be formally identified with the man I had become. It was not till a later visit that I found those little rented gardens, 'Schrebergärten', in one of which I had made the acquaintance of climbable trees; and, well beyond those gardens, a park that had been our playground in the earliest years. On an even later visit memory stabbed me like a knife. I had taken a bus to Grunewald and heard the conductor call out 'Hasensprung'. All at once that name brought back a parapet and a stone hare, the vertigo that had overcome me when I was balancing on the parapet on a walk with my father, and his calling me 'Angsthase', which means a rabbit, chicken or funk. That must have been one of my earliest traumas. The vertigo stayed with me and hit me again on the landing-stage near my grandfather's house on the river Havel, making me drop into the water like a stone. It came back some fifteen years later on an infantry assault course, when we had to walk a narrow plank on the top of high scaffolding with all our equipment on, then cross a gap in the plank, and I knew that I should drop again if I didn't hold on to something; got down on my knees and funked it, with the result that I was sent on a special toughening-up course, scaling chalk cliffs on the Kent coast, doing monkey walks on two wires strung across a river, winning a long distance walking race, swinging on ropes across chasms, but never once having to repeat the one thing I couldn't do when the vertigo threatened, balance without something to grip with my fingers. If my father had taken up psychology earlier than he did, I might well have got over that vertigo very much sooner, as over other irrational fears.

Less than a year before our emigration we moved into a new flat, in Schlüterstrasse, and discarded some of the heaviest lumber. For his consulting and waiting rooms, now transferred to a private clinic, my father went to the opposite extreme, going modern with unstained half-panelling, cork floors, steel tube furniture and a set of miniature tables and chairs for small children, all designed for him by Ernst Freud, son of the psychologist and father of Stephen, Lucian and Clement, who were our friends. It must have been about that time that my father took me with him on a car journey to the estate, somewhere in Brandenburg or Pomerania, of one of the aristocratic, landowning families among his patients — an experience memorable because it was the beginning of a new understanding between my father and me, because it took me out of the city into a way of life quite unknown to me, and because I was given a special family bed, perhaps a canopied four-poster, whose ornate antiquity seemed like something out of a fairy-tale. Only one earlier trip had left a related impression. It was a visit to a country estate in Thuringia where my great-uncle Paul hunted and fished, kept his pointer dogs and showed me a badger in a cage. I also watched a fishing ritual on a lake, involving boats and drag-nets. That caged badger and the hunting trophies on the walls aroused less pity in me at the time then wonderment and associations with the same fairy-tale world of forests and foresters, hunting lodges and huntsmen, a world of pure romance as different as could be from Berlin. It is to an earlier phase of my childhood that I attribute my claustrophobic aversion to large cities, as recurrent in later life as the urge to escape from them into open spaces less confined than gardens or parks; but I should have forgotten those two excursions, as I must have forgotten many others, if they had not made me more aware that there were other ways of living than ours in Berlin.

At about the same time, in the early 'thirties, my father did take up psychology, having learnt that most of his patients' illnesses were their parents' neuroses, though his mentor was not Ernst Freud's father but Alfred Adler, whom I remember meeting once or twice, though I think it was later, in London. Adler's visits, my sister Eva reminds me, failed to initiate a new era of spontaneity and liberation in our household. On the contrary, we had to kiss the old man when he arrived, and no one asked us whether our libido inclined that way. It did not. Perhaps that is why my sister became a Jungian analyst and I never bothered to purloin any of Adler's books, though these were available at home, like a few of Freud's.

My father, meanwhile, had become a professor at the Charité, and he had become eminent enough in his profession to be asked to give a radio talk. I forget the subject, but remember the great occasion of listening to him and hearing his voice through a box — a radiogram — that seemed hardly less magical than my paternal grandmother's ear-phones. At home we still kept no radio, only a portable gramophone that was brought out on my birthdays, when I had the privilege of being awakened by my favourite record, a military march for fifes and drums; but that ceremony, too, and the preference belong to my earliest years, since those military predilections did not outlast my sixth or seventh year. There were other records, mainly of popular classics, before the London years, when I started collecting my own, as well as borrowing my parents'.

At the age of about five I had begun to play the violin, taking lessons from a Dutch teacher. Although I could play 'classical' tunes at an early age, like an arrangement of a song by Beethoven and similar arrangements of songs by Schubert, the violin never suited me as an instrument, probably because it was not self-sufficient unless one was a virtuoso and could play unaccompanied works of Bach. If I had started on a keyboard instrument instead, and learnt to read music for it as I could for the violin, I might have developed as a musician. As it was, I'm not aware of having made any progress on the violin since the earliest years, though I liked my teacher and his wife. Yet music was my first art; and my love for it was not diminished by my dissatisfaction with the violin or my failure to master it. I did make one attempt, in adolescence, to learn the piano; but that was thwarted by my sin of impatience. I could not be bothered with the beginners' exercises set me by the teacher, but wanted to plunge straight into the kind of music I should have liked to play. So it came to nothing, and I continued to strum by ear on pianos, harmoniums, church organs or harpsichords when I had the chance and was moved to do so, without the technique and practice needed to make such playing more than a self-indulgence.

At a time when one either made music at home or went to concerts — and my parents did both — those gramophone records must have served mainly as a treat for us children. For those records I do have total recall, not only because in my early childhood I lived more by ear than by eye, but also because I knew those pieces by heart and developed a special loathing for them in later years. The records included the overtures to 'Der Freischütz' and the 'Cavalleria Rusticana' and — my pet aversion — parts of the 'Nutcracker Suite'. There were also Viennese waltzes like 'The Blue Danube' and these, too, came to be associated for me with a sentimentally escapist bourgeois culture that had blighted my childhood. Fortunately there were also records of satirical pieces in the Berlin dialect by the comedian Paul Graetz — who ended his life in Hollywood exile — and some sort of peculiar cabaret song that was a coarse skit on my father's profession, and relished for that. It began:

> Ich bin der Dr. Eisenbart —
> Wiedewiedewit bum bum —
> Kurier die Leut nach meiner Art —
> Wiedewiedewit bum bum...
>
> (My name is Dr. Eisenbart,
> Wiedewiedewit bum bum
> I cure 'em my way from the start...)

and continued with horrors of quackery that have slipped my mind some sixty years later. No visual impression has remained with me from all those early childhood years with a clarity that would allow me to reproduce it in my account. My early seeing was immediately translated into fantasy or day-dream, and I may have been incapable of taking in the pictures in our flat, just as I was totally incapable of drawing with merely childish competence. Seeing and looking were later acquisitions, developed by my interest in natural phenomena long before I learned to look at pictures.

Recollection of my first reading is also somewhat vague. There will have been the usual fairy tales, mainly Grimm and Andersen, though there were collections of others in my parents' library, reserved for adults, to judge by the state of those books. I am pretty sure that my mother had little or no time to read from them to any of us at bed-time. Like many German wives and mothers of that era, she was wholly dedicated to her husband's domestic and professional needs. Besides administering the household, though with the help of servants, she acted as my father's secretary and typist. A good-night kiss must have been the extent of her attention to us in the evenings, when we were not ill, since more often than not in those Berlin years my parents either went out or entertained guests at home. During the day my mother must have found time to keep up her piano practice and her reading, especially of the new novels that accumulated in the book-cases throughout those years next to the collected editions of German and Scandinavian authors already 'classical' by then, and probably read by her more intensively before her relatively late marriage, in her thirties, and returned to in her long widowhood. We often sensed a frustration and moodiness in her she would never have admitted to feeling, least of all to us in her total devotion to my father. If my parents had any quarrels or any differences of opinion in those years, they were kept from us in the round of duties and conventions that ruled the family life.

Among the earliest books I recall were the cruelly cautionary tales of *Struwwelpeter*, and another German children's classic, only slightly less cruel but more deeply misanthropic, the rhymed tales of Wilhelm Busch, with his equally memorable drawings. Later one of my favourite books was a 'Berlin Fairytale' about a young devil and his grandmother, his excursions into and adventures in a recognizable human world. Then there were the adventure books of Karl May and those of James Fenimore Cooper, both much concerned with American Indians, a book about Arctic exploration by H. H. Houben, and the Dr Doolittle books of Hugh Lofting, devoured by me because they were full of animals, like a book about wolves by Richard and Cherry Kearton. Very soon these were joined or displaced by factual natural history books, like an abridged version for children of the twelve-volume work by Brehm, which my parents owned and I began to refer to at an early age. (I still have those twelve volumes and still find them most useful, though the edition goes back to 1922. If many animal species had not been discovered or studied by then, many more have become extinct or almost so in the meantime, including some I looked up because I knew them in my childhood — like the European tree frog I caught and kept at one time, butterflies like the swallowtail and the Camberwell Beauty or the storks that used to nest on rooftops even around Berlin.)

We heard my father's broadcast at Kladow, the village on the river Havel where my grandparents had had what was called a villa built for themselves, their married son Fritz and the four of us. I failed to notice or to remember that when my parents stayed in Kladow overnight they rented a room nearby; it was my mother who told me so in her old age. The so-called villa, too, was in a functional style, box-like and squat except for a terrace and balconies, quite unlike the fantastic *fin de siècle* follies in Grunewald, with their Gothic, Moorish or Palladian accretions. The flower garden seemed very large to us after the Berlin flat, though — like the house — it had shrunk to insignificance when I saw it after the war, so that I wondered whether some of it had been sold off by a later owner; but my grandfather had also bought a larger plot of land on the other side of the road, with a wooded slope down to the river, on which my father had a little platform carved out for undisturbed work and rest among the pines. On the lower bank, close to the river which was so wide that I thought of it as a lake — and was corrected only after the first version of these memoirs — my grandfather grew vegetables and fruit. On the upper level we kept our rabbits and played our games, running wild, for once, like animals released from a cage.

In the flower garden there was a special shrub to which my grandfather would attach bars of chocolate for us to pick. This did not prevent us from buying more sweets at the village shop, against my grandmother's orders. Though we would run for it if she happened to be coming that way, not even she, a formidable woman, or Fräulein Baensch's successor could now keep us from doing what we pleased most of the time, at least when we were at Kladow. We got up to all sorts of pranks and practical jokes. My brother and I rolled cigarettes out of the withered leaves of my grandfather's tobacco plants and bits of note-paper. (When, later, I started stealing my father's Russian cigarettes, he gave me a cigar that put me off smoking for several years. That must have been when he had taken up psychology.) My brother found a set of black-edged cards announcing the death, at least a decade earlier, of a great-grandmother, and dropped them through the mail slots all over the village. Thinking that my grandmother had died, several villagers called to express their condolences, to be met by the fury of my grandmother, who was very much alive and in the habit of doing early morning physical jerks in the nude at her open bedroom window, to our unfailing delight. Hygiene was one of her fads, women's liberation another. She had married, or been married off, too young, at the age of sixteen, and had revolted against that state of affairs long before we knew her. Though benevolent, her disposition needed to be resisted, as it was by my father, less so by my grandfather, least of all by her son Fritz, who remained emotionally tied to her until her death, and never grew up. Our white cat, which I loved more than some of my closest relatives, was not allowed to enter the house — perhaps because, at an earlier period, my grandfather had lavished too much love on a cat whose fastidious and expensive eating habits had exasperated her, but ostensibly because cats are unhygienic. We used to ask her if she would rescind the rule if we taught the cat to wipe her paws on the mat. Our grandmother took us on long country walks, during which she said her extempore prayers prompted by communion with nature and including poems like Wordsworth's, 'I wandered lonely as a cloud'. At the dinner table she would have fierce political arguments with my father — what about I don't recall, only that she was a supporter of Count Coudenhove-Kalergi's Pan-Europe movement. One of the last things she did before our emigration was to bury a tin box full of feminist or Pan-European literature in the wood behind the garden. If that wood has not been bulldozed, the box may still be there.

For us, liberation came too late, like my father's psychology. Early regimentation and rivalry for parental affection had driven us into conflicts among ourselves, suspended only when we had to close ranks against an adult. In that situation, as a gang, we could be cruel to people who meant well, as we were to a cousin of my mother's, Kurt, who tried to act as a sort of tutor to us when we ceased to attend school shortly before our emigration, or to a woman who tried as vainly to teach us English during our last summer at Kladow. Not only did we laugh at the funny new words and tease the teacher, but on one occasion we filled a whole sack with vegetables stolen from my grandfather's plot and watched her shoulder this burden obediently when she left, not so much because she could do with the vegetables as because she was too diffident and well-mannered to refuse the gift. My grandmother ran into her on the way to the bus and thought the poor woman had stolen the stuff.

This incident elicited one of my earliest literary works, written for my grandmother at Kladow as a sort of penance or — as I now see it — as an exercise in moral duplicity. My grandmother kept it till her death in England, and it came back to me with other papers she had kept. It was called 'English lesson as I should like it to be.' The correct spelling and rather stilted manner suggest the collaboration of my older sister Maria or, more probably, of our last governess Kate Zellentin. 'I think it good if the English lesson proceeds like this: we don't sit down till the teacher has arrived. That way we learn for about an hour. Then we walk through the garden and through the rooms of the house and she explains everything in English. She needn't be so boring. Sometimes, too, she must tell us stories or read to us from an English book. My greatest pleasure is when we go with the teacher to our vegetable garden and she tells us the English name of every sort of cabbage and we secretly fill a whole sack with green stuff for her, which she then has to drag home with difficulty, but then either my grandmother or my uncle catch her and ask her what is in the sack. Then she says: the children took me to the vegetable garden and gave me a lot of vegetables. Then we get the scolding we deserve and the matter is done with.'

When not engaged in such perversities, I had grown so introverted and withdrawn that I would spend whole days and successions of days in daydreams which no outward reality could penetrate. Perhaps even the nasty trick played on the English teacher was a response to forebodings of an imminent upheaval that was not fully explained to us, when those English lessons were a preparation for our departure. I felt closer to animals and plants than to human beings. Walking through the village on my way to the pine and birch woods around Kladow and the solitary rambles I now preferred, I would pass a house guarded by a springer spaniel. Unlike most of the dogs in those parts — I had been bitten by a dachshund I tried to stroke, and my uncle had been savaged by an Alsatian trained to go for the throat — the spaniel was friendly and would join me through a hole in the fence every time I passed. We became so inseparable in the end that the owners realized they had lost their dog and offered to give it to me. I kept hedgehogs, white mice, tortoises, grass snakes, slow-worms, lizards, newts and fishes; even a baby wild rabbit, acquired when it ran into a ferreter's net. In the river I caught crayfish by prodding them with a stick and whipping it out when they clawed it. I caught butterflies, too, and beetles, because they fascinated me and I had begun to collect all sorts of natural history specimens. I caught birds in a trap made of a cigar box with horizontal and vertical sticks, which someone must have made for me, like the aviary in which I caged them until I learned that birds, too, suffer by being confined, and released those that hadn't died. One of our later governesses had tried to teach us handicrafts like carpentry; but too late, again, since we had begun to resist every sort of enforced activity, if only by apathy. When my brother or older sister provoked me in one of my trance-like states, I could fly into uncontrollable rages, attacking them with teeth and claws like an animal at bay.

It was in a daydream that I found myself on the landing-stage and compelled to go down, to undo the whole process of growing up, back to the moment of birth. If the new governess had not heard the splash and dived in to pull me out, I should not have moved a finger to save myself, though I was as unaware of a death-wish as of any other intention or desire.

Ironically enough, it may have been that new, young governess, who had reduced me to that extremity — treated as an accident by my parents, though the fact that I was a keen and strong swimmer must have made them wonder. Fräulein Baensch had been as strict with us as she was with herself. Her successor, a good-looking blonde in her twenties, resented her duties and showed that resentment — at least to me since the unit had broken up by now, and it was me whom she took every opportunity to torment and humiliate. That she once flogged me with a rope — knowing that she could count on my stubborn silence — mattered much less to me than more subtle humiliations, such as forcing me to go naked into some outdoor children's party where nudity was taboo. I think it was she who locked all four of us into a small room, with nothing to occupy us, while she went out with a lover, and there was no one about to hear our mountingly furious shouting and pounding. One of her admirers was our next-door neighbour at Kladow, a Bavarian who called her his 'golden pheasant' and once locked her into his large aviary for a lark. This neighbour was an early Nazi. When Hitler's speeches began to be broadcast he rigged up a loudspeaker in the garden, to make sure we should know which way the wind was blowing.

I knew it up to a point, because back in Berlin, at my second school, some teachers had begun to wear swastika badges. One of them started the day by ordering the Jewish boys to line up in front of the class for interrogation about such matters as their fathers' activities during the First World War. I went home and discovered that I was one of those who should have lined up. If we had been brought up as Jews, as we were not, I should at least have had something to stand up for. I had heard my father's mother speak of going to the 'temple', but that might have been a Greek one for all it meant to us, who had never been inside a synagogue, learnt no Hebrew and grown up in total ignorance of Jewish tradition. No other member of our family had so much as mentioned anything to do with the Jewish faith. Our Catholic governess had taught us some childish prayers connected with no particular creed, and that was all — except for my other grandmother's outdoor devotions.

It is only lately that I have come to guess that her husband Bertrand never forgot Jerusalem, though neither he nor anyone else ever spoke of Zionism in my family and my grandfather kept quiet about his sympathies, as he tended to do about almost everything, having been cowed by my grandmother's militant intellectual superiority. Certainly he was proud of his Jewish antecedents, had a family tree drawn up back to the seventeenth century when his forebears came to Germany from Spain, and kept a history of the Jewish community in Mainz that listed all the families, including his. From this I gathered that my father's and my mother's surnames had once been interchangeable and could also have derived from the city of Homburg in Hessen rather than from Hamburg, the Hanseatic city. Not only the advertisement taken over by James Joyce, but a collection of ancient coins and glassware dug up in Palestine, pointed to his support of the Jewish settlers there. These antiquities had been given to him as an acknowledgement of his benefactions, and someone told me that a street in Palestine had been named after him. Though in later years he bought the monumental two volumes of the English Bible illustrated by Doré, he also kept an edition of 1885 by Zunz of the Old Testament only, the Masoretic text. Because he was so reticent about his interests and allegiances it was not till long after his death that I saw these relics. The things he did show me were in line with the assimilation that had begun much earlier in both his and my father's families. Of the books owned by my great-grandparents on my mother's side I have only the four-volume Klopstock — known as the German Milton — stolen by my mother as a girl, and a Latin Sallust used by my great-grandfather Louis Hamburg in 1840 at the gymnasium in Mainz as a 'studiosus tertiae', inscribed and dated in Latin. On the other side of my family I have only one document, a letter of 1835 with the Royal Prussian seal certifying that the candidate N. Hamburger had passed the examination qualifying him for the 'educational service' ('Lehramt') in the district of Oppeln, Silesia. Unless such authorization was needed for teachers in Jewish institutions, I must assume that my great-grandfather was employed in the State system as a teacher in a secular capacity. It must have been my father, above all, who carried this secularization to the point that determined our upbringing. Yet, if he was an agnostic, he was not indifferent to religion. In his last years he contributed to a Quaker magazine and read a selection from the writings of Kierkegaard, with page references in pencil showing that certain passages were important enough to him to be noted for a book he was working on, but did not live to finish.

Suddenly, though, we were Jews — for that teacher's purposes, and others not yet clear to us. When the order was repeated, I duly lined up, but escaped the worst taunts because I had asked my father about his war record, and was able to report that he had won the Iron Cross for special gallantry while serving in the Medical Corps. What I did not say, and may have learnt of later, is that, patriotically, he had also put all his savings into war bonds that proved worthless after the war. When it came to games, a kind of handball called 'Völkerball', the teacher acting as referee divided us boys into an 'Aryan' and a Jewish team. That would have been acceptable, once the distinction had been driven home to those as unprepared for it as I was, if that master had not run with the 'Aryan' team cheering them on with the sort of expletives I was not to hear again until I did bayonet charges as part of my infantry training. Both of my best friends at that school happened to be non-Jewish; but after the indoctrination, when I was walking home from school with one of them, his older brother forbade him to have anything more to do with me, and finally went for me with a length of wire he had picked up in the street.

Those last memories of school in Berlin — a 'gymnasium', after a private preparatory school — have blotted out all earlier ones, except for some kind of solemn ceremony at the earlier school at which we had all sworn allegiance to the Fatherland — an oath I took seriously at the time, not knowing how soon I should be forced to break it. I remember the name of the first school, but not that of the later one, whose location I also failed to retrace on later visits to Berlin, though it was the one place there to which I had made my own way, unescorted. Nor do I know whether I liked or disliked my school work before that last Berlin year, when the same teacher set us extraordinary pieces of homework involving elaborate geographical charts and drawings that I couldn't begin to do, because I had no idea what they were about. Since that teacher, like others before him, ruled by mockery and intimidation, I was reduced to such despair that I could not go to sleep at night.

My father was beginning to be anxious about my state of mind, after the inexplicable 'accident' that almost drowned me; and when he found me awake and in tears one night, I broke my silence for once and told him what the school was doing to me. I think that soon after that we left school, living at Kladow and receiving (useless) private tuition there. He knew well enough, in any case, what was happening in Germany. One of his friends was a Minister in the Social-Democratic government of Prussia. As soon as the Nazis took over, this friend, Dr. Klepper, was on a black list. To escape arrest — his house had already been raided and ransacked while he and his family were out — the Kleppers went underground in the country and either stayed, or spent much of their time, at my grandparents' house, while preparing to emigrate. We saw a great deal of them and their children that summer of 1933, at Kladow, and we were warned not to mention their name to anyone in the village. That summer, too, my grandfather's chauffeur, Tietz, gave me a badge of the Social-Democratic Party. Though I had only the vaguest notions of politics at the time, I preferred the three arrows of the badge to the swastika, and pinned on the badge. When I returned from one of my walks through the village with that forbidden and provocative emblem I was told in no uncertain terms that I had endangered the whole family. Luckily, there were no repercussions. One Sunday, at lunchtime, two uniformed S.A. men came to the house. The new rulers had decreed a 'one-pot' meal for the day, and a compulsory collection for Party funds of the money saved by it. Since my grandparents had obeyed the order, an inspection of the kitchen revealed no irregularities and the S.A. men went off quietly with the money. Yet this intrusion into a private house was crass enough to serve as a warning of things to come.

I can't be sure of the sequence of events during that last year in Germany. One day I saw my uncle Fritz rush into the house, bellowing, one blood-oozing hand clapped to his face. He had been playing in the garden with the Kleppers' son, who had a toy aeroplane propelled by a catapult, and when my uncle was trying to catch it the sharp point pierced one of his eyes. I knew nothing about Oedipus or my uncle's mother fixation, which drew him to children and children's games, but the pity and terror of that moment has fused with other family scenes of that period, when my father had decided to emigrate well before the larger exodus of 'non-Aryans', and was trying to persuade other members of the family to take the same decision. Because my maternal grandparents had taken it — without telling us, as usual, the loss of my uncle's eye was inseparable in my mind from other calamities and forebodings of dissolution.

My other grandmother was too trusting and naive, as well as too unassuming, to act on my father's warnings. She refused to leave with us; and by the time she was ready to leave, after the visible atrocities, no visa could be obtained for her. My father, who moved to Edinburgh many months before we followed him there, left her what little capital he could raise. Soon after the outbreak of war he received a postcard through the Red Cross informing him that his mother 'had gone on a journey' and he knew that she would not return from it.

The only other two relatives who stayed behind, old people also, survived the persecutions and the war; my great-uncle Paul as an itinerant farm labourer with false identity papers and no ration card, my great-uncle Martin, who had been the managing director of a large steel works and an amateur show-jumper, by an exemption he owed to the connections of his non-Jewish, aristocratic wife. Of their three children, the younger son, Tino, emigrated because he was a Socialist, joined the Foreign Legion and then lived as a jockey and chess-player in Casablanca. Their other son and daughter survived in Germany. When the girl wanted to marry during the war, her mother had to certify that she was the daughter not of her 'non-Aryan' husband but of a pure 'Aryan' lover.

At the age of nine, in that last year, I wrote a piece on 'Life at Kladow', probably also at my grandmother's request, since it was preserved among her papers: 'I get up at 7.30 in the morning. I get dressed and go downstairs. I play till about 9 and then eat my breakfast. After breakfast we have lessons till 12.30. Then we go out and play with our friends. In summer we swim from our landing-stage and lie about in the sun. Often we play cops and robbers on our plot of land. In winter we skate and toboggan. Skating is very fine because on the Havel you can skate all the way to Potsdam. There is a big hill for tobogganing. That's where all the children from Kladow go tobogganing. We always keep pets here, because it's a good place for them. We used to keep rabbits and hedgehogs, and now we keep birds and tortoises and cats. At first we had two kittens, but not for long unfortunately, for they belonged to other people. But soon we shall be getting a new one. In the autumn we go out looking for funguses and wild strawberries. That's great fun. Sometimes we go out on our bicycles or on a walk. Often we build tents and play Red Indians. In Berlin there is a lot of traffic, but at Kladow there isn't.

That's all.'

It was by no means all, only the shell of a normality whose brittleness everyone tried to conceal from us. I have no clear recollection of all the preparations and partings, the dissolution of the various households and all the practical arrangements that must have been made at the time, not even of my father's departure long before ours, though my attachment to my father was a deep one by that time. I do remember seeing my great-uncle Paul weep on his last visit to Kladow. As a bachelor until his late sixties, after our emigration, he was devoted to my mother and much involved with her parents and brother, so much so that he had a flat in Berlin adjoining my grandfather's, before buying a large detached house in Grunewald. When we paid a last visit to my grandparents' large, luxurious and mysterious flat, my grandfather told each of us to choose something among its contents as a keepsake. This something had to be small, so that the elaborate toys that had been brought out for us on earlier visits did not qualify. I chose a pair of tiny enamel dishes or trays ornamented with flowers. The things were duly packed and given to us later, in England. When we chose them, we did not know that the whole household was about to be dissolved, and that anything else in it not wanted by my parents would be sold or left behind. My grandparents were to spend the remainder of their lives in hotels or rented rooms, with no further use for their old furniture or anything but a few residual possessions, like my grandfather's various collections of prints, ancient glassware and coins, and a stamp collection I was to inherit and sell.

At Kladow, that last summer, I was wholly preoccupied with a love affair — the most passionate of a succession of them that had begun when I was three or four. The first, with a little girl called Beatrice, lasted quite a few years, and was renewed whenever our families met. This one was with a girl of about my own age who lived a few houses away from ours. Probably we had met while swimming in the lake. In some secluded place on the crowded slope above my grandfather's vegetable garden we built ourselves a hide-out, spending hours on end in an intense communion we felt to be a marriage. The enforced separation from that girl meant more to me than all the other partings. She stayed behind in Germany and I never heard from her again.

The third of our governesses, Käte Zellentin, came with us when we left in November 1933, though her functions had already become more domestic than educational and disciplinarian. The journey by train and boat to Edinburgh — where my father had already begun to work for his British medical degrees, in a language he was not fluent in and in branches of medicine he had not touched since his first student years — sticks in my mind only as a turmoil of perplexity and distress, brought to a head when, at Dover, H.M. Customs confiscated the pair of budgerigars my grandfather had kept. The male, reared and tamed by my grandfather, had not only talked — German — but spent most of its time out of its cage, perched on my grandfather's spectacles or rolling napkin rings across the dinner table. It had ceased to talk when it was given a mate. To lose those birds, with so many other partings behind us, brought us up against the whole monstrosity of changing countries. Although my uncle was to write countless letters in efforts to get them out of quarantine, we must have felt that this parting was final; and its suddenness gave me an intimation of how little we could take with us into the new life; how few habits, loyalties and affections; how little continuity with what had gone before. That much of this had been far from likeable or congenial to me, did not affect the realization.

And how little of those first nine years and a half has remained with me to be written down here — with a chronicler's, an obituary writer's pedantic regard for facts! As though the subject were some public man whose face and heart could be hidden behind a screen of documents more important than he, like the faces and hearts of those gentlemen in clubs behind their public newspapers! When the chronology is in doubt, the documents are incomplete, and the dragnet of memory has cast up only what a later consciousness can make use of, discretion and squeamishness have passed for use! When my true life did not reside in any or all of those thin data, but wound in and out of them, through them, often away from them. As though a life had a beginning and an end, when even the middle won't keep still, an octopus with tentacles waving in all directions!

The way of imagination would have been to re-create this moment or that, filling it out, making it seem complete, capturing a different kind of truth by a different kind of faking; a different pretence of cohesion, of total acquaintance with characters we can never wholly know, even if they are linked to us by the legal fiction of consistent identity, by the name attached to an infant, a child, a man. To write about oneself is to write about other people, of whom one knows even less than one knows about oneself; or about events, situations, things that cannot be recollected at all, only reconstituted by invention; to bear witness, up to a point; but above all, to search for what one didn't and couldn't know. That, again, is to construct, select, impose an order, process the raw material of life. Neither the chronicler's nor the novelist's way is adequate, because too much of one's life is beyond recall, and the experience that made us what we are lies neither in moments nor in recurrences, but in a fusion of both far too subtle to be retraced.

Every day had its weather, or weathers, every room its gradations of colour and light, every piece of furniture a shape and texture that communicated something to a child. Every person I knew, or only met, aroused sensations as changeable as they were impalpable, never to be repeated or recaptured. Just as in retrospect, Berlin evokes winter for me, our flat more darkness than light, the essence of Kladow — which was freedom to me, release from oppression, the joy of letting my bicycle run at full speed downhill — was recalled not by its cottages, its cobbled streets or the villas and gardens on the outskirts, but by a smell I recognized the moment I breathed it again some twenty years later — a smell mainly of wood, of logs burnt in old kitchen stoves, it could be, or the timber in walls and gates, or the resinous trunks of the pines around the village, or a blend of all these.

And there were other people, nine tenths of each unknown, who left some impression too fragmentary or casual to be admitted in the chronicle — like the old man, a friend of my grandfather's at Kladow, of whom I remember nothing but a mouth full of gold teeth. There was a great-aunt, always kept on the periphery, my maternal grandmother's widowed sister Johanna, on whom we played another nasty trick, stealing her clothes when she was taking a nap after lunch at Kladow. There was a great-uncle on my father's side who occasionally came to lunch in Berlin, putting a great deal of salt into his soup. I liked him, was interested in him, and cannot say more about him than that. And a great-aunt in an old people's home, very old and very poor, whom I was taken to see once, retaining a smell of old age and poverty. There was a tea-party given for us children by my grandparents' cook at Kladow, Fräulein Obe, at which she sang folk songs to a lute or zither — I remember her name and the kind of cake she gave us, but not the region she or her folk songs came from. There were friends of my parents with whom I had more conversation than with some of my close relatives. One of them was Beate Berwin, who had written books on Hölderlin and Kleist and a short novel, emigrated to become a teacher at a Negro college in North Carolina and, having come to identify with them and given away her possessions, retired to a home for poor blacks and died there, forgotten by all but a few ex-students and distant friends. Because I visited her there, her end is real and vivid to me, but those childhood conversations have left no tangible residue.

There were places, in and around Berlin, too rarely or casually seen to be fitted into any pattern of purpose or locality: the palaces and ministries beyond the Brandenburg gate, or the cathedral there or the Town Hall, graceful or monstrously inflated monuments that seemed half-familiar when revisited — like certain buildings in the Zoo, certain paths or intersections in the Tiergarten, certain bridges across the Spree Canal — without being associated with any occasion I could recall. There was the small town of Spandau, where we changed buses on our way to Kladow if we were not travelling there by car, and the houses of friends at Babelsberg and other places around the Havel. Of Babelsberg, never revisited, I remember a garden fence and a dog, an elderly dachshund, photographically outlined details in a surreal vacuum; of Potsdam, only the canine graveyard in the grounds of Sanssouci — much more interesting to me at the time than the architecture or decor of the buildings. If I think I can still see the flute belonging to Frederick the Great — a grisaille oil painting of whom on horseback on a battlefield was among my grandfather's residual possessions — it may be because I connect it with Bach's Musical Offering, a work quite unknown to me then but of special importance to me much later.

Most tantalizing of all are the fragments of landscapes never to be placed, a mound on some Baltic sand dune, a bit of meadow here, a woodland clearing there, and the moment of taking it in. There it is, inside one for a lifetime, and makes no sense; was real once, may still be real somewhere, and can neither be lost nor found.

This chronicler will have no truck with such material here, though he knows it has made him what he is; knows, too, that the most intense, most formative experiences have eluded him because they have no context, no frame of reference in time and place. He leaves such stuff to the poet he has also been — in another country, another language — life not in terms of dates, events, occasions, but of 'sunlight, and how it fell'.

Two

From the moment we arrived in Edinburgh and moved into a small furnished house — stone-fronted, grey and cold — in Greenhill Place, we had to adapt to a way of life altogether new and strange. The struggle for survival began without transition or preparation when we were sent off to school, and two German-speaking boys wandered all over the buildings of what I believe was the largest boys' school in Britain, George Watson's College, and out again, looking for someone who could direct them to the right classrooms. By the time we found a woman teacher with a little German the younger of them was in tears. After too much custody and supervision we were suddenly on our own, at the very moment when we felt most helpless. My mother was preoccupied with the task of running a house in a foreign country, with no cook or housemaid for the first time in her life, with very little money and the same language difficulty that made us feel lost. As for my father, he hardly emerged from his study in that house, sitting from morning to late night over his textbooks and English dictionaries, so as to qualify as soon as possible for medical practice in Britain. His swotting was made harder for him by the cold. That winter he sat huddled over the small coal fire, wrapped in a blanket.

For us, at school, it was like learning to swim by being thrown into deep water; and it worked, in a way. This time I wanted to survive. Because I wanted to survive, my dreaminess and introspection had to be put away — at least for the duration of the struggle, until I could afford them again. Since English words were indispensable not only for school work but for what I needed most, the reassurance of being accepted as a member of the community, the words came with extraordinary speed. On my first day I stared in silent amazement at a curly-haired boy wearing a kilt, thinking that some incomprehensible custom required one girl to be admitted into every class. By the second day I had words enough to be put right about that, and to start making friends. Words, in any case, carried less weight than actions among those nine-year-old boys, and it was by an action that I won total acceptance with a suddenness I felt to be quite undeserved. It was as easy as walking off a plank — the plank being the highest of the diving-boards in the swimming-pool. No one else dared to use it. As I had been swimming since the age of four or five, quite apart from my special aptitude for falling, this feat meant nothing to me. Yet it established my prestige as no amount of fluent English or Scottish could have done, so much so that I was invited to join one of the gangs that prowled around Edinburgh after school, fighting boys from rival institutions like Heriot's and Fette's.

We spent less than a year in Edinburgh; and even though I roamed many different parts of the city with that gang or with individual friends, visiting their houses too, the city of which we had the freedom was still not that of adults, but a playground and battlefield. When I saw Edinburgh again as an adult I recognized nothing but the obvious sights and a tea-shop or two in Princes Street.

Since memory, once more, is defective, I shall translate some extracts from letters I wrote to my grandparents and uncle from Edinburgh. It goes without saying that these dutiful communications reveal only what I thought the recipients wanted to know; and what they wanted to know, above all, was that everything was going as well as could be.

December 14th 1933: '...How do you like the South of France? This letter is your Christmas present. I've settled down very well by now. At school it's really wonderful. I have so many friends, and such nice ones ...Here, we have an awful lot of mice. We've already caught a few. We always have lunch at school, so that Mummy doesn't have to do so much cooking. At break-time we always play football on our school grounds. Our school has only been up for six months and is wonderful. There's a big swimming-pool in it. But we haven't started swimming in it.'

March 10th 1934: '...This morning we played football. That was great fun. In form I'm in fifth place. On March 17th I'm having my birthday party, and I'm looking forward to that. I know you always like little pencils, so I'm sending you two. We now have two cats, one is only two weeks old and very small.'

March 25th 1934: 'Here the weather is wonderful now, so that we can walk about without overcoats. We spend the whole day in the garden, playing with our cats. I was very pleased with the chocolate biscuits. For my birthday I got 3 books, a big football, a pair of socks, a dozen crayons... At school it's very nice. Every Tuesday I have a violin lesson, but unfortunately it doesn't help much, since I'm asked to do exactly what my other teacher said I shouldn't, and it will take a long time for me to learn the new way. Eva gave me a little bedside clock which I like very much. Besides our two cats one always comes to our house. It doesn't belong to anybody. At this moment it's sitting on Maria's lap. Our big cat has an English name, Blacky, because it's completely black, our kitten is called Tiny, also an English name, because it's also a British cat.'

April 24th 1934: 'Now our holidays are over, this is our second day back at school. Today another little German boy came to school, he's only four. We know him. He once came to Kladow with Frieda, one of our maids. This morning it rained, but now the sun is shining again. In the holidays I spent a lot of time with my friends. I'm in the tenth place at school. I thought I'd do better than that. It was only because of geography. I'm top in arithmetic. My report was good. Only in geography I got 32 out of 50, but that's very hard for me. In history I got 46 out of 50. In "progress" I got "excellent".'

'The violin lesson was always horrible. Once the teacher made me write out a rule 140 times. When I start he says: "If you play one note out of tune I'll kick you in the stomach." Today Daddy wrote a letter saying I was not to have violin lessons.'

June 6th 1934: 'Many thanks for the lovely stamps. It was a great pleasure to get them. I've already got more than 1000 stamps, though I didn't bring any from Germany... Here the weather is very fine now. A week ago a German couple came to see us and brought us a goldfish. I can't write more now because I want to stick in some stamps. I play a lot of cricket now, because it's too hot for soccer and rugger...

6.30 Now I've stuck in all the stamps.'

Home life in Edinburgh was austere and severely restricted. My parents were much impressed by the courtesy calls of neighbours — a gesture almost inconceivable in Berlin — but in the circumstances these could have no sequel beyond a formal return of the call. The few people my father had time to talk to were refugee doctors in the same predicament as himself. It happened that there was a grand piano in the house, in a drawing-room known as 'the cold glory' and almost never used, because no one could cope with the coal fires. Neither my father nor my mother touched the piano while we were there, but a refugee called Adorno used to sit in that icy room, practising. I don't think I ever spoke to him, but I invested him with all the romantic glamour that was missing in the new life, and would stand in the hall for hours to hear him play.

Most of the time the house was unnaturally quiet, because my father must not be distracted from the work on which our futures depended. That quietness dominates my recollections of Edinburgh, reinforced by the quietness in the streets on Sundays, when nothing at all was allowed to go on. I doubt that I should have seen the Castle, Arthur's Seat, Holyrood Palace or the Zoo, let alone the Forth Bridge and one or two places outside the city, if it hadn't been for a few acquaintances of my parents who would take one or more of us out for the day. It was they, too, who took us to the tea-shops in Princes Street.

The strain of more than a year's uninterrupted cramming in middle age may well have shortened my father's life, but I never heard him complain. I think he felt that it was a small price to pay for the hospitality that had been offered us and for the decencies of British life, which he never ceased to praise. Uneventful though it was, that interim period changed us all. Within half a year or so the four of us had begun to speak English among ourselves, and that meant more than progress in learning the language for which I was given a special prize at school. It meant a degree of identification with those who spoke the language, an adaptation easy for none of us and different for each one. For me, it meant a drastic shift not only from home life to school life and school friends but from introversion and fantasy to a boy's world of competitive toughness, uncomplicated alliances and relative independence. That, too, was an interim state, but a necessary one, since it healed some of the wounds inflicted by recent betrayals, rejections and losses.

For my mother, who was to survive my father by forty years, the change was far more drastic and difficult. That she began to develop practical skills which, from her childhood onwards, had been left to servants, was only the outward manifestation of the change; but it did not take her long to become as excellent a cook and confectioner as she had been a pianist, tennis-player, war-time nurse, secretarial factotum to my father and administrator of a professional household. In later years she added gardening to her accomplishments. During the next war she kept hens in London. Before the war, someone sent her one leaf of a pot plant widely grown in Germany, the Sparmannia Africana, in a letter. Not only do I still have the progeny of that leaf, more than half a century later, but it is to be found in paintings by Lucian Freud, who would call on my mother for replacements of the plant for his studio.

In her widowhood, after those war-time hens, my mother kept only dogs and cats. When her children no longer needed her full-time care, she took up social work for the Society of Friends, remaining active in it well into her eighties, even after an operation for cancer. My mother never spoke of her conversion to Quakerism, if it was a religious conversion rather than a congenial opening for good works beyond the family she never ceased to care for and care about, providing a base for reunions when everything made it centrifugal. I did touch on those questions with her at times, though as reticent as she was about matters of faith and belief. She seemed unaware of any breach between her Quakerism and the agnostic humanism that had left her children no more churched than synagogued. The identity disc I wore as a soldier bore the letters C. of E., because that was the church in which, belatedly, I had my religious education, though never christened in it nor confirmed. Had he lived, I could have talked with my father about that muddle. It wasn't in my mother's nature to discuss generalities or ideas, only to cope practically and indefatigably with every sort of hardship, muddle or conflict that might present itself. She could not have done so without a faith; but, as I was to learn also, faith is not the same thing as belief. My beliefs could be shaken by experience or knowledge, and they changed over the years. My faith did not change, because it lay beyond experience and beyond reason. From her mother, too, my mother had inherited a very strong will, though one less militant than her mother's, with far less need for opinions, certainties and causes. When she was almost ninety-three, confined to bed and kept alive only by constant medical attention, I announced a visit for after lunch, because I was driving over from Suffolk. I was astonished and shocked to find her sitting up at the table, with a meal prepared for me. By telling me a story about her youth and her hatred of leave-takings, she intimated to me that we should not be meeting again, did not answer the telephone after that, and concentrated her powerful will on dying.

My grandparents and uncle, meanwhile, had left France and set up a temporary household at Hove. In the summer or autumn of 1934 we went to live with them there, while my father worked for his examinations and my mother made arrangements for a permanent home in London. For a term or so I attended the Brighton and Hove Grammar School, getting on well enough to remember nothing about that institution. In Edinburgh I had watched a rugby match between Old

Watsonians and a rival team. At Brighton it was county cricket, including an invitation to tea with a Lord Mayor whom my grandparents must have got to know. I never took to either game, as it happened, preferring soccer, rowing and boxing at school, swimming and riding in later years.

From Brighton Pier, where we spent our pocket money on slot machines and ice-cream, I did most of my fishing, though more often than not it was dogfish I caught, small spotted sharks which at that time had not been promoted to the dignity of 'rock salmon' and were either killed, with difficulty, to be cut up for bait, or thrown back. I respected the leathery strength of those streamlined predators and never killed them, but sometimes needed the help of old locals to get them off the hook.

It must have been towards the end of the year that we moved to an early Victorian semi-detached house in London, 45, St. John's Wood Park. When the lease expired during the war it remained empty and derelict for many years, before being demolished, like almost all the old houses in that street. Although my father also kept a consulting room in Upper Wimpole Street, certain patients came to the house, to a room that served him as bedroom, study and consulting room, with a small waiting-room adjoining it. Unlike later emigrants from Germany, my parents had been able to take their furniture and possessions — a strange assortment of the old and new, from the Berlin flat, the ultra-modern clinic and the functionally plain villa at Kladow. In the top-floor bedroom which I shared with my brother we slept on beds designed for Kladow — with hinges and collapsible legs, so that they could disappear behind curtains against the wall, giving us more room for the games we might have played if we had got on well enough together.

St. John's Wood Park was a triangular street, with a central island formed by large detached houses and their gardens. Motor traffic was minimal in those parts. Neither my family nor any of the close neighbours owned a car. Marlborough Road Station, later replaced by St. John's Wood, was only a street or two away from the house. There was so little noise that one could hear the lions roar in the Regent's Park Zoo. Another familiar sound, in the early mornings, was the clatter of horses' hooves when the soldiers from the barracks on Ordnance Hill rode out for exercise. There was something archaic even about the street musician we knew best in the street, an old harpist who sat there playing as though he enjoyed it and that pavement were the chosen setting for his art. We had many conversations with him, as with a pavement painter we passed on our way to school.

My father was no longer a professor, and his private practice, at first, was reduced to a few families, mainly of refugees, since in England it was unusual for paediatricians to function as family doctors. As he got to know more colleagues, who sent him patients, his practice grew, but there must have been no end of money pressures at the best of times, even when he had become a consultant at a London hospital. A cook and housemaid were still considered indispensable; and so were private schools for the four of us. Yet my father found time for some of his other interests. Not only did he and my mother take up music again but many eminent musicians played in our house — Feuermann, the cellist, Max Rostal and Franz Osborn, Lily Kraus and Szimon Goldberg are some of those I remember meeting. Marlene Dietrich brought her daughter as a patient, and I caught a glimpse of her. The Kordas were also among my father's patients. They invited me to their Denham studios, where I was initiated into the mysteries of film-making, such as the cutting of film tapes, and saw Rex Harrison and Merle Oberon at work. At the White City stadium, where my father took me, I saw Jesse Owens win a race.

My father's psychology books began to interest me, almost as much as the natural history books of which I had quite a library of my own. I used to borrow the odd volume of Freud and read it in the lavatory — though that must have been some years after we moved to London. I could now talk with my father about almost everything, but sexual matters were an exception. It was a residual puritanism in him, I suspect, that kept him faithful to Adler, for whom I had little use, even when my father became active in a child guidance clinic which he helped to found. Neither my own puritanism nor my innocence was much affected by early attempts to read Freud. I couldn't understand my parents' amusement at finding me in bed with the last of my childhood girl friends, Cornelia, when she was staying at our house. We were reading a book together, and we were comfortable there.

Reading, in fact, was more of an addiction than going to bed with girls. Even in my prep. school years, at The Hall, Hampstead, I spent most of my pocket money on books, stopping at Miss Waterhouse's bookshop in the Arcade at Swiss Cottage, as I continued to do for many years to come. In addition I collected anything to do with nature:

skeletons, skulls, a stuffed long-eared bat, snakes in bottles, a beautiful chain of Egyptian scarabs, a rose of Jericho — the miraculous plant that will sprout again years after its death, whenever placed in water — shells, rocks and crystals. Our next-door neighbour, an old man called Yeatman-Woolf, shared this mania and gave me many precious items from his collection, finally parting with a whole cabinet of tropical butterflies and beetles, which my father bought from him and gave me for a birthday. Yeatman-Woolf had also published one or two books of comic verse, and he had a large collection of gramophone records, some of which he passed on to me. I still have one or two of his original Caruso and Galli-Curci records, with one side of the heavy discs left blank.

The Hall, Hampstead, under its headmaster Wathen, was an efficient processing factory for potential public school boys. The buildings were drab, almost seedy, but the turnover was satisfactory. For games we were marched in crocodiles along the Finchley Road, to the playing fields or the old municipal swimming baths and gymnasium. I took up boxing, too, and was better at it than at most games. The Scottish boxing coach had a peculiar method. 'Punch me on the nose', he would invite us with disarming gentleness, and when we complied rather gingerly he would retaliate with a terrific whack on the chin, teaching us to keep our guard up.

There was much savagery and bullying at the school, especially in the small back yard that served as a playground between classes. For some strange reason old car tyres were provided for our exercise there, so that at any unwary moment one was likely to be hit by one of those formidable toys. The fighting there and in class-rooms was less clean than our street fights in Edinburgh, because it was more personal, the expression of real hatred and rivalries, exacerbated by the competitiveness of the whole school system. Bullying was against the rules and punishable by beatings with a gym shoe; but this didn't prevent some large lout from jerking a knee into one's groin, quite casually, in the back yard, and gloating over one's agonised contortions. Only a weakling would report such an incident. The code demanded reprisals, if practicable, or else a stoical acceptance. The Headmaster who did the beating with gym shoes, had once been sued by a parent for victimization, but had been acquitted or rehabilitated. He seemed genial enough, a bit eccentric in his teaching — he taught us French syntax in rhythmic units repeated in chorus by the class, while he conducted the chanting — and otherwise conventional. This doesn't rule out the possibility that he derived pleasure from beating boys, or certain boys. Repressed homosexuality was part of the system, inherent in it.

I did well enough at that school and at the next, having learnt to stand up for myself, to get by, to do what was required of me while reserving more and more for my private pursuits, hobbies and friendships. One of my sparring partners, Timothy Hallinan, became my closest friend in those years. He was serious, especially about politics, inclined to priggishness like myself, and like me had two elder sisters and a younger brother. His family was Irish-American and his father a political journalist. His home in Belsize Park Gardens was congenial to me because the children were treated as persons with minds of their own. There was conversation about politics and ideas. Timothy's sisters became friends of my sisters, and his younger brother, at one time, a patient of my father's. In later years we drifted apart, not only because he went on to Gordonstoun, but because my increasingly aesthetic leanings struck him as somehow frivolous, lacking in moral and intellectual grit. Frivolity was what he could not abide. I remember defending the younger of his two sisters against his disapproval when he called her a 'social butterfly'; but that may have been because I found her attractive.

Another school friend, David Cairns, lived in our street. I spent a weekend with his family at their country house near Arundel, but got into trouble because we talked about rabbits. When he mentioned that his rabbits didn't breed as rabbits proverbially do, I explained to him that they couldn't, because the buck and the doe were in separate hutches. I supposed that this revelation of the so-called 'facts of life' was referred to his parents and that they thought I must be utterly corrupt to know them at my age. In any case I was never invited there again. My early acquaintance with country matters may have cost me the joy of another stay in the country, but the friendship was taken up again later.

My mother's parents and brother were still in close touch with us. When they were not in the South of France they lived near us, in a service flat in Fitzjohn's Avenue, then in Belsize Park Gardens, where my grandfather died. We were fond of him, though he was touchy, moody, and embittered by decades of conflict with his wife and son. To his grandchildren he was more than kind, but with a reserve bound up with the suspicion that we liked him more for his gifts than for what he was. He was deeply offended when in some skit my sister and I improvised for one of his birthdays there was a passing reference to an inheritance from a rich grandfather, a mere parroting of something we had heard or read. In his last years he had nothing to do but worry about his investments and buy the odd old stamp for his collection. I inherited a few books from him as well as a collection of old woodcuts and etchings, mainly Dutch and German — but I don't recall ever seeing him read a book. Not till many years after his death did I see the sketchbooks, of 1900 to 1911, that contain his impressions of landscapes visited on holiday, portraits of his friends, and painstaking copies of paintings and sculptures. The activity itself, like the execution of those pencil and crayon sketches, was conventional enough, but his delicate response to certain kinds of scenery, especially alpine, made me realize how little of himself my grandfather had been able to communicate to us in his old age. His collecting of paintings and engravings, too, seemed more essentially related to the man he was; and so did his solitary gardening under the wooded slope of his plot at Kladow. His very silences about what he thought and felt became something I could recognize and understand, for he had passed them on to my mother, and she had passed them on to me.

While he was alive we had spent part of each summer as our grandparents' guests, at Combe Martin, Bournemouth or Torquay, staying at hotels and passing the time much as we had done at Hove, except that we mixed more and more with other children and adults. My parents could not afford many holidays. They spent the summers in London, though once my mother went abroad, to meet her uncle Paul on neutral territory, at Karlsbad.

For a few years I kept up my violin practice and lessons, begun in Germany when I was five or six. My violin teacher, as it happened, moved to London at about the same time as we did. Much as I liked my teacher, a Dutchman, who became a psycho-analyst when a paralysing illness forced him to give up the violin, he could not arouse much enthusiasm in me for the instrument, and I gave it up as soon as pressure of school work provided an excuse. Ever since my early childhood in Berlin we had known a girl violinist, the daughter of a Russian émigré and former professor of music. Though at least ten years older than the oldest of us, she had climbed a tree in our little rented garden in Berlin. When we saw her again in London she was no longer merely tomboyish and odd, but gradually slipping into acute schizophrenia. She must have had a special attachment to my parents, for she would turn up at our house during her worst crises, frightening us with her incomprehensible behaviour and remarks. She had been a brilliant violinist. One day she started playing in the street, then gave her valuable violin to a passer-by. After a frontal lobotomy she fell into complete apathy, became quite unrelated to her past life, and finally killed herself. At about the same time we knew a boy virtuoso on the violin who disappeared into a mental home. I don't know whether these two acquaintances put me off the violin by association, or whether I simply wasn't good enough at it to get much satisfaction out of my playing. Later, when I was fifteen, I wanted to take up the piano and the organ. One of my friends at Westminster, Colin Turnbull, played the organ and had permission to practise in the Abbey. I sometimes joined him there and indulged in experimental strumming when he had finished. By that time my father could no longer afford lessons, and I was too busy trying to get through the School and Higher Certificates. For the rest of my life I have had to content myself with clumsy and barbarous improvisations on the piano. There were periods in my life when I had much more use for music than for literature, including poetry, and felt that words could never be more than pedestrian, beggarly aspirants to 'the condition of music'.

Compared to central Berlin, residential St. John's Wood seemed half-urban at the most, mainly because of the scarcity, at that time, of large blocks of flats. True, the working-class terraces in St. John's Wood were already being converted into fashionable and 'desirable' residences; but it was the war that made way for large-scale redevelopment. Perhaps it took old flat-dwellers like my family to appreciate the garden of our house, the wrought iron steps leading down to it from a conservatory, the sycamore tree as tall as the house, and the little pond in the garden. Just before we left Berlin my mother had turned her bedroom into a veritable birdhouse, with cages on the top of every wardrobe and every other suitable surface. In St. John's Wood we could keep a succession of cats and kittens, budgerigars and tropical fish in the conservatory, goldfish in the pond. To these I added whatever other aquatic and amphibian creatures I could catch in the country, though many of them, like the eel I brought back from a holiday, can hardly have felt at home in a London pond. By force-feeding with milk my father managed to save the life of a sick hedgehog we had found.

I still hankered after the real country, for open spaces less knowable than Regent's Park, Primrose Hill, or even the plausible show of wilderness put up by Hampstead Heath. London had other kinds of wilderness to explore, but we hardly penetrated beyond the West End, with Kensington and Chelsea as our Far West. The City, the East End and the Docks — not to mention everything beyond the South Bank — remained almost unknown to me until the war had begun to transform them.

Some time before his death in 1936 my grandfather took us to our first opera — a performance of *La Bohême* that left me with the image of velvet jackets as emblems of the artistic life. The squalor and death by consumption that went with it didn't detract from its fascination, but heightened the appeal of living dangerously, amorously and melodiously to the end. The cinema was another belated discovery of those years, especially forbidden horror films like *Frankenstein* or *Dr. Mabuse,* with the early Tarzan films as close runners-up.

Our cook and housemaid at that time were Austrian, and one of them used to tell me stories about the depravities of Vienna night life. It never occurred to me to ask whether they were based on first-hand experience or picked up from lurid magazines. To me they were as real and unreal as the case histories in Freud, the novels I read voraciously or the films I saw.

In 1937 I left the Hall for Westminster School. My father, who could barely afford to send me there, had got me admitted after an interview with the departing Head Master, Costley-White. Luckily, the son of the German Ambassador, Ribbentrop, had also left before my first term. I was just tall enough not to have to wear the Eton jacket prescribed for shorter boys, and could begin as a fully-fledged gentleman in morning coat, striped trousers, top hat and obligatory umbrella or cane. That uniform — abolished during the war — must have been an effective means of inculcating the sense of superiority which public schools were intended to inculcate, combined with other qualities far less questionable. There were things one couldn't do in that garb. In fact there were precious few things one could do, if one was a day boy, except walk or ride to school and back with as unselfconscious a dignity as one could maintain in the face of stares, rude or sarcastic comments in tube trains, and the occasional stone aimed at the top hat by less privileged boys in the remaining working-class streets of St. John's Wood. Yet a silk hat is a very much tougher thing than it seems. Mine withstood several drenchings under the changing-room shower, being used as a football in Dean's Yard, being hit by missiles, being sat on, trodden on, bashed with umbrellas and sticks.

A feud began almost as soon as I went to the new school. A boy called Meyer, half German and half Scottish, went into the changing-room saying that anyone who opened the bathroom door while he was in it would be beaten up. I couldn't resist the challenge, opened the door and started a private war that lasted for years, in and out of the boxing ring, and ended only after an ambush that left my face permanently scarred — a moral victory for me, who had usually beaten him in straight fights, but a physical one for him and his assistant.

But this was a private war, and Westminster had nothing to do with the tensions that caused it. Relations between most boys at the school, and between most boys and me, were peaceable and easy-going. The only two older boys who threw their weight about in my House, Busby's, were a Yugoslav and an Iraqi, and even they were good-natured at heart, and could be dealt with if one stood up to them. The Yugoslav, Ivan Račič, used to order small boys to scrub his back under the shower, a privilege to which the strict rules of precedence didn't entitle him. He counted on the greater amenability of English boys, but would admit defeat if he was not obeyed. When he and the Iraqi, Ali Jawdat, taunted me about Germany and the Jews, what began as an attempt to brow-beat me turned into a political discussion that ended quite amicably. Even fagging proved less humiliating than I had feared, because the House Monitor whom, for a term or so, I had to serve in his study was too sensitive and decent to demand more than formal attendance.

At school I joined the Madrigal Society, singing in a performance of the St. Matthew Passion — not very well, because my voice had only recently broken and hadn't found its true range, and because my sight-reading was poor, so that I had difficulty in keeping to the right part. I also entered for an inter-House boxing tournament, though my liking for the sport had already cooled, and I had better things to do in my spare time than train in the gymnasium. I got as far as the Finals, nonetheless, only to suffer a bloody defeat. My opponent was a friend of mine, and he had asked me not to punch him too hard. By the time I resolved to go back on my promise it was too late, for he had winded me in the first round with a punch to the diaphragm, and proved too quick for me after that. The occasion mattered to me because my father was among the spectators, so that I felt ashamed of my poor performance and blood-stained vest. He and I were given a lift home by the father of my arch-enemy, Meyer, and that made it worse.

In the summer of 1938 we stayed at a farm in North Wales, near Betws-y-Coed, at the invitation of my grandmother and uncle. My father joined us there for a few days, my mother for a slightly longer stay. I got on well with the farmer's children and found their way of life so attractive that for a long time I wanted to be a farmer. About thirty years later the same thing happened to my son — in Teesdale — though his infatuation didn't last as long as mine. It was not till later visits to North Wales that I grew aware of the extreme hardships that beset the sheep farmers there. To play with the farmer's children in the hay loft or feed the poultry was one thing, quite another to make a living out of that land. On my walks I collected wildflowers and ferns, some of which my father planted in our London garden. This, too became a habit, and I still grow wildflowers, much preferring them to most of the highly hybridized variants, and did so even when our garden was a city one.

Westminster School was close not only to the Abbey, where we attended morning services, but to the Houses of Parliament; and political passions were bound to penetrate into Dean's Yard even before the Czechoslovak crisis, when the school was briefly evacuated to Sussex. As far as I am aware, the sons of Labour M.P.s at school outnumbered those of Conservatives, even at that time, before the school's liberalism had become overt. Lively meetings of the Political Society were held at the houses of masters or parents, and these, too, tended towards the Left. I remember such meetings at the houses of Andrew Wordsworth, a master, and at the Wedgwood-Benn's. Another master, M. W. Blake, stood for election as a Labour candidate. In a school play written and produced by a later Head Master, J. D. Carleton, I played the part of Hitler. What may have been my first published poem appeared in our House magazine, *The College Street Clarion,* in April 1939; it was a pompous Petrarchan sonnet on the German annexation of Czechoslovakia, 'The Death of a Nation'. In the same magazine I published a very different piece of verse called 'The Science Master in Love'. I kept no copy of it, but found it again recently in a Digest of extracts from the *Clarion* for the years 1938–1948. The sonnet was produced in class as a verse-writing exercise. This piece was spontaneous and slap-dash, written for the fun of it:

> Thy sparkling eyes like manganese dioxide seem,
> Thy rosy mouth doth like acidic litmus gleam,

Thy waving locks are of a fine sulphuric shade,
Thy teeth like chalk (as that which in the lab. I made).

The sight of thee, my dear beloved Felicity,
By twelve per cent reduces my acidity,
The sound-waves of thy voice add sugar to thy charms,
With nine ergs' pressure I would lock thee in my arms.

Thy flowery breath hath strong ammonia's pungent smell,
Thy song resounds just like a chromium-plated bell,
Thy touch corrodes like H_2SO_4 (dilute),
To win thee I would give the leather of my boot.

O dear Felicity, consent to be my wife:
And lessen by a twenty-sixth my cost of life...
And when the calcium of my bones returns to soil,
And I have shuffled off this platinum wire coil,
When foul bacilli eat my decomposing flesh,
Then sodium chloride tears will be released afresh.

My grandmother, who kept copies of most of my early literary exercises, had no use for such frivolity. She did preserve the script of a speech I prepared for the school Political Society, opposing the motion that 'This House considers that the German nation should be annihilated after the war'. That must have been after the school's evacuation to Lancing College. The solemn high-mindedness of the speech was of the same order as that of the sonnet, which my grandmother also kept and translated into German. For a long time this sort of high-mindedness was to get in the way of my development as a writer, which demanded not generalities and commonplaces but a grasp of the particulars of experience, if only those picked up in the chemistry lab. At the same period I was obsessed with the rival claims of science and of poetry, or of 'progress' and nature, the subject of another piece of verse fustian written in 1939, 'The Beast's Farewell', and of several poems written over the next few years.

In the debate I said: 'The annihilation of the German nation would constitute a great loss to the culture of Europe. Germany has produced the majority of the great philosophers of the Western world. It is to Germany that Europe owes most of its finest music.' That was a mere appendix, of course, to my main argument, summarized like this: 'A nation consists of individuals. Most men would hesitate to condemn individuals indiscriminately to death or misery, yet they are prepared thus to condemn a nation. As long as such a view prevails there can be no progress.' Yet it was through German culture that I tried to preserve some continuity with my own childhood. The earliest translation of a German poem I remember doing was of a sentimental piece by a minor nineteenth-century poet called Theodor Körner, and its theme was loyal friendship maintained in the teeth of separation. I did it in December 1939, describing it as a 'poetical translation', which seems appropriate:

Last Visit to the Brook

The boy sat near the water's edge
And listened to its murmuring sound.
He understood the whispered pledge
As words of one in friendship bound;
And while his brothers roamed o'er meadows wide
He watched the brook, sat silent by its side.

However, that boy feels 'deep longing surge and rise', and decides he cannot stay there for ever:

'The joys of peace no longer soothe my heart.
To seek the stormy world I must depart.

But should I see thee flowing fast,
Thy thundering passage onward wend,
In foaming waters rushing past,
I'll recognize my faithful friend.
Now we must part until another day.'
With one last glance he wandered far away.

The diction of that exercise points to the fact that my favourite English poet to date, before Shakespeare — three of whose plays I was to know almost by heart, because they were set as examination texts at various stages of my school career — was Thomas Gray, whose *Selected Poems*, vellum-clad and edited by Edmund Gosse in 1885, I bought in 1939. The next was Tennyson. In a waxed and glossy leather binding suitable for Victorian coffee tables, I acquired his *Collected*

Poems at school, either buying it from a friend at Busby's or swapping it for something other than a book. It was Tennyson's 'Tithonus' and 'The Lotus-Eaters' that I learned by heart, attracted by their languid melancholia; and that influence was so apparent in my poem 'The Beast's Farewell' that my sophisticated friend Freddy laughed at its inflated and outmoded rhetoric.

The first translation was followed by others, rather less 'poetical' of Goethe's would-be Pindaric free verse poems 'Das Göttliche', 'Gesang der Geister über den Wassern' and 'Grenzen der Menschheit', to which I was drawn by their high-mindedness rather than by their superiority as verse to Körner's tear-jerker, though my father has intimated to me in a letter that Körner might not be the best of models for my own first efforts, and I had taken the hint to heart.

Another literary work I produced in 1939 was a short story called 'War Aims', which I had the cheek to submit to the magazine *Lilliput* — handwritten, on lined school exercise paper! Being rather more down-to-earth than my political speech, this war story was anti-pacifist and ironic. Its point was the difficulty of reconciling the kind of humanism I had expounded in the debate with the realities of war, as I imagined them at the time. The story was returned with a non-committal rejection slip, the first of many I was to receive.

By this time, at the age of fifteen, poetry was beginning to replace natural history, music and politics as my dominant concern. One of the more advanced of our masters had introduced the class to the work of T. S. Eliot, in an anthology, at a time when T. S. Eliot was far from being regarded as a pillar of the Establishment for educational purposes. Eliot's poem or poems made little conscious impression on me till some two or three years later, when I was won over not by 'The Waste Land' but by the earliest of the 'Four Quartets' to come my way. When I submitted something to Richard Wollheim at school for a very avant-garde magazine to be called 'Bogueur' he was planning to edit, he told me to read Dryden. Though the title alone was provocative under the reign of J. T. Christie, our Head Master, I am told that the magazine did materialize. Far from being ready to contribute — I was never to fit into any sort of smart set in literature or outside it — I must have missed that publication completely, because I thought it had never materialized until my friend Freddy told me he still had 'one, if not two issues' of it in 1977. Nor was I ready to take the sound advice about Dryden, who might well have knocked some of the maudlin romanticism out of my verse.

The ambiguous 'Bogueur' — it had to be French, because everything smart was French in those years, and much of that smartness was bogus — reminds me that homosexuality was the bugbear at that school, tolerant and liberal though it was in almost every other regard. Needless to say, the school was full of it, simply because most of the boys, even day boys, were either passing through a homo-erotic phase or leading lives that made contacts with girls impossible. The forbidden thing, therefore, was sexual and erotic need itself, since its existence was not acknowledged; and the more it was repressed, the more likely it was to break out in its most forbidden and generally abominated forms. The assumption was that decent boys do not know, and do not need to know, anything about sexuality. In practice, a good many boys at Westminster may have got through their school years without any sexual experience, though few of them can have avoided some sort of homo-erotic, sublimated hero-worshipping attachment. Those who could not resist physical contact — if only puppyish 'fun and games' — or were seduced into such common practices as mutual masturbation didn't necessarily become homosexuals in later life; but something of the surreptitiousness, 'filth' and 'shame' of those lapses was likely to stick to all sexual activity, with obvious consequences. What astonished me, when I was told about the later lives of some of the boys I had known at school, is how many of them have remained exclusively or sporadically homosexual; and how many more, with wives, children, and outwardly conventional careers, remained entangled in a social, ethical and emotional nexus set up in their school years. I doubt that in any country but Britain one can look at a prominent man, statesman or writer, and suddenly see the face of a prep. school boy, a public school or grammar school boy, thinly masked by skin that has managed to wrinkle.

The friend I saw most of at Westminster was a veteran and inveterate homosexual who had already been expelled from his prep. school. The friendship was viewed with suspicion by the masters who knew about it, though it was an intellectual friendship based on the attraction of opposites. What attracted me to Freddy Hurdis-Jones was a precocity, eloquence and self-assurance that were respected even by those who found him most repulsive, the paradigm of everything a public school boy ought not to be. In fact it was difficult to think of Freddy as a boy. At the age of fourteen he seemed formed and finished

— perhaps 'finished' in more senses than one, because the pattern in which his life was set seemed to leave little room for development or fulfilment. I can't presume to be sure about what he got out of our friendship, unless it was that he needed someone who appreciated his wit while disapproving of his glibness. Commenting on my account in a letter of 1977, Freddy wrote: 'I think I enjoyed opening your eyes to the iniquities of the world you saw through your Biedermeyer spectacles (horrid metaphor!)'. We were certainly useful to each other, if only as antagonists who could strike sparks from the clash of their personalities. Even that exchange may have meant more to me than it did to him, because I was the one with the greater capacity and the greater need to grow. He may have needed me only as an actor needs an audience. Nobody else at that school could have given me what he gave me — a perpetual testing and stretching of my faculties against a suppleness quite beyond me.

Freddy had made an amalgam of his two masters and models, Disraeli and Oscar Wilde, and it was impossible to say to which of the two he owed the florid prose of his conversation, spiced with paradoxical aphorisms, his gold-topped cane, his signet ring and the green note-paper to which he applied it. Freddy lived in St. John's Wood, and we usually took the same trains or buses home, often walking up and down either his or my street for half an hour or more before parting. Since I was as self-conscious as he was disdainful of the *profanum vulgus,* his dandified appearance and affected or outrageous talk attracted attention which I should have been glad to avoid. If Freddy was a physical coward — he hated all games and never fought back when attacked at school — at this time I was in acute danger of falling into the moral cowardice of conformism. That was one thing I learnt from our ambivalent relations. More than anyone I knew, he could puncture my self-esteem and the self-righteousness bound up with that cowardice. By provoking me to the point of physical violence against him, he brought me up against the limits of a self-protective rectitude, and exposed its dishonesty. That, of course, was a subliminal effect, since most of the time we exchanged opinions, not judgements of each other; but the opinions left no permanent mark. Because we were so utterly different, Freddy could make no more use of my opinions than I of his. What really went on between us was something his flippancies and artificialities helped me to gloss over — as though a man who turned his defeats into epigrams could have no heart. Freddy's provocations didn't probe deeply enough, after all. Not till much later did I realise how much was at stake for Freddy in those early years.

Freddy's almost boastful frankness about his sexual exploits kept me informed about the school underworld. It included a number of semi-professionals — or 'pathicks', as Freddy called them — who were paid in money or 'tuck'. One of them continued to solicit Freddy when he had fallen in love with another boy and had only contempt for the boy he had formerly used. Yet I imagine that Freddy gave him more sympathy and affection than he received from anyone else in the school. He was pale and weedy, and his wide blue eyes had a way of positively begging for maltreatment. I was to run into him again during and after the war, when he had become a Fascist, achieving brief notoriety through some escapade with a German prisoner-of-war. He seemed as gentle and cringing as ever when I met him in Miss Waterhouse's bookshop, where he bought German books and tried to explain his ambiguous interest in the work of German-Jewish writers. The last time I spoke to him he was studying the German colonial record in Africa, engaged in an equally ambiguous attempt to vindicate that record and bring about a revival of German influence in Africa. I know nothing about his family, but he shared his surname with a distinguished Jewish theologian. Whatever his background, I am sure that his early homosexuality and masochism were inextricably bound up with his political pursuits in later life.

Freddy, too, was never to disentangle complexes set up in early childhood, when his father disappeared and his mother took possession, living with him in a state of complicity so intimate that the two of them sometimes struck me as the male and female halves of a single person; but somehow Freddy seemed to draw vigour and bounce from this extraordinary union, as though his vigorous and bouncy mother were still suckling him. It occurs to me now that what he got out of me, a father-dominated boy, was contact with the missing half of his world. When he was angry with me he called me 'the Prussian Ape'; and he regarded me as an object both of mockery and awe — awe, because I half belonged to that other distant world, the world of his moralizing persecutors, while being flexible enough to be fascinated by him.

Although he was a year or so older than I and never in the same form, Freddy and I met almost daily, both in and out of school. His knowledge of history — as egregious as his reading in other fields, from Rabelais to the more obscure French decadents and English aesthetes — made him an excellent guide in our explorations of the Abbey, and I think it was he who introduced me to the Little Cloister that became my favourite part of the precincts. What we talked about there, on walks in St. James's Park and on our way home from school, in the tuck shop or the House changing-room or up-School, between prayers and announcements, is irretrievable, and I shan't attempt to retrieve it. Our correspondence didn't begin till later, when we were separated by circumstances to do with the war and Freddy's expulsion from school.

Not long before the outbreak of war Freddy fell in love with a younger boy in the House. One day he was surprised with this boy in some compromising way and reported. As a friend of Freddy's I was summoned to the House Master's study, belatedly initiated into the 'facts of life', with preliminaries about flowers, insects and mammals, then reduced to blushing confusion by the sudden question: 'Hamburger —', puff of smoke from his pipe, 'do you know what buggery is?' I don't remember my answer, if any. Knowing Freddy, I could hardly help knowing about his *summum bonum;* but the more I said I knew, the more I must incriminate Freddy. The surprising thing is that Freddy got away with it — that time; and my reputation must have emerged untarnished from that interview, since little more than a year later I was a House Monitor, though my friendship with Freddy was known to have continued right up to his expulsion.

From a School Roll of 1938 I see that I obtained the first place for examination results in my form, the Modern Remove, with my enemy Meyer in second place. Freddy was fifteenth in the Modern Transitus, though he knew incomparably more than I did about most matters outside the curriculum. Freddy or no Freddy, for me there was no escape from the compulsion to be good; and goodness, most of the time, was not yet strained and complicated by the conflict between an inner absolute and the mere observance of outward rules — the conformism that is the super-ego's concordat with the world. Before the end of my school years the division had grown acute: if one served conscience one couldn't serve respectability, couldn't do what was expected of one, and pocket the rewards. That much was brought home to me by Freddy's immoralism, consistent at least, and damaging to him because it was consistent. If Freddy had to pay the price of his immoralism, I must have the guts to pay the price of my righteousness; or admit that I was no better than he was, only different, subject to other compulsions, other weaknesses.

In 1938 and 1939 I won book prizes for my work. Since those for 1939 were science books — I still have one of them, Eddington's *New Pathways in Science* — I deduce that the prize was for one of the subjects, like mathematics, that I liked least; and that would not have been out of character. On the other hand, I remember choosing Wilde's *Salomé* with Beardsley's illustrations for one of my prizes, and hints that my choice was not approved, perhaps because it betrayed the influence of Freddy. Yet I received the book. The Head Master also awarded me a special prize or *digniora* for a scripture essay, in the shape of a piece of Maundy money, a silver fourpenny bit. I kept the coin for more than thirty years, till it was stolen by a couple of amateur house-breakers in South London. The *Salomé* disappeared long ago, 'borrowed' by a friend.

In the summer of 1939 Freddy and his mother went to France. Our correspondence began after his return, for Freddy did not go to school for a while. His letters convey more of his style and character than anything I could write about him: Sept. 4th 1939: 'Thank you so much for the elephantine sheet which greeted me upon arrival in my own country on Saturday morning at the ungodly hour of 7 a.m. We got what was literally the last boat out of France, and never have I felt more thankful to see an English policeman and the lights of a British port. To follow your example and quote from the rich heritage of our national verse, I select the bard who sang:

> I travelled among unknown men
> In lands beyond the sea.
> Nor, England, did I know till then
> What love I bore to Thee.

'We had been to the Belgian coast, and on to Brussels, and concluded with a week in Paris, from which city I sent you a postcard, which I presume you did not receive. The political part of your epistle is interesting, though I can hardly be expected to accept all your statements without reservation. We were "bombed" at 3 this morning, and I suppose you were too, but it is my view that these "raids" are fictitious, and that their object is to ascertain the reaction of the public to such an emergency. I have received no information from school and thus can give no statement regarding my plans. I should love to come down and see you one afternoon, and ask you to invite me, but I fear I must wait until the Green Line runs again.

'I presume that in your bucolic retirement culture is conspicuous by its absence. When you reply, tell me and I will send some books to enliven the hours unoccupied by the maidens of Hitchin...

'Believe me, my dear Michael, I am honoured to remain

Your most devoted friend...'

The name is partly obliterated by the green sealing wax stamped with Freddy's family crest.

When war was declared, shortly after my father had obtained his British naturalization, he was posted to Hitchin in Hertfordshire to await the expected bombing casualties. We moved there, to 1, Hitchin Hill Path, and he stayed there for a few months, while his London practice fell apart. The older of my sisters, Maria, had left home before this time, because she did not get on with my father, and was living at an unknown address in the Midlands until my other sister, Eva, managed to find her again. My brother was at a co-educational boarding-school not far from Hitchin, St. Christopher, chosen through a connection my father had formed with the Society of Friends, to whose journal he contributed an article on child psychology. My father made use of the relative leisure of this waiting period to prepare a psychological book which he did not live to write.

That summer I was taken on a tour of England by car with a friend, George Schindler, and his father. We must have visited most of the cathedral towns in England and caught a glimpse of the other prescribed sites, including Stratford-on-Avon. What I liked best was the Lake District, where I began to swim across Lake Windermere and had almost got to the other bank when my friend's father panicked and sent a boat to fetch me back — to my extreme disappointment and disgust.

In September 1939 I went to Lancing College, where room had been found for Westminster School. When I could not get home for weekends, either to Hitchin or to London, my father would meet me at Brighton or Shoreham, even when he was already ill with the disease, not yet diagnosed as Hodgkin's Disease, of which he died in August 1940, at the age of fifty-five. Almost to the end, too, and after collapsing in the street, he saw his remaining patients. In February 1940 he had also begun a course of lectures on medicine and psychology, given to some two hundred foreign doctors. The good reception of these lectures, as he wrote to me, helped to compensate him for the decline of his practice; but it didn't alleviate his financial worries, which increased as his illness progressed.

Lancing, at first, offered me compensation for the second break-up of my home life, in the form of walks on the South Downs. Yet the stricter rules of boarding school life — and of Lancing College, whose High Anglicanism and more-public-school-than-thou pretensions rubbed off on its guests from London — soon began to oppress me.

On September 7th Freddy wrote to me:

'I must begin by asking you to pardon this letter, for it will abound with seemingly stupid questions. These are in reality necessary, for I wish to obtain an accurate and impartial impression of conditions and so forth at Lancing, with a view to my returning there.

'For a work of this kind I know of no one less likely to tinge with romance or to ornament or embellish the truth than your solid, but excellent self.

Questions

1. Roughly, how much work do we do?
2. Do we have to wash up, clean boots, or perform other tasks unworthy of our dignity and position?
3. Do we get a reasonable amount of free time, thus can we smoke, play cards, or engage in more congenial occupations, such as "Hunt the — " (the name of a boy), "Kiss in the Ring" and similar games suited to my exotic and oriental tastes?
4. Do we have to play games, throw ourselves about, or indulge in rough sports so clearly detrimental to a female in my delicate condition?

A lucid and intelligent answer, such as I know you only too capable of giving, to each of those questions, will greatly assist me in deciding whether to join the school or not. Several factors are, of course in my favour, as, for example, I imagine that discipline will be greatly relaxed, which will, no doubt, be of great service to me. I note with satisfaction that Rigaud's (a school House) are going to Hurstpierpoint, so I shall be for ever rid of that blessed little parasite, — , whose continued importunities are enough to drive me to drink or worse. I am making great efforts to discover whether the Cert. will be held next summer. This, of course, is the only reason that I contemplate a return to incarceration...'

Freddy did return, despite my report on conditions at Lancing. When work, and Freddy's 'more congenial occupations', permitted, he and I went on longish strolls on the Downs, where we smoked cigars or cigarettes in relative safety and continued our pre-war dialogue. However frankly he conducted it, I couldn't know just how ruthless and reckless he had grown in those other occupations, how close to the point where even a liberal institution was forced to expel him. A diary he kept for the Lent Term of 1940 is almost exclusively devoted to his passionate pursuit of one boy, though Freddy was also doing well in class, acting in *The School for Scandal,* and virtually editing the House magazine. What strikes me on reading the diary he has lent me is how easily his dominant concerns fitted in with the general life of the school. Not only his primary pursuit at the time, but his more casual affairs with other and lesser loves, involved all sorts of boys not markedly homosexual as go-betweens, accessories or rivals. Against the background of school life Freddy's exploits seem as natural and self-evident as the amorous intrigues in a Restoration comedy or the Sheridan play in which he acted a female role. It wasn't so much what he did as how he did it that precipitated Freddy's débâcle.

Needless to say, the diary shows no awareness of the effect that Freddy's advances might have on the object of his passion, a boy who had recently lost his father, who was susceptible to the interest and admiration of anyone older and more self-confident than himself, yet shrank from the kind of interest that Freddy made only too clear to him — to the extent of physical assault on one occasion, in broad daylight, and in the presence of 'friends' who chose to encourage Freddy to do what they would have liked to do, but were inhibited from doing. Freddy would have had to be even more mature than he was, and less of an insider at heart, to care about the damage he was capable of inflicting on someone he professed to love, rather than about the risks he was prepared to take in breaking school rules. Even his precocious knowledge and experience didn't go that far, though his sensibility might have done, if it had occurred to him to apply it to the other boy's position. If Freddy had any scruples beyond the school code, and the dangers of infringing it, he kept them out of our conversation, just as he kept them out of the journal.

As for me, I should be even less aware of any side of the business but for recent meetings with persons more immediately involved in it than I was. In Freddy's diary I appear as 'the Hun', and as one of a number of boys with whom he had 'interesting' or 'stimulating' conversations. Only one of our walks received a fuller entry in the diary. Early in February Freddy, Douglas Harley and I composed a letter — in

Freddy's most Disraelian manner — complaining about the food at Lancing. Freddy compared it unfavourably with that in the Neapolitan jails visited by Mr. Gladstone in 18-, whatever it was, a detail that would have sufficed to give away Freddy's part in the authorship. The food was abominable. I remember rabbit stews with bits of fur that stuck in one's gullet. Yet it was war-time, and we'd been put up with great difficulty in emergency quarters. Freddy and I had no intention of posting the letter. It was Douglas who sent it to the woman in charge of catering at Lancing College.

Next day, at Latin Prayers, the Head Master read out part of the letter before the assembled school, trying to keep a straight and solemn face, and emphasizing the discourtesy done to the host establishment. The anonymous author was asked to identify himself and report to his House Master. We did so, and I received my first and only caning at that school. The three strokes given to Freddy brought his total up to forty-seven, as the journal records. Nevertheless, he called the day 'momentous' and the scandal 'shameful in the extreme'. He also mentioned that 'the Hun's pride was wounded, and we went for a walk to try to console him'. In the same spirit, Freddy's summing-up at the end of the journal grants that 'the Hun is a good, though moody, friend'.

One reason for my moodiness was the deterioration in my father's health, which I noticed long before he admitted that he suffered from fevers not yet diagnosed. That was not till May. 'It is a very strange case,' he wrote on the 24th, 'and my friends are racking their brains for a remedy.' A week or so before that he had suffered more anxiety when two officials had turned up at Lancing to take me away for internment. Apparently my father had forgotten to inform the Head Master of our naturalization before the war, but this did not prevent the Head Master from standing up for me so valiantly that the two officials left without me. Many errors of that kind were made at the time by the Home Office, since there was a sudden scare about 'enemy aliens'. My uncle, who was living with my grandmother in Gloucestershire, was interned for a few months; but he had remained a German subject.

Most of the time, though, I was working desperately hard for my School Certificate, which I sat for and passed in December 1939 at the relatively early age of fifteen, obtaining credits in six subjects. My father had suggested that I take it early, without telling me that he was afraid I might have to leave school for financial reasons. For the same reasons he had to ask me not to take music lessons. He was still optimistic about political developments, thinking that the Soviet-German Pact would lead to resistance in Germany and to peace feelers, because the aristocrats and officers who had supported Hitler's rise to power would begin to feel threatened by the pact. That reliance on circles with whom he had had professional and friendly relations was soon dashed both by political developments and by the news of his mother's deportation. As a firm believer in the psychosomatic origins of almost all illness I attribute his fatal disease to a combination of stresses that became acute at this period.

On December 29th 1939, Freddy wrote to me at Hitchin:

'I find a large part of your epistle is occupied by observations regarding what you are pleased to term my "position at school". The triumphs for which I have long laboured are mine at last, and the well-deserved spoils of conquest I now enjoy. In the plenitude of my success it is interesting to reflect upon the disparity visible in this sinful world, between fact and its superficial appearance. For I have never worked at my lessons with smaller application; yet my report contains unparalleled praise from every master; the frigid — unbends to laudatory remarks concerning my intelligence, and it needs not you to assure me that I have none; the solid — observes that I "pull my weight" yet I daily corrupt the youths in his charge, and neglect all duties of the House...

'It has not been roses all the way, though I now tread the primrose path to the sound of flutes. I have, during my passage, offended many worthy persons, among them yourself, whose talents I have never doubted but whose conduct I have sometimes despised... If the path leads but to the gates of Doubting Castle and the dungeons of Giant Despair, I shall be the last to wonder... But meanwhile (to vary the metaphor) I'm safely launched on the Ocean of Success and shall pray Priapus my helmsman that he will steer me through the storms with less danger to other shipping. I know that a spirit generous as yours is unable to refuse a penitent, however vile his sin, and in that knowledge I again subscribe myself

Your devoted friend.'

In September 1939 my old feud with Meyer had come to a head. I was riding my bicycle at some speed down a lane when Meyer and his friend Ferrers-Guy — later killed in the war — jumped out of a hiding-place and grabbed the handle-bars. Somehow I was catapulted on to the tarmac and scraped a good deal of skin off my face. There was no one at the school to do the necessary patching. My forehead, cheek and chin healed by themselves, but not my nose, which was dented, twisted and discoloured for life. Meyer and Ferrers-Guy were horrified at the bloody pulp they had made of my face. I promised not to report them, and told the House Master that I had run into a lamp-post or a wall. That was the end of our feud. Relations with both boys became quite friendly or neutral until I left school. My pugnacious years were behind me in any case, and I had more serious worries.

Despite them I was planning a cycling tour for that summer with George Schindler and Elinor McHatton. Both were at Frensham Heights. Through George I had begun a correspondence with Elinor, whom he was to marry later. Our cycling tour fell through when Elinor decided against it. On June 1st I wrote to her from Lancing Manor: 'It is probably unnecessary for me to write this letter, but I think our short correspondence might as well continue long enough for me to tell you the latest developments. I wrote to George telling him of your refusal, and, as far as I can gather, he does not seem to have much hope of going away at all, after the news. I shall probably do some harvesting on a farm instead. I perfectly understand your attitude, though I sympathize with George, who seems slightly depressed. You need not have apologized to me, for, although I was looking forward to the holiday, I am the least affected.

'I don't think that I am a genius, and so I have every hope of getting the Higher Cert. However, I'm working as hard as I can, and I have a kind of blind faith which tells me that I shall succeed, even though my reason tells me that it's impossible. At any rate, it is not absolutely essential for me to get it this year. I think you are very sensible to wait till next year.

'I hope that despite all the complications we shall meet some day. This is all rather unusual: two persons write to each other without having met, and then cease to write without having met. It's rather satisfying to think that it's all against the conventions of society, that is, of prim, respectable society, but apart from that our correspondence was not very happy...'

The letter ends rather formally: 'Wishing you all possible happiness, whatever happens,

I remain
Yours sincerely,
Michael H.'

— a style that points to the example of Freddy's 'epistles'. Elinor and I not only continued to correspond but met, and continued to meet over the next thirty-odd years. Our later differences, of which there were many, tended to be explosive. Even at the age of sixteen Elinor must have laughed at the pomposities, earnestness and public school tight-lippedness of that letter.

In June I went home for half-term. My parents were back in St. John's Wood, though my father's practice was now minimal. Before I left Exeter, where the school had moved from Lancing, my father had tried to reassure me about his condition, writing that it had improved. His letter was typed, but he added one line of postscript in his own hand which proved the contrary, since it was shaky and almost illegible. When I got home I began to fear the worst. At the same time my father's fears for his family had communicated themselves to me, so that I worked frantically for the Higher Cert, which I took that year.

When I got home again my father was dying. I remember the meal my mother gave me the day I got back, and the effort of eating it. I talked with my father once before he fell into a coma, trying hard to tell him that I was now able to look after myself. Because his illness was a sort of cancer of the lymph glands, he had swollen up with fluid. Most of the time I could not bear to talk to anyone, but locked myself up in my bedroom, listening to gramophone records. Then came the death rattle, loud enough to be heard on the staircase all over the house.

I was not fit to help my mother in any practical way, and did not attend the cremation. My sister Eva, who was a medical student before breaking off her studies to join the WAAF, took care of the things I could not bring myself to do. The practical problems must have been acute, since my father left no capital, only a life insurance policy. Even the lease of our house hadn't long to run. Complicated arrangements were made between my mother and her brother, who had inherited what remained of my grandfather's wealth, but I wasn't interested in those.

Freddy wrote a letter of condolence on August 5th. Though in his usual style, it showed real understanding: 'In this sad moment of your bereavement, I would wish to express the profound sympathy which I feel for you. I am conscious in what degree you revered your father, and I could not fail to notice, in the short space which I had for such an observation, the complete concord which existed between you. There is little I can say at such a time that would lighten your grief; but know that I realize and appreciate the terrible shock which this your sad loss must be...'

That, in a way, was the end of my boyhood, though I had another year to get through at school. After taking the Higher Certificate in

July 1940 I could concentrate on Modern Languages and work for a scholarship to Oxford, winning a Westminster Exhibition to Christ Church early in 1941. My father had been amazed at some of the German texts set for the Higher Certificate — an almost forgotten Naturalist like Sudermann and an early novel by Hermann Hesse — but had supplied me with all the necessary books, even if they were not in his library. The master in charge of the Modern Languages VI, G. C. Claridge, was an impressively eccentric character, whose pessimism and misanthropy pointed to experiences of which we knew nothing. I remember his drawing a mouse inside a cheese on the blackboard, in no obvious connection with French or German but as an emblem of the human condition. He once called my friend Freddy 'a lavatorial effervescence'. I sometimes disagreed with him over German usage, since the residue of my childhood German was more colloquial than literary, but in most instances that I referred to my father he had found Mr. Claridge's German correct, if rather old-fashioned. When my first book came out in 1943 I sent Mr. Claridge a copy, but he did not care for the poet, Hölderlin, whose work I had begun to translate while under his charge. When the school returned to London after the war Mr. Claridge stayed in Herefordshire to keep a bookshop.

Bromyard in Herefordshire was more like what Freddy had feared Lancing might be like, with a good deal of digging and other manual labour to be done, and it was there that the school took on its new informality, maintained after the war. At Bromyard we had to rough it, became less and less conscious of our 'dignity and position' more and more conscious of the war and its inevitable austerities. Emotionally numb as I was after my father's death, I did my best to carry out my duties as a House Monitor, though with increasing reluctance, since one of them was caning boys for offences, such as smoking, which I committed as a matter of course. By the end of 1940, when my mother had moved to Bangor because Eva's College had been evacuated there, I was eager to leave school as soon as possible, so as to get a taste of independence at Oxford before joining up. My guardian, Dr. Teale, thought that I should stick it out at school. My mother didn't mind my leaving, provided I obtained the Head Master's consent. With his help I managed to get to Oxford one term sooner than I was meant to do, in the spring of 1941, when I was just seventeen.

In London, about two weeks after my father's death, I went to the house of my friend George when his parents were out. We raided their wine cellar, drank several bottles each, and got so drunk that George had to abandon his bicycle in the street when he saw me home. I got as far as my bed before being sick. My mother cleaned up the mess and said nothing more about it. Freddy commented in a letter from Buckinghamshire: 'I read of your orgy with disgust; not, God knows, from any Puritan convictions, but from an epicure's standpoint. The consumption of the divine juice of the grape in conjunction with vermouth, a substance fit only for the dilution of cheap gin, and Benedictine, sugared beverage of dowagers, is a gastronomic disgrace. The reasons for your failure to enliven your depressed spirits are not far to seek. I hold that the results of drink are connected with the spirit with which it is approached. To be merrily drunk, one must drink in a well-lighted room, too hot for comfort, and surrounded by noise and people; the only effect of earnestly sitting down to drink, as, indeed, of doing anything earnestly, is to produce fatigue in the earnest one and disgust in the beholders.'

At about the same period my sister Maria returned to our house in St. John's Wood. It was through her that I met David Gascoyne and another friend of later years who has forbidden me to name him in these memoirs. His objections to what I had written about him, followed by the demand that I do not mention his name, brought me up against the impossibility of writing anything like a truthful account of my life. I had tried, in any case, not to elaborate on events, to evoke no half-forgotten place, interpret no half-forgotten gesture, describe no one's appearance, claim no more than partial or passing insights into anyone's motives or character. Yet even the little I had allowed myself to write about that friend offended him, because my recollections of him did not tally with his image of himself or his view of his circumstances; and this after a more unbroken acquaintance, more unreserved exchanges, over a period of thirty-two years, than I had with any other man.

That shook me, as it was meant to do, and almost made me take my friend's advice to scrap the whole book. Discretion was not enough: I had to question my discretions as much as my indiscretions, since to withhold part of what one knows can be as deceptive, as distorting and misleading, as to add to it. Fiction, after all, seemed the more honest medium, just because it doesn't pretend to be anything but selective. My scruples had not only cramped my style but failed to spare my best friend what he feels to be the indecencies of biographical exposure.

His response was unreasonable, of course; but it was the same extremism of his responses that had attracted me to him in the first place, when Maria gave me a folder of poems, saying it had been left behind by a friend and asking me to take it round to his lodgings — an amply furnished flat, he says; the barest of rooms, with books piled on the floor, according to my recollection. (It could be that I merely handed the folder to him on the doorsteps, then transferred this first meeting to a room in which I visited him later; but I cling as stubbornly to the impression that remained with me as he does to his version of the facts.) There he was, anyway, the first poet I had met, and all that my adolescent notions told me a poet should be. Though ten years older than I, ten years and ten days, he seemed to have no job, but spent much of his time in the British Museum Reading Room, where he had studied philosophy and literature only because he was devoted to them. He seemed a solitary figure, with a family and educational background far less conventional than mine, but he knew the strangest people I had ever heard about before my own excursions into London bohemia. He was lean and pale, and could put away such quantities of food when he came to our house that my mother was positively alarmed, and I thought that he must be close to starving. (He denies that this was the case, and gives other reasons why a man may need to consume large amounts of food when being entertained as a guest. I accept those reasons, confirmed by later experience of other people. He regards the inference that he was close to starving as a hostile comment. To me, at the age of sixteen, it was one of many attributes that made him fascinating and authentic.) He had been married briefly and quixotically, to a girl who wanted his British nationality. I must have sensed from the first that he was unhappy, dissatisfied, tormented by conflicting impulses and unfulfilled ambitions. Of the two of us it was I who stuck to poetry, while he became a novelist, dramatist and specialist in the occult. Only a few of those poems in the folder were published over the next few years. To get his more substantial writing done, while earning a living in various ways, my friend had to discipline himself and change his way of life. Yet he remained unpredictable and extreme, Dostoievskian in his grasp of irrational impulses as a writer and his susceptibility to them as a man. No one taught me more about the intrinsic ambivalence of human behaviour; and no friend was more closely interwoven with the textures of my outer and inner life. Since I can't cut him out of this memoir, as I said I should in my anger at his objections, he will appear in this book as 'X'.

Because, after a gap of some fifteen years, X and I made it up, and he was generous enough to give me a bundle of letters I had written to him from 1940 onwards, I am able to fill one of many gaps in my memory. When I wrote the first version of this book, I had totally forgotten that at Christmas 1940 I was back in Edinburgh with my family, and that my mother considered settling there once more, at least for the duration of the war. The lapse must be due to the state of mind I was in after my father's death. On Christmas day I wrote to X from the Grange Hotel, Chalmers Crescent, Edinburgh: 'Our resolution to write to each other, like most resolutions, was not realised. In my case it was due to a scholarship examination I had to take last term, and for which I had only one term to prepare and revise. However, by luck or merit, I succeeded in winning an exhibition in Modern Languages for Christ Church, Oxford. I shall not be going up to Oxford next term, because I am rather young.' (I was still sixteen). 'You have succeeded in turning me from my poetical effusions, which I now treat with contempt and negligence, an attitude which I usually reserve for the productions of others. I have not devoted a minute to poetry of any kind since I left London. I have now kept to a strict diet of Auden, Spender, the revered Eliot, with occasional lapses in the form of Richard Le Gallienne, a very bad poet of the 'nineties, whom I find very entertaining. However, despite my valiant efforts and intellectual asceticism, my poetic thoughts still flower into the ancient and conventional forms which you so despise, with only a rare line worthy of this age. I have adopted the "désespoir paisible", which is my attitude to life when I can afford an attitude to life, in regard to my poetry. We shall probably be removing what is left of our furniture to Edinburgh, since our home has been badly damaged by hoses putting out a fire next door and by an explosive bomb. I prefer to live in London, even in war-time, but now we shall not be returning.'

My mother must have panicked briefly, after the loss of my father, and, with her new responsibility for her four difficult and intractable children, all about to go their own, and very different, ways. Not only had the bombs begun to fall in our street, destroying a number of houses and badly shaking up the rest, but the lease of our house did not have long to run. What had been the cook's room in the basement of our house — there was no question of keeping servants now, without my father's earnings and no capital — had been reinforced to serve as an air raid shelter, but I don't recall ever making use of it. I do recall walking the streets at night with bits of shrapnel falling all around me and an enormous blaze from a gas main that had been hit in Ordnance Hill — but that may have been later. When the lease did expire and my mother bought the lease of a house near Maida Vale, I refused to budge and was still in bed when the removal van arrived. Though nearly nineteen by that time, I resisted another disruption, attached as I was by now not only to London, and the beginnings of literary relations there, but to the house that offered at least the semblance of some sort of continuity in our lives. Most of the treasures of my boyhood and adolescence had already been discarded — the cabinet of tropical butterflies and beetles sold, the scarabs, skulls and skeletons, even the rose of Jericho, cleared out before I could salvage them.

Meanwhile, though, I had to go back to school and pretend that my boyhood had not ended. On January 21st I wrote to X from Buckenhill, Bromyard, Herefordshire: 'I am going to read Dostoievsky's "Idiot"; I don't get much time to myself, and so I shall leave school after this term and spend one term with my mother before going up to Oxford. Today I had to beat a boy (I am a "monitor"). The only way to overcome one's distaste at such an occupation is to force oneself to feel contempt for the creature being punished; fortunately this is usually not very difficult, though I'm told that I did not cane hard enough. How shameful! I will try to be more conscientious next time.' One of the boys I had to cane was to be a Cabinet Minister, and one of the few for whom I never felt contempt. In the same letter I reported: 'I read Eliot's "East Coker", and after reading it four times, I have come to appreciate it more than any other modern poem.' (I was to discover Yeats soon after, in a Bangor bookshop, with consequences even more formative for my early work.) 'I am not going to write any more dead poems; that means I will probably write no more poems. I am very depressed by my failure to write in anything but a "worn-out poetical fashion". I wish I could express myself in symbols taken from real life.' Pages of self-dissatisfaction follow in that letter, as in hundreds of others. Because of so many pressures on me, the one thing I could not learn for years was patience. In my outward achievements I was precocious, in myself I was prevented from growing by that very precocity, by perpetually forcing myself to leap ahead intellectually of my emotional needs and development.

No wonder, therefore, that by February 18th I had forgotten all about the drastic alternative in my preceding letter — fulfilment or silence! — no more than another attempt to jump ahead of myself: 'I'm sending you an altered and revised form of my last poem, which you criticized in London; I have changed the poem completely, and retained only some ideas and the best lines. Please criticize it mercilessly, and tell me whether you think it is of any use. I believe it is influenced by Eliot's style. A pity.' If it was an attempt to imitate Eliot's inimitable manner, that would have been a pity only if I had been ready at all to write poems of my own, as I was far from being; but, as the same letter tells me, I could not wait for anything at that period: 'I have sent my translations of Hölderlin to John Lehmann' — at the age of sixteen! — 'I don't expect an answer, but one must attempt the impossible to get any success. He will probably consider me damned conceited, impertinent and so on; but who cares?' Incidentally, that letter bears out my first impression of X's lodgings: 'I am sorry about your father, more than about the furniture; if you really want some, I am sure you can have some from our house, which is not being used much. Don't be too proud to tell me if you want some. I'll settle it with Mother... Do you still correspond with Maria? I wrote her a letter, but it was a disgustingly helpful sort of letter. No wonder I got no answer. The trouble is, I feel I have some responsibility towards her, and I can't set about it, because I hate interfering with people because I hate being interfered with.' My sister Maria was two and a half years older than I, and better able to look after herself than I was of looking after her. The 'responsibility' was an inheritance from my father; the misgivings about it belonged to a different code, taken over from my British education. The letter continued: 'I have been trying to leave school this term. This continual play-acting and hypocrisy get me down, and I want to get away from it. But I can't. My mother and my so-called guardian or adviser are against it. So I shall have to stick it for another term. I am so used to having my own way in matters regarding my own life that I was really surprised at having failed this time. You can't imagine what this is like. It was all right while I could break rules and laugh at discipline, but now I am the representative of authority, and my job is to repress any signs of an individual mind. Ludicrous, but very annoying. Have been reading Auden's latest poems, *Another Time;* some excrementally vulgar, in the style of jazz tunes. Others, however, are very fine, and I can see aspirations to a new perfection of style, or rather an old one... I have bought Gascoyne's *Hölderlin's Madness;* very good translations and some original poems. His translations are much more free and personal than mine, and the mad poems definitely better, but I *think* that my translations of the sane ones are as good as his, or better. Probably only conceit... I am very tired and bored and rather depressed. The only consolation is the country. Say what you like, laugh at me, but I still like nature better than any amount of streets. I like both, but nature is more refreshing, and sometimes even gives me hope: romantic drivel, perhaps, but true... I hope to come to London some time to pack up some things, but I'm not sure.'

X's response to my poem cheered me up for a while. On February 27th I wrote: 'I rely on your criticism more than on any other, because I know that, first of all you are yourself a true poet and secondly, that your criticism is frank and just and that it can be ruthless when necessary... you have given me hope, in the same way as you made me realize the futility of my previous attempts. Please don't think that you are "talking down" to me, or that I think you are. Your experience would justify a far more patronizing attitude than yours is. Besides, I feel I know you too well to feel wounded in my pride by advice from you, since only people I do not like or understand can do that. Also, I'm rather precocious and conceited, and must try to cure myself of those faults. That reminds me: you very justly remark that it is rather presumptuous of me to lay down the law, as I did in this and many other poems. I can't excuse this, because you are right, but I can explain it: as soon as I try to put some problem or feeling into words, I have a violent inclination to get to the fundaments, often to generalize stupidly, but, above all, to get beyond the purely personal... I have read more than I have lived, and thought more than experienced, and all this is sure to show in my poems. I am too much like a Huxley novel: no action, no movement, only ideas and sterility. Perhaps I shall have time to live profoundly, but I fear not. I feel worn out already... I have been trying to get Baudelaire's letters; I can't. I was very fond of the little bookshop in Swiss Cottage. I can't really picture you sitting there with a cup of tea; but I should think it is not too bad, since you can read.'

Miss Waterhouse's little bookshop in what was the arcade of Swiss Cottage Tube Station not only laid the foundations for my library, from the time I spent my pocket money there as a schoolboy, but it became a refuge for several of my friends, whom she employed. Long after the disappearance of her shop I discovered that a tramp-like character with whom I talked there repeatedly across a language barrier was one of the best Yiddish poets surviving from the diaspora and near-destruction of that culture, Itzik Manger, and that he owed his survival in London to Miss Waterhouse's help. Her generosity and kindness, especially towards writers or potential writers, were concealed behind a sad and embittered face and a manner easily mistaken for surliness or moroseness. In her shop I bought not only English classics but German and French books otherwise unobtainable in the war, out of the libraries of refugees who had congregated in that part of London. In later years it was Bumpus's bookshop in Oxford Street — and its foreign language department — that served me as a day-time social centre, library and information bureau, as well as a place in which to buy books.

By March 19th it had been decided that I could go to Oxford on April 25th, after my seventeenth birthday, and I hoped that I could get to London before that. 'Today I visited a barracks, and I have seen a hell which I have not yet experienced.' Since I was expecting to be called up soon, some of my impatience was due to the conviction that I should be killed soon and that 'all my work for scholarships will have been in vain,' as I wrote to X on February 27th. On April 5th I wrote from 8 Menai Terrace, Bangor: 'I am now in Wales with the family. Maria arrived today' — from Nottingham, where she was living as a dress-maker — 'and she has been talking about you. The weather is very dark and dismal, and that depresses me more than I can understand. I have finished school... I am coming to London on the 20th or so, and hope to see you... John Lehmann answered about my translations; he seems to like them. I'm going to see him when I go to London. What about your poems and *New Writing* which he edits? Does *Poetry* ever print translations? I have been translating Rilke lately. Maria says that London is very quiet now and very empty. Still, I would rather be there. I hate small towns: either a cow-shed or a capital, but no compromises.'

By the time we moved out of St. John's Wood Park in March 1943, very few houses in the street were inhabited. Our own had lost all its windows and the glass roof of the conservatory. One exception was that of the sinister ex-lawyer E. S. P. Haines, who lived with two large dogs — which once had to be sent away for treatment after he had flogged the hide off them — a manservant, a plentiful supply of spirits and a collection of rare erotica. I got to know him when the almost derelict street was an appropriate setting for a survivor like him, and he would bathe in the water tank that had been set up against incendiary bombs. He asked me to tea once or twice and showed me some of his books; and I seem to remember calling on him with my Oxford friend John Mortimer. He did not show me the whips he used on his dogs and — so it was rumoured — employed his manservant to use on him.

For years after that I revisited the street and our house, roaming the wilderness that had sprung up where the gardens used to be. As late as 1950 or 1951 I wrote and published a poem, 'Derelict Street', about 'the almost reverted wood', trying at once to raise and exorcise the ghosts of the 'obstinate fool' who had his being there and of the 'wittier one, his friend' — Freddy. The evocation failed not only because of its Yeatsian machinery, inadequately handled, but because in the poem's own words,

> ...the years have raised a wall
> Hard, though invisible,
> Proof against all intrusion:
> From its surface touch and sound,
> Gesture and glance rebound
> Into the mind's confusion...

Because my obstinacy, like my reluctance to leave that house, was a vain impulse to resist change; and because, by 1950, I knew better, at least half in love with the wilderness that was blotting out the traces. Equally obstinate though they were, my father, too, knew the limits of his human loyalties and affections. His last will was that his ashes be scattered on the Swiss Alps.

Three

In one letter, written in August 1940, Freddy signed himself 'your devoted chronicler'. That is what he shall be here, in part, because his letters are a great deal livelier than anything I wrote in those years. Freddy, in his way, was producing 'literature'. A postscript asks me to keep his letters, since if he was not mistaken about himself they would be worth £10 a piece one day. Freddy may have been mistaken about himself, but I kept his letters, and am glad that I did.

That same summer Freddy actually took some exercise: 'During the last two days I have been crippled in one foot,' he wrote from Buckinghamshire. 'This is the result of walking 107 miles in six days. Consequently, I have been working for the first time in some years. I have taken notes on three great volumes dealing with James I, and my overwrought and complex constructions in this letter are the result of reading Coke on Purveyance or Bacon's views on Divine Right.' Another letter gives the reason for this unusual exertion: 'My orgy of heartiness in walking is, in reality, a glorified pub-crawl, and I think I have tasted the vintage of every licensed house within ten miles. "Nothing in excess" is a device suited to the conventional and timid, and a precept which I have never had occasion to follow.'

Freddy and I met again in London that August, but he was not returning to school. The reading mentioned above was the beginning of his preparations for an Oxford scholarship that he won without any help of any institution or tutor. In September he moved to Cheltenham, the home town of the boy from whom his expulsion had separated him in term-time. For the same boy he wrote a poem that September, 'An Apology for Puberty', far less involuted and anachronistic than his prose in the letters. As Freddy explained in a letter, he had read no contemporary poet except MacNeice, and that makes its tone even more astonishing, at a time when Freddy was immersed in Walter Pater. The poem begins:

> Baker Street looks dead on a Saturday evening;
> Only a few tarts and taxis plying for hire:
> The winter nights are drawing nearer, nearer,

As I would draw near the fire.
But fires cost money. Money, the curse of my life.
It surrounds me, but I have not
Happiness: outwardly opulent, carnations, cane and tie-pin,
But within, the stench of dry-rot.
But soon, I suppose, I shall have to exist on fifty
Cigarettes a week:
Alas, I shall never inherit the earth like a Christian
(Blessed are the meek)
All I shall ever inherit is a few hundred,
But not till twenty-five,
Eight years ahead, and in the meantime
I must keep alive.
Alive, i.e., for me, not crusts and water
But Abdullas and decent wine,
Orchestra stalls and limited editions
And polished nails that shine
In the light of candles set in silver sconces ...

The poem goes on for several pages with reflections on Freddy's recent 'débâcle' and very serious misgivings about his future. As Freddy himself commented, 'these verses are my first and, I suppose, only attempt to be sincere in literature'. His letters continued in the old style:

November 3rd, 1940: 'Pause a moment, in your manual task, and, wiping the perspiration from your fine brow with a silk handkerchief of that soiled white which is characteristic of a dying culture, be seated amid the barren solitudes of Buckenhill while I, your chronicler, seek to portray for the delectation of your enforced exile some few images less mirthless than the bleakness of Bromyard, or the high-life of Herefordshire.' This leads to a long disquisition on boredom — 'the least sterile of negations' — on the literature of boredom and, inevitably, on Proust's Charlus, Wilde and Lord Alfred Douglas, Praz's *The Romantic Agony*, hence to Freddy's love life. In the next letter, of November 15th, he addresses me as 'Most Monitorial Highness', and continues: 'Hear, from the Olympian austerity of your exalted mercy-seat, the plea of a humble suppliant. I have not had talks with gods and Monitors, and others of that kidney, but there is one question I've always wished to put to them: Is it cold up there?'

In his previous letter Freddy had asked for news about his boy-friend, and I had refused to act as a go-between. This offended Freddy: 'Without further proem or preamble: I must take exception to one sentiment in your otherwise delightful letter. I have asked you to be ponce or pander to no unholy lust, to further no besotted or filthy scheme of debasement; to corrupt no youth and to stain no reputation; and yet, to my enquiries concerning —, you reply as though I were a Borgia before the Seat of Judgement. You know, far better than the rout and crapulous rabble who turn me to ridicule, you know how true is my affection for —, and how constant. It is to you alone that I've spoken of these things in earnest, and your advice thereupon has been respected, though seldom taken ... Now, at a moment when dreams (I dreamt of him last night) and fevered fancies are the sole consolation for a life barren as I assure you is mine, come your reproaches and your refusal to help me, even in so small a thing. I have never required you to pimp for me: you should know in what measure I revere your immaculate conscience ...

'But revenons a nos moutons, and let me again assume the cap and bells, the motley of Folly, my vocation by necessity. Your warning of my stagnation is timely. I have felt it myself. In fact:

My brains decay, my brains decay and fall,
Abdullas weep my talents to the ground;
Maid comes, and makes the bed: I lie beneath
And after many a slumber comes the dawn ...

(Note: in the third line, it is the bedclothes I lie beneath, not the maid. Mais ça va sans dire.)

'This process of pulverization is further aggravated by the constant perusal of critical works, biography, memoirs, history, and other displays of dusty desultory erudition.'

To counteract this 'pulverization' Freddy had sketched out some short stories 'with a possible view to offering them to *Horizon*. One was to be about Wilde, another about Verlaine and Rimbaud. Like most of Freddy's literary projects they were abandoned. After his one sincere poem most of his writing did not get beyond parody — like the above lines based on lines I used to recite from Tennyson's 'Tithonus'.

It was Freddy, not I, who should have been still at school. Though less mature than he in most ways, I could derive no more satisfaction from it. When I wrote to Freddy that I disliked being a Monitor, he elaborated all the joys this office would have given him. He belonged to that enclosed world of hierarchically graded achievements and could have flourished in it if it hadn't cast him out for deriving more pleasure from it than the code allowed. The same code that limited his freedom protected him from the political and social changes that he had more reason to fear. Though he was to cut a figure for a while at Oxford, that expulsion was his downfall, and he knew it. All he could do was to put a brave face on it with gestures like describing his profession as 'dilettante' when applying for a ration card.

On December 18th he wrote to me: 'I see nothing in the *Telegraph* about Election this morning: but I need not written proof of your success, which I know is assured. You deemed me fortunate once: our positions are altered.' This must refer to my Exhibition to Christ Church, which I should have been unable to take up but for special funds made available by the college at the Head Master's request. Nor should I have got to Oxford in a bye-term without his support of my wish to leave school as soon as possible. Freddy could not understand my impatience, if only because he had no intention of doing military service. I couldn't understand his very different predicament, or I shouldn't have written him the 'homilies' which he begged me to continue, since he could take them from me, if from no one else.

Freddy, meanwhile was also working for his scholarship and had been able to obtain a reference from the school in spite of his expulsion. He was also preparing for Oxford in a different way, assuring me that there was no danger of an estrangement between us, because 'the baroque barbarities of my Westmonasterial personality will not be suited to the austere quadrangles of Oxford: there, the maturer delicacy of the rococo will be required. Oxford provides the perfect setting for my talents. There are none of the galling restraints of a public school, the company is charming, and the ogre of sex-starvation is absent. Those who require women may find women, and those with some taste in the matter may continue unhampered their appreciation of subtler delights. And, when finally caught in flagrante delicto, there shall be none of the distasteful enquiry so dear to the sadic —; a short note from the Dean, and I shall leave unostentatiously to linger as a legend when the oarsmen of Brasenose and the prigs of New College are forgotten.'

That was an accurate prediction, as far as Freddy is concerned, except that he was to be forced to leave Oxford not for his 'subtler delights' but for debts incurred over them. I did not read Hobhouse's *Oxford* or *The Life and Times of Anthony à Wood*, which he recommended to me. Nor was I mature enough to avail myself of the less subtle delights he thought were available there. My Oxford was to be not rococo but severely Gothic.

In the same letter of January 1941 Freddy took up the dissatisfaction I had expressed with my verse written at school: 'I am pleased to hear that you abandoned the conventional mode of poetry. "The roaring of hungry lions"' — a reference to my dreadful piece of didacticism 'The Beast's Farewell' — 'was useful as an experimental exercise in the structure of words and metre, but bears no more relation to poetry than does 'la plume de ma tante est dans la jardinière' to the obscene sonnets written by Verlaine in bed with Rimbaud ... Beware of too much Eliot, as he tends to have a mentally constipating influence, and the costive condition of some younger poets is due to him. The school of Auden is trying to get away from this rarefied atmosphere, but at the expense of often writing worthless pieces. MacNeice is a healthier and more desirable model.'

I wish I had taken more notice of that warning than Freddy took of mine, about other things. T. S. Eliot's influence combined with Oxford Gothic were to constipate me both mentally and emotionally for many years to come. Eliot's doctrine of impersonality, taken too literally, kept me locked in a cage of decorous generalities, so securely that I could make no use of his own comments on my poems telling me how to get out. His 'objective correlative', improperly understood, made me distrust the data of my immediate experience, though his own poems should have put me right about that. His religion set me off on a protracted, agonizing, and finally fruitless, quest. But no one forced me to choose a father figure so ascetic, and use him for my own self-defeating ends. 'Influences' are only another word for our own compulsions and needs.

In February, Freddy described the extraordinary effort he was making to win that scholarship: 'I have been born and bred a voluptuary. My remotest memories, my immediate lineage, were of the world and the Flesh (and perhaps of the Devil). Now, I ask you to believe, that since the fifth of this month I have worked from eight to ten hours a day. This is done on tobacco and the mortification of the flesh. On about 35 cigarettes and 2 cigars a day, I can take some 50 pages of notes and read at least two books. Thus, today, I have read Belloc's

Napoleon and Petrie's *Bolingbroke*, and taken about 30 pages of notes on 17th-century Holland. It is now 11.30. I have sat at this desk since 9.30 a.m., with breaks for meals and ½ hr's walk this afternoon ... Any honours I get will have been earned.'

When Freddy received a telegram from a number of masters at school congratulating him on his scholarship, he was triumphant: 'You will have a delightful time,' he wrote on March the 18th, 'but not so perfect as mine will be, surrounded by all that can make my blood circulate once more.' Yet he also quoted: 'To fresh defeats he still must move.' In February he had sympathized with my attempts to obtain permission to leave school: 'For once, your woeful protestations have a cause ... Make a resolute attempt to persuade those in charge of you that remaining at school will be a waste of time and money.'

I had lent Freddy my copy of W. H. Auden's *Another Time*. He commented: 'The common opinion that *Miss Gee* is cruel neither touches myself nor Auden, who share a perversity: spinsters disgust us both. But the mood and metric of that section of the book are cheap, and they are stupid. The first poem I think the best: "Beneath the hot incurious sun".' He asked me to copy that poem for him. In the same letter he comments on my search for a publisher for my Hölderlin translations: 'I doubt whether there is enough anticipation of Marx in Hölderlin to appeal to Lehmann, but the effort is praiseworthy, and I wish for its success. If they publish it, you might dedicate the book to me, as you will then be sure of at least a posthumous sale.' I did not dedicate the book to him when it was accepted for publication some two years later. Hölderlin and Freddy did not go together; and by 1942, when I was waiting to join the army, we were seeing little of each other.

I, too, was keen to go to Oxford, but before I got there I tried to join the Merchant Navy. Like a later attempt to get into the Royal Navy, this one was thwarted by my German birth. I was also one of the few boys at Westminster who had failed to pass out of the O.T.C. Freddy had dropped out of the O.T.C. in 1937 and had no intention of doing any kind of war service: 'I have decided to object, if not conscientiously,' he wrote in February. 'There is probably a higher percentage of kissable young men in the objectors' camps than in the line regiments; and, anyhow I have a rather determined intention of emerging alive from the war.'

Freddy was unable to visit me at Bangor till the summer of that year, but in April we met in London. In Bangor I had found three books of Yeats's poems — new copies still in the shop six years after publication in one case, *A Full Moon in March*, less in the case of *The Herne's Egg* and *Last Poems and Plays*. Many years later, around 1950, Yeats's manner became so obtrusive in my verse that one critic, G. S. Fraser, described me as 'ghosting for the ghost of Yeats'; and that criticism now strikes me as fair.

When Freddy and I met in London, just before my going up to Oxford, I left all my belongings behind at the Dutch Oven in Baker Street. Freddy retrieved them and wrote: 'The woman in the Dutch Oven said, "He must have been very much in love." I asked whether you looked like that. "Oh, I never saw the man," she answered.'

At Christ Church I had rooms in Peckwater, at first in an attic, later on the ground floor. After the barrack-like dormitories at Buckenhill, our bomb-damaged house in St. John's Wood and the drab lodgings in Bangor — where the mad landlord had chased my mother with a carving-knife — it felt strange to live in an oak-panelled room, waited upon by a servant. My mother had provided me with what remained of the contents of my father's wine cellar in St. John's Wood after the raids on it by my sister Maria and her boy friends. Those pre-war relics included a bottle of green Chartreuse which attracted all sorts of visitors to my room. Although the college was full of Old Westminsters, most of them were older than I, so that I had no immediate social contacts and had to look for new friends. One of these was John Mortimer, whose college, Brasenose, had been quartered with Christ Church, much as Westminster had been with Lancing College.

Not long after my arrival I received a large parcel with the instruction 'not to be opened', followed by a telephone call from my former House Master at Bromyard, asking me to see him at once. It turned out that two friends of mine at Westminster had broken into the Head Master's house, and that the parcel contained valves and other parts removed by them from his radiogram. When I was still at Bromyard the same two boys had caught a duck, killed it with the greatest difficulty, and begun to roast it over a fire of sticks before having to return to their dormitories. The half-roasted duck was left in a drawer there for days, and had begun to stink when I was accompanying the House Master on his evening round of inspection. He smelled a rat, or duck, and was getting pretty close to it. Since I knew about the escapade I did my best to keep him away from that drawer, and succeeded that time. The duck was then disposed of. This new escapade was more serious, and there was little I could do for my friends. One of them decided to leave after a threat of expulsion, and I later managed to get him into Wadham College, whose Warden, C. M. Bowra, told me that he would take anyone expelled by J. T. Christie from Westminster School. It was a wasted effort, since this friend did no work, hardly ever left his room, did not want to meet anyone, and left after a term or two.

That sort of situation, soon to recur at Christ Church, sprang from an ambiguity in myself. All the people who interested me enough to become my friends seemed to go in for pursuits which I couldn't share, had no wish to share, or was inhibited from sharing. If these got them into trouble, I was implicated and plunged into a conflict of loyalties. What I couldn't see was that my self-righteousness was a compulsion quite as perverse, and often as destructive, as their pursuits. Freddy was no more 'of the Devil' than I, at heart, was on the side of the angels, if that meant the side of hypocritical respectability; but it would have been easier for me to become a monk than to imitate his sensuality, quite apart from its direction.

For the benefit of X, who had educated himself in London, mainly at the British Museum Reading Room, I wrote this description of Christ Church life in a letter of May, 1941: 'It consists of four quadrangles. There are eight to twelve rooms on each staircase. I live right on the top of one, in a garret, no. 12. The undergraduates are of many kinds: Those who come up to have a good time, wine, women and swing. Those who come up to talk: potted culture, the right books, music reduced to an intellectual skeleton. Then, the compromising mediocrities; and finally, oh, how glamorous!, the unapproachable, exclusive eccentrics. These are various: some are poor wretches who are simply abnormal: they are usually ignored. I don't mean those. The real eccentrics practice eccentricity as an art, with subtle nuances of vice, the dressing gown specially made for the purpose of flashing, long hair, velvet waistcoats, even cosmetics, and usually a lot of money to throw about. Most exciting. As to work, I see my tutor three times a week, and he sets me quite a lot of work to do. There are also lectures, outside the college, which I very rarely attend because one can learn more by reading. Meals take place in a large Hall, and tea takes place in one's rooms. It is usual to invite others to tea or to sherry at 6.30p.m. After dinner at 7 one can go out until midnight, but I very rarely go out at night, because I am not very fond of the pictures.'

In another letter to him of that month I describe the state of shock that was also at the root of my dissatisfaction with the verse I was writing at the time: 'Things are beginning to appear strange: today I walked through the crowded streets of Oxford, and it seemed to me that I had seen every passing face before. The spring seems unreal, the flowers and the warmth are out of place, part of something that is passed and buried in the subconscious.

At first I kept apart from company, but then I gave in out of weakness. But it is no use: even in fascinating company I am alone, because I just don't react. Oxford is very pleasant to live in after school, because you are left alone. I realize how fortunate I am to be here, and I only wish I could appreciate it more.'

X and Freddy, meanwhile, were meeting in London, where I must have introduced one to the other. 'We have both altered our first impressions of one another' Freddy wrote in May, 'and I find him interesting and delightful.' Contrary to all my expectations of Freddy, too, he was undergoing a temporary change, becoming less flamboyant and cultivating not only a plainer style in his letters and dress but a new calligraphy, 'not wholly legible', he wrote, but with the merit of 'looking important, which ever was the aim of your very devoted Freddy.' That month his mother and he gave up their house in St. John's Wood. Freddy was planning a book about Otto Weininger, at first as a psychological study, then as a novel. (Otto Weininger, a homosexual of Jewish descent, became famous for his book *Geschlecht und Charakter* (Sex and Character), published in 1903, in which he attributed feminine characteristics to the Jews as a race, providing substance for a pseudo-scientific anti-semitism already widespread at the turn of the century. The self-hatred that drove Weininger to suicide was propounded so delicately and forcefully in his writings that the philosopher Wittgenstein — of mainly Jewish descent also — was among those intrigued by them.) Freddy hoped to get down to work on it after Responsions, in July, but nothing came of either project. 'I have come out of that Saison en Enfer called puberty', Freddy wrote '— the most vitiated and futile hell ever conceived — and feel that at last my prejudices and predilections are in some static form. You will also find this peace soon, and your correspondents will hear less of languor and depression, and more of new things being written, and fresh experiences tested. If I may be didactic for a moment, it will be to advise a break with your tradition of repressing natural impulses. If you were once to have a physical experience, the ensuing calm would reflect itself, not least in your writing. When you shrink from this and hide your head in the sand, you adopt an attitude the more ridiculous because it is untenable. Oscar could live up to his blue china, and I to my Beardsleys, but you cannot carry your celibatory ambitions to their conclusion without doing violence to your nature, and, thus, to your art. Should your innocence be a pose (and I assume it is not), then it would be more ludicrous: it were as well to pose as deaf, or as mentally deficient. I know you, who have so often and charmingly preached to me, will forgive this temporary assumption of Elijah's mantle, by him who was your gaudy, and is your sincere friend, Freddy.'

To the end of our close friendship — which was near — I remained incapable of profiting by Freddy's greater maturity or by the shrewdness of judgement he could now reveal whenever he was not preoccupied with his own ambition of 'looking important'. In June he commented on my hero-worship of Stephen Spender, whom I had met that year; 'You probably see more in Spender than there actually is, but I think it is no bad thing to have a hero, however inadequate. It saves one from cynicism and narcissism. I have no hero myself, but am possibly more self-contained than you.' In the same letter he outlined the fascinating plot of what had begun as his Weininger study but turned into a very personal exploration both of his own motives and those of his early Westminster 'pathick', whom he was seeing again at this period. Another instance of the development in Freddy is that his stylistic models for the book were not to be Pater and Huysmans, but Henry James — and Kafka, a writer who was only beginning to be appreciated.

On May 19th I reported to X: 'I had a letter from John Lehmann today in which he says that he will soon discuss my translations with Spender, but that even if he likes them the difficulty remains: how and where to publish them. I had hoped for a book, but am used to disappointments.' A month later I wrote to X: 'These last days have been very eventful for me. Both Freddy and David Buckley came to see me, and stayed for some days. (D.B. is the silent boy whom you met the last time I saw you.) I was amazed to see what an enormous influence you have had on Freddy, an influence you seem to exert on almost everyone you come into contact with. Freddy talked like you, expressed all your views about literature, and even modelled the intonation of his voice on yours. Unfortunately your influence, though great, has not been sufficient: he behaved in a disgustingly vulgar fashion. On the last evening he gathered all his Oxford acquaintances together in my room, with the object of making an impression. For an hour he talked about himself in a most offensive, conceited manner, and on being laughed at he broke down completely. This was worse than his bloated self-satisfaction: he said that there was nothing in him, that he was a mediocrity, who cultivated eccentricity only to satisfy his inferiority complex. Unfortunately this confession corresponded with the general view of his audience, and his chances of popularity have been destroyed.

John Lehmann visited me on Wednesday. He had been giving an interesting lecture the night before on contemporary literature.' (This was at the university English Club, in which I was involved as an organizer, together with Philip Larkin.) 'He wants a Shakespearean giant, a Tolstoy, a poet who can interpret his age in literature. He did not say, however, that such a giant must be very sure of his ethics; and who can be, today?' I then ran through the candidates, Eliot, Auden, Spender — with great hopes for the last, after reading his 'September Journal' in a recent issue of *Horizon.* In my next letter I return to Freddy: 'He has had a very unpleasant time (he was incessantly bullied at school) and has developed an inferiority complex, together with a desire for revenge which he occasionally satisfies on his friends. When I complained of his behaviour here, it was not because I objected to it, but because he defeated his own purpose by it and made himself quite unhappy. I agree with you when you say that 'even beneath the humility and Christianity of the great Tolstoy there is an overbearing and incredible conceit.' Dostoievsky says: 'In the abstract love for humanity one always loves only oneself.' I admit that I have looked for 'a friend who will satisfy me in every particular', but I never expected Freddy to fulfil this hope; it is only the natural urge to find something ideal, which — one's reason tells one — is really foolish and ludicrous.'

I wrote a letter to Stephen Spender when drunk, after being introduced to him at Oxford by John Lehmann, then tormented myself with self-reproaches about it, probably because the letter was a hero-worshipping one that could only embarrass him. X also visited me at Oxford towards the end of the term, but a conflict arose between us after he had taken me to the house of a Communist friend of his called Ridley, to whom I did not take. That altercation and my remorse precipitated another of my long and wordy juvenile poems. X had reacted just as negatively to one of the Christ Church aesthetes and dandies I must have introduced him to, known as 'The Black Tulip'. Very soon I had no more use for characters of that kind than he had.

I spent part of my first vacation at Oxford taking notes for the Introduction to my Hölderlin translations. Then I went to Bangor to stay with my family. From there, in all seriousness, I informed X of a new political party I had founded together with my school friend David Buckley, with a six-page manifesto of its programme, and asked him to join it! The nearest thing to the party's programme, although I did not know it, was Plato's Republic. The country was to be ruled by an 'elected council of experts, scientists, artists, scholars and engineers', rather than philosophers. Socially, it was to be a welfare state in which everyone would 'live in the most harmonious and congenial conditions possible.' There would be 'no large-scale capitalists, and everyone will only receive money for what he has done and promises to do. There will be no inherited fortunes. We want no dictatorship of the proletariat, as in Russia, or of the businessman, as in Britain. We want to abolish social classes.' But for the evidence of the letter in which I expounded this programme, assuring X that it was no joke, I should not believe that I was ever capable of such presumption. In my very next letter from 4 St. James's Drive, Bangor, written on July 22nd, I had second thoughts: 'About the political idea: I was not surprised by your rejection. Since I wrote the letter I have thought more coldly about it and have read Plato. Naturally I realize that utopias are practically impossible. Nevertheless, I believe that it is necessary to have a totally different society, and although the fundamental idea is utopian, it should also satisfy the practical needs of the people, and the utopian principle would only be a distant aim. You are right when you say that politics are not my cup of tea ...' In fact, the political programme was one of my precipitous and precocious leaps into generality, in this case out of frictions that had become acute during X's visit. On the level not of ideas but individuals, it was a frantic attempt — as surely doomed to failure as my poem on the same theme — to reconcile Ridley's Marxist dogmatism with the Black Tulip's freedom to parade his useless finery. X must have understood that. If they had not amused him, he could not have been as patient as he was with my monstrous follies of those years; and they would have got me into worse scrapes than they did if I had not been lucky enough to have a friend ten years older than I was.

In Bangor that summer I was studying the prose writings of Baudelaire and taking notes on them for work on him that I was to do years or even decades later. I then turned to Rimbaud, also reading a biography, probably Enid Starkie's, that gave me material for the poem 'Rimbaud in Africa', written three years later, but not salvaged for publication till forty years after that. On August 2nd I 'spent the day on Snowdon, or rather climbing it. It was pleasant to look down on the clouds for a change, but otherwise the heights were not impressive.' I also wrote to X: 'I agree with you that my poetry is not individual or only sound enough to justify publication, but I have a terrible impatience as regards my poems. I am always thinking that I shall not go on living very long, I don't know why, but I cannot imagine myself growing old at all, because death seems so actual and life much more dim. It may be only a fancy, but nevertheless I can't rid myself of this impatience.' At Oxford I had also met Dylan Thomas, and dreamed about him at Bangor. Curiously enough, in the dream he looked 'bloated', as he did become in later years, but was not when I first met him; and he was 'flashily dressed', as he wasn't at that time. I recorded that dream image in a drawing, and offered to send a copy to X, but it must have got lost. I was reading Thomas's *Portrait of the Artist as a Young Dog*, and raved about the stories to X, who did not share my enthusiasm for them.

In September I went to Llangrove, near Ross-on-Wye, in Herefordshire, to help with the harvest on a farm. 'I like hard physical work occasionally, because it makes me feel a different person altogether. Besides, I would rather be a farmer or even a bricklayer than an office clerk.' From there I wrote to X: 'Here I have very little time to write. I work nine to ten hours a day. On the whole I enjoy being a farm labourer, though of course it is very tiring ... I have been mildly in love again recently, but nothing will come of it. I mean that my attachment will fade away because it is not very deeply rooted. At present I am still friendly with the girl in question. She is a student of English literature at Bangor. She is beautiful in a wild Irish way, very unsophisticated.'

Before the beginning of term I stayed in London briefly, seeing my friends there, including X and Freddy, then went to Torquay to stay with my grandmother, who was in lodgings there. From Torquay I wrote to X: 'I shall not forget the last communal meeting at your room. Freddy was conscientiously pointing out trivial mistakes in your ms., and I knew that whether he was right or wrong he would discourage you. I could do nothing about it, because I know how easy it is to become uncertain about one's own work and how difficult to regain faith in it once one has been discouraged. If I had told him to stop, you would have thought that I too believed that the corrections were justified, but wanted to prevent him from revealing how bad the novel is. As a matter of fact, I think that some of the corrections were necessary, or at least advisable, but entirely unimportant ... I have discovered that a girl I knew some time ago is living in a village not very far away. I shall pay her a visit, and this has made my stay more exciting. I am also having long discussions with my grandmother which are at least stimulating for both of us. She has enquired about you, and likes you.'

In June Freddy had written to me: 'I had a letter this morning from X, whose esteem I value very much. Were it not for his praise and your constant support, I should more often succumb as I so lamentably did the other night. You are very good to forgive me after having behaved so in your rooms. But that is not all you have forgiven; years of abuse and satire, incomparable rudeness; you have forgiven these. I remember in what anxiety I waited for your return to Exeter last year in the middle of that tragi-comedy; and how, when I found, contrary to my anticipation, that you were not taking your cardinal opportunity of revenge; that you, who knew all my secrets, whom I had so often and so lately insulted, who had more than a slight acquaintance with the instigator of the affair, were remaining silent: then I felt a gratitude and sincere affection which, until now, I have been too timid to express.'

This must refer to the circumstances of Freddy's expulsion from school, and I have forgotten all about them, just as I've forgotten the offences against me of which he accuses himself. Our relations, as I said, were based on the attraction of opposites, and I can consider myself lucky to have had a Mephistopheles like him to make fun of my Faustian compulsions.

A chance meeting with an army officer on his way to Buckinghamshire prompted Freddy to make another discovery about himself — about his kind of romanticism, snobbery, about his Toryism, and the degree to which he ought to have been an insider, and would have been but for his homosexuality. This officer was 'late of New College, Eton before that, a historian, hates the army, in for diplomacy, intelligently unassuming, a Roman Catholic, broad-minded, heterosexual, Tory, healthy-minded, but has brains.' Freddy went on: 'Dabble as I may in anarchism, it is to this I come as to home. It is these people, charming, insincere, sympathetic, and above all well-mannered, who put me at my ease ... You will never see what I mean, because it is quite foreign to your appreciation, but Etonians are like honey to my social qualities.' In such people, Freddy wrote, he found peace. 'It is not in Wilde, and it is not in me, for whom it is unattainable, therefore admirable.' This was the chink in Freddy's armour and the point where his shrewdness deserted him, for he was to ruin his Oxford prospects, and all his prospects in England, by trying to keep up socially with a set which, at best, found his oddities amusing for a while. In the process he lost most of his former friends.

Freddy was disgusted with the political idealism to which he attributed my work as a farm labourer that summer: 'My summary rejection of your warm gospel probably did not cheer you up; but, really, you will outgrow this sort of thing. Never having been a child myself, I have not been prey to such fancies. I think I was born cynical, and can remember even as an infant rejecting the tasty morsels of morality held out by relatives on the ends of their respectable umbrellas. At some time or another we both made our first acquaintance with the life of Shelley: you were entranced (and still are, slightly) but, I thought him a pretentious humbug; wholly without wit, a village schoolmaster's mentality in the body of an anaemic pathick, a bumptious poet ... If he had tempered his wild-eyed zeal with complete disdain for his pretended objects of enthusiasm, it might have been better; but he was that most boring manifestation, an egoist who has not the sense to realize it. Who wants to lead the Workers' Movement, or even be President and Chairman of the Housewives' Auxiliary Service Council Committee for the Preservation of Votes for Cockatoos except in order to be glorified and lauded? Such people are beastly anyway; all enthusiasts are beastly; but never more so than when they pretend to disinterestedness.' Our differences were now crystallizing, so much so that it was difficult for them to interact. Though Freddy came to Bangor in September, and we got on as well as ever there, his going-up to Oxford in October, to a different college, put an end to the phase of our friendship that mattered to us both, because it was a vital confrontation.

In his next letter he refused to continue our political discussions. Instead, he wrote about Proust and homosexuality: 'It is rather terrible, but I always despise whom I love. It is as though the other person pays a price for loving, or being loved by, me; a price of pain and calumny and insult. Read *The Cities of the Plain* in *À La Recherche*, for Proust there sets out the blasted sterile heath of homosexual love in all its tragic colours.' In another letter he tells me off for being rude about his new association with the boy who had solicited him at Westminster, 'first, because it contradicts the principle of toleration which is supposed to underlie your philosophy, and also because each man makes the thing he loves, and, as I love him in a way (why should I be ashamed? I am not above emotions, thank heaven) you are depreciating me, which is beyond your intention.' It was beyond my intention, and I accepted the rebuke, though at one time it had been Freddy who inflicted his contempt for the same boy on me. And two years earlier, in October 1939, Freddy had composed a formal document in which he addressed me as 'Sir', apologized for slander against me, and drew up a sort of contract for our future relations:

'This afternoon, while we were separated by a large table, I took advantage to besmear your name with foul abuse, to heap calumnious libels upon your character, and doubt your loyalty to our Gracious Sovereign.

'These untruths, both in the manner of their delivery and in their substance, were, I unreservedly acknowledge, an unjustifiable and opprobrious slander, unbefitting my position and rank; reducing me to the level of the guttersnipe who pelts the passing traveller with mud while lying concealed behind a wall ...

'Besides, Sir, I fear that I am not of the mannish make; I have a woman's weapons, a slanderous tongue. It may appear an affectation to declare that physical violence is nauseating to me; but I fear that it is true.

"Therefore, since I do most earnestly and upon my bended knees conjure and beseech you to refrain from attacks upon my person, it is also meet that I should refrain from further logomachy ... '

This sort of nonsense had long been left behind. Our disagreements now were real ones, as when Freddy, in the same letter, played down my high seriousness about poetry: 'I am sorry to hear about your poem, but you are talking rubbish when you say your life depends on it. On art, perhaps; but you know the opinion which "X" and I entertain of poets and poetry. Such an adolescent activity is made only to be grown out of, like the other addictions of public intellect — atheism, *À Rebours*, rhodomontade. Try a prose work: you have several very good things to say which a poem won't hold, and the hard work will discipline your talents. I am not one to talk, for "Paul" is hibernating, although I am determined to finish it this year.'

Freddy concluded: 'I advise you to throw yourself more into the world,' very sound advice, if I had been ready for it. Freddy had made his peace with the world, on his own terms: 'You seem to be trying to sell me a back-bone,' he had written on July 3rd, 'but the homosexual is a parasite. I am not a parasite in the particular sense, and such living on a person I dislike; but a parasite on society, to which I must hold, however bad or stupid or unpleasant, for fear of worse ... When you and the others set out to find Utopia, having launched the lifeboats from the sinking ship of 19th-century liberalism, if I were to get on board with you someone would say, "Dirty creature! Throw him in the sea! Row, brothers, row, comrades, leave the wretch to drown!" ... I shall go to Oxford: I shall get a double first, and a triple thirst, and a fellowship. There, I will be in contact with the most intelligent men in Europe, and the most charming boys in England. I shall be more than one of these dons who, like your tutor, mumble the same eternal platitude. I shall write, read, and live at that pressure suited to my temperament. I shall keep Oxford pure, and attempt to defeat the machinations of Nuffield. Unambitious? Vegetable? Perhaps; but I will, at the risk of being very vain, say this. I really believe that, were I obliged to, I could do anything, a diplomat, a demagogue, a preacher, an actor, a politician, a prostitute. I have chosen Oxford, because it is the only safe Ivory Tower ... One is respected, not because an ancestor plundered a monastery or despoiled a Stuart to get a title, not because one's heart is in the right place (hateful), but because of what is on one's shoulders. "Use Your Head" is the only device worth having: "Use Your Heart" will end in tragedy.'

It did, for Freddy, who never got his degree, let alone his fellowship, and published only one book, the melodramatized story of his Oxford débâcle. The world — even the little world of Oxford — was not to be had on his terms.

By October 12th I was back at Oxford, 'well installed in the artificial paradise,' as I put it to X. The following week I wrote: 'I have been infernally busy doing uninteresting things. Oxford life is, on the whole, a great disappointment, if you are stupid enough to be disappointed. You meet so many people with fascinating facades, and when you know them better you find how desperately they are clinging to their little personalities, or only the pretence of a personality. I'm not blaming them for that. I'm no better myself. Sometimes my work consoles me (I am now finally typing out the Hölderlin) but often even that makes me thirsty ... When I'm not drunk I'm sober and damned depressed. However, I don't want to become dependent on drink for joy, and, besides, it is too expensive. So I'm usually depressed, which is rather funny.' In November my sister Eva was seriously ill with pneumonia, and that jolted me out of my Oxford preoccupations. 'When you are faced with (the possibility of) other people's deaths, your problems shrink and become ludicrous ... That is why, also, I find it so difficult to write anything in war-time, and I think most people do. There is always a still, small voice saying: to hell with your words and worries, we've got to die. Really this seems wrong. We are also going to die, and trying to create something valid before we do.' That month my Hölderlin script was rejected by Faber, though I must have submitted a later version in the following year, when T. S. Eliot wrote to me about it.

That October I also came close to being sent down, after a visit by Dylan Thomas to the English Club, which I had joined at once, becoming a committee member and — after the war — its President. There are two accounts of this visit in letters to X, one written immediately after the event, in October, the other in December. Neither mentions the intention of people outraged by Dylan's obscenities to throw him into Mercury, the Christ Church fountain, but I distinctly recall that threat; and it must have been more than my 'raving' that did enough damage to my room for me to be reported to the Junior Censor and almost sent down. Here is the fuller account of December 5th: 'I met him first at the English Club, which he was addressing. He read out several parodies of contemporary poets, George Barker, Spender, Auden and Eliot. He also read two new poems of his own. The room was more crowded than it had been before. We sat on the floor and could not stretch our legs. The parodies were good. When D. T. left, he was surrounded by a crowd of undergraduates who followed him and swarmed about him as though he were the queen bee. They finally dragged him off to this college and brought together all the liquor that could be obtained. We settled down to drinking and the telling of obscene stories. Dylan was excelled by none, not even Freddy, whom D. T. described as an 'American homosexual Jew'. I kept rather aloof, but got more and more drunk. At midnight Dylan had to leave the college. Then I proceeded to rave, and three friends attempted to tame me.

'The next morning I met D. at a sherry party, without any sherry, or a cocktail party without any cocktails. He was sober then. We talked culture, and he expressed his contempt for most of his contemporaries, except Eliot and Vernon Watkins — the latter, I suppose, because he is a Welshman. We then went to a pub — Freddy, Dylan, Wollheim and I. We continued to talk culture, while Dylan consumed pints of beer. He developed a theory to me about dignity, and the necessity of losing all *external* dignity before you can find out whether you have any *real* dignity, integrity. The others went off to have lunch, and I went on talking to Dylan, then brought him to this room. He criticized one of my poems, and said he liked it. Various people came in, and he told them what they were or would be: Wollheim — do you remember him? — a conductor of homosexual traffic. Croft, whom you have met, he described as 'smug and smutty' . He said that I would be a friend of Lucian Freud's. It so happened that I was some years ago. (Lucian Freud is a young painter of promise, friend of Stephen Spender's, grandson of the great F.)

'I met Dylan last at Freddy's room, where he was illustrating his *Twenty-Five Poems* for Freddy. I expect Freddy will show you the copy. As for Dylan's character, I can only say that he is very clever, witty and good-natured, utterly unprincipled and self-confident. He does not care about public opinion and would willingly relieve himself at a social gathering. He has amazing vitality, and gets drunk almost every day.

'As for his poems, they are not as undisciplined as you think. He writes only when he is sober and often rewrites a poem countless times. The effusive effect is calculated and, to me, attractive.' It is the earlier letter that mentions my being summoned next day to the Junior Censor's, but let off with a warning, because of my youth.

Dylan not only became a drinking companion, whom I met night after night in Soho when I was on vacation or army leave, but one of a succession of models for the derivative verse I was writing in those days. The poem I showed him, 'Childhood', was written in Wales in September of that year — in 'less than half an hour when I was ill and had a temperature', as I explained to X when I sent him a copy. Whatever Dylan found to praise in that poem, he certainly did not encourage me to write more such exercises in his own subliminal manner. Typically, though, I must have taken his detailed criticism to heart, because the version of the poem I kept among my papers bears very little relation to the early version I sent to X. The spontaneity I thought I had achieved under the influence of Dylan and a fever proved no more satisfactory than my more cerebral agonizings of those years.

Earlier that year, still at school, I had written a dialogue between Poet and Scientist no better as verse but much more pertinent to those quarrels with myself out of which I managed to make rhetoric, not poetry:

> No more dreams of immortality,
> Or recherché immorality
> Or riding on retired war-horses
> In Rotten Row.
> No more gazing on imaginary stars,
> No sublimation of sex;
> The heart has played its part,
> And the soul is on the dole:
> Only truth ...

This, of course, is the scientist speaking. The Poet despairs of truth, concluding: 'We can only find new ways/ Of saying nothing/ But we will say it' — a travesty of the Eliot *Four Quartets* I must have been reading at the time. That winter, at Oxford, I wrote the earliest of the poems I was to publish in my first book, the *persona* poem 'Hölderlin'. An earlier descriptive 'potted biography' poem on the same subject, written in March 1941, had come to grief. The later monologue was written under the influence not of a literary text, for once, but of one movement of a late Beethoven quartet — the Cavatina of the B flat major. (A recording of that movement only had been given to me by our neighbour in St. John's Wood, Yeatman-Woolf.)

Freddy had come to Oxford, to Magdalen, that term. 'I don't see very much of Freddy', I reported to X in November, 'He has at last become a social success by joining all the Conservative associations at Oxford, and so I no longer matter very much to him. I now believe that he always thought of me as a dustbin for his emotions, better than no one to talk to. I am not shocked or disappointed, because he is living by his standards, which are not mine.' By December I wrote to X: 'I have finally broken with Freddy, and we are no longer on speaking terms. He is becoming no more than a social puppet, telling everyone that he is "the man in fashion ..."'

I spent the Christmas vacation in London, in a 'useless and dissipated way', meaning parties and pubs. As a reaction, I plunged into work on my return. 'As long as I can read and write', I wrote on January 22nd 1942, 'I am not only happy but, in a quiet way, ecstatic ...

Oxford is a wasteland, and at present books are the water (or only the rocks?). I see very few people, and then very briefly. There is Ronald Cohen, whom, by indulging a certain Nietzschean strain in my character, I try to raise from servility and one of the most pitiable inferiority complexes I have ever seen. (He was the host at Dylan's Last Supper). His way of overcoming inferiority is generosity in money matters and, as he admits, the belief that he can buy companionship and recognition. Strangely enough, he is beginning to develop a sense of pride and greater confidence.' (Ronald Cohen, later a photographer, had been a friend since my prep. school.) 'Another is John Gowrie, not an undergraduate, a very eccentric and adventurous character who writes philosophical poems of great length in a formal, rhetorical eighteenth century manner. One he has just written describes the spiritual metamorphoses and development of man through the ages.' (John Gowrie, whose real name I may still have to withhold, was to be the editor and transcriber of a long 'philosophical' poem of my own published as a booklet while I was serving as a soldier overseas.) 'I wish you would come here. Freddy has made you a famous figure through his repetition and imitation of your remarks to him, real and imaginary. I have seen him once or twice. All bitterness is gone, but we have now hardly anything in common, and I dislike his role of clown and entertainer, and the way in which he popularizes his friends, chiefly you, and now also Dylan — intermingled!'

On February 4th, I told X that: 'I have had my translations refused for the fourth time, but since they may be the only work I can finish before leaving for the sea, I am going to rewrite the introduction for the fifth time and try again. On Tuesday I have to go to Reading for a medical examination and interview, and I shall ceremoniously end my days of freedom by being registered for the Navy. I now work most of the day, because I want to get my war degree in case I come back after the war ... ' I was rejected by the Navy, and mistaken about the 'war degree' that was no more than an interim examination. Such practicalities and formalities were beyond my comprehension. On the 26th I wrote: 'This term I formed an attachment to a girl that promises to be as unhappy as all my former ones. The fault is in myself, and I am too easily seduced by beauty, instead of virtue or constancy. It seems to me that love has to be studied, and is chiefly a matter of diplomacy. As in international politics, the victory belongs to him who can shout loudest, present the most impressive array of weapons, and bluff most convincingly. It very rarely comes to fighting.' The girl in question may have been my friend Rosemary, whom I saw from time to time, too shy to talk to her about anything but the most indifferent matters, over tea at Fuller's or dinner at the George Hotel. Those polite sessions, with their small talk about the Modern Languages course we were both taking, books and acquaintances, were excruciating, but there was nothing I could do to break the ice. It was she who broke it, years later, too late, when she actually kissed me good-bye because I was on embarkation leave! The heat engendered by that kiss, the first and last physical contact between us, was proportionate to the duration of the ice; and a different sort of pain, since she didn't answer my letters after that and soon married another man. John Mortimer had warned me off what he called the 'tennis-playing virgins' of Oxford; but he was more essentially mature and a great deal less inhibited than I was. At the English Club, where I met Rosemary, another attractive girl had come up to me and asked me whether I knew what young girls feel like in springtime. The question precipitated an embarrassment as acute as the House Master's had done back at school, when he was telling me 'the facts of life'.

My other infatuation at Oxford, on the rebound from the frigid one with Rosemary, was much more puerile still, since I hardly so much as spoke to the girl, Diana, who was already engaged to a medical student and university wrestling champion. I had seen her on one of my rare appearances at the Taylorian Institute, the Modern Languages building of the university — for a lecture by Enid Starkie, probably, since I attended very few others — and was overwhelmed by her radiant beauty. One night, when I was drunk in John Mortimer's rooms, I wrote a note to her fiancé challenging him to a duel! He was old and sensible enough to ignore it, and he laughed about the incident after the war, when I ran into him and Diana in Cornwall. On another occasion I rushed into Diana's college at a time when men were not admitted, got through to what I thought was Diana's room and found another girl there, in bed. The other girl was charming about the intrusion, but my romantic monomania made me rush out of the place as blindly as I'd rushed into it. Although he was old enough to be my father, and married, my Soho friend Tom Good was also bowled over by Diana on a visit to Oxford; but all his life he remained a 'Platonic lover of too many girls', as I called Gérard de Nerval in one of the potted biographies in sonnet form I had begun to write at Oxford.

On February 26th I wrote to X: 'I live the life of a recluse, in a state of more or less pleasant mummification. Sometimes the odour of the balm (of my books) predominates. I have also begun to read Burton's *Anatomy of Melancholy*. Unfortunately I have very little time to read it. I am now almost exclusively taken up by Old French, philology, and 19th century French literature. I am beginning to know the last very well; too well. The more I read the dull novelists and poets of that time, the more I appreciate the few great ones and above all, Baudelaire.' I begged X to come for another visit, promising that it would be less disagreeable than the last one. 'It is strange', I wrote in my next letter, 'that the more I believe in literature and appreciate it, the less I am myself able to produce any. This may be partly due to the fact that my mind is continually occupied with the work I am doing for my degree. I work nearly all day, and when the strain becomes too great I get drunk and play the fool.' I did have time to read Yeats's *Last Poems*, which I recommended to X; and to attend talks by Dylan Thomas and by Louis MacNeice at the English Club that March.

In my last term Cyril Conolly asked me to review a selection from Hölderlin's poems that had been published for educational purposes. I sent in a brief notice and was asked to expand it. Having no idea of the requirements of a magazine, and too many ideas about Hölderlin and other things quite irrelevant to him, I then produced a script that would have filled about half an issue of *Horizon*. Astonishingly, this was even set up in proof. It never appeared, of course, and I never submitted more work to *Horizon*, because I had begun to dislike the *Horizon* set and had a guilty conscience even about my one submission, apologizing for it to X because I knew that I had been asked to write the review on the strength of personal relations.

At the same time, April 30th, I was still urging X to revisit Oxford, as he did at the end of May. I had also sent a novel or prose fantasy by X to Herbert Read, who liked it, but could not accept it for publication by Routledge. Meanwhile I had received a warning that 'unless I work superhumanly hard, I shall fail my exam, which is next month. It will be rather annoying to fail, and get no degree after all the work I have done. Even if I pass, I shall get a degree only after being in the Army for about a year.' On June 6th I took the first examination, an oral one, but was 'so distracted and so apathetic that I did not hear all the questions addressed to me.' I duly passed, anyway, and left for London to wait for my calling-up.

One thing I had never mentioned in my letters to my friends is that all those four terms I had taken full advantage of the river, rowing, sculling and punting, as well as swimming. This, and the walks out of Oxford that meant so much to me that I kept on returning to places like Binsey after the war, had no place in my strenuous, impatient ambitions. So I kept them out of the letters too.

As for Freddy, there was to be one triumph for him before his débâcle, when he played the title rôle in Peter Brook's London production of Marlow's *Doctor Faustus* at the Torch Theatre in 1942, with favourable notices in the daily papers that added to his celebrity and notoriety at Oxford; but there was to be no sequel to that success, though he was to take minor parts in other plays after leaving Oxford. His next two letters, written after a long silence between us, when I was abroad in the army and we were to see little more of each other, will serve as an epilogue:

(*April 30th 1946*) 'I would have replied to you sooner, only I was in Oxford, and your letter was here when I returned. This place is becoming very much more its old self as people come back, and I saw quite a few people we knew ... It was pleasantly sad to see them again. Sad, because today and for us so much is sad. I am more melancholy than I had ever believed possible: that is, the depression is not only deeper, but the intervals are ever shorter and less frequent. This is not only because I know myself to be a *raté,* to be one who has talked too much and achieved nothing: that is not quite the whole story. There is, I am finding, an absorption of mine in the spirit of the time, a recognition that its political atmosphere, this English crypto-totalitarianism that I find so detestable and which seeps through armour and dykes howsoever thick, makes irreparable breaches ...

'I cannot work here at all, surrounded by nostalgia and regrets.

'To you I write all this, because we have talked of these things before, and shall, I hope, soon talk again. In those days I thought you precociously disillusioned (I still think you should have had *some* youth) and perhaps it was my dim feeling that you were right that made me so often stigmatize you as unusually gloomy. You have now the barren joy of seeing me agree with your then views. And our two blacks will not make white, but, it seems, everlasting darkness.'

(*May 14th 1946*) 'As for Oxford, yes, they are all back. So few of them, alas, are changed; even those most severely maimed. As one of the latter said to me (it may be sensibly), "It's very nice to be back, and to feel that one can take one's time over getting a degree." I think you'll find, when you yourself come back, that it's not the old place, and that Oxford has become a sort of sausage-machine for turning out "cultured persons" as quickly as is compatible with the least academic demands.'

That summer Freddy left England never to live there again. In Paris, where I saw him in 1948, he gave me a poem he had written:

I do not mourn the lonely child
Who perished in the storm:
Where he has gone
Where he has gone
He will not be alone.

I do not mourn the hungry man
Who stiffened in the dawn:
Where he has gone
Where he has gone
There's neither bread nor stone.

I have no tears for child or man
Woman or beast or worm;
I only mourn
I only mourn
That flesh still shrouds my bone.

With that poem Freddy passed out of my life, and I did not meet him again until I was writing the first version of these memoirs, when he lent me the school diary from which I have quoted. In a letter he wrote me in 1950 he mentioned that he had lost 'all sentimental attachment to the past'; and though he made an exception of me in the letter, even our correspondence ceased for more than twenty years. As I leave him I must return briefly to 1941 and record not how I saw him then, before our estrangement, but how he appeared to an observer less romantic than I was at the time, a Christ Church acquaintance to whom I had introduced both Freddy and X: 'I feel that X is, all the time, trying to justify himself; this applies equally to Hurdis, whom I have seen quite recently. How much more pleasant X would be if he had £400 a year; not, I mean, that he isn't interesting now. You know that it takes a lot to shock me but H's homosexuality is so glaring, sometimes vulgar when you are not in the mood for it that, for me, it is essentially boring. Both H and X are like rifts in the strata of society: they have no background really and, most important of all, their family environment is reversed ... When you compare them to people like G, W, and, may I say?, yourself, you can see the difference: there is a background, and it is relatively stable; they (and you almost!!) are part of society, in so far as the artist can be ... One more thing: I wish, when talking to Hurdis, I could talk to Hurdis's mind only — this is the best part of him, and sometimes his physical repulsiveness bursts in on you.'

The writer of that letter, as far as I know, was homosexual also, but not 'glaringly' enough for it to have damaged his career. Whatever I wrote in defence of my friends in reply, I preferred, and still prefer, those 'rifts' in the strata of society to people who succeed by playing safe. If that meant being only 'almost' a part of society, this 'almost' linked me to Freddy despite all our differences. What came between us at Oxford was not his failure and fall but his short-lived success in a set too smart for me.

Four

Though I published early, and had made literary connections even at this time, without being aware of looking for them, the only success I wanted was to write good poems — an end far more difficult to attain than Freddy's Ivory Tower or the social acceptance he craved. It is easy enough in retrospect to see why it took me so long to write my *own* poems, good or bad. All my responses were exaggerated, inwardly over-dramatized, as it were, and utterly unstable, because I was trying out one stance, one identity, after another. The same Oxford acquaintance who disparaged my friends told me that I should never write good poems because English had not been my first language. It may be that my linguistic transplantation at the age of nine has something to do with the distrust of verbal virtuosity that became acute in my later work. 'Word-scepticism', as Hofmanthal called it, is as prevalent in twentieth century poetry as its antipole, 'word-mysticism', — and much has been written about the aspiration of poetry not to the 'condition of music' but to the 'condition of silence'. Yet long before my word-scepticism became effective or explicit in my writing, I marked this passage in Jeremy Taylor's *Holy Dying*: 'We form our words with the breath of our nostrils, we have the less to live upon for every word we speak.' I can only wonder what made me mark that passage at the age of nineteen, when I had been far from sparing of words in my writing up to that time; but when I opened that book again at random, and re-read the marked passage, it struck me as a strange anticipation of the whole complex, word-scepticism and word-mysticism, that opposed the pull of silence to my writing in later years. To write in a language that is not one's first is to be at one remove from the seeming identity of word and thing. The gap made by that remove can be bridged by close adherence to convention — the over-assimilation to which 'naturalized' subjects are prone — as in my early verse, or it can be accepted, left open, explored, as in my later.

An even more daunting obstacle was something to which Freddy alluded when he wrote that I was less self-contained than he. For at least another decade my work was so variously influenced, apt to wander off in so many different directions, that I often despaired of finding my own way. Because of that uncertainty in myself I needed the response of friends and critics, yet could never be satisfied or reassured if that response was favourable. 'I know you want some recognition', X wrote in the June of 1941, 'You will grow to laugh at it.' And he was right. In poetry there were no ends, only new expeditions after every arrival. X was also right about my need, in youth, for heroes and mentors, due to the same uncertainty in myself and the early loss of my father. 'All men struggle for self-advancement', he wrote, 'and there is nothing more mutable than friendship. You are more likely to be hurt by this than most people. He who makes idols will always be picking up the pieces.'

For all my chronic dissatisfaction, I got a great deal out of my first stay at Oxford, becoming so deeply attached to the place and its surroundings that a decade later I would still go there whenever I could on visits, often returning with the nucleus of a poem. There was much about the university life that I disliked, since the war had not yet changed the social structure, and much of the would-be intellectual life struck me as distinctly decadent. Yet I was half-fascinated at first by the tall, stooping figure of Simon Asquith, who would recite poems in a booming voice after midnight as he crossed Peckwater Quad to go to the lavatory; even by the deathly white powdered face of another undergraduate who rose at noon, walked to some unknown destination, impeccably dressed, and never talked to anyone I knew on the way. The place was full of people putting all their energy into strenuous and futile efforts to be different. One of them described himself as a 'male lesbian' and made a fetish of the soiled bedclothes of his friends. There were parties attended by bizarre hangers-on of the university, like Professor Robert Sencourt, a friend of T. S. Eliot's, who molested me with invitations to dance with him until I had to run away and hide as the only alternative to knocking him down. He told me about his contacts in neutral countries that would soon bring the war to an end. In my own primitive fashion I, too, was an intellectual, and it seemed impossible to escape that sort of company if I was to have any social life at all. When I was in the army, Sencourt tried to pick up my friend X in London.

On the whole, though, my puritanism and purism — priggishness, I'd call it now, but didn't and couldn't then, because I hadn't yet seen through the machinery that compelled me to live up to some idea of myself projected by my super-ego, my taskmaster — proved stronger than my curiosity and adventurousness. As soon as I was in danger of simply enjoying myself, the task-master rapped me over the knuckles. Any enjoyment more gross than that of literature, music, scenery, architecture, painting or theology wasn't good enough for him; and if it wasn't good enough for him, it mustn't be good enough for the encapsulated sensual man whom Freddy recognized in me, but couldn't help to liberate. My older or more mature friends knew perfectly well that my depressions were bound up with this repression, but nothing said or hinted at could make me admit as much to myself. In 1943, when I was in the army, Stephen Spender wrote about his impression of me at an earlier period: 'The trouble, I think, with you is that you let yourself get too depressed. Life is not so easy that one can stand being depressed by other people more than a certain amount, unless one is insensitive or unless one makes up one's mind to help the other person, and pay some price. I didn't feel that I could help you, so I didn't want to be depressed by you. On the whole I've developed a useful (to me) form of selfishness, which is not to see people when they're unhappy.

'If you could possibly see your way to being a little happier when you are with other people, you would get more out of them.

'Personally I don't think I could have borne to know Hölderlin — at all events not after he was 25. Our own romantics, Shelley, Keats, etc. were very cheerful and companionable people, when with each other. I hope our New Romantics will take note of this, and not be depressing company.

'I don't in the least criticize you for being unhappy, but I think you ought to make up your mind to prevent its showing too much and too long; or it will affect your relations with your friends. A year or two of unhappiness will not do you any harm. But I hope that later you will find that you are able to develop a group personality which belies your sad solitary personality. I am all for the smile and grease-paint on the clown in company, and the broken heart when he is alone ... Forgive me for writing like this, but you raised the subject, and I feel you need a father, which I prematurely am in some lives ...'

Stephen Spender was quite right, of course, in terms of the accepted understanding of relations between writer and society in Britain, at a time when reputations trickled down from dominant social-cum-'cultural' sets into what one could still believe to be a general public.

Although I came to see the necessity of good manners, as a regulator of formal transactions, including political ones, between individuals and groups, I never learnt to wear the mask or make-up that would have made me acceptable in such a system. If, for reasons of my own, I could not enter into a party game, I had no choice but to be a wet blanket and drop out. To try to become a poet at all was duplicity enough, where poetry could never fit easily into any order outside it or have any function in it that was more than decorative; and where one had to take on other functions to make a living and survive. That was a grim prospect, and if one did not face it grimly, the chances were that one would be diverted from it into one of the roles — including the clown's, the charmer's and the shocker's — for which society did have a use.

Earlier, when I was at Oxford, Stephen Spender had also written to warn me of the dangers of hero-worship, and the burden placed on the hero by the worshipper; but I must have destroyed that letter because it came closer to the root of the trouble than the one I have quoted, and threatened the self-delusion by which I lived at that time. My hero-worship of Stephen Spender, in any case, was long behind me when he wrote his letter. For a father figure I needed someone as unapproachable, exacting and austere as T. S. Eliot, whose poems I could not imitate and whose pronouncements I could take to heart only to punish myself once more with demands of 'impersonality', classical rigour and ascetic spirituality; which reminds me that at Oxford I imposed long fasts on myself, only to test my will and prove to myself that I could do it.

During my first term I had made friends with a girl older than myself — the girl I planned to look up when I was at Torquay — but she had gone down in the summer and become an A.T.S. officer that year. I wrote to Joy at the vicarage her father had left twelve years earlier, and she begged me not to look for her there: 'Please may I ask you not to try to find me anywhere unless you have definitely heard from me that I shall be there at the appointed time', she wrote in October, also remarking very perceptively: 'You seem to flourish on wild goose chases, lost addresses and the like!' In September she had thanked me for writing her 'a reasonable letter' for once. I saw her from time to time over the next year or so, when she could get to London, and she was one of my few links at that period with a world less inbred than my Oxford or London circle of artists and intellectuals; and she was more intelligent than a good many of those intellectuals. 'In fact occasionally I am tempted to envy you your morbid preoccupations and to weary of the active energetic life which you presume is mine.', she wrote from Winchester in March 1942. At one time I almost involved her in a very different sort of life when I took her to a London night club to which I had been invited by the mother of an Oxford friend, and the mother decided it would be good for her son to see more of Joy; but she was too sensible to fall for the glamour of an aristocratic demi-monde. At the same time she urged me never to become a private soldier, a warning I could not obey, when it transpired that the Navy would not have me. 'You must have someone to laugh at you, Michael,' she wrote in 1942, 'You take yourself so seriously. Nevertheless I am very sincere when I say that I am looking forward to reading your book.' If only I could have seen more of her, and hadn't lost touch with her entirely when I joined up, Joy could have done more than anyone I knew at that time to make me human. The 'someone' I needed to laugh at my absurdities had to be a woman.

The Oxford poets I knew at this time — Sidney Keyes, Drummond Allison, John Heath-Stubbs, David Wright and Philip Larkin — were far less outrageous in their behaviour, dress and way of life than the vaguely literary aesthetes of the smart set. Sidney Keyes came to see me at Christ Church and asked me to read the typescript of what was to be his first book of poems. He was also interested in German poetry and knew of my Hölderlin and Rilke translations, still unpublished at the time. We were fellow contributors to an anthology of Oxford and Cambridge writing that appeared in 1942, in which my very first published poem appeared; and to *Oxford Poetry 1942-1943*, another anthology. Though older, Sidney Keyes was only a little less shy than I was, and as serious about his work. I am sure that my comments on it were of little use to him; and it was his second, posthumous, book that impressed me more. Our acquaintance was very brief, since he left in 1941 and had been posted abroad by the time I joined his regiment. The one meeting with Desmond Allison I remember took place not at Oxford but in Soho, at the Swiss pub in Old Compton Street, where Allison's talk proved as vivacious as Dylan Thomas's.

Philip Larkin kindly acted as a go-between after I had gone down and was waiting in London for my call-up. John Lehmann had spent a year or more 'considering' my Hölderlin translations and leading me to believe that he would publish them, but had asked J. B. Leishman, an established translator, to produce a book of Hölderlin translations instead. When I heard about this, belatedly, I found a new publisher for my work in Tambimuttu, at the same Soho haunt, and a ridiculous race began between the two publishers. Philip Larkin dropped a hint to Leishman over dinner: 'Perhaps I seemed rather rude', he wrote to me on October 2nd 1942, 'because having cheerfully embarked on the subject (I know a man whose life you have ruined) I was in an awkward position: I didn't want to appear holding a brief for you, yet I didn't want to suggest your versions were inferior in any way to his (or else the story would lose its point), nor did I feel like suggesting they were superior (not across the dinner table). Nor did I want to stress the only other aspect — that he'd got the job simply because of name etc. — So after a brief exchange on the difficulty of getting even German texts in these days the subject dropped uneasily among the salt-cellars.' It was an impossible undertaking, and my life wasn't ruined either. Tambi won the race, it turned out, because I had been first in the field and he had a head start on Lehmann. Later I was to meet Leishman, as he suggested to Larkin I should, and the rivalry was forgotten.

I must have commented on the reddish-mauve notepaper of that letter 'one of my indulgences', Philip called it — which may have struck me as out of character, though he hadn't yet taken up his no-nonsense stance of later years. His next letter was on plain white paper which he hoped was inoffensive. His way of life was as austere as I could wish: 'I work all day and still only paddle on the fringes of the vast ocean to be chartered by next June. Consequently I get very little time for reading. When I go down ... I shall begin reading English literature. This occupation will take up the rest of my time until I am dead ... Genuine appreciation of literature (which at 20 must come, generally speaking, in isolated explosions rather than a calm survey of all and seeing it is good) is I think not only unnecessary in schools but a definite handicap!'

I had written something about the need for tradition — probably parroting Eliot, whom I'd begun to misunderstand and misappropriate with self-maiming zeal — and Philip wrote that he didn't understand that word. 'To me the "tradition of poetry" is, quite simply, emotion and honesty of emotion, and it doesn't matter who it is written by or how, if this is conveyed.' He also asked me to remind Dylan Thomas that he was due to revisit the English Club — where he must have been a quite uncommon attraction even at this period, when this would have been his third appearance there within eighteen months — and that 'many breathless freshers are awaiting him. I trust he is well and cheerful. I know this reads queerly but I am strangely solicitous about him as a sacred vessel of, among other things, poetry.'

The 'other things' were mainly drinks. Dylan Thomas was hardly well or cheerful, however ebullient before he had drunk himself into unconsciousness. Many of his drinking bouts in Soho pubs would end with his being carried out to a taxi, sometimes because he had provoked the largest Canadian soldier he could find there and been knocked out — as if total oblivion had been the objective of all his drinking. Before that he would be witty and inventive enough, talking Shakespearean blank verse for an hour or more on one occasion I recall, only gradually slipping away into self-absorbed muttering incoherence. Once or twice I met him in day-time, when he was more or less sober, and once he took me to a cinema where he chain-smoked cork-tipped cigarettes the wrong way round, suddenly discovering that they tasted foul. Once he took me to a special drinking club that opened in the afternoons, and was disgusted again, by his failure to physically excite a tomcat there. 'Even cats are getting degenerate', he muttered.

All this may have been after my Oxford terms, for Soho was my club and second university, where I spent night after night whenever I was in London during the war, but especially the period between the summer of 1942 and June 1943, while I was waiting to go into the army. As I mentioned in passing, at Oxford X had taken me to the house of one of his working-class friends of earlier years, a writer of Communist tracts, and the meeting had precipitated a quarrel between us — the first of many we were to have much later from very different political positions — because I reacted vehemently either to the man's fanaticism or to the squalor of his house. I had to blame what I called my 'instinctive snobbery', and felt so ashamed of my flight from the place that the incident got into a poem I wrote at Bangor in August 1941 — 'An Evening'. The poem, too long and cerebral, like many I was writing then, contrasts the decadence of Oxford aestheticism and élitism with a proletarian philistinism I felt to be directed against civilization itself:

> The smell of mongrels and no air
> Stirs up the palaces in brain and blood.
> And slumming aesthetes soon renounce
> Their mite of basic brotherhood.

> The years are sick and yearn for home,
> For Eve and ape and apple-tree.
> Time cannot turn, nor reconcile
> Aristocrat and aborigine...

and so forth. All the four sections of the poem search for a *tertium quid* that eludes them, because the antinomies are false in the first place, derived not from seeing and living but from thinking. It was all a matter of delicate gradations to be grasped only by experience and understanding. In my lack of either, the incident had forced me into the very reverse of the position I had taken up in my arguments with Freddy, who regarded me as hopelessly 'progressive' and utopian. When I quarrelled with X he had poured scorn on my romantic notions of art, saying that art was a sort of excretion. That ought to have been taken as a corrective to my nonsense, but merely outraged me, precipitating more nonsense. In fact, X was to devote his life to writing in the teeth of indifference and rejection; and without the advantages conferred on me in those years. Knowing that in my heart, I had to take back what I'd said about his friend, though his kind of monomania remained unacceptable to me when the nonsense had been knocked out of me.

Friendship meant more to me than opinions; and that, in many ways, could be dangerous or embarrassing. The friend whose mother had invited Joy and me to the night club was reputed to be a fascist, and said to have been beaten up by students at Glasgow for his anti-war convictions. On another occasion, when his mother took us out to dinner, she treated me to a long anti-Jewish diatribe. According to my friend, whom I shall call by his pseudonym of John Gowrie, I listened in pained silence until she said something like: 'Of course you wouldn't know about these things', to which I replied: 'Oh, yes, I would, madam, because I am a Jew myself.' The subject was never raised again, as far as I recall; but I had forgotten the whole affair before my friend reminded me of it, decades later.

Nor do I remember how I came to know John Gowrie. With his gashed forehead, stooping gait, wide-brimmed black hat and threadbare old-fashioned dress, he looked so sinister a figure that people had been known to run away when they saw him approach on an Oxford pavement. Everything about him was shrouded in mystery. As far as I knew at the time, he was not an undergraduate, and I was never sure exactly what he was doing at Oxford. One rumour made him out to be the illegitimate son of the lady I met, a Countess, and someone told me that his father was an M.P. In fact, his legitimacy had been established in a lawsuit, but we never spoke of these things. John had been at Eton, as long as his mother could afford it, and had then been sent to Dartmouth as a cadet where his health deteriorated and he took up his anti-military stance. While serving in the Navy at Portsmouth he broke his back, not long before our first meeting. He had come to Oxford to sit for a history scholarship, like Freddy, as he did three times, and had registered at a college. At Oxford he was living on a midshipman's pay, and was often close to starvation. From time to time his mother would turn up and take him out to an expensive meal. He had literary interests and ambitions, writing and publishing poems at this time, but no sympathy with any current trend. His poems combined eighteenth century, if not Miltonic, formality with the blackest romantic gloom. I can still hear his sepulchral voice intone the lines:

> I have a box wherein to lay my bones,
> And, all around, a heap of quarry stones...

and this, in one instance, to an audience of Mayfair ladies, his mother's friends, to whom she took pride in exhibiting her unworldly and unhappy son from time to time.

John Gowrie would come to my rooms at Christ Church, lie flat on the floor — because his back gave him constant pain, and he was being treated by an osteopath who recommended this form of relief — drink a glass of water, and proceed to wolf every morsel of food I could provide. Bookish as both of us were in those years — though he was less so than I, having been knocked about variously in the world — our conversations were about literature rather than politics. If I suspected him of having been mixed up in fascist activities, I put those down to his circumstances, but especially to a need to make his peace with his mother and step-father, the Earl, whose political views inclined that way. (John had never seen his father, who, he told me later, was in America). During the war, at Oxford, the Earl had his right arm set in plaster, into what looked like the Hitler salute. When he met John in a street he said to him: 'I hear you call yourself the Hon. — Kindly call yourself the Dishonourable.'

I was fond of John Gowrie, who was as different as possible from those Oxford sophisticates whose cautious and devious crypto-fascism repelled me. For all his Eton and aristocratic connections, I felt him to be not only essentially an outsider, but as underprivileged socially as those who came from the poorest of broken homes. He would probably have put down the sympathy between us to our being born under the same astrological sign, with only three days between our birthdays. (His mother was much involved in occultism.) Both of us were what our horoscopes would have called 'accident-prone'. At the time I could only feel the sympathy, unable to foresee or understand how much more serious his accidents were than mine, how much more extreme his exposure to every kind of violence and stress. His broken back and gashed forehead were only the beginning. I was to have my mug's game of being a 'recognized' poet to keep me occupied, very busy, engrossed, and out of mischief most of the time. He was to move from one lost cause to another, from one conflict and disaster to another, involved to a degree I could not be in the world of politics, business, sensational journalism, litigation, and suffering the worst penalties those activities can inflict, between physical and nervous breakdown.

Remote from that world as I was, I should never have learnt anything about his later life if the writing of the first version of these memoirs had not led to a single meeting before his emigration. We remained friends for some five years, corresponding copiously when I was in the army, until in 1946 there was a misunderstanding between us. With the best intentions, John Gowrie published a poem I had sent him, as a booklet, with alterations by him in the text, a new title, countless misprints and mis-spellings, even of the author's name, and a 'biographical' introduction so embarrassingly and wrongly eulogistic that I had to have the pamphlet suppressed — not before a few copies got into libraries, because I was abroad, and there was a time-lag. My poem was a bad, inflated piece of writing in the first place — just how inflated, I didn't know when I sent him the poem, being full of apocalyptic notions and fantasies which I mistook for vision. In the published form it was not even my writing, since John had excised some of the more personally authentic images and replaced them with decorous, second-hand items from his stock. My anger at this affair ended our correspondence, and twenty-seven years passed before I saw him again. In retrospect the cause of our break seems unimportant, except as one more instance of the accidents to which both of us were prone. The one kind of business in which my profession involved me, relations with publishers, tended to be as troubled, if not as drastic in effect, as John Gowrie's enterprises in later years. Something compelled us again and again to stick our necks out. In this case we both did so at once, and collided — each of us high-mindedly and high-headedly dedicated to standards and objectives that would lose their validity even for himself.

For all my vacillating moods and exaggerations of those moods into generality, at Christ Church itself I was fairly sociable most of the time — much more so than during my second period of residence — with contacts in the most various groups and circles, dropping into people's rooms for drinks, or meeting in the Buttery. One day I stopped at an open window in Peckwater Quad, fascinated by music I had never heard, Purcell's *Dido and Aeneas*, and was promptly invited in. It was easy to make friends with almost anyone, before one's sympathies and antipathies had begun to set. As I was still rowing at the time — later I confined myself to sculling, a solitary pursuit, only once entering for a race — I wasn't bothered by the accepted antagonism between brain and brawn, though it was brought home to me at least once, when one of the Oxford intellectuals, a homosexual and a Fascist, jeered at me from a bridge for being out in a sculling-boat. In retrospect it strikes me that my continued use of the boathouse and of sculling-boats had more to do with my aesthetic needs than with sport, since I wasn't interested in the competitive or the social sides of belonging to the Boat Club. What I remember of the Christ Church boathouse, at the junction of the Isis and the Cherwell, is moments of an almost day-dreaming absorption in the interplay of light on water and foliage; but, most vividly of all, a fight between two cob swans, the repeated attacks with wings beating down on neck and head, until one neck floated limp as a water-lily stalk. As for the sculling-boat, its flimsiness and delicate balance made it respond to every ripple and current in a way that made one feel closer to the river than one could in any larger or heavier craft. In a four or eight one had to concentrate on one's rowing, caught up in a rhythm neither one's own nor the water's. Punting was different again. Somehow it called for company, and its most memorable moments, for me, are bound up with people, or with accidents half-deliberate that were part of the fun.

Yet the more lasting associations were with people who shared my literary concerns, like John Mortimer — a painter and poet at that time, rather than a novelist and playwright — and John Pettavel. He, too, was to publish stories and a novel, before taking up medicine and becoming actively interested in Maurice Nicoll's work and the Gurdjieff-Ouspensky teaching. At this time he was writing poems, mainly in French, since he was bilingual, having been born in South Africa of a Swiss father and a French mother. Two collections of his French poems were published during the war, under the pseudonym of Jean Brienne, one at Oxford and one in Canada, where he was serving in the R.A.F. When I met him at Christ Church he was enigmatically reserved, with few of the fashionable aesthetic affectations but a mundane elegance that concealed religious preoccupations, and literary accomplishment far in advance of his years. (He was the only person I knew at Christ Church younger than myself.) Throughout the war, and for the next ten years or so, we remained in close touch.

Social relations with dons were restricted to the odd routine sherry party, though through the English Club I once dined with Lord David Cecil, whose nephew Richard, killed in the war, was a Christ Church friend. From time to time I was invited to A. J. P. Taylor's house at Hollywell Ford, where his wife Margaret held a salon for writers, painters and musicians. In the grounds of their house, right on the river bank, there was a little shack of which I saw much more than of the house. At that time it was occupied by Vera Leslie, an art student at the Slade who was also translating Kafka. I spent a good deal of time with her and her friends, helping her with the Kafka and contributing a small translation of my own to the collection *The Country Doctor* which was published in 1945 by a small ephemeral press, *Counterpoint*, with illustrations by Vera. The same shack was to be occupied by Dylan Thomas, then by a later Oxford friend, Alan Beasley, his wife, Marie, and their enormous Pyrenean mountain dog.

Friendships were not only mutable, as X wrote, but continued to involve me in the strangest complications. One of my Oxford friends was one of the few undergraduates I knew who actually had a mistress — at least there used to be a girl in his rooms who served tea but was never introduced to his friends, never took part in the conversation, and seemed to have no other possible relationship with him. Another friend, who had been at The Hall with me, invited two boys still at his public school to Oxford, where we all met. The friend whom I had taken to be heterosexual, if anyone was, conceived a violent passion for one of the two boys. In the middle of the vacation I was summoned to the Dean of Christ Church and put through an interrogation more gruelling than the one in which Freddy had involved me at school. It turned out that in one of his letters to the boy, which had been intercepted by the boy's headmaster, my friend had written: 'Michael Hamburger sends his love.' It can't have been difficult for my friend to explain that those words were a mere formality. But so, I had reason to suspect, was my exculpation. That didn't matter to me. What did matter was that another of my friends had been disgraced and sent down. Since he was my friend, I was involved in his disgrace, regardless of whether the College authorities really believed his explanation.

What was more, one of the senior dons in the College, generally known to be homosexual, used to offer each freshman — or perhaps only those he liked — instruction in the 'facts of life'. When my fifteen-year-old brother came on a visit to Christ Church in 1941, he was allocated a guest room in that don's apartment and promptly offered the treatment, which he didn't need, if only because he was at a co-educational school. He was then bombarded with letters and asked to come back. I advised my brother to ignore the letters. He wrote back: 'I shall take your tip about not writing to old — again. I heard from him for the third time and he still wants me to come & stay with him again. If ever you're thirsty you can always go to him for a pint!' Three weeks later he wrote: 'I got a letter from the old boy and mainly it was about sex advice. He put a special note on the bottom that I was to burn it after reading. I could blackmail the blackguard with it. But enough about him.'

The duplicity that allowed the College to put up with that routine of thinly disguised seductions on the one hand, and expel a brilliant undergraduate for a single infatuation — 'passion' is what my French tutor at Christ Church, F. A. Taylor, harped on as a peculiarly French phenomenon, as though in this country it hadn't yet been discovered — was one of the things that made me reject the possibility of a teaching career at Oxford, when it arose later. Another was that, after army service, the very attractions of the city, the Meadows and gardens, the overhung river, the splendid buildings, seemed like a seduction, an invitation to drop out of the real world. The disparity between Oxford life and the war in which I felt I should be taking part began to make me restless even before the end of my first period of residence. My failure to take the examinations seriously enough to find out what they were meant to qualify me for, while working moderately hard for them because most of the work interested me, had to do with that restlessness.

At the same time I was well on the way to becoming a professional writer, — partly, I now think, through unconscious pressures from the insecurity precipitated by my father's death — when I should have been learning to relax. Yet even by 1942 I had begun to submit my poems to older writers for criticism — to Stephen Spender, to Herbert Read, and to T. S. Eliot. To Eliot, more as a revered poet than as a Faber editor, I also sent my Hölderlin translations. He wrote about them on November 12th 1942: 'I am very sorry for the considerable delay over your Hölderlin translation. After a good deal of deliberation and consultation we have decided that such a book is a luxury for which we could not spare the paper at a time like this. While I admire Hölderlin's poetry and should like to see it more widely known in England, the sale for translations of poetry is always small. It is not a direction in which we feel justified in using our supplies at present. I hope very much that your admirable translations may be published by someone and, of course, if paper were unlimited, the ideal way would be to publish the text and translation on opposite pages. I think that the chief value of translations is for people who have some acquaintance with the language but cannot read an author of any difficulty with ease ...' About my own juvenile verse, which he returned with a few annotations about a year later, he wrote to me:

'I have been a very long time over your poems and you may say that the result of my opinion is not valuable enough to justify it, but I do like to keep poems for a considerable time in order to lay them aside and re-read them. I think I see what Herbert Read means by saying that this is rhetoric and not poetry, though I should try myself to find other ways of putting it. I have made a few minor comments on the text, but those are not important. What I feel is that I do not find each poem to be a separate and distinct experience, and the general effect is of your being more interested in a persisting mood of your own than in the particular occasion. This helps to give a generality which partakes of what Read calls rhetoric, and a certain monotony out of which no specific sensations emerge. The actual writing is all right on the whole, though no word ever seems to be invested with a new life in the context. I don't know what will happen but I shall be glad to see the next stage ...'

Of Eliot's comments, which I didn't preserve, I remember this one placed against the word 'bird': 'What sort of bird?' — and that question had the weight of pages of general criticism. I hadn't yet learnt to use my eyes, for reasons connected with Eliot's general strictures and my extreme introversion at this time. The things I saw evoked moods and sensations, but I wasn't interested enough in their quiddity. The real birds I had both observed and read about were not the birds I put into my poems.

It was in 1942 or 1943 that I first met Eliot — at the Spenders' flat in Maresfield Gardens, Hampstead. He had been to dinner there, together with E. M. Forster, Julian Huxley and Geoffrey Faber, and I arrived later, in time to hear Natasha Spender play a Beethoven sonata. I don't remember a word of what was said, only my awe at being in the presence of the living poet I admired more than any other. E. M. Forster, in fact, was far more inclined to be gracious, but I wasn't interested in him — a mere prose writer! Graciousness, in any case, was not to be expected of the High Priest of an austere, ascetic cult — who may well have been talking about wine or cheese. It was enough, much more than enough, to be in that room, breathing the same air.

While at Christ Church I had also begun to correspond with an earlier, and very different, hero of mine, Hermann Hesse, whose books I devoured at school, buying those not in my parents' library in Miss Waterhouse's shop or borrowing them from a fellow devotee, a childhood friend of my mother's recently turned psycho-analyst, Hannah Ries. At Oxford I wanted to translate *Der Steppenwolf*, my favourite, and wrote to Hesse in Switzerland. He replied that he could not grant me permission, since the rights were tied up with his German publishers, with whom he was not in communication, but he sent me a number of privately printed works. Later, he informed me that the novel I wanted to translate had already been published in England before the war. He added: 'Certainly *Steppenwolf*, in exceptional cases, can be read by a very young person without damage — if the reader is a potential poet or has a related vocation.' The correspondence dribbled on into the 'fifties, but my admiration for Hesse's work hardly outlasted my adolescence, and I was never to translate his work. (The only exception, some lines of verse set by Richard Strauss in his *Four Last Songs*, doesn't count, because the translation was commissioned, and because translating words for music is a peculiar activity I have never felt happy about.)

'I like your lines about him,' Herbert Read wrote to me on November 15th 1943, 'but I think it is frightfully difficult to be successfully elegiac. I mean that the very consciousness of the attitude or expression is somehow false. I feel this even about a poem like *Adonais*.' Herbert Read was commenting on a poem I had written for Sidney

Keyes, who had been reported missing in North Africa and — as the same letter confirmed — almost certainly killed. I took the indirect stricture to heart and never published the poem.

When Herbert Read died I took his advice again, though no elegy I might have written for him could have been quite as inadequate as those early conventional lines, written for someone I liked and respected as a poet but had known only briefly as a friend. For more than a quarter of a century Herbert Read was a friend to me, and the words quoted are an example of the special kind of friendship he was generous enough to give a writer more than thirty years younger than himself. I don't remember how it came about that I got to know him when I was only seventeen. His earliest letter to me, of December 1941, suggests that I approached him at that time, sending him a poem. Possibly we had already met, either at Oxford or in London. What his letters bring home to me now is how much I owe to his advice and criticism in those early years. It is characteristic of the man, and of the role he adopted towards me, that his letters reveal more about my preoccupations over the years than of his. Herbert Read was shy, gentle and reticent; but he was also unassuming to the point of self-effacement. That is why he could take on young people like me without expecting any sort of allegiance, let alone idolatry or adulation. As he knew well enough, my supreme idol in those early years was T. S. Eliot, whose very remoteness as a person made him a better object of idolatry; but Herbert Read himself was devoted to Eliot, and never tried to assert any kind of authority that might have counteracted the other. For the same reason there was never any need for me to revolt against Herbert Read's guidance, as I had to revolt against Eliot's authority before I could begin to be myself; and the simple human affection which I felt for Read from the first could grow without strain or disturbance.

Herbert Read's letters to me are a record of unselfishness in a thankless task — almost inevitably thankless, because I simply wasn't able to help him in the way he helped me — not, at least, until the last years of our friendship, and no letter records the meeting at which our roles, for once, were reversed, and Herbert broke his reticence to tell me about the harrowing stresses and frustrations of his life. It was then that I urged him to reduce his public and professional commitments before it was too late, and to return to the kind of work which I had always considered his true vocation — the work that included his poetry, his novel *The Green Child*, the auto-biographical *Annals of Innocence and Experience*, essays on literature like those in his early book *The Sense of Glory*, and some of his writings on anarcho-syndicalism. Only his illness forced him into the partial retirement which he had desperately needed since his middle years, but thought he could not afford. It may have come too late, after all.

For a long time I took his kindness too much for granted; perhaps all the time, since it was the shock of his death that made me re-read his letters and discover the extent of his self-effacing furtherance of my work. If this sounds like conventional piety, as false as the elegiac sort, I must be specific here and confess a real sin of omission. It was Herbert Read who did more than anyone to bring about the publication of my *Hölderlin: Poems and Fragments*, a translation whose progress he had followed and encouraged since the beginning of our association. I cannot understand what made me dedicate the book not to him but to the memory of Arthur Waley, a man I never met or corresponded with. Was it a ghostly residue of Eliot's doctrine of 'impersonality', haunting me still? A temporary absence of mind or heart? A perverse kind of tribute to the unselfishness of Herbert Read's motives? Whatever the cause, I was taking his help for granted, long after I had learnt that his readiness to be bothered has always been rare among writers, and is becoming still rarer than it used to be.

In his own quiet and uncomplaining way, Herbert Read was one more victim of the philistinism that punishes British poets with more neglect and indifference than most of them can bear, while insidiously tempting each to become 'somebody', which means almost anybody other than a poet. Herbert Read preserved his innocence and his romanticism, but those very qualities proved detrimental to some of the activities — such as art criticism, sociology and psychology — into which he was drawn by genuine enthusiasms, only to find himself trapped in a variety of institutionalized functions. The elegy which I cannot and will not write was written by himself — in the form of a tribute to Hölderlin, the same poet who presided over our friendship, linking Herbert's last letters to his first. It is the poem 'A Gift for Scardanelli' from Herbert Read's *Moon Farm*:

> The clouds are unanchored: they might
> fall from the sky to cover you
> I have brought you a basket of figs

and some fine linen
but alas
no white goat to slaughter
and fingers have faltered
that should have played the flute.

I wish I could be sure what poem I sent Herbert Read in November or December 1941, but I should think it was the persona poem 'Hölderlin', written at about that time, and the first poem I published after my contributions to the school magazine. Herbert Read wrote: 'I like it very much. I would like to read it again & perhaps I could say something more critical when we meet.' His letter was from his office at Routledge, but he gave me his home address in Buckinghamshire and suggested a meeting in London. Our earliest meetings were over tea at Yarners, near Broadcasting House, and once we were joined there by George Orwell, whose gaunt appearance and forthright manner impressed me, though I scarcely knew his work at the time. During those war years, too, Herbert Read once came to my mother's house to look at a collection of ancient glass phials and jars — Phoenician, he said — that had belonged to my grandfather. The visit stands out not only because it was an instance of Read's extraordinary kindness — such glassware, it turned out, was fairly common and of little archaeological interest to an expert — but because I recall only one later meeting on either's home ground, in the flat which the Reads occupied for a time in London. Most of our later meetings were over lunch at his London club — where he introduced me to tripe and onions, a plain demotic dish as incongruous with the menu of the Reform Club, even in war-time conditions, as Herbert Read himself was with London club society. From time to time we met in other people's homes or in wholly public places like the Institute of Contemporary Arts. In 1964 I was to have stayed with the Reads in Yorkshire, but the lecture that was taking me to York was postponed, and the new date clashed with an engagement of his elsewhere. Of our meetings all I can say is that all of them were a delight, since he bridged the thirty years' gap between us without effort or condescension. He never seemed bored or moody, though he had the habit of suddenly absenting himself inwardly from indifferent social gatherings. When there were silences between us, they were congenial to me, and as relaxed as our conversation.

Herbert Read's letters of 1942 are mainly concerned with my early Hölderlin versions, which he read in typescript but was unable to accept for Routledge, and to a surrealist fantasy by X which I also sent him. (This work — a prose poem rather than a novel — was declined 'chiefly because of its awkward length', and it has never been published.) In February of that year I invited Herbert Read to address the English Club at Oxford, but he replied: 'I only manage to get through my work by a strict rationing of such obligations, & I am afraid I have more than enough for the next six months.' I was too young and inexperienced to realize that he had more than enough for the next six years, or sixteen years; but the more I saw of him, the better I understood that business and busy-ness were his chronic affliction. 'I am really sorry to have missed you this time,' he wrote in April, 'but I have been so overwhelmed with work and business. I have to address two conferences next week, & have had to prepare the lectures, in addition to my usual work. And all kinds of engagements in town.

'I am returning your Hölderlin translations, after reading them again. I like them very much — they don't read at all "literally", but at the same time they give such an exact rendering of the form and tone of the poems. I wish I could be more optimistic about publication, but I don't see much chance as long as the present conditions continue. But I think that when publication does become possible, you ought to make a substantial volume — a long introduction and *all* the best poems ... I hope you will write about Blake. I would like to see a fresh point of view on a poet I am so devoted to.'

The really substantial volume had to wait another twenty-five years or so, and it was published by Routledge when Herbert had already left the firm. The long introduction, on the other hand, got written in time for the 1943 edition, packed with all my youthful pseudo-learning and miscellaneous references to almost any writer who preoccupied me at the time, including Blake. That long introduction had to be scrapped for later editions, and I was never able to replace it. The older I grew, the less expansive my writing became, and the less value I attached to opinions.

By October 1942 I must have begun to feel uneasy about burdening Read with my work and letters, but his answer was characteristically generous: 'The apology should be mine, for neglecting your letter. But you know how busy I am, & you must never feel conscience-stricken if I seem indifferent. I am always glad to hear from you and wish I could find more time to see you.

'I have read the poems with real interest, & do not find anything for definite criticism — but that rather implies, & it is true, that their virtues are rather negative. If only there were more lines like: "To the soft tyranny of drums" — that gave me the authentic thrill. But mostly I find just the clever twist of rhetoric. It interests me, but it does not move me. The Hölderlin poem is surely the best.

'I am being honest with you, because that is my way of encouraging you. I don't want to dismiss you with conventional praise — I want you to press on, & show me more of your work in the future ...'

No one could have done more for me than that. The 'clever twist of rhetoric' was not to be expunged for a long time, because ideas remained more real to me than people, places and things. I could not act on Herbert Read's advice until that had changed — and it was a matter of learning to live, rather than to write. Yet at least I knew what was needed — thanks to that letter, and another, of April 15th 1943: 'The relatively leisurely intervals of a conference at Oxford give me a chance to catch up with my correspondence. I have, since I got your letter, read the poems three or four times. "Profane Dying" is an ambitious & on the whole successful effort. I think it is rhetorical rather than poetic — a distinction I am always in the habit of making. The images are apt, the expression forceful: but not essentially poetic. But this does not mean that it is not worth writing. Fine rhetoric, indeed, is an art we don't sufficiently practise these days & perhaps we have lost the tradition. It demands a high degree of technical "finish" & in this respect I think your poem falls short. The rhythm is occasionally too staccato & there are awkward compressions and ellipses. But the force of your poem wins through.'

It wasn't Herbert Read's fault that I took this response to be ultimately favourable. My principle in later years was to ignore all favourable comments on my work and make what use I could of the unfavourable. What I took to be his approval in this case made me publish that poem sequence — written at fever heat while I was waiting in London for my call-up, over several days and nights of such intense absorption that I refused to talk to anyone and had to have food brought up to my room — only to freeze with embarrassment every time I was confronted with the printed text. Yet the point about rhetoric did sink in, leaving an irritation that made me look for a remedy.

In November Herbert Read wrote again to praise the Hölderlin book and comment on the elegy for Sidney Keyes. By then I had almost finished my infantry training in the same regiment, the Royal West

Kent, in which Keyes had served, and Herbert Read expressed the hope that I wasn't having too bad a time. We met again once or twice when I was on leave in London; but my first literary — too literary — phase was over, and for many years I struggled to come to terms with experiences that made all I had written seem worthless. I must have said or written as much to Herbert Read, who tried to reassure me in a letter of March 1945. In his letter of January 19th 1946, advising me how to deal with the matter of the poem published by Gowrie, he mentioned that he hoped to see me, but would 'probably be in the USA from mid-March to mid-May.' I doubt that I saw him again until after my demobilization and return to England in the summer of 1947.

The following year, on July 12th, he wrote about a new batch of poems I had sent him, (telling me that he had been travelling a great deal since receiving them — 'USA and twice Paris'). Again he found a 'lack of essentially poetic expression' in the poems, and I agree with him in retrospect, though I could not take his advice to try drama. 'I feel you need a dramatic myth to give pregnancy to what you have to say,' he commented; but after my early persona poems I was trying to get away from myths and fictions of every kind, reacting too strongly towards a prosy literalness. 'I am glad you found the Adelphi article of interest,' he added in one of his rare references to his own work. 'Now that even Middleton Murry has given up pacifism, I feel very lonely.'

My long absence from London and the anti-romanticism induced by my army life, or by the impact of what I saw in Italy and Austria, must have caused a temporary estrangement between us. I notice that in his letters of 1948 and 1950 he reverted to the address 'Dear M.H.' after the 'Dear Michael' of earlier letters. Something of the kind is also suggested by a note of January 24th 1948: 'I am always glad to hear from you & I don't want to lose touch with you or your work. So please don't feel that you are being a nuisance. If I lived in London I would try to be more social, but my few days every week are taken up with "business" of various kinds. I shall hope to see you occasionally & to hear what you are doing.' We never lost touch, but I sent him no more poems for criticism. Though I was still far from being satisfied with my work, I no longer believed that anyone else could help me to make it better. It was not a question of this word or that, this line or that, but of finding a modus vivendi between the poet and the anti-poet in myself.

In 1950 I added to Herbert Read's too many commitments once more by asking him to see a refugee German poet, Peter Höfler, who wrote under the name of Jesse Thoor. The desperate financial situation of this extraordinary poet, of whom I shall have more to say, was perpetuated by his absolute refusal to do anything only for money, and by a state of mind close to paranoia. Herbert Read wrote on 24th April: 'I will see Peter Höfler, but I have not much hope of being able to help him. I see so many of these refugees & it is always the same hopeless outlook. If he is a good silversmith, it would be possible to make a position for himself. The Clerk to the Goldsmiths' Company might help ...' I have forgotten whether that meeting took place. Even if it did, it can only have ended in a total misunderstanding. What Peter Höfler wanted was a gesture of recognition, not a recommendation to the Goldsmiths' Company or commissions which he would not have accepted in any case, preferring to live on horse meat and give away the jewels and ornaments which he made. The tragic irony of it was that Höfler, a self-educated visionary who had lived either as a vagrant or by his various manual skills, came as close as any poet alive at that time to embodying Herbert Read's ideas about 'the grass roots of art', and his anarcho-syndicalist theories generally — quite apart from Höfler's striking facial resemblance to William Blake. But there was a difficulty of communication; and the pressure on Herbert Read that made Höfler only one more of 'these refugees'; and the stubborn pride in Höfler that resisted efforts to give him the help he needed, if it wasn't offered in the right spirit. My elegy for Höfler, 'A Wreath of Thistles', was to appear in a book of mine which Herbert Read accepted for Routledge. That was one elegy I couldn't help writing, because Höfler's life and death imposed themselves on my imagination like a legend.

By this time Herbert Read had moved from Broom House, near Beaconsfield, to Stonegrave House in Yorkshire. After 1952 our relations became cordial once more. In that year he advised the Bollingen Foundation on a project, their Hofmannsthal edition, in which I had some part as a translator at the time, together with Stephen Spender. After long delays and complications I took over the editing of the two projected volumes of poems and plays, to be published by Routledge in England. In 1955 Herbert Read was also instrumental in getting Routledge to accept a book of my essays and my third collection of poems. He had also tried to get them to publish an enlarged and revised edition of my Hölderlin translations, which another firm brought out in 1952. Most of our correspondence of those years was confined to those matters. In 1955 I reviewed Herbert Read's *Moon*

Farm, showing a preference for those poems in which he presented images rather than arguments. He thanked me for the review and commented: 'It is very perceptive, and I agree with you (and not the general public) in the estimate of the relative merit of the two kinds of verse which I write.' He had probably forgotten that it was he who made me wary of rhetoric and cogitation in verse.

On January 25th 1961 Herbert thanked me for sending him the Penguin *Hölderlin*: 'I had been looking for it on the bookstalls. He is the one poet I return to again & again, my German being so imperfect, I need just this kind of edition ... I wish I could see you occasionally, but it is my fault for being so inaccessible.' In September of the following year I wrote to tell him how much I liked his essay 'What is left to say?' in *Encounter.* The diffidence and vulnerability to criticism that beset him in his later years were distressingly evident in his reply: 'I had been rather shy of the appearance of that *Encounter* article — they have had it for more than 12 months & I thought there must be something wrong with it. It is good to be reassured by you.

'I am glad that you like Ned O'G.'s* poems. They have been badly received — very few reviews & not a single good one. I thought that there must be something wrong with the judgement of Kathleen Raine & myself, who recommended them to Hamish Hamilton ... I have just returned from 5 weeks' absence & have to go to Washington on October 20 for the National Poetry Festival, at which I am "the voice from abroad". Not an easy assignment.'

The same number of *Encounter* contained a contribution by me. Four days after that letter, on September 28th, Herbert wrote again: 'You must have thought (me) very self-centred not to have mentioned your article on Nietzsche when you had been so kind about my piece in *Encounter.* The truth is, I did not look into the magazine until last night, when I read and was quite absorbed by your essay. I was, as you know, a Nietzschean in my time, one of the circle around Orage. If only we had known how the Master had been betrayed by those nearest to him we might have remained more faithful!'

I never thought Herbert Read self-centred — and his accidental omission of the 'me' in that context bears me out — but wished he had been more so, if that had meant more securely centred in himself. Yet his dependence on the judgements of others was inseparable from his

* Ned O'Gorman, the poet.

fatalism and his humility. 'My life has been guided by chance,' he wrote in the same *Encounter* essay, 'and that I accept as a natural condition. The people I tend to dislike are those who have successfully planned their careers: there is no conflict or contradiction in them because they have imposed a human ideal (of logic, of purpose, of consistency) on the divine irresponsibility.' That is a poet's creed, a re-affirmation of Keats's 'negative capability'; and in his best work Herbert Read was open to this 'divine irresponsibility'.

That year I had to find a new publisher for my next book of poems. Herbert Read wrote in July: 'I am sorry about this. Routledge has a habit of dropping an author just at the moment he is about to make good. It has happened so many times that I have become cynical about it. But it does the author no harm ... I could fight for your retention, but in such cases a victory leaves unhealing wounds. So you had better go, for your sake.

'But I should be glad if you could exclude the Hölderlin volume from any transfer of options. This is something I have worked on behind the scenes, as you know, and I would like to keep it under my wing ...'

One way in which Herbert continued to work for it, even after leaving Routledge, was by sponsoring me for the Bollingen Foundation Fellowship which enabled me to complete what I hoped was my definitive selection and rendering. His wish was fulfilled, though his wing was no longer visible over the book by the time it appeared — all the more reason for me to have acknowledged it my dedicating the book to him.

That same year I decided to try to live as a writer once more, after twelve years of university teaching. 'I believe (or hope) you are wise to seek freedom,' Herbert wrote on August 8th. 'I feel like a new man (at 70!) since I left Routledge. I wish now I had broken away long ago. As for London, I share your views and never want to go near the place again.'

My projected visit to Stonegrave that autumn fell through. 'I am spending the weekend with Henry Moore,' Herbert wrote on October 1st, 'collecting information for a book on him (biography) which I have to write, & for various reasons I can't change the date. It is a great disappointment to me, and one more reason why I should dislike politics.

'I've been to Germany (Berlin, Kassel) for a fortnight — a congress of poets in Berlin, but no evidence of any poetry. Ingeborg Bachmann, whom I had hoped to meet, did not turn up. I met Günter Grass & rather liked him — perhaps I will make another attempt to read his books, which hitherto have defeated me.'

Our last meeting, over lunch at his London club, must have taken place before his retirement from Routledge, since it was then that I begged him to give up some of his many functions and commitments; but my unchronological memory tells me only that it began like earlier meetings, with Herbert as a quietly attentive adviser, before taking the turn I have mentioned. My only regret is that this did not happen sooner, and that we never met again. It had taken me too long to grow up and understand that being a father — literary or otherwise — is at least as hard as being a son.

In 1966, before leaving for America, I received this answer to a letter I had written Herbert about his recollections of T. S. Eliot: 'Thank you for writing about my T.S.E. Memoir. I am glad Wesleyan sent you a copy & that you enjoyed it. I did not know you had been to Wesleyan — we enjoyed our two visits there very much. I went to Mount Holyoke once to give a lecture & it seemed a very pleasant college. You should be happy there ...

'I come to London as little as possible. I find it very exhausting. But I would like to see you again & will let you know when there is an opportunity. I am very sorry I missed you when you came to York, but I hope you will come again & then you must stay with us. I saw a little of the University & they were kind enough to give me one of their first honorary degrees.

'I always read your poems and reviews with pleasure when I come across them & hope you will always keep me in touch with your published work.'

I did so, and he read it carefully enough to point out one or two technical errors in *Hölderlin: Poems and Fragments* so serious that part of the edition had to be withdrawn and reset. His wing was over me almost to the end, for it was in his letter of February 26th 1967 that he did me this service. On January 23rd he had written: 'An advance copy of your noble Hölderlin volume reached me this morning, & I rejoice to see the fruition of so many years of labour. I shall spend many happy hours with your book, especially in my present invalidish state, which has reduced my extrovert activities to a minimum ...'

Alarmed by this reference to his illness, of which I knew nothing, I wrote to ask him what it was. His reply gives precedence to the errors in the book. It continues: 'You ask what is wrong with me, so I will tell you — cancer of the tongue. It is accessible & therefore can be effectively treated, but I have had three separate manifestations. But at the moment it seems to be under control & I feel well enough. I hope to go to Portugal for a holiday in about four weeks' time.

'I am sorry you have had such an exhausting time. I did too much at your age & can only advise moderation.

'If you come this way we would love to see you, at any time — there is always room for a guest or two. Yours affectionately, Herbert.'

That was his last letter to me. If I wrote again, as I think I did, offering to take up his invitation, he did not reply; and I was half-reluctant, in any case, to intrude on him now that his illness had given him something like the leisure which he ought to have enjoyed throughout his active life. Yet I am sure that his illness did not change him, that he remained stoical and unselfish to the end. As late as 1962 he had written to me: 'I no longer understand poetic standards in this country. But I did enjoy an article by an unknown (to me) person called Falck in *The Review* — do you know anything about him?' I was able to tell him something about Colin Falck, and he returned to this in a later letter.

Sketchy and faint though it is, this record may have the negative merit of not falsifying that side of Herbert Read which he chose to reveal in letters to one of his many friends. His more essential self should be looked for in his works. For the greater part of his life Herbert Read was a neglected and misunderstood writer. His public honours were awarded to the public man he became out of a mixture of excessive modesty and a fatalism rooted in the trauma of his experiences in the First World War. The essential Herbert Read could have been honoured only by a realization of his vision, or at least by the kind of sympathy and concern with which he responded to the works of other men.

If I had presumed to write an elegy for him, it would have had to be as unassertive as the best of his own poems, with the quiet strength often concealed by his outward faltering; as unassertive too, as the man whose tragedy was of the distinctly modern kind recognized long ago by Hölderlin, when he wrote in 1801: 'For this is tragic among us, that we leave the realm of the living quite calmly, packed into a container, not that devoured by flames we atone for the flame which we could not master.' Hölderlin went on to write that this modern predicament was 'less imposing, but deeper' than that of the ancient tragic heroes; and that noble souls confronted with it will 'persevere in the teeth of exasperation'. Herbert Read was often exasperated and often isolated; but the constancy of his affections is one instance of his power to persevere.

When I left Oxford to wait for my call-up papers — for nearly a year, it turned out — my mother had moved back to our bomb-damaged house in St. John's Wood. My sister Maria had moved into a flat of her own and was working in factories, my sister Eva had broken off her medical studies and joined the WAAF. My brother, I think, was still at his boarding-school. X was working at Miss Waterhouse's bookshop, where Freddy had stood in for him for a while before going up to Oxford.

In my morbid adolescent romanticism I took it as a certainty that I should die in the war. (Joy told me off for this assumption in a letter.) That may be one reason why the Introduction to my Hölderlin translations was so inordinately long: I had to put everything I thought I had to say into that one book, whether it was relevant to Hölderlin or not. Another reason was my extreme bookishness at this period, my still unshaken conviction that books were the chief repositories of the good, the true and the beautiful. That the essences each contained didn't always mix, but could well neutralize one another, was something that hadn't begun to disturb me. If an author excited me, no matter why or how, that author must be relevant in any context. The Introduction, though, was already finished, and I wasn't dead yet. So I got down to a study of John Donne and Metaphysical poetry, even working in the British Museum Library despite a library phobia that was to keep me out of it when my academic career demanded that I do 'research'. This study was completed before I joined up, and published in Stefan Schimanski's year-book *Transformation*. Like the earlier attempt at criticism it presented a great lump of unassimilated material — this time, material to which I had been led by T. S. Eliot's essays. For the next two years or so I concentrated on the Master's canon of sacred texts, packing my kit-bag with the works of countless minor Jacobean dramatists and filling my army diaries with notes on them. When I came to re-read the diaries I was so furious to find all those literary notes, instead of a record of my army experiences, that I tore up the lot and burned them.

Most evenings I went to Soho, to talk and listen over half-pints of bitter which I didn't particularly like. What I did like, from time to time, was to get really drunk on stronger stuff, which I couldn't afford. What drew me to the Soho pubs was that they broke down barriers of class and nationality. Though predominantly upper-middle class, or parasitical on the upper-middle class, the war-time and pre-war bohemia could accommodate the Welshness of Dylan Thomas, the Scottishness of W. S.

Graham, of John Burns Singer and of the two Roberts, Colquhoun and MacBryde, the East End Jewishness of Willy Goldman. Paul Potts was a Canadian, Tambimuttu a Ceylonese. There was a very young Polish boy killed in an accident a year or two later. There were painters like John Banting already out of fashion; and others — like John Craxton, David Haughton, John Minton, Keith Vaughan, Lucian Freud or Francis Bacon recently established or not yet at the height of their reputation. Among the rarer visitors Bryan Howard — better known as a character than as a poet — was as affectedly and self-consciously elegant as Anna Wickham was negligent of her appearance, warm-hearted and bluff. If professional envy or competitiveness affected those drifting configurations, I wasn't aware of it. In many cases I didn't even know what those people did in the daytime — if they did anything at all. The youngest of the three Bernard brothers was said to be a boxer. Another familiar figure, Stephen Fothergill, said he was a lamp-lighter. I talked to Bill Belton for years before discovering that he was a painter. There were quarrels and fights, of course, but I don't think they had anything to do with the ambitions and intrigues that made me avoid literary groups in later years. The cult of success was still considered vulgar. There are other objections one could raise against the cult of failure deep in the hearts of quite a few of the Soho regulars of those years, but they didn't occur to me till much later; and even now I would rather fail on my own terms than succeed on other people's.

When the pubs closed we made our true descent into the underworld, in the form of a dive — that seems the right word — known as the Coffee An' (non-initiates called it the Café Anne, unaware that the An' stood for nameless amenities other than coffee, but not necessarily culinary). It was a large basement somewhere near St. Giles Circus. I never saw it in daylight, and never really asked myself whether it existed in daylight, let alone exactly where. One drifted there in small groups to sit at long tables, drink coffee and eat. The proprietor was a Greek Cypriot with a scarred face and a notorious readiness to draw a knife when provoked. At least one alsatian dog also belonged to the premises. I remember an occasion when Lucian Freud quarrelled with the proprietor and was chased round the tables; but fights were more likely to break out in the pubs or on our way through the streets, where there were gangs unfriendly to 'long-haired boys.' Dylan Thomas, I think, rarely got as far as the Coffee An', but either dropped out at the drinking stage or went on to more exclusive clubs to do more drinking. I recall only one meal with him, when an Oxford friend took us to a restaurant and Dylan was sober enough to compose parodies of Hardy, Housman, Auden and Spender on the back of the menu.

To some extent the Soho circle overlapped with my life outside it. John Heath-Stubbs and David Wright were two Oxford friends often to be found in the other place. David (at that time Anthony or Ricky) Sylvester — not yet an art critic but jazz musician, poet, literary critic and painter — could also materialize in broad daylight, in St. John's Wood, where we visited each other's homes. Tambimuttu, incredibly enough, was sometimes to be seen in a real office, in Manchester Square, when he had become the first of my many publishers. Philip O'Connor became a friend and correspondent for many years, with meetings in various parts of London, in Suffolk, in North Wales and in Berkshire.

With *Horizon* I felt less at ease than with the Soho drinkers, a few of whom contributed to it. Through Stephen Spender I had met Cyril Connolly and Peter Watson, who financed the magazine, but something other than the circumstance that I wasn't good enough to contribute always kept me well beyond the periphery of this circle, with its adulation of whatever happened to be the latest thing in France. French literature had been my main subject at Oxford, and Baudelaire, Rimbaud and Mallarmé were among my poet heroes. Yet I had the feeling that the French orientation of so many British intellectuals of the inter-war and war years had less to do with literature or the arts than with a sophisticated life-style against which I had begun to react. When Peter Watson invited me to stay at his country house, Tickerage, during an early army leave, not even the presence there of David Gascoyne could induce me to accept, though Watson was a charming, intelligent and generous man. After a whole series of painfully ambiguous situations, not all of which I have mentioned, I had also grown wary of personal entanglements with any homosexual, however charming, intelligent and generous.

It was in war-time Soho that I first met Thomas Good, who remained a close friend until his death in 1970. Tom had been an actor in the Midlands, where he was born in 1901, then a High Anglican priest in the Society of the Sacred Mission. He fell in love with a girl met through his work in the Mission, lost his faith, was defrocked and put in a mental home. For a time he became a Nietzschean, and it was through him that I met Nietzsche's early translator and advocate, Oscar Levy, at Oxford. Tom Good had had contacts with the Orage circle and contributed one or two small pieces to Eliot's *Criterion.* In the 'forties he still published poems, criticism and translations in periodicals like *Poetry Quarterly*, and a book of his poems was published by the same short-lived Oxford press that produced Vera Leslie's Kafka book. By the 'fifties, he was almost unknown or forgotten. His marriage had broken up. Soon his only son was to die of diphtheria. He had prevailed on his doctors and psychologist to confirm that he must not live in England, ostensibly because of the climate, in reality because he could not face up to the disruption of his ties and aspirations there. When he lived in France with his wife before the war, he had a small private income. After the war, living abroad meant drudgery as a language teacher in France, Lebanon and Italy, year after year of solitude in furnished rooms, White Goddess celebrations of girl students and embarrassed visits to prostitutes. When he lost his last job in Italy, where a third book of poems had just been printed, he had to return to England with his meagre savings, no pension and no prospect of anything but an old people's home. In January 1970 he drowned himself in the Thames near Richmond, where he had been staying in a residential hotel. Six weeks after his disappearance from the hotel I had to identify his body.

Though Tom was old enough to be my father, he was not a father figure to me. In fact I was hardly aware of the difference in our ages, even when he had become officially old and economically 'redundant'. An unquenchable youthfulness was one of his troubles; one motive, too, for his suicide, when the alternative was to accept his official age and wait sedately for death. Like most of the inveterate outsiders I have known, he was connected by traceable lines of communication to the inside. In his own chirpy and mischievous way, he remained priestlike — not so much the bad or spoiled priest he sometimes accused himself of being as a naughty one. The actor and the priest combined when he entertained his friends with mock sermons, sang old musical hall songs or played Irish jigs on his tin whistle. Nor did he ever forget that he had been at Oxford, that an uncle had been an important person in Nottingham, that someone in his family had known Yeats and Yeats's sisters in Dublin, that someone else had borne the surname of a noble family. To the end he remained a student, filling exercise books with notes on his reading, sketches for works he never had the concentration or incentive to write, names and addresses of people likely to arrange the American lecture tour for which there was no demand. His old-fashioned manners didn't allow him to betray his acute depressions to his friends, though his manic cheerfulness and endless flow of disconnected reminiscences could be at least as hard to take. If he were alive now, his habit of living in the past — with unrealizable projections into the future — would have helped out my defective memory. He would amaze me by telling me what I said to him on such and such a day twenty-five years ago, when we were walking from this place to that, and he must have seemed what he always seemed, a man who didn't listen to anything or take anything in but perpetually trod the wheel of his own mind. But, no: once the thing said or seen was there, in his mind, it was there to stay, to be turned over with the rest as long as the wheel turned.

Tom Good's poems, and most of his prose, lacked incisiveness. That a poet can be dedicated for a lifetime to his craft or Muse, sincere within the limits of his self-knowledge, skilful within the limits of his sensibility, and yet remain not good enough (not Good enough?), is the most extraordinary of the risks entailed in the vocation to which Tom was committed. I, too, was committed to it by now, with no more certainty that my work would ever be adequate by standards nowhere defined, in no reliable or definitive relation to outward success or the absence of it. 'A mug's game', T. S. Eliot called it, aware of the risk he shared with those whose persistence was a blind obstinacy, a waste of themselves and of others. Or wasn't it — even at the worst? Where even the best is for ever being re-examined and re-assessed, where any new development could be a falling-off or a final defeat, mightn't it be enough to go on trying?

These were some of the questions that worried me as I waited for the event that would push them aside, at least for a good while, but never far enough to give me much peace of mind. The old house, meanwhile, had to be given up for a newer, more practical one to whose suburban pseudo-Tudor I had the bad grace to object, as though I, not my mother, were to be responsible for running it. Glad as I was to stay there in future years, on leave or on vacation, years of barrack-room squalor didn't quite cure me of a purism about styles that could have been due to social conditioning, aesthetic fastidiousness or an amalgam of both. It took me decades to be less affected by the destruction of a good building than by the destruction of a human life.

I don't remember whether it was just before my joining up or on an early leave that David Gascoyne came to stay at my mother's house and insisted on reading out Henry James's letters to me at two or three in the morning. No more exquisite torture could be devised, and I recommend it to policemen who may be unfamiliar with the involutions of Henry James's mind. I do remember less involuted conversations between David Gascoyne and my grandmother, who spent her last years at Kew, taking long daily walks in the Gardens and discussing the state of the world with her familiars there, including a former Archbishop of Canterbury. When she fell off a chair while replacing an electric bulb, and broke an arm, she marched off to the hospital and asked them to put it right. Yet from time to time she succumbed to depressions as total as the zest and energy with which she had taken to new occupations like housekeeping. Then she would retire to a darkened room and lie there for days with her face covered, unable to speak a word. Perhaps it was her experience of such states that made her sympathetic to a man as tormented and hallucinated as David Gascoyne, preoccupied not with Roosevelt or Churchill, as she was, but with the 'Christ of revolution and of poetry'. My mother took no part in such conversations. Though Henry James was one of her favourite authors, she considered it her function to be practical and look after unpractical people like David and myself.

War-time London worried me too, but in an apocalyptic fashion, impersonally, since no one close to me had been killed or wounded in the bombing. My religious preoccupations made me look for transcendental hints where I should have been trusting my senses. In the poem 'London Nights' (published by Gowrie as 'Later Hogarth') what I suppose was a buzz-bomb became 'the metal humming bird whose breath is fire/ Whose beak is our undoing' — with an appendix of metaphysical speculations about 'Chance, Destiny or Providence'. A few shorter lyrics written in 1942, and published in *Oxford Poetry*, were at least felt, if somewhat vaguely. In my London waiting period I was seized by a veritable frenzy of what I took to be not only inspiration but revelation. For several days I locked myself up in my bedroom, refused to talk to anyone or go down for meals, while I produced the monstrous piece of rhetoric on which Herbert Read commented, the sequence 'Profane Dying', later published in a special book-size, hardbound and all too durable issue of Tambimuttu's *Poetry London*. This long poem too had a section called 'War in the City':

> Already streets are stirring,
> Though we have not reached the sun,
> And even now a purring
> As of distant cats is heard.

Silence is pierced soon after
By some huge exotic beast's
Insanely swelling laughter,
Now subsiding to a wail,
Hysterically changing,
Like a jungle symphony.
Usurping beams are ranging
Through surprised, awakened skies ...

When the paper currency ran out, there was no petty cash of simple observation to fall back on. It was high time I got away from some of the reading matter I had picked up in the wake of Eliot's essays, but as much of it as was portable, including Jeremy Taylor's *Holy Dying*, was still to be devoutly studied amid the profanities of barrack-room talk. How I wish I had recorded those profanities in my army diaries, or been ready to enter without reserve into the realities of profane living! Very gradually some of the intellectual clutter began to fall apart, making room for things heard, seen and felt; but again the break was too drastic to let the different orders of experience coalesce and the whole man move at once.

One night in Soho I got into conversation with an attractive and intelligent woman — in her thirties, I imagine — and went home with her. She was living in a Chelsea studio that may have been her husband's or ex-husband's, since she was not a painter but a literary critic, of all things. To the initiation that followed I reacted rather like a Stendhal character — 'Can that be all there is to it?' — but also with an agony of guilt over the casualness of the event and what I felt to be my betrayal of the untouchable girl I was still in love with. Since the guilt was far more acute than the desire or its satisfaction, that was all there could be to it. In the early hours of the morning I walked from Chelsea to Hampstead, where I called on X and his greater experience in such matters. Though he concealed the irritation he must have felt at being knocked up at that hour of the morning, to be used as a father confessor yet have any absolution granted thrown back in his face, the affair was cut off at that point. It opened another gap to be slowly bridged over the years. In one way and another it took me an inordinately long time to grow up.

Five

In June 1943 I joined the Queen's Own Royal West Kent Regiment at its Maidstone depot, to do my infantry training there, in the first place, though I was to stay there till April of the following year, apart from a special 'toughening-up course' at Shorncliffe, between Dover and Folkestone, and a signalling course in Yorkshire.

I ought to have been fairly well prepared for army life. I had been a Wolf Cub and Boy Scout and a cadet in the O.T.C. I had gone on a walking tour with my sister Eva and some friends shortly before the outbreak of war, staying at youth hostels, and on another tour with a school friend on which I had scaled a rock face, for the fun of it, and found myself suspended by my fingertips while my friend chatted away facetiously on firm ground and I groped desperately for a foothold. I was physically fit — A1 — and convinced of the necessity to fight that war. During my last year at school, in Herefordshire, I had got a foretaste — however genteel — of the manual chores expected of a private soldier. I had slept in dormitories organized on much the same lines as barrack-rooms.

Yet Oxford and Soho, my two universities, were hardly the best of all possible preparations for a life of service without responsibility or independence. My very first day at Maidstone was a fall from grace so sudden as to be traumatic. To be shorn like a convict, issued with bits of second-hand clothing and equipment as rudimentary as a mess-tin, herded and yelled at like cattle, fed and watered from buckets, bedded on straw in sacks — the palliasse without sheets — one didn't need to be a decadent aesthete to find this induction abrupt. At my first meal I felt sick, and should have been unable to eat but for the coaxing of an old soldier, who took me under his wing at once, telling me that the food wasn't as bad as it looked and that the first five years were the worst.

There, immediately, was the other side of the army, too. That same old soldier looked after me with a humorous and delicate solicitude which I had no right to expect from anyone there, least of all from him, saving me from the consequences of my awkwardness by laying out my kit for me before inspections, with a neatness still beyond me, and in other ways I have forgotten. Wherever I went in the army as a Private I received the same kind of help from people who must have found me utterly strange — *because* they found me utterly strange, but respected the strangeness. When I took my test as an infantry signalman and got into difficulties over some complicated knot used for mending cables, a corporal on duty in the examination room picked up my bungled knot in passing and substituted a correct one, getting me through the test. I had been advised to change my surname before joining the army, but even that proved unnecessary. After the internment alarm at school I had gone to the House Master to suggest that it might be best to change my surname for the duration at least, but he had said: 'What? Hamburger? A good old English name!' — and the very zaniness of that response had confirmed my own dislike of disguises. As far as 'other ranks' were concerned, I needed no disguise as long as I was one of them.

The initial shock was recorded in a letter to X from Maidstone: 'I don't know where to begin my account of the first days in the Army ... It seems as though I had been in the Army not two days (this is the third day) but at least a fortnight. Time passes very slowly. Besides, we get up at 6 and go to bed at 10. Secondly, I wish that I'd taken your advice and stayed out! I flattered myself that if it was going to be really bad I should break down mentally; but if I do break down it will be physically ... I am referred to as "The Scholar", and this word is pronounced with an expression of wonder, respect and incredulity. All my fellow privates and most of the N.C.O.s treat me in a very friendly way. I have not yet met a single one who likes the Army. In fact the only thing that keeps them going is the belief that this training only takes six weeks and that "we're all in the same boat". Unfortunately, I can't quite feel myself to be in the same boat, or rather I could do, but am beginning to fear that I shall be absorbed. The Army is run on the principle of "bread and circuses". There are about six meals a day, and the wireless (Forces Programme) is kept on continuously in the feeding and sleeping rooms.

'Today I can hardly move. After being inoculated I was moved to a different camp and had to carry all my kit and a suit-case containing my civilian clothes for about two miles. I completely broke down several times during the march — but so did most of the others — and, since one should rest for at least 48 hours after the inoculation, my arm and shoulders are swollen and very painful. When we arrived at the new barracks, we were left outside in the rain, while new quarters were found. At that moment I had a terrible fit of exasperation. When a sweating horse is left waiting outside a house, the coachman usually covers it with a blanket or tarpaulin. But private soldiers are below horses in the social scale. If I don't succeed in getting an intelligence Corps job after these six weeks, I shall have to start thinking.

'The worst of it is that I shan't be able to correct my proofs and get my book out.' (The Hölderlin book) 'The proofs were sent off three days ago, and I haven't even received them. As for writing poetry in the Army, it seems like sailing a ship on the barrack square. But if and when I return to civilized life, I shall most certainly have profited by this baptism of fire. Please don't tell any members of my family about these "revelations", because I want them to think that all is well. But try to persuade Paul to rely on his psycho-analyst when the time comes ...'

My younger brother, Paul, chose to be a Bevin Boy — an emergency coal miner — when the time came for him. X was kind and generous enough to visit me at Maidstone during my first weeks there. Still in June, I sent him a self-pitying poem I *was* able to write in my barrack-room, thanks to the civility of my fellow soldiers. Sending it, I wrote to him: 'I had two interviews with officers today (one of them a psychiatrist), and they both intimated that the Intelligence Corps is out of the question as far as I am concerned. They spoke of clerks. If I became a clerk I should have to count out pay or keep ledgers, but at the same time I should have to fight when the occasion demands it and therefore undergo further infantry training. As for the psychiatrist, he refused to believe that I am extremely neurotic and on the brink of insanity. If he doesn't see to it that I am given a suitable job, he may be obliged to change his mind ... Naturally they brought up the question of my nationality and birth, and made this a reason for disqualifying me. I am rather sick of being an Englishman when it suits them and a German when the question of my own predilections arises.'

After the initial shock of becoming something less than a human being, by civilian standards, what bothered me most at Maidstone was the unpredictability and corruption of some of the regular staff, beginning with the 'Mad Major', as he was called, who would order elaborate kit inspections in the open air — of the kind that preceded embarkation — and forget to attend them; or, if he did attend, indulged in capricious games of his own quite unrelated to the occasion, at the expense of anyone he picked on as a stooge. Many of the platoon sergeants sold week-end passes and accepted bribes for other favours and exemptions. There were private soldiers there who boasted of having their names struck off draft lists, and at least one who attended roll calls and pay parades, but crept out of camp each morning to work in a butcher's shop. This kind of thing was demoralizing to conscripts and volunteers who hadn't joined up for a 'cushy job'.

On July 5th I wrote: 'Your letter was so full of substance that it remained in my mind when I returned to the barrack square for drill. I completely forgot to slope arms, and merely waved my rifle about in an aimless fashion. The sergeant merely called out, "Wake up, Wimpey" (my nickname), and all was well. He is very indulgent and quite used to discovering that my mind has strayed miles away from the barracks ... I entirely agree with what you said in your letter concerning my attitude to the army. I have decided to forget that I was a poet and to consider myself no different from my fellows — in fact, as you put it, to "sink into anonymity". A great deal of humility is required for that, but I shall try. What you call my pessimism is, of course, a rather cowardly safety precaution. By preparing myself for the worst I have now reached the stage where nothing can surprise or disconcert or shake me, as far as the Army is concerned. There are certainly moments when I am caught and taken by surprise — for example when I wake up in the mornings, and from one minute to the next exchange my private dreams for an impersonal and anti-personal reality; but that is only a brief moment, though it occurs every day. Another instance occurred last weekend when I read two plays by Shakespeare. I returned to the barrack room after reading *The Tempest* out in the fields. I must have been still under the influence of Shakespeare when one of the men called out: "Hey, mate, what's that book?" I replied, "Shakespeare". He said: "I've got no time for people like Shakespeare". At any other time I could have ignored this remark, but I suddenly found a terrible fury within me, and could have attacked the man, a very decent fellow.' This was followed by pages of self-analysis and self-questioning in my old manner; but I was soon to get out of that habit.

On July 9th I wrote: 'I was very interested to hear of your meetings with Tambimuttu. I have been treated in exactly the same manner, and your account didn't surprise me. Nevertheless I don't think he is a bad egg, but simply that he is very childish and very unbalanced, besides suffering from delusions of grandeur. On the one occasion when someone pointed out to him that he had treated me in a most insulting way, he became very contrite and later apologized. He is quite unaware of behaving badly, otherwise, as you yourself pointed out ... I am now beginning to feel that I am entirely divorced from the old life, the civilian life. I have noticed that even my dreams have become military, and my dreams were the last link between the old life and the new ... I have heard nothing more about my future. I shall know what my next destination is in a fortnight's time ... I have decided that I may as well remain a Private. I have found that I do not belong to the officer class any more than to the other ... It has come to my ears that officers resent the presence of private soldiers at my place of refuge, the Royal Star. Although I hate the place and its air of pretentious and stuffy provincial snobbery, it is the only place where I can read and write in peace. For that reason I continue to go there, except when the weather permits me to read in the open air ... But I don't eat their meals, even though the menu is written in mis-spelt French. It is possible that I can preserve more independence and integrity as a private soldier, in spite of all the indignities and humiliations that Privates suffer ... Don't think that I have been "broken in", that my spirit has been broken. On the contrary, I feel stronger than ever before, though I have been stripped of a certain arrogance (often disguised as modesty) peculiar to artists and those who consider themselves to be such. I am more grateful for the extraordinary consideration and delicacy which the sergeant of my platoon has shown whenever I suffer lapses of absent-mindedness and dreaminess, and more surprised by them, than for all my little successes with literary people. I shall tell you more of my experiences in the next letter; for example, of an outing that began at 7.30 p.m. and lasted till 2 o'clock in the morning, when we dug trenches up in the hills, in complete darkness and with rain pouring down. (I had been put in charge of a section and supervised the digging of one trench). Then the return to barracks, still in the rain, and every man so tired that his feet moved mechanically, in perfect rhythm, while his mind was already asleep ... Then, after four hours' sleep, another seventeen hours of strain.'

Soon, in an undated letter from Maidstone, I was to tell X: 'I am now going through a phase when poetry loses all meaning. I can neither read nor write anything. Verse suddenly appears as a series of words and nothing but words. It is much as though you were to look at a face of one whom you know and love, and see nothing but bones covered by skin and other excrescences. That is what the face is composed of but it is not the face; it has lost its meaning. The meaning of poetry, and even of the thoughts expressed, is in the music. Some thoughts have more musical value than others. The meaning of a face is in the expression, the symmetry, and in the symbolical representation of the soul behind the face. Perhaps this is rather trite, but I'm trying to explain something rather difficult to express.

'Lately, I've been running away from my duties. I spent a whole day trying to avoid training. I played hide-and-seek with several sergeant-majors, running from one corner of the camp to another, crawling through a gap in the barbed wire which surrounds the camp, and spending hours in a little café outside which is out of bounds. I succeeded the first day, but when I decided to be honest the next day, I was put on a charge for being ten minutes late on parade. I was on trial today, and the case was dismissed because we found a very cunning excuse. (I was put on trial with several other offenders.) The whole thing was quite amusing but rather childish, besides being nerve-wracking.'

On July 29th I reported: 'I am now living in a small tent, together with seven other men. At night I can't move my feet without touching another man. The whole thing is arranged on the principle of a birthday cake. The worst of it is that there is no room for clothes and weapons and equipment. About eight times a day (at least) we have to empty our kitbags to find some object or other. Within two or three minutes the object must be to hand and the kitbag refilled. It is these things that play on one's nerves: the continual rush, the shouting, the scramble. I shall no longer be able to go out in the evenings, for all one's spare time is needed to keep the tent tidy etc. Now we're beginning to go on route marches up to a distance of 30 miles, some of them at running pace. I need all the strength I have to keep myself together under these conditions ... But still, I am determined to emerge from this business, intact if possible; for, after all, it is Purgatory, not Hell. (In Purgatory *hope* and *faith* remain, in Hell they are dead) ... The three books I have kept with me give a great deal of trouble. They must continually be shifted from place to place, hidden in blankets or in the straw mattress, or stuffed into the haversack when it's not being used or inspected. Since they're not part of my equipment, I should be charged with breach of discipline if they are found. Tomorrow a General is inspecting the camp, and today we spent eight hours on preparations for this occasion. I shall most probably be on leave for 48 hours in four weeks' time, but I shall try to change the date so that I can give the lecture on August 27th.'

One piece of news that cheered me up momentarily while adapting to army routines was a meeting between X and Arthur Waley, who told him that he liked my book of Hölderlin translations and kept it on his bedside table. Arthur Waley's translations from the Chinese had already begun to encroach on my awareness. His version of the Tao te Ching, as it was then transliterated, *The Way and its Power*, became not only a bedside book but a second Bible to me in later years. That may be why I dedicated my much larger and later book of Hölderlin translations, *Poems and Fragments* to Arthur Waley's memory, though I never met him or only corresponded with him, and when it was Herbert Read who not only saw to the publication of that book but had encouraged me almost from the start to persist in my work on Hölderlin. Since my friend Alberto de Lacerda, whose first book of poems Waley had translated from the Portuguese, confirmed Waley's interest in my Hölderlin version in later years, it may also have been Alberto's urging that brought about what I came to feel was a lapse on my part. I have changed the dedication in what is likely to be the very last edition of my versions. The change does not detract from my gratitude to Waley as a mediator, but it was Herbert Read whose mediation was personal and active. Almost the only translation I was to include in my *Collected Poems* is a translation from the Chinese, a language of which I remain totally ignorant. Because I cannot even judge how far this version of mine — a solicited experiment — is a translation at all, I was able to include it among my poems.

As for training, I was awkward at anything to do with mechanics; could shoot pretty accurately with a rifle and bren gun but couldn't throw hand grenades straight — a peculiarity that had arisen earlier, when trying to bowl at cricket, but became rather more alarming when the missile was a live grenade; loathed arms drill, inspections, ceremonial parades, and could be relied on to lapse into my normal stride and tread on the heels of the man in front; quite enjoyed route marches, before one grew so tired that one's mind withdrew from one's body, and was one of the lucky ones who needed no treatment after the longest route march, when feet were inspected and shreds of wool separated from blood and skin. Assault courses were all right, except for the balancing act already mentioned; bayonet practice unpleasant, because of the visceral instructions and commands that accompanied it.

In a crowd — or 'shower', as the drill sergeant would say — as mixed as a war-time unit it wasn't hard to find friends. A group of former Manchester Grammar School intellectuals soon joined the battalion, and in March 1944 I met a Welshman called David Evans who wrote poems and became a close friend until his death a year or two later. On route marches one could talk and sing — while one had breath to spare. There were moments during exercises when one lay on one's belly in some quiet spot, as close to the earth as could be, feeling as though one were free and alone, with all one's senses alive. On such exercises, too, after days on iron rations, one learned what hunger is, and I remember digging up a turnip with my bayonet to eat it raw.

Life outside the barracks didn't amount to much, in Kent, because the local population kept aloof. If I went to pubs or dances in Maidstone, they made no impression. My first army poem, written at Maidstone Barracks in June, 1943, registers disillusionment with a death that is 'stale, is daily fare, not worth the dying'. Yet the astonishing thing is that I was able to write and read at all in my barrack-room, thanks to the considerateness of men who felt no need to do either. By the autumn I even worked at Hölderlin translations, though my book was already out and about nine years were to pass before an enlarged edition.

My first book had appeared about the time I joined up. In connection with it I received an invitation from the Poetry Society to give a Hölderlin talk and reading. In the midst of my training nothing seemed more incongruous and remote, so I excused myself. The Poetry Society then wrote to my Company Commander. I was marched into his presence by the Company Sergeant Major, expecting some kind of reprimand or punishment for one of many possible offences, and was benignly but firmly advised to accept the Poetry Society's invitation and represent the Regiment at this function. I had never given a lecture or a reading; and now I was to talk about a German poet, in my new uniform, in the middle of the war against Germany and my endeavours to learn the names of the parts that make up a Royal Enfield Mark II rifle, at the command of a British officer. It was more than I could face. I asked my friend Alfred Marnau to read the paper for me, and John Gowrie to read the poems, while I hid in the audience, doing little honour to the Regiment. Yet if I had asked myself at the time why that war was worth fighting, I should have said, because such absurdities are possible in Britain, and there was nothing I wouldn't do to keep them possible.

My devotion to this German poet, whom I was to translate and retranslate for fifty years, might have been put to a more severe test if I had known that a special 'field selection' of his poems had been prepared in Germany for the edification of the Wehrmacht; but I had heard something of the use to which Nietzsche's works — or a selection from Nietzsche's works — had been put by Nazi propagandists, from a refugee scholar, Karl Kilian Mayer, who was preparing a work on Nietzsche (left unfinished when he died). Hölderlin and Nietzsche were also the authors of the most ferocious indictments of Germany ever written by Germans. That the same authors could be exploited by the manipulators of German 'idealism' for their own realistically political purposes might well have shaken my own 'idealism' at this stage. Yet the essential difference between German and British attitudes to 'culture' would also have had to be taken into account. It simply didn't occur to people in Britain that poetry could be used to oil the war machine, as indeed it couldn't have been, in Britain, because British culture was a way of life, not a set of edifying national exemplars that could be carried around in books.

At some point after my basic training I was given a test, mainly of my capacity to hear and distinguish sounds, and was found fit to be trained as a signalman, as I duly was, at Richmond, Yorkshire. The dating of a poem written there tells me that I was at Richmond in November 1943. Shortly before that time I had heard about the death of Sidney Keyes and written my elegy for him at Maidstone, with the usual dearth of concrete and sensuous particulars. An irregular sonnet with half rhymes written at Richmond that November showed the beginning of a response to a winter landscape there, though the ploughed fields and 'sharp stubble' and haze are still subordinated to a subjective mood, a personal nostalgia:

> Rather (now in the foggy season) yearning
> For London, a background of grey, dimmer
> Webs of pride by trembling fingers unfurled.

Apart from an ear trained by listening to music, I had very little aptitude for the special skills of an infantry signalman — wireless telegraphy, telephony, semaphore, laying and mending cables — but I managed to pass the course. This meant that, for a time, I was spared a few of the more general fatigues like peeling potatoes, cleaning latrines and scrubbing the floors of officers' messes. Yet the worst routine, because there was no end to it and no purpose except to remind 'other ranks' that they were 'other ranks', was that of 'turn-out', 'spit and polish', 'bullshit', ceremonial parades and inspections. Decades later I had recurrent nightmares about brass inadequately polished, belts inadequately 'blancoed', boots inadequately dubbined, rifles inadequately oiled or pulled through; and of being back in the army as a Private, trying in vain to tell people that I'd been commissioned, pointing at pips on my shoulder that had suddenly become invisible.

After my training I expected to be posted abroad — the most likely place being Burma, where a battalion of my Regiment had been very nearly wiped out. In December I got as far as embarkation leave, but for a reason I still don't understand my name never appeared on those posting lists. Back at Maidstone in January 1944, I wrote about these uncertainties to X: 'My posting to battalion has been delayed for a week or two. I had a medical inspection and was reported "unfit for posting as A1". I don't know what will happen now; probably I shall have another and more thorough medical examination. At any rate, the delay is very welcome to me, since my nerves were in a bad state as a result of the holiday in London. Civilian life seems very complex and difficult compared to life in the barracks. The things that really trouble me, such as personal relationships, the frictions of two different nervous systems, ambitions and the need for self-expression, rarely occupy one in the Army. That is why military life is so sterile: the friction is necessary. It is true that there is a personal side to the Army, but in order to endure military life it's necessary to think of it as a mechanism. Once you consider the personal motives at play, you're liable to burst with resentment, contempt and hatred ... I was interested in your remarks about my reticence. I assure you that there is a reason for that reticence. I'm charged with highly explosive neurotic tendencies, and if I ever relaxed my habitual restraint, God knows what would happen.'

These medical troubles are specified in another letter of January from Maidstone: 'I am still waiting here. I have had one examination by a specialist, ear, nose and throat, and am waiting for another one (chest). I don't feel too fit, especially since coughing and blowing my nose keep me awake at night. If I didn't, I'd suffocate in my sleep. Unfortunately the authorities have got tired of X platoon, which consists of odds and sods not actually being trained, and have just decided to put us on the kind of training we did previously. Unless I can evade this (by various exploits) before Monday morning, I shall probably be in hospital. But all these considerations are neither here nor there.' To fortify myself, I had translated a poem by a seventeenth century French poet, Maurice Scève, enclosing my version with the letter. It is of Dizain CCLXXVIII:

> Hardly had white Aurora crowned her head
> Wholly with roses and with gleaming gold,
> When my sick soul, which striving powers had led
> Into a deep confusion's tightening stranglehold,
> Through the two guardian shutters that enfold
> My eyes, returned and armed me against death.
> But you (and it is you alone) whose breath
> Can calmly soothe my whirling destiny.
> Shall be as myrrh to me, a shielding wreath
> Against the worms of my mortality.

Soon after, in another undated letter, I told X: 'My military situation is still very confused. I have now been thoroughly X-rayed and examined and am awaiting the results. It is unlikely that I shall be re-graded. I am now going to volunteer for the Palestine Police, as I told you in my last letter. By rights I should be overseas by now, but all these complications have delayed the draft. To explain the situation as clearly as possible I shall give you a list of the possibilities:

1) if I am refused for the Palestine Police, but not re-graded, I shall proceed to battalion, and thence overseas, anywhere
2) Enter the Intelligence Corps and go overseas eventually
3) Go overseas in any non-combatant capacity.

If I get into the Palestine Police I shall go to Cairo to be trained as a policeman, and thence to Palestine for the duration of the war or for three years (whichever period is the shorter).

At present I can't say what will happen.'

In retrospect it is clear to me that the Army itself did not know what to do with me and that my German birth prevented my posting to a combatant unit, just as it disqualified me for my first choice, the Navy, for the Intelligence Corps and the Palestine Police. I was never to be told so.

By early February, the impasse was temporarily broken by my failure on an assault course and my being sent on a Command Conditioning Course or Reconditioning Course to Shorncliffe on the Kent Coast. I had assumed that this would be a gruelling punishment, but took back my apprehensions about it in a letter of February 2nd: 'I must retract. Siberia indeed! A holiday on the seaside. The information given to me at Maidstone and my growing paranoia were responsible for an entirely distorted conception of this place. Even if the discipline were what it was described as being and the physical training as intense as it could possibly be, I should be compensated by the situation of this camp, the sea wind and, just below this cliff, the bewildering and fascinating sea (which I haven't seen for years). We are near Folkestone and opposite Calais. Owing to the channel guns, the civilian population of this area has been largely evacuated. This circumstance and the presence of the sea make an atmosphere of desolation and vastness which I love. The course is merely one of intensive physical training, including the usual assault courses, runs, marches and scaling cliffs with the aid of ropes.'

In April 1944 I joined the Seventh Battalion, which was stationed at Blackburn, in a disused cotton mill. It was a relief to be out of that Maidstone depot. In Lancashire, too, we were immediately struck by the friendliness of the civilians, who invited us to their homes, talked with us in pubs and bought us drinks. 'For soldiers everything is free of charge — even the pox,' I noted sardonically at the time. Over Easter we were on a route march, singing bawdy songs. The Platoon Commander, a young subaltern, protested mildly, saying, 'After all, it's Good Friday.' About Blackburn I wrote to X on April 8th: 'I've been walking about in this town. There is a fair on at present. I have never yet seen a town whose inhabitants are so ravaged by syphilis, undernourishment and every sort of disease. At present there is a great deal of money in circulation, but it has merely served to add a kind of lurid gloss to the underlying misery.'

From Easter Monday onwards I worked in the Signals Platoon — serving the telephone exchange, laying cables, going out with a 'walky-talky'. One of my ex-Manchester Grammar School friends, Stanley Kerry, took me to his house at Burnley, a former mill town with cobbled streets and disused factories that struck me as more desolate than any part of England I had seen. True, it was a Sunday and it was raining; and a cousin of Stanley's excused himself, saying, 'Well, I must be going to worship the Lord.' A dutiful sort of church-going and a puritanical morality were more widespread at that time among the working classes than they are now. A fellow soldier at Blackburn, a Pioneer called Tom Kember, said about the night life there: 'They goes in a pub and get their belly full of beer, and then they pick up a tart and blows it off on her' — and that summed it up more neatly and accurately than anything I noted down at the time; but a letter to X reports: 'The girls, and there are surprisingly many of them, are more or less asking to be picked up. They're particularly fond of soldiers ... And all this against a background of grimy factories and cotton mills, slums and rainy weather. Today I was transferred to Headquarters, the signal platoon. This is a considerable improvement. When I leave this place, after embarkation leave, I shall go to one of three places: Italy, North Africa or Burma. If I went to North Africa, it would be as reserve (reinforcements) for the Italian front. If the second front opens meantime, I could be sent elsewhere. In fact I don't know where I shall be going.' Possibly because of censorship rules, most of my letters of this period are undated and without place names, so that I can't be sure about their sequence. Even letters were hard to write: 'I could tell you some interesting experiences connected with my removal from Blackburn, but with this bloody censorship on and the general craze for "security" I don't know what I'm allowed to tell and what I'm not, so that I prefer to say nothing at all. The nearer I get to "the other side", the less I think about it; and that is a good thing.' Censorship wasn't the only hindrance: 'As I'm writing this letter, my attention is being claimed by a soldier (whom I have never previously seen) asking me such questions as "Tell me, sir, why does man use all his energy to destroy?" and "Can you honestly say that you know what we're fighting for?", etc. He has also talked about his wife and son, and is just about to open his mouth again. Since he is in greater need of my infinite wisdom and experience than you are, and I can't possibly tell him to shut up, I must close down for tonight.'

Nor had I given up trying to read. It was out of reading Shakespeare's, 'The Tempest', my favourite play at the time, that I wrote my monologue, 'The Tempest: An Alternative' just shortly before leaving Blackburn. I sent it to X. 'There isn't much to tell you. I have written a poem, but ... you know all the rest. I write it every time I send you a poem: apologies, excuses, reasons why I can't write in *this* environment, at *this* time ... Still, I was glad to write even this. If it makes you read 'The Tempest', on which it is based, it will justify its existence; please do — Shakespeare's last play. This is very evident in a certain way, though of course Shakespeare's feelings on leaving his vocation are "objectivized", so that most readers wouldn't be struck by the *subjective* content of the play; nor would they be interested, nor did

Shakespeare intend them to be interested in his own feelings. The great qualities of the play are: the transformation of blank verse, which developed from its primitive stage of being a definite metre to its consummation in Shakespeare's last plays, in which it has become completely flexible and hyper-sensitive, capable of reporting every subtlety of thought and feeling; secondly, the play is completely imaginative: at this stage Shakespeare no longer needed a historical background, a story or contemporary conditions to justify his characters; they just *are*, and nobody can dispute their reality. It is a pity that you don't read Shakespeare. I think that once you've overcome the first strangeness ... you'll read all the works of Shakespeare in the same way, at the same rate, as you've been reading Dickens.

'I have to rely on coffee entirely as a substitute for sleep, and this means living on borrowed energy ... I am trying to do too many things at once: be a more or less conscientious soldier, keep up a pretty large correspondence, write a longish poem, translate a German medieval poem, occasionally speak to the people I know here, read two books (I haven't been able to begin "The Possessed" yet), drink occasionally, walk occasionally (as distinct from marching), see something of the Lake District etc. This, you will realize, is as strenuous as a literary life in London, with all its intrigues, ambitions, complexities, depressions and elations ... Two nights ago I dreamed a strange dream in which my mother's chickens had been killed by foxes, and I saw maggots on the ground and in the carcasses. Yesterday, the day after the dream, I spoke to a farmer who was shearing his sheep. He talked mainly about foxes carrying off lambs and chickens, and then showed me a piece of sheep's wool full of maggots. Is this a coincidence?'

Only a fortnight later, on April 19th, I was part of an advance party sent to Ulverston, in North Lancashire, to prepare new quarters there. I travelled with the signalling equipment on the back of a truck, propping up wireless sets with my back and legs. In pouring rain we laid cables, under the supervision of an officer who became a friend through his censoring of the copious letters I wrote at the time. The Officers' Mess, which I had to scrub on at least one occasion, was a Victorian Gothic building called Stone Cross. In the bathroom there was a stained glass window with the inscription: 'Wash and be clean. The blood of Christ cleanseth of all sins.' But for us, the proletariat, there was very much less opportunity for sins in those parts, only a landscape that captivated me like none I had seen in Kent.

We were billeted in a place called Ford House, another delightful change after Maidstone Barracks and the cotton mill. Two musicians, one of them a Christ Church organist, Allan Wicks, the other a tenor, Barry Hall, were among my friends there, and life became relatively civilized again. Allan and Barry gave informal concerts in pubs. The locals joined in and invited us to their houses for more music-making. I found it hard to understand why the daughter of one of our hosts at those sessions began to weep whenever Schubert's *Marche Militaire* was played, but refrained from asking her, in case it was through some personal association. In a church, Allan played the organ and Barry sang a Handel aria. I had been almost starved of music for a year. To X, I put the difficulties of my life at Ulverston like this: 'Last night, afternoon and this morning we were either marching or operating a switchboard, taking down messages in Morse etc., so that I am rather worn out. I had two hours' sleep in a barn, but the effect of smoking cigarettes and pipe all night (to increase consciousness of being alive) and a great deal of concentration needed to work the switchboard, together with bodily fatigue of forced marching etc. have left me rather flat.' On April 28th I wrote: 'I heard today that I shall have to do another seven weeks' training before I get my embarkation leave — a pity. The spring and the fine weather oppress me, by making me conscious of confinement and the more than natural drabness of my present existence. Wars should be fought only at certain times of the year, mainly in autumn and winter. Of course this doesn't apply to Burma and other remote countries. Sometimes I suffer fits of distraction when I move as though I were in a trance, and those who speak to me (usually roughly and coarsely) seem to be entirely unrelated to me. I move and obey mechanically, but sometimes I blunder badly. Today was such a day: I did everything wrong and couldn't force myself to care. I knew that they couldn't reach me. Incidentally, I saved a hedgehog's life the other day, by paying a fellow two shillings to set it free. He was treating it abominably and was about to sell it to some village boys. It's the only charitable thing I have done for years.'

In May at Ulverston I received an offer from the Fortune Press to publish a book of my poems. Sure as I was that I should soon be dead, I considered this possibility for a while, and X went to see Caton, the owner of the press. 'I was very amused by your account of the Fortune Press bloke. There's more of Dickens in you than I suspected. I literally roared with laughter when I read: 'a tall, black-hatted, shifty-eyed, unshaven bugger comes up ...' I don't want my poems published unless I die in the war, which would mean that I shall never write anything better. I herewith solemnly appoint you my literary executor in the event of my death and give you access to all my mss, to be published at your discretion. My mother knows where they are. I also leave you my books, or as many of them as you wish to have. This is in earnest.'

Meanwhile I was also trying to live. In the same letter I recorded: 'I was bored on Saturday night, and drifted into a performance of some mediocre comedy by the local dramatic club. One of the actresses caught my eye, and after the performance we talked and made a date etc. She is a pretty girl of 19 ... She was the reporter (social gossip) for some local rag and would like to be sophisticated. She told me about a symphony concert and about one sublime piece of music in particular. It was so peaceful, she said, that she fell asleep. She told me also that she's had five proposals of marriage (one from an American *officer*); apparently she collected them, and wants me to join the happy throng of the rejected. I have been trying to impress on her that I shall be gone by the end of the week — the implications are obvious — but she insists on talking about the future, love, etc. when there is no question of any of these things. I've got another date with her, but hope that I shall be on guard duty that night. I don't like the idea of necking on a park bench — either one thing or the other.'

Guard or sentry duty was the subject of the only poem I wrote at this period — at Ulverston — that came out of my military experience proper, as distinct from my hyperbolic rantings about war, death and destruction. Somewhere behind that poem is a figure like the girl of that letter; but in the sonnet she had to be a siren! I had a long way to go before persons or things could be only themselves, and I could make poems out of something other than literature and theology. A sort of long sermon cluttered another of my undated letters: 'I do think that death is not an accident but comes when it must; but at the same time we have free will, and the problem and difficulty are to know how and when to act, and when and how to refrain from acting. If one could identify completely with Providence as the will of God these difficulties would not exist; but as it is, our knowledge of God and our faith are imperfect, so that we act perversely, sometimes in accordance with Providence and sometimes against it. It is not a question of following *instinct* or *intuition*. Our instincts and intuitions are as false and corrupt as our conscious impulses, often more so ... If there is any hope, it is in the guidance of our discerning intellects. For the intellect can be trained to preserve a conviction, once this conviction is known to be true, but the impulses and instincts preserve nothing, and learn nothing. They can be disciplined but not educated — like dogs.'

I apologised for this 'pompous' letter and promised only to write frivolous ones in future. 'What can I do? Wander about in the streets or the fields, meditating corruption or the orgasm of spring? I prefer to talk with the stupid but unsophisticated girls of the district, drink myself numb and dumb, or crack jokes with the soldiers (feeling like death warmed up) ... I like old men best. I talked with an old farmer today. He has lost all his family and all his labourers. He said that he had a family, "but they're all married or buried." But he was quite cheerful, and said that he could find enough to eat in his garden. He also spoke of the peace after the war — he is nearly seventy — when there would be "bags of labourers" and one or other of his children might return. Soldiers don't know anything about life; they don't see much of it either. Soldiering is a substitute for life.'

In May, the Battalion was dissolved, and the Honorary Colonel of the Regiment, Sir Charles Bonham-Carter, came for the ceremonial parade. On his round of inspection he stopped to chat with private soldiers informally, a condescension never shown to us by officers below the rank of General. On leave in London that year I ran into him in the Charing Cross Road and absent-mindedly saluted him, though I was in civilian clothes. When he stopped and I apologized for the reflex action, he claimed to have recognized me from the ceremonial parade and thanked me for the salute.

Soon after the parade my friend Tom Good arrived at Ulverston, staying for a week before moving on to the Lake District. In my free time we went on long walks around the Estuary, through copses of rhododendron trees just beginning to flower. We went to Bardsea across pasture land smooth as a park lawn, moors with pools of salt water and sheep that grazed right down to the beaches. Tom and I also went to a dance at Ulverston, where he teased me about my shyness. I think it was about that dance, or a similar one, that I wrote a new turgid philosophical poem in several parts. Another long poem written there, in June, was one of several dramatic monologues or *persona* pieces of those years, 'Rimbaud in Africa'. Though some of my friends liked it, I left it out of my first book of poems. It had an epigraph from a letter by Keats and another from one by Tom Good: 'I meet so many boys who ask me if I like WAM-BO who wrote the BATEAU IVRE. The streets are littered with them.' The Keats quotation also points to one effect the army was beginning to have on me, a puncturing of my monomaniacal literariness: 'As tradesmen say every thing is worth what it will fetch, so probably every mental pursuit takes its reality and worth from the ardour of the pursuer, being in itself a Nothing.' That was the gist of 'Rimbaud in Africa,' which began:

> Poems? you would like me to write more poems?
> About dusk in the deserts, perhaps, dates, camels and thirst?
> Mirages?
> Certainly — if you pay me well.

Another theme of the poem was religious, and this, too, connected with my own preoccupations at this period:

> I was clever when I was young;
> (Good at Latin, better at blasphemy),
> I built myself a hell and furnished it,
> Mocking the comfort of another's heaven.
> My hysteria transformed the world.
>
> But a little wisdom has made me dull;
> All my curses are prayers now, and if
> I were to sing, my song would be
> Desolate, holy and quiet
> As the desert sands ...

And so forth, at excessive length, as in most of my more ambitious work of those years. At the other extreme were the sonnets I continued to write. The sixteenth was written at Ulverston in July and published and in my first collection as 'Sentry Duty'.

In May, Barry Hall took me to see an Irish priest, Father Moirissy — one of several clerical associations of that time, for Captain Browne, too, was to become a clergyman when he left the army. He and Tom Good had met when Tom was at Ulverston, and they had got on well enough, though they were moving in opposite directions.

Towards the end of the month I went to Grasmere, returning for the night operations in cold, wet and windy weather on June 1st, to lay cables and operate signalling equipment. Only three days later I was able to take another trip, this time to Coniston and Hawkshead, together with Captain Browne and a fellow signalman, Graham Durrant, whom I visited in Cornwall after the war. After a third Lake District excursion to Rydal, on June 21st, I was sent to Catterick for a War Office Selection Board, possibly because Captain Browne had recommended me as a potential officer. On June 18th I was at Elterwater, Westmoreland, 'deep in the heart of the Lake District, as the Americans would put it — a little village of less than thirty houses and one inn. The inn was full up and we were directed to a little cottage, where I am at present, waiting for lunch to be served. I love this part of the world. The only things that relate the inhabitants to the war and goings-on in general are a few wireless sets here and there, and tourists ... Early on Tuesday morning I'm going to Yorkshire, to a W.O.S.B., where I shall be for four days. During that time you may not hear from me. Those days will be rather strenuous — assault courses, psychiatrists, intelligence tests, cross-examinations, etc.' I managed to write another letter the very night before my departure, continued at Richmond: 'Well here I am, ready for the ordeal. So far the place seems pleasant enough. There are sheets in the bed, for the first time since I joined the army, and bath-tubs (also for the first time). There are quite a few refugees of various nationalities among the candidates.'

On June 27th I told X: 'I believe I have failed the W.O.S.B. at Catterick. If so, I shall be leaving Ulverston on Sunday, to go to Lancaster. There I shall join a battalion of another regiment for a few weeks' training, after which I go abroad ... I have been comparatively happy here, but one can't expect things to last.' Since all the intimations I received about my movements were confusing, the letters don't clarify them. Whatever I did in Lancaster, it was not what I thought it would be. 'There are about two different versions of what is to become of me in the immediate future,' I wrote on July 4th, 'and so I merely wait.' On July 1st I had reported: 'I have definitely failed my W.O.S.B., owing to the psychiatrist's report. He recommended that I be interviewed by yet another psychiatrist, who will decide what kind of employment I'm fit for, if any ... For the last week or so I've been in continuous suspension, packing my kit at one moment, unpacking the next.' And five days after that: 'I still don't know what is going to become of me. I could get a discharge from the army if I tried, but this would have such a bad effect on my future state of mind that I shall do my best to be useful in some way. I don't want to be a Maclaren-Ross. Also, after the refreshing simplicity of army life I'm afraid that, in my present condition, I should break down when faced with the complexities of civilian life. I should have to rely on other people to remove the sticks & stones from my path, as I've done in the past. Literature will have to wait, and literature doesn't mind waiting.'

At the interview with the President of the W.O.S.B. that preceded tests of various kinds, he told me that he thought me perfectly well placed where I was. This damped any keen ambition I may have had to improve my status in the army. At Ulverston, in any case, I did feel that I was well placed, for reasons that had nothing to do with status. Nevertheless, the various tests of physical fitness, and one in elementary tactics went well enough. The trouble began when I was interviewed by a psychiatrist and presented with a word association test card which I left as blank as my mind became in face of that prying into my subconscious. What my subconscious associated with the word 'Mother' was my business, not the army psychiatrist's, even if it had obliged me with an association in those circumstances. Perhaps I ought to have faked the thing, but in a way I had already become reconciled to my lot and acquired a sense of solidarity with the peelers of potatoes and the scrubbers of floors. At any rate, when I returned to Ulverston I knew that I should never be an infantry officer. In the report, one of the reasons listed for failure was, 'He likes writing poems'. That, by army psychiatrists' lights, must have been the equivalent of 'He wets his bed'. Just over a week later I was sent to Lancaster for another interview with a psychiatrist.

Back among the 'other ranks', I had cause once more to admire their almost saintly forbearance. On the night of July 1st an old regular soldier came back drunk. At two o'clock in the morning he tried to get into a young conscript's bed and pissed all over him when rejected. Instead of beating him up, the young soldier talked to him for about half an hour, gently persuading him to get into his own bed. Such leanings were described as 'Eastern habits' and attributed to long service in the more exotic outposts of the Empire. If uneducated people were capable of such tolerance, I could only feel ashamed of the fastidiousness I owed to my upbringing.

At Ulverston my time continued to be divided between indoor and outdoor signalling duties and trips to the Lake District with more general chores like night-time guard duty in between. On July 11th we had to vacate Ford House and move into the stables of Stone Cross. I wrote a rather sentimental poem about this event, since it pointed to the break-up of the unit and the end of a relatively pleasant phase. After a day-trip to Bowness and another to Ambleside, which was full of evacuee art students, and a swim in Rydal Water, I prepared for another blind departure that might take me anywhere in Britain or overseas.

My frictions with psychiatrists — I have forgotten why I went to Lancaster and what happened there — were trivial compared to the stresses of some of my friends who had remained civilians. At some time in 1943 or 1944 my sister Maria wrote to me from London about David Gascoyne: 'I have seen David again. He left me with an extraordinary scrap-book with cuttings of underwater and cave pictures, etc. He is gradually deteriorating but has now decided to go to a doctor. He has, in other words, reached the stage where he realizes that he's suffering from a disease rather than thinking that the voices he hears are those of real people. He is still giving his weekly poetry reading, in South Terrace, Thurloe Square. Do you know that house? If you do, tell me what you think of it.' My sister, too, was undergoing psychoanalysis, and so were other friends.

In May 1944, David Gascoyne wrote to me from his parents home at Teddington in his stylized and elaborate script of that period, and with more than Jamesian hesitations and suspensions: 'This isn't the long, long over-due letter that I've always wanted — alas! If for once I tried to be really articulate, these pages, I know only too well, would never get to you at all; remain eternally unfinished — to write to you ... — to establish any sort of intimacy means such a protracted struggle, in the ordinary way, in London, unless perhaps one happens to be living in the same house with a person; English everyday life, I rather think is organized against intimacy ... I have been seeing something of your sister Maria recently — not nearly as much as I should like (perhaps just because I should like so much to see her oftener, something in me that I've never yet managed to nullify or eliminate shrinks in cowardice away and tries to arrange my outward affairs in such a way as to reduce opportunities of contact to a minimum). When we meet I must try to tell you more — ask you more — about my poor complicated obscure and inhibited strugglings towards establishing some sort of an exchange of human feelings with someone else — ...'

Those difficulties of communication were to increase in later years, till they affected not only David Gascoyne's personal relations but his literary work. When the brilliant graphologist Hans Jacoby, to whom I had been introduced by X, saw a specimen of David's handwriting at about this time, he was alarmed, and discouraging about his prospects. The kind of robust sociability to which I'd grown accustomed in barrack-rooms and billets made it difficult for me, in turn, to adjust to the intricacies of a mind like David's. After seeing him in September I noted: 'I feel disgustingly worldly in his presence; and he wearies me so much that I had to run away from the house when he was staying there. I haven't the virtue of being able to look after people ... He is a walking sensibility, a phantom; and what little flesh remains on his frame — he is terribly emaciated — is simply a burden he drags around as a matter of form.' The word 'worldly', I now think, should have been 'earthy', for that was what I felt in relation to David, if not in relation to most of the soldiers I mixed with. For all his unworldliness — not only at this critical period of his life — David was more mundane than I was, though he could never cope with the grosser necessities of practical life.

The place to which we moved from Ulverston on July 23rd, travelling overnight and arriving at one o'clock in the morning, was Mersham-le-Hatch, an eighteenth-century country house near Ashford. As we marched there from the railway station, the sky was bright with searchlights directed at flying bombs. I was to see many of them shot down in the area. We were billeted in the main building. I was fascinated by the old books that had been left in the library, though the shelves were boarded up to protect them from the curiosity of intruders. Later, it was the large park, almost reverted to a wilderness since the outbreak of the war, that attracted me, and I wrote a sonnet about it in the autumn. By a strange coincidence the book in which I included the sonnet in 1950 was published only a few miles away from Mersham, at Aldington, Kent. During one of my explorations of the park I found wild strawberries in September.

At a pub in Ashford I met the first American soldiers with whom I had any conversation. One of them told us stories about the precocious virility of his kid brother, who used to make love to older girls on their way to school in the back of a truck, at the age of six!

Four days after arriving at Mersham I was able to go to London on a week-end pass, returning to see four flying bombs shot down near Mersham. Two of them burst into flames in the air. For a time I was on fatigues in the NAAFI canteen, before taking over the battalion telephone exchange together with my friend Graham Durrant.

My frequent visits to London from Mersham — I went almost every week-end — made me conscious of an element of unreality, of escapism almost, in the life I was leading. I was neither fighting in the war nor grappling with the problems that beset my civilian friends. To X, for instance, writing was not a luxury but a struggle to establish himself and earn a living, though in fact it was journalism to which he had to resort for money, writing his novels at night after an office job. The novel he was writing at this time, which I particularly liked, was never to be published. My old London preoccupations began to reassert themselves, in the rather morbid manner apparent in the sequence 'London Nights', which I wrote in August. I had no wish and no need to publish this or anything else I was writing at the time. On one of my leaves Fred Marnau did ask me to translate some aphorisms by Novalis for the miscellany *New Road* he was editing, but that didn't make me a professional writer. The people I saw on leave in August and September were school friends like Freddy and David Buckley, Oxford friends like John Mortimer, and London friends like David Gascoyne, Peter Vansittart, Fred Marnau, Count Priuli, and a German refugee writer Heinz Priebatsch, who had got in touch with me when the Hölderlin book appeared. For years I was to translate a novel of his that was never published either in German or in English.

In Kent I was beginning to see something in a landscape that appealed to me far less directly than North Lancashire and the Lakes. I noted that the Kent landscape needs sunshine to offset it: 'In dull weather it's rather like a dirty tablecloth.' In the evenings I would drink at the Farrier's Arms at Mersham and attend dances at a little shed opposite the pub that served as a village hall. Returning to the billet one night I rescued a drunken soldier who'd fallen into a ditch and was lying face down in the water. That was a simple practical act of a kind that was rarely called for in my relations with civilian friends, who demanded so much more sympathy while being so much more difficult to help, if only because I had hardly begun to experience the kind of emotional involvement and economic pressures that made life hard for them. It was the disparity between the two ways of life that made me note in September: 'What is known as neurosis really depends on the degree of one's awareness of places and people. In London I am a neurotic, in Kent I am not.' I also noted that the army is a 'sort of Spartan republic in which duty takes the place of ambition, and trifling offences take the place of original sin. It's a simplified civilization, unrelated to any other.'

My literary studies and projects had not been put completely aside. In September, I was reading Baudelaire and Ronsard, discovering affinities between them on which I sketched an essay never written. At the same time I planned a translation of Baudelaire's prose poems on which I did set to work soon after.

In August, I had seen my brother, on sick leave from the coal mines to which he had gone as a Bevin Boy. Our relations were still in a rather harmonious phase that had begun after my father's death, when I could act the part of adviser — if not of keeper, for which I saw too little of him. In September he wrote to me from Merionethshire, where he was staying with a friend, and told me about a love affair he was having. 'I can just see your face as you're reading this letter and I feel certain that you're feeling your little brother is really deep down in the dregs. But, dear Michael, you need never worry about me, as underneath I am quite sensible and the air of frivolity and carelessness which you might have noticed is nothing but a blind to cover my sadness and depression. I have always played a rather false part in life but it has usually only been a blind. On the whole I've had a miserable existence and nothing quite seems to satisfy or engross me. But still, these things will change.' When things did change, I couldn't share the interests that satisfied and engrossed him — if they did — and my squeamishness got in the way, much more so than over the confession in the letter. In fact, when he wrote 'disgust, another product of my chronic upbringing, about sexual matters is wearing off', I probably felt that he was well ahead of me in that regard. The army wasn't conducive to progress in that direction. In 1945 he wrote from Newbridge in Monmouthshire expressing a different sort of disgust — with the royalties I was to receive for my next book, and saying: 'I think you had better employ me as your manager.' I never did, couldn't accept the advice he was now ready to offer me, and continued to fall into all sorts of booby traps over publishers' contracts. At this time Paul had literary plans of his own — a book on the Bevin Boys and the mines, which he discussed with Victor Gollancz, and a play about a bookmaker; but nothing came of these, just as I was never to have the financial success he wished me.

While on sentry duty at Mersham for the last time, I had a long conversation with a regular soldier who had just joined the Battalion after being a prisoner-of-war. He had served in the Army for fourteen years, eleven of which he spent overseas. He had seen half the countries that surround the Mediterranean, fought in France and Africa, travelled in Turkey, Egypt and the Aegean islands. He had been a prisoner-of-war in Italy and Germany, and suffered all kinds of hardships on land and sea. I hadn't been out of the British Isles since I arrived at the age of nine, and was full of silly notions about the experiences I had missed. Yet all that soldier remembered — and this in astonishing detail — was the amount of money paid out or not paid out at such and such a time, in such and such a place. What I learned from him, as from other old soldiers with whom I had talked, was that Egyptian beer was bad and expensive, Turkish vodka was cheap, and that nothing he had seen or suffered had changed his outlook or prejudices. After his last repatriation, while working as a stretcher-bearer, he had persuaded his girl friend, an ambulance driver, to give an Italian prisoner-of-war a lift in the ambulance, though she knew how he felt about Italians and had refused the same request before. This time he pointed out that it was raining, and that 'the poor bastard was drenched'. This didn't prevent him from pushing him out of the back of the ambulance when it was travelling at 40 m.p.h. 'Never 'eard nothing more about it,' he said, and didn't care whether the man was dead or alive. 'But the ATS tart wouldn't speak to me for three weeks. She got the wind up in case the Eyetie 'ad the number of 'er ambulance.' In my poem 'Rimbaud in Africa', written a few months earlier, I had written: 'My journeys are as a soldier's,/ Passionless ...'; but perhaps that cold-blooded act sprang from the nearest thing to passion that man was capable of.

The very next morning, on September 18th, I set out on another journey, to Aberdeen, on our way to the Shetlands. The crossing took a long time, for the boat had to change course to avoid German submarines, passing west of the Orkneys instead of east. It was the worst sea voyage of my life. Even the sailors were sea-sick. Not only were the decks flooded, but towards the end we were wading through the corridors, trying to save rifles and other equipment floating or submerged in the bilge. On top of everything I was ordered to clear up the mess-room after breakfast. Cold porridge and bacon rind, in those conditions, had a distinctly queasy effect, though I had held out till then.

Garrison duty in the Shetlands was unlike anything I had experienced in the army. For one thing, all parades and ceremony were discarded, probably because even the officers were too bored and too demoralized to insist on them. The Germans were in Norway, very close, and had in fact sent over occasional raiding parties, despite the barbed wire coils on the beaches. Yet, at that stage of the war, nothing seemed to be happening or likely to happen. Soldiers lounged about in their Nissen huts on the moors, trying to pass the time as best they could. The Norwegian sailors also on the islands were perpetually drunk on rum.

Censorship did not allow me to describe the crossing to X: 'The island is bleak', I told him on September 21st, 'but the sea breeze is lively enough and more stimulating than anything on land. The town, like most Scottish towns, is built of granite, which always produces a hard and puritanical atmosphere. There are no pubs on the island, and the inhabitants expend all their spare energy in endless dances. I am sure they must have all sorts of secret vices, like the Americans in the years of prohibition.'

Only two days after my arrival I got down to work on my projected Baudelaire translations. Since I couldn't work on them all day long, I asked for some sort of employment. On September 28th I began an 'educational' job that consisted in going the rounds of various camps with a portable gramophone and a number of classical records. I would set this up in the NAAFI, where a few soldiers were drinking beer or tea, and put on the *Coriolan* overture. After one or two minutes the soldiers would walk out of the room. I would play as many records as I wanted to hear, and move on to the next camp. Those walks were not always easy, because of the high winds. At times one had to lie back on them as on an air cushion to avoid being pushed down the other way. Yet those rounds did keep me employed. They gave me plenty of exercise and a chance to listen to those records until I'd exhausted them. In fact, I had other duties, as a letter of September 28th tells me, but it is only the walks across the moors that stuck in my mind. 'I have begun a new job, entailing various educational activities, from providing tools for leatherwork to selecting programmes for gramophone concerts and giving lectures on citizenship. I shall hold the temporary rank of sergeant.' A few days later I added: 'I am learning a great deal whereas before now I worked only for myself, and wrote with no readers in mind, I am now learning how to "put things over", to adapt to a certain standard of intelligence and knowledge, a pretty low one as it happens. For example, I'm trying to dispel the prejudice against good music, by introducing gramophone recitals and ascending very gently from the sentimental to the emotional, and from the emotional to the spiritual or sublime, or whatever you want to call it. I shall try to do the same thing with literature and particularly poetry. Mind you, this isn't easy for me (or for anyone), since there is a great deal of opposition and very little likelihood of success. Also, is it worth doing at all? It is possible that in making a man more sensitive to works of art one is not doing him a favour but putting a curse on him — especially a working man. The wealthy need something that can alleviate their boredom, but others want an emotional laxative, dance music for instance ... I wish I could send you some local curiosity. Would you like a sheepskin, woollen gloves of many colours, a barrel of fish or a Shetland pony? Or some oat-cakes? ... The only eventful thing here is the weather, whose moods dominate everything. I have seen a rainbow in moonlight and the Northern Lights (Aurora Borealis).' On October 9th I wrote: 'Tonight I gave a gramophone recital to an isolated part of this unit. The audience was small but appreciative, and I enjoyed the evening. I am not too well physically, but otherwise indifferently well. The damp climate has brought back my catarrh, cough, nose-bleeding etc.; but these are by now so familiar that I hardly notice them, especially since no great exhibitions of physical prowess are expected of me at present ... Don't worry. All one's (literary) worries are due to impatience, and impatience is due to one's dependence on something that doesn't exist, namely time ... "Sufficient unto the day is the evil thereof". This has nothing to do with the Epicurean doctrine of "carpe diem", or the Old Testament equivalent of "eat, drink and be merry, for ... etc."' My promotion to Sergeant/Instructor did not materialize in the Shetlands. 'I may yet be promoted, but not at present. My duties are various. Our typist is on leave, and at present most of my time is spent as an inadequate substitute for her. However, today I had to write a history of painting, from Leonardo da Vinci to John Armstrong; for educational purposes. I had 2 hours for research and another 2 in which to write and type my learned dissertation. For 2 hours I was surrounded by massive tomes encyclopaedic, which I tried to swallow whole in order to gain time ... The Army Education Officer was surprised that I refused to sign it even with my initials. Strangely enough, even this orgy of activity taught me something.'

I was growing less communicative: 'I have given up all correspondence except with yourself, my family and John Pettavel', I wrote to X. 'I simply can't think of anything to write. I've got into the habit of using words only for the communication of essential statements and questions, such as "What's the time, please?", "Yes, sir", "No, sir" etc. Occasionally I swear very obscenely, just to prove that my silence is not due to a sense of superiority, as in fact it is not. Perhaps I should become a Trappist monk when I leave the army : they dispense with talk altogether.' The same letter goes on to my reading of St. Thomas Aquinas and his way of defining the nature of God 'by a process of elimination, by pointing out all the things that God is not ... as though God were an x in an equation. No one today would have the courage to base his belief in God on reason and logic, rather than on faith.'

In Lerwick there was little social life. Most of the native population found it hard to communicate with all those foreigners in uniform. One of the local industries, fishing, had been suspended for the duration. All that remained was sheep, the curing of sheepskins, and the various traditional skills connected with wool. I don't remember exactly how I came to be invited to one house or cottage, belonging to the Shetland aunts of an evacuee from London, a woman pianist, but my two musician friends had something to do with it, through musical activities similar to those at Ulverston. Somewhere I heard her play a Brahms *Rhapsody* and a Beethoven sonata; and towards the end of my stay at Lerwick I took her to a recital of recorded music that somebody had arranged. In any case, we fell in love; and that was hard on us, since she was married to a man serving in the Army abroad and she had a small son.

A cynic would have pointed out that between the vigilant aunts and a small, puritanical, tightly knit community on the one hand, the inhospitable moors and the barricaded beaches on the other, it was easier for us to suppress our impulses than it might otherwise have been. But we did get away, walking an icy road at night by the Northern Lights, at a time when I should have been back in barracks and she at home. No blizzard or snowfall would have got between us if conscience had not. (Though conscience needn't be more dependable than impulse. When, later, I wrote a poem about the relationship, conscience had defected to the other side, blaming me for having been made a coward by conscience. As for her, she was twenty-five, as against my twenty, and sensible enough not to deceive herself with cant about 'Platonic love'. Her conscience plagued her because she had wanted the affair we didn't have, though she loved her husband and wrote to him about the encounter.)

Two months after disembarking at Lerwick I was on a boat once more, leaving as suddenly and unaccountably as I had arrived. She was on the quay-side, but didn't know which boat I was on. I saw her, and didn't care whether we had done the right thing or not, only that we weren't likely to meet again and that, even if we did, there would be no way out of the trap.

The return crossing was smoother than the other, but I was sea-sick again, because I felt sick the moment the boat pulled out. As she told me in her first letter, written on December 23rd, she too had fallen ill at once. She had to hide the letter she was writing from one of her aunts. 'By the way', she wrote, 'did you notice her last words to you and the way in which she said them? The words may have been Christian enough, but the tone was that of an old witch pronouncing a curse.' Her next letter was written on a Sunday, when the aunts had gone to church. Yet she was reading 'religious and missionary literature, not in order to save my soul but because there's very little else in the house. The doctor was quite shocked to find *Sin and its Remedy* at my bed-side.' When I told her of the poem I'd written for her, she commented: 'Now I know why people write poetry (& I've often wondered) — because they dare not say things plainly in prose!'

The Battalion moved to Hastings, where many of my friends, including Allan Wicks, were posted abroad, and I, too, expected a posting. When it still didn't come, I began to agitate and press the Company Commander. I had had enough of doing useless things, sitting around and waiting for something to happen.

That parting, together with all the uncertainties and delays of my army life, precipitated another crisis. All my army travels had only brought me back to my starting-point, the South of England; and the proximity of London, where I now went frequently on short leaves, brought the literary scene closer to my awareness again. 'I haven't yet left school as far as my poetry is concerned' I wrote to X 'In my poetry I'm always sincere but never natural.' But I was less worried about that deficiency than before. After a meeting with X in London, I wrote on January 6th: 'Since I can't express myself in conversation, I shall try to do so in writing. My attitude to all things that matter has changed considerably. First of all, literature : poetry has ceased to be a religion and obsession. I don't worry about my poems now, and I never force myself to write ... The emphasis has shifted from poetry to living. The mere condition of being alive and perceptive has acquired a very definite value and a very definite *importance*. I believe that this is something permanent and independent of circumstances, something I

(above) Father at the time of the First World War.

(below right) Mother in the early years of her marriage.
(below left) My maternal grandmother Regina at Kladow, about 1930.

(above) The Hamburger, Freud and Mosse children at Kladow: Lucian Freud is second fron left in the back row, Clement Freud on the left in the front row; I am on the right of the front row.

(left) I visited our bombed house in St John's Wood after the war: these are the stairs to the conservatory.

could preserve in any situation whatever. It is founded on religious convictions that have become stronger since I joined the army but which I cannot discuss even with you. You asked me the other evening whether I thought the army had profited me. The answer is that it has changed me, but that I'm not sure whether you would consider the change an improvement. Very often I, too, think that it is a deterioration, but my more lasting conclusion is that the process of shedding I have undergone, like a tree in autumn, is necessary and valuable. I have completely lost my sense of being different, of being superior. I have decided that poets are not demi-gods, but people who are often grossly inferior to the simplest peasant; that the mere fact that one is filled with a desire to write great works does not put one into a class apart and does not give one the right to despise anyone at all, humanly speaking. No man is a genius until 300 years after his death. While he is alive, he is merely a mortal and subjected to the same criteria and the same laws as anyone else. This, in brief, is my present position. It doesn't matter what I do or where I go in future. I believe in the literal truth of the phrase: Everything comes to him who waits ...'

As far as the military life was concerned, though, something did have to be done. By January 1945 it looked as though I should be sent to the Western Front, but once more I got only as far as embarkation leave. By this time I was really exasperated. When I applied to become an interpreter on the Western Front, I was told that I couldn't be transferred from the infantry because of my medical grade. At last I prevailed on the Company Commander to have me down-graded — on the strength of a letter to the Medical Board saying that I was apt to puff and wheeze when running, the whitest of white lies — and my grade was duly changed from A1 to B1, on January 22nd. Four days later I was sent on infantry work again, on a rifle range. On February 9th I was sent on a course to Bamber Bridge, near Preston, Lancashire, but this turned out to be not an interpreters' course but a general educational course, on which I attended lectures on music given by Eric Fenby! How and why I was there, I shall never know, when I was not to be transferred to the Education Corps until much later, after being an interpreter.

From Cuerdon Hall, Bamber Bridge, I wrote to X: 'When I said that I'd transferred the emphasis from poetry to living, I didn't mention that this (at present) leaves me in a kind of no-man's-land, where I am a stranger ... At present I'm a donkey starving between the hayricks of poetry and life ... The instruction here is excellent — the War Office at its most genial. A sort of inferior Oxford, where everyone is treated as a gentleman, except the poor bastards who do the dirty work — the same work that we do when we're at our own units ... There's plenty of work for people like myself, in the Army, I mean — "re-education for civilian life", they call it.'

My depression, frustration and restlessness showed in letters to my friend at Lerwick, and she gave me a 'little, simple piece of advice': 'If only you could just think about the "little things" for a while: concentrate on not losing your personal belongings and not forgetting things. And then, having put the minor details of life right, go on to bigger things.' That was sound, womanly advice, but it didn't apply to that particular situation. It was the little things of army life, conscientiously attended to in a vacuum of purposelessness, that were getting me down. At Hastings, on December 11th, I noted: 'Today our despatch rider was found embroidering a handkerchief with the arms of the Royal Artillery. When asked why he was doing this, he replied: "It's for the husband of the girl I go out with. He's in the R. A., you see."' If only I could have been as realistic as that, about love, war, or anything else, I might have been content with little things, and counted myself lucky for being out of the fighting.

On January 24th I was in London, cycling with Elinor through blacked-out streets and being chased by a policeman on a bicycle for having no lights. We gave him the slip by going off in different directions, so that he didn't know which of us to pursue, and meeting up again.

At Hastings I spent most of my evenings in the old part of the town, talking to fishermen in pubs. Of my friends there, Tom de Tivoli, a middle-aged man whose health was poor, was trying in vain to get his discharge on medical grounds, while I had been downgraded, was perfectly fit, and was doing my best to be sent abroad. On March 13th, I went to the War Office for a language test, which I probably passed quite smoothly, though many more months, and the war in Europe, were to go by before there were any results.

At that period I began to do new versions of my Hölderlin translations, for a new edition not published until 1952. My Baudelaire translations had been finished at Lerwick and accepted for publication by Tambimuttu. For a time I had considered publishing a book of my own poems, but thought better of it. I was still very far from being satisfied with my work as a whole, and my doubts had been confirmed by others. In January 1944, T. S. Eliot had written to me: 'I am sure that if you have it in you to be a poet you will not be discouraged by the severity of Read's and my criticism.' I was not discouraged by it, inasmuch as I went on writing, but the kind of development which I knew was necessary couldn't be forced by hard work. It was a matter of learning to live more fully and unreservedly, and that is where my dissatisfaction with army routines linked up with the other.

From March 27th to April 5th I was on leave again, seeing my London friends and visiting my grandmother at Kew. On a visit to Oxford I met the widow of the German scholar Friedrich Gundolf, Stefan George's most influential disciple and advocate in the universities. She had written to me after the publication of my Hölderlin book, asking me to do something for her husband's works in England. When I managed to interest Tambimuttu in a translation of Gundolf's book on Goethe, she suddenly changed her mind and tone, asking me how I had the impertinence to suggest such a thing. She had been notorious in the George Circle for alienating her husband's friends. At an earlier period, in 1941 or 1942, X had introduced me to a George disciple, Karl Kilian Mayer, and his wife, Runhilt von den Steinen, and Mayer had helped me with my Hölderlin studies. Through them I had also met Friedrich Gundolf's brother Ernst, a scholarly and retiring man who produced a drawing, usually of a German landscape, every day in his London exile. He, too, was not on speaking terms with his sister-in-law. After Karl Mayer's early death I kept in touch with Runhilt von den Steinen, who practised as a doctor in Wales, but I could never respond to the Stefan George cult or the strange élitist assumptions current among his disciples.

I was much more impressed, but also depressed, by my one meeting with Dora Dymant, the woman with whom Kafka had lived in Berlin towards the end of his life. I went to see her somewhere in Hampstead, to sit talking for an hour or two in a room where nothing seemed to belong to her but a photograph of Kafka. There wasn't much she could tell me about their life together, and I wasn't a biographer in any case. What she communicated to me was the sadness and loneliness of her present situation as a refugee.

Later in April I was on the march again, on a so-called 'scheme' or exercise, passing through village after village — Brede, Westfield, Guestling, Broad Oak, among others. The war was coming to an end, at least in Europe, and I was still playing soldiers. Immediately after that I was in London again, going to a party at John Mortimer's in Chelsea. I stayed too late, couldn't get a taxi, and walked from Chelsea to London Bridge in pouring rain. At 3 a.m., in a Fleet Street café, a reporter told me that the fighting in Europe was over. At 4.05 a.m. I caught a mail train back to Hastings, soaked to the skin and frozen.

For me, the war games weren't over. Two days later I went to Moor Park to join the First Airborne Corps. I spent the night at my mother's house, and returned to Moor Park next morning, to be taken in a truck to some unnamed place in East Anglia. The games became more and more farcical, for my part in that exercise was to impersonate a German soldier. I was issued with a German uniform. Perhaps this was the outcome of my language test at the War Office. I was shuttled from one place to another, from one bed to another. The only place I could identify was Bury St. Edmunds. While rumours of peace circulated I began my rôle of German soldier, and was taken prisoner by a brigade of Polish paratroopers. I spent a sleepless night under interrogation, with intervals of casual conversation with the Poles in a stable. Later the Poles disappeared from the exercise, which was considered important enough to be visited by the Minister for War. In due course I became a British soldier again and returned to my unit.

On V.E. Day, I was in London. I went to a party given by Tambimuttu, then to the Gargoyle Club, a favourite haunt of Dylan Thomas. In the course of our celebrations I climbed the Eros statue, or rather the boarding that had protected it during the war, and brought down the flag that had been planted on the top — a feat about as useful as my other contributions to the war effort over the past two years.

At last, in June 1945, I succeeded in getting myself sent abroad, though still not to Germany. On the long sea voyage I also managed once more to lose my personal belongings, but this time it wasn't my fault. They were stolen by a fellow soldier while I was asleep in my hammock, with my uniform folded under my head. Somehow he managed to get at the pockets through the meshes, taking my money, pocket watch, silver cigarette case. He also rifled my kitbag. This turned out to be awkward. Not only was there no compensation for such thefts, but when I disembarked, in Naples, my papers, too, had been lost, I didn't exist officially and could draw no pay. The whole posting, perhaps, had been a mistake. In any case I was stuck in a transit camp in Naples, with nothing to do once more but the most extraordinary fatigues, such as unloading sheep in the harbour and herding them to a camp of Muslim Indians for ritual slaughter. I could eat and sleep in the camp and draw my cigarette ration. Since I also needed money — if only to give to the beggars, before I became inured to misery more abject than any I had seen or believed possible — I was reduced to selling a tin of fifty cigarettes on the black market. The proceeds of that sale kept me in petty cash for a month or so, and even allowed me to replace the cigarette case and the watch.

The impact of Naples was so powerful that I still remember the drive by truck from the quay to the transit camp. I had never been south of the English Channel. Even the sea voyage, with glimpses of the Bay of Biscay, the Spanish and Portuguese coast, my first sight of the Mediterranean, a brief landfall at Capri — where we swam in the Blue Grotto — and countless unidentified coastlines, was a major experience. What overwhelmed me on that truck was not the beauty of the city — nor its sordidness, at that point — but the strangeness of its air and smells, as exotic to me as the tropics or the remotest Orient. The circumstances didn't need to be propitious. During long roll-calls at the camp, the only parade of the day, at which fatigues were also assigned — even to people whose official existence was in doubt — soldiers used to faint and drop in the heat. At night, on the other hand, in our tents, the cold sometimes kept us awake. The camp was chaotic, its population more mixed and fluid than any I had known in the army. On July 9th I summed up my first impressions in a letter to X: 'I have been here for four days, and am still waiting to go to Austria. All the documents relating to my appointment as an interpreter have been lost, and I was very nearly sent to an infantry depot. It is difficult to describe Naples in one letter, especially since I don't know how much of the misery is due to the occupation, how much is due to the laziness and inefficiency of the Neapolitans. The town itself is beautiful enough, spacious, well-designed and situated, but the stench is quite overpowering, and I am glad that we sleep in tents, about four miles from the town centre. Black-marketeering and prostitution are the main, almost the only, industries ... But at the same time there is plenty of *joie de vivre*, laughter, shouting and brawling. Also, there are luxuries that don't exist in war-time England, wine and fruit of every kind, the opera etc. Books are pretty cheap, if you know where to go for them, and I've bought as many as I can accommodate. Many of the soldiers sell their cigarette rations to Italians. Stealing is very widespread in all the camps. All our army kit can be sold to Italians very profitably, and that's why it's stolen by British soldiers.' That four mile stretch between town centre and camp is what I remember best, because I must have walked it at least twice every day, and it was also the road along which I drove a flock of sheep on one occasion. Not all the smells along that road were of open drains. The air was also impregnated with the rich vegetable smells I was to breathe again on every visit to the European or American South. It was on that road, too, that I stopped to chat with local people at times, practising my rudimentary Italian picked up from the books I was reading.

The few letters I wrote from Naples had no answering address, because I was in transit without an official identity. On the 15th I wrote: 'Now that I have seen Naples from several angles, I can understand the pessimism of writers like Leopardi and Foscolo and their laments for a degraded Italy ... Last night I went out with two soldiers who were looking for a girl to pick up. They talked to a little boy of about eight who tried to sell them his sister and gave a detailed description of her merits, her past and her price. There are hundreds or thousands of boys in Naples who are employed in the same way, also as agents for black-marketeers, usually members of their own family ... I expect that I shall be moving on to Rome either on Monday or Tuesday.'

In the city itself there was the literally palatial NAAFI, the former Royal Palace, with a soprano purveying local produce like *O sole mio* to largely indifferent ears. Since the marble walls kept it relatively cool, I spent many hours there over drinks, learning Italian or chatting with anyone I happened to meet. I was learning Italian not because I might suddenly find myself employed as an interpreter for that language — anything was possible in the Army — but because I wanted to be able to speak with Italians and read the Italian books I was beginning to buy. The foundation was a bilingual Dante I had brought with me; the next, incongruous, layer, snatches of colloquial Neapolitan picked up in my endless prowlings around the somewhat dangerous back alleys of the city; the one after that, any later works, from Alfieri's autobiography to Chirico's, just published, that I picked up in the bookshops. Grammar had to be assimilated in the process, or not assimilated at all.

Outside the Royal Palace life was rather different. At every second step one was accosted by someone who wanted to sell or buy something — anything — or be given alms. 'Hey, mister, you want drink? Good vino, spumante? My sister, she only fifteen, virgin. Want to sell cigarettes?' And so forth. At first I couldn't resist the beggars, who looked as though they would drop dead if they didn't eat within the next five minutes, but there were simply too many of them. Quite a number of back streets were out of bounds to soldiers. We had been warned, too, that soldiers who went there for drinks or girls had been robbed or knifed. It was the small boys who not only sold their sisters but developed the highest skill in theft. One day, when we were waiting outside a railway station with our kitbags on the ground, a boy ran up to a soldier and spat at him. The soldier tried to catch him, and his kitbag vanished so fast that none of us saw it go. On a night train journey kitbags disappeared just as mysteriously from luggage racks, during a few minutes' halt in some poorly lit station, with the owners sitting right underneath them.

Somehow I managed to do a bit of sight-seeing around Naples, going to Pompeii, to Caserta, to Amalfi and Sorrento before my papers arrived and I made my way north by slow stages. Of Rome I saw nothing but the monumental railway station, but got to know Bologna, Milan, Udine, Venice, and a variety of small towns not on the tourist circuit. On the way I picked up an infection, hepatitis, and had no sooner joined my new unit in Austria than I had to go to hospital for three weeks. This was in August, and the hospitalization had an awkward sequel. As I was travelling in an ambulance to the Convalescent Depot at Velden, near the Wörthersee, the driver offered me a bottle of very rough Italian brandy. I had been told not to drink for a whole year, but in my unsettled frame of mind I ignored the warning and drank the greater part of its contents. When the driver noticed that I had passed out, he grew afraid and threw me out into the road. I was in a coma for several days. I came to, once, on the roadside, and tried to get up. There was a barbed wire fence behind me that tore my army tunic from top to bottom as I collapsed again. When I next regained consciousness I was back in the same hospital by the lake, with anxious doctors at my bedside. They told me I was lucky to be alive. The immediate effects passed very quickly, but from that time onwards I had trouble with food and drink, finally being reduced to a fairly strict diet and no alcohol at all.

My new home bore the euphonious name 'J Divisional Dump Unit'. It consisted of large sheds full of captured enemy equipment, and the stores were loaded, unloaded and maintained by German prisoners-of-war, under the supervision of a very small British staff. It was at Lienz, a small town in East Tyrol, near the Glockner and Heiligenblut. My job was to act as interpreter to the officer in Command, Major Hudson, and pass on his orders to the Germans. From the first a friendly relationship was established between Major Hudson and myself. That was lucky for me, since I returned with a letter from the hospital saying that disciplinary action was to be taken against me for disobeying a medical order and endangering my life. Major Hudson laughed the matter off, and nothing more was heard of it. I was afraid that the ambulance driver didn't get off so lightly.

On August 24th I wrote to a friend from hospital: 'Wherever I go some German or Austrian discovers that I know the language and attaches himself. After that he tells me that he is out of communication with his family, and expects me to sympathize as voluminously as he complains. In future I shall conceal my knowledge of German except when I'm on duty. I have seen no poverty in Austria, at least nothing comparable to what I saw in Southern Italy ... Lienz bores me stiff.' It became rather less boring as I became engrossed in the affairs both of our small unit, including the prisoners-of-war, and of the Displaced Persons in nearby camps. The mountain scenery, too, became more and more attractive, especially when I took up riding. The unit had acquired a strange assortment of horses, including a former circus horse — a white stallion — and two Cossack mares captured from the Cossacks who fought on the German side. These Cossacks had been rounded up when British troops entered Austria and handed over to the Soviet Army. I was told that they had been shot while packed into trains bound for Russia.

A German groom attached to the unit taught me to ride, in a pretty informal manner. I got on a horse, he gave it a great whack on the backside, and off it went at a gallop. If I kept my seat, as I managed to do, he considered that I could ride. That was all the tuition I ever received, but it was enough to keep me riding happily in all weathers, over snow and ice, through forest tracks on the foothills of the Alps, along lake shores, as long as I was in Austria, but especially at Lienz. The Cossack mares became my favourites, because they combined sensitiveness with stamina. I became so attached to one of them that when the unit was disbanded and the horses put up for sale, I very nearly bought that mare, though I shouldn't have been able to keep her either where I was going from there or back in London.

As I recovered from my alcoholic coma I looked out on to a green valley, and was very glad to be alive, after all, even if the old subconscious death wish had been behind my drinking. The first letter I received from X after Naples told me of the death of Hans Jacoby, the brilliant graphologist, whom I had met once or twice in London. I wrote another of my elegies on his premature death, no better than the one for Sidney Keyes.

By August I was back in hospital. On September 10th I wrote to X: 'I've been in hospital for three weeks now, or is it four? I don't know. Time doesn't seem to matter. All I know is that the summer has ended in the meantime. All I can see from my bed is a bit of the sky and the top of some mountains. I recovered from the jaundice, but now I've got some other bloody disease that comes and goes, makes my temperature jump up and down, my head ache and my stomach incapable of taking food. I wouldn't mind getting my discharge, since all this business is a waste of time. The occupation is completely useless, nobody is doing anything to re-educate the Austrians. They bow and scrape at every Englishman, and behind his back they say, "Aren't the English soft?", because nobody shouts at them or kicks them now that the "master race" has left. I've heard a good many first-hand accounts of the Russians in Vienna and elsewhere, and their behaviour is atrocious ... Jewish refugees come from the Russian zone into the British, when they can. They have to be smuggled to Italy, thence to Palestine.'

My contacts with civilians at Lienz were mainly with Displaced Persons, beginning with the two Russian or Ukrainian girls who worked as secretaries in our unit. Through them I came to visit the camp they lived in, though D.P. camps were out of bounds to soldiers, and became fascinated by the customs and dances of the various East European nations represented there. Yugoslavs, I think, were in the majority, and I learned to dance the Kolo. My access to the camp was made easier because a school acquaintance was one of its administrators. Through my acquaintance with a Serbian who had fought as a Partisan with Tito, but fallen out with him after the fighting, I was initiated into the political and ethnic conflicts in the camp — especially among the Yugoslavs, once more, since that camp had thrown together Fascist Ustashi, Royalist Cetniks, Social Democrats and Communist deviationists like my friend. Several Democrats were murdered in the camp by men in the pay of the Ustashi, who had smuggled gold coins out of Yugoslavia. The older ethnic rivalries added to the complications. I remember the uproar when a Slovene girl was elected 'beauty queen' at one of the fêtes I attended there. Besides the Yugoslavs there were Russians, Ukrainians and Balts. I was much taken with the pale beauty of a Latvian girl I met in the camp, but she was closely guarded by her mother and grandmother, and language difficulties also helped to keep her inaccessible.

About my Serbian friend, Popovic, I wrote to X: 'I have met a very interesting Yugoslav revolutionary. He was Tito's personal friend and at one time his adjutant. Later he revolted against what he called the tyranny of the Communist leaders and, with 300 men, went over to a small democratic group that was also fighting the Germans. Now, of course, he is in disgrace.'

Earlier on, at Klagenfurt, on my way to Lienz, I had got to know of the official Yugoslav claim on certain areas near the Wörthersee inhabited by Slavonic-speaking people, and there had been a certain amount of tension there, with pro-Yugoslav slogans to be found here and there on walls.

'Fraternizing' with Austrians was also strictly forbidden, but the cook in our unit was having an affair with a local woman. When her husband was discharged from the German Army and returned to Lienz, our cook kept him quiet with gifts of tinned food stolen from our rations, and continued the affair. Such deals — and they were common at the time in Italy and Austria — were still so shocking to me that I avoided speaking to that cook. Very gradually I began to question both my own moral code and the more general perfectionism with which it was bound up. This process led to a revulsion against the romanticism and idealism of my earlier verse, and a decided change of tone in the sequence I began at about this time, 'From the Note-Book of a European Tramp'. The reaction was too extreme. In my endeavour to be direct, unliterary and true to life, I fell into triteness and flatness. Sending a poem in the old manner to X in January 1946, I commented: 'I don't know whether it's good or bad, but suspect that it's the last poem of that sort I shall write. I should like to get rid of the moralizing strain once and for all, but perhaps I have nothing to replace it. I shall need a few more years in which to develop a sense of joy ... To be a poet one must eternalize the moment, not be momentous about eternity.' At Christmas I wrote to X about festivities for the event: 'The preparations are made by our two Russian office girls, who expect to be sent back to Russia in January, where they will be imprisoned or killed — at least, so they believe. Last week I came to their rescue when the Austrian Police raided their camp and confiscated most of their possessions, but I doubt very much I shall be able to help them when they get the order to move. What a life! For all I know, nothing may happen to them, but I can't bear being surrounded by people who consider themselves sentenced to death. Of course they were traitors to Russia, and I can't believe that Papa Stalin will, as he says, welcome them back with open arms, except with a vengeance. They'll probably try to escape to the American zone.' The girls were not deported, but probably settled in some remote foreign country after the unit's dissolution.

In January 1946 I asked X to ring up or send a postcard to the Times Literary Supplement 'asking them not to review the damned poem' — 'Later Hogarth' — 'since it was published without the author's consent etc.. Briefly, I don't want to take legal action or to avenge myself, because as you say, J. G. probably thought he was doing me a good turn ... Did you know that the waxing and waning of the moon affects the fall of snow, as well as one's moods? I thought at first this was a mere superstition, but it seems to be true enough.' On February 22nd I wrote: 'Our correspondence isn't up to much these days. It is not only the distance in space that sets us apart, but the fact that our activities are so very different and that neither of us is as fond as we used to be of abstract statements and arguments. Your job, your family life and your novels probably take up most of your energy and your time ... Within the last year my outlook (and perhaps my character too) has changed so much that I'm now overhauling the whole mechanism. My poetry now is a mere ritual bearing no proper relationship to what I am, and I must either change it radically or give it up ... By the end of June up to group 32 will have been released. My number is 53, and you can calculate how much longer I shall have to serve, even assuming that the release does not stop entirely after a certain group, as it may do. I have no idea what I shall do as a civilian. I may be able to kill a few months at Oxford, but during that time I should have to decide. This week I'm going to Villach, the nearest town of any size, to celebrate something or other with a party of Yugoslavs. Horse-riding and drinking schnaps (the most revolting distillation I have come across) are my main recreations. The first is really exhilarating, and I shall be sorry to give it up.'

Meanwhile I had received my first promotion in the army, to Lance-Corporal, a rank that must have gone with my duties as an Interpreter. Major Hudson's treatment of the P.O.W.s was liberal in the extreme. He even allowed them to 'fraternize' with Austrians at dances held in the camp. After a time, though, stores began to disappear from the sheds. I had been given a few badly needed items, such as fur-lined gloves and a pair of riding breeches, unfortunately of S.A. provenance, but the only ones available. These and a pair of despatch rider's boots were my riding outfit. The stores now missing were of a different order and quantity. We guessed that there must be a regular smuggling ring, very well organized, among the P.O.W.s. Since they functioned as a largely autonomous unit, governed by German army discipline according to army rank, it seemed unlikely that such a ring could exist without the knowledge and complicity of at least one officer. Major Hudson worked out what point of the camp periphery was most suitable for smuggling out stores. One night he and I hid there, complete with loaded revolver, saw the stuff — mainly blankets — being passed over to civilians, and made our presence known. It remained to establish exactly who was involved in the operation. A young lieutenant, relatively fresh from the Hitler Youth, readily admitted to having initiated it — on idealistic grounds of course, for the greater glory of the German cause and the greater comfort of his men, since the proceeds were to be used to buy black market commodities for them all. Days of interrogation passed before the German Regimental Sergeant-Major admitted his part in the operation. It was a strange experience to hack away at his arrogant and self-righteous denials to the point where his toughness — feared by all his subordinates in the camp — suddenly cracked, and he burst into tears. Once again, only the highest motives — concern for the welfare of his soldiers and an order from a superior in rank — had impelled him to collaborate. When the shell of authority broke, there was nothing inside it but a boy confused by the conflicting demands of two fathers. More sobbing followed when I pointed out to him that Major Hudson had gone out of his way to improve the living conditions laid down for P.O.W.s, and that none of them was in fact suffering any deprivation.

My services as an interpreter were also called upon for a rather different interrogation — of the witnesses at the trial of a British soldier who had killed an Austrian guard on a train, only because he was travelling without a pass or ticket after going to see his Austrian girl friend, and was afraid of being punished for a relatively minor offence. This soldier, who was barely articulate, offered no self-justification of any kind, least of all on idealistic grounds. When his girl friend was called as a witness to his movements at the time, he winked at her. His attitude was one of neither knowing nor caring whether and why he had done what the prosecution accused him of having done. That was their concern. His concern had been to get from one place to another.

This would have been a more fruitful subject for my writing than the second-hand ones — Faustus and Don Juan — that still occupied me in 1945. These two, and Sir Walter Raleigh, were to be the last of my literary and mythical personae for many years. The figure of the

European Tramp who took their place was at least a contemporary and my own invention, though his inverted romanticism and traditionalism were a transition, at best, to the openness I was after, an openness to immediate experience.

Meanwhile I was reading Russian novels recommended and sent to me by X, and making half-hearted attempts to learn Russian, because another area that had opened up for me was that of Eastern Europe; but this opening, a mere chink, came too soon after my discovery of Italy. Europe, altogether, was too large and too diverse to be gulped down and assimilated in this voracious manner. Another book I was studying at this period was Burckhardt's Renaissance in Italy; and I was also beginning to be interested in the differences between German and Austrian culture, at a time when I felt that both had collapsed. There was simply too much to be taken in and sorted out.

'I got rather a scare the other day,' I wrote to X in November, 'when I heard that all soldiers whose release number is higher than 35 will be sent to the Far East. That's the last place I want to visit in uniform. However, I don't think I shall be sent, because I'm a "key man" or specialist or something or other. I can't say that I like the prospect of another two years' service. The lack of all social intercourse gets one down more quickly than I thought at first. I said "social" but perhaps "sexual" has something to do with it. One man in this unit has actually volunteered for another year because he wants to marry a Latvian girl and is waiting for official consent. It's really extraordinary how women are handed on from one person to another. A sergeant going on leave will lend his girl to another sergeant until he returns — but not to a corporal. Of course there's a practical motive behind this: he knows that the other sergeant will "keep her warm" for him, whereas if he left her without a partner she might find an officer while he's away, and he'd lose her for good. Most of these military mistresses are well-experienced, because they were German camp-followers before they were taken over by the "victorious armies". Rather a sordid business, "love" in this place, don't you think? ... At Christmas we're throwing a party. We're getting some wine from Italy. At present we can't even get drunk. Roll on Christmas! as they say in the army.'

I remember our wine and spirit buying expedition to Italy through the wintry Puster Valley, in a jeep. That winter I spent a short leave at Cortina, getting stuck on a broken-down ski-lift and almost freezing to death, and taking up ice-skating again, a pastime I had dropped after my Berlin childhood. The conflict between Italy and Austria over the South Tyrol or Alto Adige was not in evidence at this period, but I was to get an unpleasant taste of it on a later visit to Lienz. As for Austrian politics, I wrote in the same letter:

'Today Austria is voting. There is no enthusiasm, in fact nobody cares a damn, because one party is so much like another, except the Communists, whose posters are usually torn down or covered with swastikas. The Socialists will win, I believe, because they've put up more posters than any other party. Or possibly the Volkspartei, because it sounds attractive.'

Had I been to Vienna at this stage, I should have qualified these observations which were based on a superficial knowledge of local affairs. For personal reasons, I needed to keep them superficial. On one of my first days at Lienz I had gone out to the outskirts of the small town and was reading or writing on a bench facing the mountains, when a man sat down next to me and spoke to me in basic English. I answered in German, and he was eager to know how I came to speak German so well. I explained the circumstances. He jumped up from the seat in a weird frenzy of astonishment, repeating, 'An Israelite, an Israelite', as though this marked me as the last surviving specimen of an extinct species. Perhaps he had believed in the total success of Hitler's 'final solution', or was amazed to find that I didn't look like the Nazi caricatures of Jews. In any case he wanted to tell all the people in the village about his discovery, asking me to go back with him to be exhibited. I declined the offer, explaining to him that there was nothing extraordinary about my origins or function, and that there were many people like me serving in the Allied armies. And now would he please let me get on with my work? He didn't take kindly to the brush-off, and left, sulking. After this I was careful to confine my conversation with locals — mainly the shopkeepers — to necessary exchanges.

In December and January, I was worried about the poem printed by Gowrie, not knowing then that even in its authentic form that poem was among those I should only want to suppress. In January, too, I was trying to get a letter through to my great-uncle Paul in Berlin, and had to ask an army friend serving in Germany, Denis Andrews, to help. Even he couldn't send it by post, but had to look for someone going to Berlin who would deliver it by hand. There was no official communication between the B.A.O.R., the army in Germany, and the C.M.F. in which I was serving. My friend was at a school of Military Intelligence at Bad Driburg, and Berlin was a different zone again. So he had to find a middleman who would deliver my letter by hand to my great-uncle, and went to great pains to do so. My great-uncle's reply — he was overjoyed to be in touch again — reached me in the same way.

X had recently finished a sort of picaresque novel, the first of his novels to find a publisher. My comments in a letter of February 1946 show that I was reacting strongly, perhaps excessively, to earlier literary preoccupations: 'As for the novel, my opinion is that the old form is capable of development, just as in poetry. I have come round to a very conventional view of literature. *Finnegan's Wake*, in small doses, is quite amusing, but only to those who trade in words. It is *not* a novel; it is the consummate product of the author's self-bestowed divinity, which has made him an absurd appendix of society. An author is one who writes books which others may *read*, not one whom others may write about. If the novel can't go forward along the lines of increasing subtlety and sensibility, if Henry James & Proust are a dead end, then it can go forward or back to a new simplicity, crudeness if necessary. That's the way of art: it is never exhausted.'

In much the same vein I wrote on March 1st: 'Incidentally, the Austrians are just discovering Kafka, via France and America, and they'll probably start translating him back into German. He is now celebrated not as a writer but as an "influence", to which the whole intellectual West has succumbed.'

The unit was now about to be dissolved, mainly because most of the P.O.W.s were due for discharge and repatriation. I was put in charge of a party of them who had to be taken to a transit camp, and was issued with a revolver for this escort duty. When we reached the camp the approaches were poorly lit and slushy, and the lorry got stuck. I got out to direct the driver, standing on the running-board, but had to give up and ask the Germans to walk the rest of the way. When we had almost got to the camp I noticed with alarm that the revolver had fallen out of its holster. Losing a revolver was a court-martial offence. I halted the prisoners, wondering how I should retrieve the revolver in the dark and in all that slush. I was pretty sure that it must have dropped when I was trying to direct the lorry, but couldn't be sure. At that point one of the prisoners came up to me, smiled sheepishly and handed me the revolver, saying he had picked it up and thought that perhaps I had lost it. That was by far the worst of all my experiences of losing things, since the revolver was not a personal possession but something that had to be signed over again as soon as I returned. It would have been more humiliating than it was if my relations with the prisoners-of-war had been such that a revolver was needed, if only as an emblem of authority; but, apart from the smuggling operation and the interrogations that followed, there had never been any friction or unpleasantness in our dealings.

After all, I had grown quite attached to Lienz — most of all to my horses, but also to the countryside they enabled me to explore, though I had noted: 'When the sky is overcast the landscape here is drearier than any in England. It's the light that makes all the difference. Instead of fiddling about with atoms the scientists should be building a vast artificial, private sun for the British Isles.' It was light and sunshine that made the Alpine winters exhilarating despite the extreme cold, so that it was a joy to ride out into the snow.

On March 10th, I was in Klagenfurt, at a larger depot full of Russian, American, German and Italian equipment, including fire-arms, on my way back to Italy for a course at the Army School of Education in Perugia. Since I seemed not to be needed any more as an interpreter, I had decided to transfer to the Army Education Corps, which promised more interesting work than any other I was likely to be given. From Klagenfurt I wrote: 'Last night I had my first serious trouble with German prisoners-of-war. There was a dance here, and the German band played the Horst Wessel march, disguised as a dance tune. I told them to stop and gave them a warning. They replied by denying that they had played it. I told them they were liars and a heated scene followed. All the women (Austrian), of course, were on the Germans' side. So were some of our soldiers, whose principle is peace at any price. The Germans here are doing as they please ... at Lienz I never needed to raise my voice. The Germans there were well-treated and well-disciplined. Here they've taken advantage of the atmosphere of laissez-faire broken by thunderstorms (but mock-thunderstorms) issuing from the mouth of the soft-hearted Guards Corporal. But individually they're abject cowards. If you shout at them in the manner to which they're accustomed you can see them crumple up ... They despise the English, even when laxity is due to kindness — which, in this case, it isn't on the whole. Nobody gives a damn for anything but women and black-marketeering. You can imagine that I'm glad to be leaving this place. If I stayed on I'd have to fight a terrific battle, and should probably lose it as well. One lance-corporal versus one captain, two sergeant-majors, six sergeants, etc., and a few hundred Germans! It isn't cricket.'

In Perugia I fell ill once more, with a malaria-like fever that had complicated my jaundice and recurred for many years whenever I went to Southern Europe. A different kind of fever was generated by the mere circumstance of being back in Italy, and in a city which I described as 'wonderful', 'one of the most impressive in the world'. The Umbrian landscape delighted me as much as the medieval buildings. I went to Assisi, too, 'not because of St. Francis' — though I had been reading the Fioretti — 'but because of its position and the landscape'. As for the educational course, my comment was, 'the less said of that, the better ... I'm going to give a lecture on fish, to everyone's disgust. I can't take these things seriously. But I may pass this course and become a sergeant-instructor, because I possess a thing called education which is like a dinner-jacket hung up in a wardrobe: no one cares whether it was bought ready-made, given to me by my father, or acquired in candlelight. It's an education, and it's mine.' While on the course I made a new friend, Geoffrey Wickham, a painter, whom I was to meet regularly for many years after our war service.

Contrary to my wishes, and despite all my efforts, the pamphlet poem was reviewed. I wrote about this to X in April, from Seeboden in Austria: 'I have been acclaimed, recognized and praised to the skies! Who by? By none other than the Book Review editor of Psychology, Marple, Cheshire, that illustrious organ of public opinion. He heads his review: A poet uses a Hammer and Steel Plate: "Later Hogarth" by Michael Hamburgher (sic). I must quote a little section of the review: "It is not an elegant piece of work. In fact it still bears hammer marks ... but it is vivid, real and alive. Because of that it is worthy of a front place among contemporary poetry." Then he quotes three chunks of Gowrie-Hamburgher's masterpiece ... He ends up: "You'll remember his name won't you? It is Michael Hamburgher." Exit Michael Hamburgher, who won't be heard of again by the readers of Psychology, Marple, Cheshire.'

Having become a Sergeant-Instructor, I was teaching current affairs to fellow soldiers, also elementary English for illiterates, and a number of other subjects for soldiers preparing for an examination equivalent to the School Certificate. 'But it's teaching me something,' I wrote, 'because it obliges me to take an interest in such matters. I'm reading Burnham's *The Managerial Revolution*, which is really good. I have also re-read *Gulliver's Travels*, which is more than really good. Tomorrow I'm lecturing on the

British Press.' An additional duty at the 78 Div. School of Education was that of 'N.C.O. i/c Entertainments', in which capacity I went in search of a dance band leader, and rejected the overtures of his wife.

Seeboden, on the Millstatt Lake, now became my base and favourite location in Austria, even when I changed my occupation. When we had moved from the disused factory at Seeboden to a small castle on the lakeside at Millstatt, in many ways our life there was almost too idyllic, too much like a lakeside vacation, since the work was undemanding. The building occupied by the College helped to remind me why we were there. Much larger and more pretentious than most of the villas and chalets around the lake shores, it had served as one of those Nazi stud farms where selected specimens of Nordic manhood were mated with selected female stock. Only the landscape and the very young girls who worked for the unit as servants were innocent of that past.

Once again I managed to get hold of a horse, though not a Cossack horse. I also did a good deal of swimming, rowing and fishing, though I lacked the tackle needed for catching the giant cat fish at the bottom of the lake, and even the lake trout. Most of the time I caught perch — a welcome addition to army rations. On long walks I explored the mountain pastures, where one could come across a cow-herd boy who seemed to belong to some primitive bucolic order difficult to reconcile even with those lakeside towns whose inhabitants included dance band leaders and amenable wives. But there was no tourism at that time. In later dealings with the civilians there I came to distinguish a peasant stratum from a small-town, lower middle-class one, with a very strong preference for the former. Many of the tradesmen and craftsmen I found devious, disingenuous and obsequious in their relations with the occupying power. Many of them, at heart, were still Nazis, while trying to do as well as possible out of their new employers.

Yet I was now trying to understand people rather than judge them, and it was high time for that, at the age of twenty-two. 'Opinions aren't very important,' I wrote to X in May, à propos of some difference between us. 'But I'm sorry to say there isn't much left of that severity you valued in me. Severity now would be hypocrisy.' By this time, I think, I had met a D.P. girl, half-Ukrainian, half-German, who lived not in the camp but in a little shack near the lake, too primitive to be coveted by native Carinthians in nearby villas and chalets. She came to a dance at our school and offered to give me Russian lessons. These, while they lasted, were chaperoned by her mother, but they didn't get very far. Soon we went out for walks in the forests instead, and became lovers of a sort. That idyll, too, was incomplete. The pine forests that began immediately above the shack were innocent of the past; but it never became clear to me how Manya's family had come to leave the Ukraine, whether of their own free-will or as captive imported labourers. Nor could I help being reminded again and again that Manya needed someone to give her a home in Europe and a new nationality, the only alternative being emigration to South America; and this motive, which may have had little to do with her feelings for me, though it accounted for her mother's approval of the association, set up a resistance in me that made me half-hearted about the affair. This, in turn, led to self-doubt and self-questioning. To be half-hearted in a love relationship, no matter how good one's reasons, is always to be in the wrong. Often I found myself wondering whether I hadn't made her situation the excuse for my own reluctance to be tied down, at least at that stage, and to her. Even now I can't disentangle that web of guilt and suspicion, nor blame our circumstances for the temporariness and surreptitiousness of the affair. When that web broke, as it did from time to time, we didn't care about the circumstances or the motive. In the end she taught me no Russian other than a piece of mildly anti-clerical doggerel. She taught me to mistrust the moral perfectionism that had made me mistrust her, but not soon or completely enough to escape being hurt by it. I taught her rather more English than she taught me Russian, and hope that I taught her no more than that. The poems I wrote for her, a sonnet sequence full of tortuous metaphysical justifications of my bad faith, were a shoddy acknowledgement of what she gave me. To read them now, or to think of her as she was then, playing her few records of songs by Tchaikovsky in a shack more suitable for storing winter fodder for cattle, is to be brought up against the cruel absurdity of the letter 'I' and its pretence of continuity. There we were, two persons variously displaced and fortuitously brought together, soon to part again. The 'I' that records it is a stranger to the 'I' to whom it happened, just as she is a different person from the girl recalled, whatever may have happened to her since, and wherever she may be.

A document I kept informs me that on May 14th 1946 I went all the way back to Southern Italy for an interview; but if I really did go on that journey, no trace of it, or of its objective, remains to be recorded. Here, then, is the text of the document itself — as cryptic and as inexplicable as the event:

MOVEMENT ORDER

78 Div. School of Education
Seebach
14 May 46

14632152 *Sgt./Inst. M. Hamburger, A.E.C.*

1. The a/n. N.C.O. is required for Interview by CEO.
2. He will be conveyed by R.T.C. Villach on 14 May for outward routing to GHQ. Caserta — train booking arranged.
3. Unexpired portion of day's rations will be carried.
4. Authority: HQ. BTA. 30334/Educ.

At some time that summer, probably in August, I went home for ten days' leave, bringing back presents for Manya. During that leave a friend took me to see Aleister Crowley at Hastings. He was in a relatively genial mood and put no curse on me — as he did on my sister-in-law-to-be when the same friend took her to see him — even though we were in competition over Baudelaire, having both translated prose poems by him. Crowley disappeared from time to time behind a screen to inject himself with heroin. He was also drinking whisky or brandy. We talked about Baudelaire and other things. I was less impressed by his intellect or his 'wickedness' than by the sheer physical stamina that kept him not only alive but active and vigorous, after excesses that would have killed a whole stableful of horses. He didn't seem to notice the incongruity of his last retreat, a boarding house that seemed deserted and remote, though quite comfortable. Even if he put no curse on me something rather sinister happened years later, when I was living in a Campden Hill Gardens flat. In the corner of the book-case that contained a few of his books and John Symonds's biography of him, giant fungi appeared. Before these had been diagnosed as dry-rot — they didn't look dry to me — the rot had eaten through several books on either side, leaving his intact. I began to wonder whether he hadn't cursed me, under his breath.

That summer, too, I was commissioned, after all, with a minimum of fuss and in the teeth of the W.O.S.B. report. It happened 'in the field', from one day to the next, with no more ceremony than an invitation to an Officers' Mess, where a pip was attached to each shoulder. It took me rather longer to get used to this change of status, and I wasn't at all sure that I wanted it, after three years of learning to identify with 'other ranks'. Suddenly one had to get rid of one's stock responses not so much to commissioned officers as to the immediate enemy, the Sergeant-Major, whose bark now could be and must be ignored since his bite was reserved for others. At the same time a 2nd Lieutenant — or Subaltern as he is also aptly called — was a new boy, and in no rank was one more exposed to the risk of making a fool of oneself, even if one's reflexes hadn't been conditioned by years of servitude. I did make a fool of myself, frequently. What was worse I had to leave Carinthia for an office job at the GHQ in Graz, as assistant to a Major responsible for educational matters at a high administrative level.

The promotion did mean something to my mother and to my grandmother, who wrote to me on July 25th 1946 from the Solent Pines Hotel, Bournemouth. She was seventy-eight by now, and was to die in 1949, indomitable still, but tormented by the love-hate of a son who could not break his emotional dependence on her. 'I hope it gives you some satisfaction,' she wrote, 'and the feeling that you did not waste your time. Life is learning, and you can learn where you are living, if you want to. Another piece of good news is that at last you will come on leave for some weeks, and this will be a great joy for me and the whole of your family. This year of separation was by no means an easy one and brought to mind very hard facts. I don't like to be pessimistic, but I wish very much I could be more hopeful. It would help in my present state of health. I had two bad months in May and June, but it is much better now and I hope to return to London in August. I very much enjoyed the sea and, as I cannot have the mountains which I loved so immensely, I am thankful that I had the opportunity to live here for such a long time. I heard from your mother that you had very interesting work to do in organizing and supervising teaching. There was a long article about it in "The Times" and I cut it out for you.' Since my grandmother's main interests remained political, the pessimism she was trying to resist must have been to do with the Cold War that was becoming blatant at this period.

After a mainly outdoor life among mountains and lakes and forests, with very light teaching duties — which, in any case I preferred to the writing of official letters — I felt claustrophobic about Graz and the tiny room allocated to me in the tiny flat of an Austrian couple I neither liked nor trusted. That my privacy there was incomplete became painfully and embarrassingly clear to me when Manya suddenly turned up from Carinthia, prepared to move in and live with me. I couldn't doubt for a moment that Manya's visit would be reported by that couple. For one thing, she had to use the bathroom I shared with them, and it was clear enough that they resented even my use of it. Since my promotion to the status of temporary gentleman had come too late, at a time when the persona of my poems was a European tramp, I could have faced up to any scandal likely to ensue. But to live with Manya, as far as I was concerned, would have finalized the relationship. It was my shrinking from this finality that made me fail the test, fail her and ask her to go home. There was no way of explaining to her that I should have failed the test of cohabitation, too, in that little room and my claustrophobic state, with a hunger for solitude increased by the office job and years of enforced sociability; and no explanation, in any case, would have made any difference to the finality of my failure. Manya forgave me, and we did meet again; but, for me, there was no going back after that betrayal.

The beauties and amenities of Graz were lost on me. I may have gone to a concert from time to time, but remember only the ordeal of listening to two or three Bruckner symphonies in succession, and that may have been later, in Vienna. Most evenings were spent either in my room, reading and writing, or at the Officer's Mess, where I learnt to play roulette. After consistently losing more of my modest pay than I could afford to do, only for the sake of sociability, I hit on what I thought was a system, though it may have been nothing more than a series of strategic withdrawals or abstentions based on a very dubious 'law of averages'. Whatever it was, it enabled me to win more often that I lost. That was not playing the game; but, with demobilization at least in sight, and an obsessive determination to hold out as a writer after it, I did not feel like contracting a temporary gentleman's debts. My gamble was a different one, and I would stick to it even if it made me unacceptable in that Mess.

Once I went out riding with a group of fellow officers; but what had been my favourite recreation in Carinthia, pursued for its own sake, became another test in Graz. My mount had to be a race-horse much larger and less co-operative than my Cossack mares. All went well at first, though the horse sensed the primitiveness of my horsemanship and played me up. As soon as we got into open country it ran away with me, making straight for the one branch of a tree low enough to knock me flying. I suffered no injury except to my pride and prestige, but I didn't ride again in Graz, since I couldn't ride alone. Graz was a place where nothing went right for me.

It may have been Manya's visit that saved me. At any rate Major Gladstone knew that my heart wasn't in my work or in the place, and he was considerate enough to have me posted back to Carinthia after only a few months. It was also Manya who had made me keep my distance from a witty and imaginative Austrian girl who worked in our office and who began to write to me after I had left. If I'd been capable of a new involvement at that point, or if I'd known exactly what new job awaited me in Carinthia I might have felt less relieved and delighted when the posting came.

The new job was the headmastership of a co-educational boarding school for the children of British soldiers and military government officials in Austria. Perhaps 'headmastership' is misleading, since I took my orders, mainly by telephone, from a Colonel and a Lt.-Colonel at HQ. My title was Officer in charge, Children's Boarding Wing, Army College (C.M.), C.M.F. My position, from the first, was an awkward one. I was responsible for everything that went on in the school, and responsible to senior officers, yet my authority was restricted not only by my low rank but by the difficulty of overcoming the resistance of my staff, many of whom were older and much more experienced than myself. Most of them were N.C.O.'s, but the Matron in charge of the girls' dormitories was a British civilian, and it was she who was most obstinately opposed to my way of running a school. This was distinctly unorthodox and libertarian. I had never taught children, and never concerned myself with educational theories. It seemed self-evident to me that children should not be intimidated, that there should be no corporal punishment, and that the business of a teacher was to understand and try to satisfy each pupil's needs. That, of course, was easier in principle than it was in practice, and I was prepared for a good deal of conflict between the needs of different pupils, as well as between the needs of the children as a whole and those of the teachers. Yet the system — if it was a system — worked very well, as far as my relations with the children went. That I overworked to the point of illness and almost of nervous breakdown had to do not with the spirit of the school but with its military framework, shortage of staff, and internal resistance.

I was on duty without a break from seven in the morning to ten o'clock at night. I did the paper work, was present at every meal, taught English, French, German, Current Affairs and Musical Appreciation, took the children out for walks, swimming and fishing, acted as boxing coach to boys who wanted to box, organized football and cricket, dealt with the Austrian domestic staff and their problems, went out in search of plumbers, electricians and the like, conferred with my colleagues, fought for equipment and books. I had no secretary or personal assistant of any kind and found it hard to delegate duties, since I hated giving orders even to those who were bound by military discipline to obey them — another psychological effect of serving in the ranks for so long. Needless to say, I also took the rap for everything that went wrong. In a girls' dormitory, for instance, there was an outbreak of hair-lice. I had been told that the girls' dormitories were the province of the civilian Matron, and that I was not to enter them. When the hair-lice appeared, so did the Lt.-Col. from HQ, and it was with him that I first entered the forbidden region — to find that the place was filthy, with plates of old food tucked away under the beds. The obvious thing to do would have been to sack the Matron. But, no, the lady was irreplaceable, and I was not. So I was responsible for what I had no authority to control.

The age of the children ranged from about seven to sixteen. It was the older girls who took advantage of my informality at first, with provocative and flirtatious teasing, but they dropped this when they found out how little I cared about the dignity they were out to deflate. On my twenty-third birthday the senior class lay in wait for me as I came in and bumped me. By that time I was no longer in charge; but the stricter discipline introduced by my successor could not change the relationship that made this kind of behaviour seem quite natural to me.

Some of the children went home at week-ends. After one of these week-ends the Colonel at HQ telephoned me to say that he had received a complaint about the morals of the school, and that I was to give the children instruction in the facts of life. The offence in question, it turned out, was that a little boy had kissed a little girl. The little girl was a Brigadier's daughter, and she had told her father about the kiss — received from the son of a private soldier! The result of the instruction I had to give them was that a nine-year-old boy crept into bed with a fourteen-year-old girl. With the help of an ATS warrant officer who had joined the staff, and with whom I was friendly, I managed to hush up the discovery, which would almost certainly have put an end to the school if it had reached HQ.

The school was regarded as an experiment and as a showpiece — I believe it was the first co-educational boarding school ever set up by the Army. It was considered interesting or important enough to be visited and inspected by a variety of VIPs, including Field-Marshal Montgomery and the then Lord Pakenham. Every time one of these visits was due the whole school had to be smartened up, if not re-organized for the occasion. When Field-Marshal Montgomery arrived, in the winter of 1946–1947, the whole school was lined up in the snow outside the building, a former factory, to be inspected like an army unit. I was introduced to the Field-Marshal by the Colonel, and told to follow him on his round. When he finished his round, there I was again, at the other end, so he shook hands with me once more. After the tension and discomfort of waiting for the Field-Marshal's arrival, this repetition affected the children like a scene from some silent comic film, and more silent gestures were needed to induce them to keep their mirth under control. The moment of crisis came later, when they were lined up once more to see the visitor off, and were in no mood for the prescribed cheers. Yet they did wait — just — till the Field-Marshal was in his car before starting a snow-ball fight. Lord Pakenham, if I remember rightly, arrived unexpectedly, coming into my class when I was teaching musical appreciation, and asking me to continue after a brief chat. On other occasions I received orders to change the normal time-table for the visitor's benefit — an irksome addition to my administrative burden.

By December the strain was proving too much for me. I had found no way of breaking the civilian Matron's resistance. On at least one occasion I had found her sitting with a little asthmatic girl — an army schoolmistress's daughter who had grown neurotic through being separated from her parents and deprived of affection — trying to force the little girl to eat a cold fried egg left uneaten at breakfast. The longer they sat there, the more nauseous the egg became to the little girl, and the more the woman insisted that it must be eaten, though the girl claimed that she was allergic to eggs. I remonstrated with the Matron, tried to explain, finally ordered her to leave the child alone — all to no avail. If I had referred the matter to my superiors at HQ, they would undoubtedly have come down on the side of the Matron's notion of discipline. So I fretted and grew exasperated. One night when I was in my office after a particularly bad day, trying to read or relax, another member of the staff, a sergeant, came in to bother me over some trivial matter, with a persistence which I felt to be deliberate bloody-mindedness. I lost my temper with him and shouted at him. Soon after that outburst I fell ill with a violent fever.

X had suggested in a letter that melancholy is a creative state of mind. In December, I replied: 'I don't know whether melancholy is creative; there are so many kinds. But with me it's not creative; it's simply a state of utter exhaustion. It's so nearly a physical illness that recently, when I was ill, I was walking about with a temperature of 102, still under the illusion that I was suffering merely from acute melancholia and mental weariness. Melancholy can be so heavy that it hurts merely to speak a few words. But perhaps that is not melancholy but a nervous disease with a less familiar name.'

When I finally retired to bed, in my billet near the school, my peasant landlady looked after me. My relations with her, and with all the peasant families connected with the school, were excellent. One boy who worked in the school as an odd-job man committed some petty theft and had to be sacked; but from visits to his parents' farm I knew the poverty that had driven him to it, and I was able to help him and his family with presents and references. One of the few walks I was able to take during my headmastership was the cross-country one to that farm. The school was at a tiny place called Seebach, near Seeboden, close to the Millstatt Lake once more, but not on the lakeside. That little bit of countryside assumed a strange significance and attraction for me, perhaps because it was the one escape I permitted myself from the school and a rare one at that.

Since I was devoted to the children at that school, it was with the greatest reluctance that I applied for leave; but I knew that if I didn't, I should suffer some form of breakdown. 'I've often wondered,' I wrote in the same letter, 'how schoolmasters endure life. Now I know that there is something in the relationship to children that sustains them ... something like Platonic love but more reliable and more lasting and without the element of distorted sensuality. I've observed it in all the teachers here. It's quite different from the frustrated sodomistic lechery of scout-masters (and of course certain schoolmasters too).'

For once in my life I did almost no writing, simply because I had no time and no solitude. X was circulating a collection of my poems among publishers, but I kept changing it and finally asked him to withdraw it — rightly so, since I wasn't ready to publish a book of my poems. John Cullen of Methuen wrote about it. 'The best things in the collection are the sonnets. These, and one or two shorter pieces, bear the writer's personal signature. This cannot, in our opinion, be said for the longer pieces. In most of these his imagination has been stimulated by literature and art and, although they may be good as criticism, they seem to have no sense of completion as poetry. The general standard of interest is not sufficiently high for publication, although some of the poems show that the writer is capable of fine things.' That was almost too generous a judgement.

I got my leave in December, going home to London for about ten days, but that leave lost me the headmastership. When I returned, an older man and a former schoolmaster had been appointed in my place. This made life easier for me, especially as I got on very well with my successor, Captain Murphy. He did introduce at least the appearance of stricter discipline, including corporal punishment, into the school, and almost the first thing that happened after my return was a mass protest against the new régime, in the form of a walk-out. The children disappeared in the woods. I had to go out and persuade them to come back. I could do so with an easy conscience, since in practice Captain Murphy's running of the school proved as non-authoritarian as mine. At about this time the school moved from Seebach to Spittal.

After my return, with only reasonable teaching and administrative duties, I took up literary work again, continuing my European Tramp sequence of poems and revising my Hölderlin translations. In a letter of January 25th, I complained of headaches 'due to the madhouse din and lack of exercise'. I missed the opportunity to go out riding, though I did as much walking as weather conditions permitted. I had another lucky escape when a jeep in which I was being driven somewhere crashed into a wall at about 40 m.p.h. Accidents were frequent on those mountain roads in winter conditions. I never learned to drive while I was in the army, and always preferred to walk in any weather, if there was time enough. All the moving about I had done in the army hadn't sated the intense wanderlust of my early years. 'I almost believe that there is no other joy than motion without a purpose,' I wrote to X at the time.

In March, I decided that I'd had enough of the school and applied for a posting, which was refused. Early in April, I had to escort some children to Vienna for the Easter holiday, and spent a few days in the city, staying at the Hotel Sacher in the sort of luxury the Army now provided everywhere. My civilian travels were to be very austere in comparison. I described Vienna as 'just another overgrown capital with a gracious exterior, a history, and inner decay'. Since I knew no one there at the time, and had a powerful prejudice not only against large cities generally but against the urban population of Austria in particular, I had nothing to do but look at the sights, as I did conscientiously. On later visits, as a civilian, I realized that many of the virtues

I saw in the Austrian peasantry were also to be found among the Viennese working class.

Since I destroyed my diaries of those years I can't be sure whether it was during the last phase of my army service or in the summer of 1946 that I spent a leave in Venice, staying at the Danieli. On the Piazza San Marco I ran into an old school and Oxford friend, Ronald Cohen, much as I had run into him at some transit camp in Villach, Carinthia, on my way up to Lienz in 1945. My enthusiasm for Italy was such that I made no distinction there between city and country, townspeople and peasants, but approved of everything and everyone. In Venice, too, I did the usual and prescribed things, but with gusto: went out in gondolas, swam at Lido, took boats to Torcello and the other islands, sat on café terraces in the squares, looked at the cathedral, the churches, palaces, museums and art galleries. The closest I could get to explaining my delight in all things Italian was, 'there is some quality in the air you breathe there which alters the whole meaning of life'. I can only wonder what I meant by that.

As my demobilization approached I grew more and more restless, more and more dissatisfied with the writing I had been doing in recent years. 'Of course I see the difference between your position and mine,' I wrote to X in May, 'and realize that I've been unusually fortunate. If I'm depressed it's not because I think that I'm less successful than I deserve to be but because my work is not as good as I want it to be. If I believed firmly enough in the value of my poems I would not have asked you to give up circulating them. I had an easy start and must have thought that the rest would be a steady and comfortable ascent. But the real difficulties are yet to come.'

In April or May, I became a full Lieutenant. This made no difference to my status at the school, but must have incremented the gratuity I received on my release, and this meant a little more leisure to get on with my literary work. It was not till June, 1947, about six weeks before my release, that I took steps to clarify my position at Oxford, and found that I had gone through the army with false pretences, under the illusion that I had already obtained a wartime B.A., after four terms of residence! 'It's a curse,' I wrote to X, on being corrected about that, 'since I don't feel like studying philology. If I could begin again I would study a science, preferably zoology or psychology (but the latter is not scientific enough).' On June 26th, I wrote: 'As for me, I'm just hanging on till my return home. The other night the Muse paid me an unexpected visit and

I was able to scribble down a verse or two. I'm busy making arrangements for the end of the school — setting & marking exam papers, preparing for the Sports Day (a great occasion, since the Commander-in-Chief will be there), etc. I've applied for leave to visit Berlin very briefly before my return home, but I don't think this will come off. Frankly, I'm not keen on the trip but promised my great-uncle that I'd visit him if I possibly can. Berlin has very powerful and terrible associations in my mind, and I'd rather keep away from it. Often I feel morbid enough as it is, without going back to the nursery of my neuroses.'

The trip did materialize, though no official leave or travel documents could be granted, since there was no official communication between the two armies, C.M.F. (Central Mediterranean Forces) and B.A.O.R. (British Army of the Rhine) Captain Murphy and the Colonel at H.Q. simply told me: 'You're free to absent yourself for seven days. Get there if you can, and good luck to you.' Captain Murphy also did more than that. He lent me his dress uniform — I had never bothered to acquire one, but was content to wear my old battledress or khaki drill outfit — complete with three pips and his campaign ribbons. This certainly helped me to get there, though it also made me feel an imposter as well as a stowaway. No conclusion to my army service could have been more bizarre than this trip without papers, in a borrowed uniform, to the heart of the former enemy's camp — on compassionate grounds, bearing gifts of tinned food. To me, it also meant a return to the birthplace I had left at the age of nine and almost expunged from my consciousness; and a meeting with relatives I had not seen since that time.

The trip was fairly straightforward as far as the American Zone of Austria. This could be done by civilian train. At Salzburg I had to obtain some kind of permit to cross over to Germany but, when I succeeded, found myself going not to Munich, the obvious place, but to Carlsruhe in Baden. I arrived there in the small hours of the morning — on July 6th — and wrote a note to X: 'I have been terrifically busy. I'm on my way to Berlin — at least I hope I am. At the moment I'm sitting in an American H.Q. waiting for somebody to arrive. (Everyone is still asleep.) I've got to get this permission to travel on an American train to Frankfurt; thence to Berlin. If they refuse I'm stuck here. Yesterday I had nothing to eat until 9.30 p.m. ... And I've got to be back in Spittal by the 12th. If everything goes smoothly I can spend 2 days in Berlin and get back in time.' When a duty officer arrived I had quite a struggle to convince him of the pressing need to let me travel to

Berlin; but, once convinced, he put me on the most luxurious train I ever saw the inside of, with a panelled sleeping compartment to myself. (I suspect that this was a train specially built by the Nazis for delegates to the Party Rally at Nuremberg.) I needed all the sleep I could get. At Frankfurt I had literally to barge my way on to one of the overcrowded civilian trains of those years. In the end my compartment was shared by only one German, and I stretched out again on the narrow wooden seat for more sleep, making a hard pillow of the provisions I was taking to my relatives.

I got to Berlin, and was directed to guest quarters in the former Olympic Games Stadium. Cars could be obtained immediately by telephoning for them, with no questions asked. My first visit was to my great-uncle Paul and his wife Ilse, whom I hadn't met, since they had married after our emigration. She had stood by her much older husband throughout the war, working with him as a casual farm labourer with false papers and moving on when there was a risk of detection. My great-uncle was now nearly eighty, and his time was spent in efforts to obtain restitution of his confiscated property, including a house in Grunewald. He was suffering from various ailments due to undernourishment and hardship — they had had no ration cards while living underground — but this didn't prevent him from acting as a guide to me through the ruins of the city. At first I recognized nothing — not even the street I was born in, or the block of flats I was born in, though it was almost unchanged. Even the old concierge, Herr Wolff, was still there, and I talked to him, naïvely asking him whether his tom-cat was still alive! (My great-uncle Paul and his wife were to stay with us in London before he died. He told us about the death of most of his Berlin friends, but wept when he came to the loss of the last of his pointer dogs, given up when he and his wife went underground. He got angry when somebody made a sweepingly anti-German remark, saying that he was a German still, and that he and his wife would not have survived if they hadn't been decently treated by many Germans during the war. He did not live to move back into his Grunewald house, which was returned to his widow.)

The visit was too brief and hectic for me to begin the long process of recognition among so much rubble and empty spaces. If some street corner or shop front did assert its familiarity, I passed by too fast to weigh up the assertion and await the confirmation of memory. This became clear to me as I walked down the Kurfürstendamm with my other great-uncle, Martin. Despite his short, slight, jockey-like figure and eighty-two years he moved at a speed with which I found it hard to keep up, though not many years before I had won a long-distance walking race! As though no time had passed, in the teeth of food shortage and rationing, my great-uncle Martin insisted on taking me out to lunch at one of the few restaurants functioning for civilians in those years. (We had seen little of him as children, and had found his tremendous extraverted nervous energy rather daunting when he did appear, with presents of chocolates. He had been the managing director of a large steel works and had lived a style too high for us in Düsseldorf, with coaches and outriders and the horses on which he won prizes as a show jumper. He had been given an honorary doctorate for his services to German industry, and had been protected during the war, though a 'non-Aryan', either by this record or by the connections of his aristocratic wife. One of his two sons — the other had emigrated — had been drafted for forced labour as a half-Jew, but only towards the end of the war.) His wife, my great-aunt Wanda, was in a suburban nursing-home, where I visited her and delivered my gifts of food. I remember the embarrassment of being treated as a sort of war-hero both by her and by the nurses at the home, including one who was memorably beautiful, and trying to tell them how little my borrowed campaign ribbons accorded with my utterly undistinguished war service.

A year or so later this great-aunt who had survived the bombing of Berlin and her marriage to a 'non-Aryan', was murdered in the street by a man wanting her handbag. In 1955, when my great-uncle celebrated his ninetieth birthday, my mother went to Berlin for the occasion, and his long-lost younger son returned from North Africa, where he had served in the Foreign Legion and then lived as a professional jockey at Casablanca. Soon after the birthday this son crossed over to East Berlin, to die in mysterious circumstances, seemingly by suicide. I last saw my great-uncle in 1956, when he was ninety-one and living in an old people's home at Nikolassee. 'No senile slip except one,' I noted then. 'His sight and hearing still keen. Showed me his diplomas, letters of congratulation from Vice-Chancellor of the Republic, etc., also from present owners of the industrial concern for which he had worked. But seemed to have forgotten about his wife and her death — and his conventional allusion to the suicide of his son Tino. Altogether, he seems to have no feelings or emotions. That's probably how he's managed to go on living for so long. He seems to have no values other than the outward ones of power and success — even at the age of 91 — living in a little room in a home for old men. He has a private room, of course, but downstairs the place is like a doss-house. Took him a bottle of claret and 2 grapefruits — he has a "passion" for grapefruit, as far as he has passions at all.' That impression may well have been superficial. I never got to know the man at all, perhaps because he didn't relate to people easily, certainly never to us when we were children or later. Nor could I ever understand people of his kind, dynamos activating something outside themselves or nothing.

My remaining relatives in Berlin were my great-uncle Martin's daughter Erika, her two young daughters, and her brother Kurt, who had once tried to act as tutor to us at Kladow but was now working in industry also. I had last seen Erika in London when she was a dancer in the Ballet Joos and was on tour. Of my father's family there were no survivors in Germany except a cousin living in Hamburg, with a non-Jewish wife. I had no time to revisit our house in Kladow, and there would have been no point in going there with no leisure for exploration.

As I travelled back to Carinthia I could make no sense of anything I had heard or seen in Berlin. What little I had known of the city was largely destroyed, and any pattern of relations set up in childhood with the persons revisited had been broken up by long estrangement and differences that would have become acute even if there had been no enforced separation. Only my great-uncle Paul had been close enough to me in childhood, and was bound to me still by an affection strong enough to have made the trip at all meaningful; and time had been too short for a real exchange of our disparate experiences. By the time I returned to Berlin and began to reorder all the jumbled fragments, he was dead.

After that, nothing remained but to prepare to go home, wind up the school — with final group photographs for the record — say goodbye to my civilian friends, the employees at the school and a few other locals, and pay a last visit to Manya, whom I had met from time to time right up to the end of my stay. I never saw her again, but heard from her sporadically until she emigrated to somewhere in South America. Four years later I revisited those parts, on our honeymoon, and out of a perverse need I have always felt to keep my fingers on all the threads of a life lacking in any obvious or natural continuity, took my wife to see what was left of Manya's shack.

One sequel to my service in Austria suddenly arrived in 1988 in a letter not from Manya, but from another woman, received more than

(left) Tambimuttu and David Gascoyne in the 'Forties. (Courtesy of the Tambimuttu archive.)

(below left) Vernon Watkins. (Courtesy of Gwen Watkins.)

(below right) Kathleen Raine. (Courtesy of Kathleen Raine.)

Anne Beresford and I just after our marriage in the autumn, 1951.

forty years after the events. One of the servants at the school, a maid-of-all-work, she called herself, was a very young girl with blonde pigtails of whom I had been especially fond, often talking with her and once asking her to go fishing with me on the lake — though that must have been considered fraternization at the time. When I was ill after my breakdown it was this girl, Steffi, who brought me food to the lodgings near the school to which I had moved.

Towards the end of 1988 I received a 24-page letter from her, going over our relations and life at the school with a minuteness quite beyond my selective memory, and with bitter reproaches to me for not returning her love for me and, worst of all, not saying goodbye to her when I left. She had traced me by way of a broadcast and of the publishers of books of mine translated into German. She was now married, a mother and grandmother. She enclosed a photograph of herself in 1946, as Steffi Feichter, probably at the age of sixteen and more child than woman still, and a group snapshot of staff and children from the school, including me, by a river. Later she sent delicate drawings by her husband of the small castle at Millstatt in which the school for soldiers had been housed, and of the lakeside road to it I had often travelled, passing a solitary little Gothic chapel on the mountainside.

'I fell in love with you at once', she wrote, 'You always had such a friendly smile for me if you happened to be looking into the scullery through the open sliding door from the dining-room at Seeboden and always called me "Cinderella". I was to have been engaged as a waitress, but Mr. Hull said at the interview, she looks like an innocent angel, so we will put her in the kitchen — and so I came to do the washing up.' She then went on to give an account of every meeting between us over the next year and a half, the removal from Seeboden to Millstatt, with the dog-roses in flower. She reminded me that I used to play the piano there — by ear, as always; and that I did say goodbye to her when I left for Graz, telling her to be good, and precipitating more tears than she had already shed over me. (She also knew that the British commandant of the unit was living with the sixteen-year-old daughter of another member of staff, the Austrian chef, who agreed to that arrangement in the hope of advantage to himself, 'selling his daughter', as she wrote.) At the place to which the children's school moved from Millstatt, a hotel at Spittal, Steffi asked to be taken out of the scullery and allowed to wait at table, a request I granted at once. Then came my failure to speak to her before I left the school. Probably, it was deliberate on my part, because I must have sensed something of her feeling for me; but though I dreamed about her once in one of my fevers, to me she had always remained a child, like the other adolescent girls under my charge, only one on the wrong side of the political and national divide. I made enquiries about her when I returned to those parts in Carinthia on our honeymoon, but did not know her married name and was unable to trace her.

Of my repatriation and release no detail has stuck in my mind, only having a choice between a number of civilian suits all of which were drab and badly cut, and being allowed to keep my old battledress, though it was issued to me before I was an officer, as well as my officer's trench and rain coats, which lasted me for at least another ten years. To this day I use the green canvas and leather hold-all that replaced my kit-bag when I was commissioned, and I still have the despatch rider's boots I wore for horse-riding in Austria, though the Cossack mares are a distant memory.

The temporary discharge certificate issued to me on July 22nd, 1946, when I received my Emergency Commission, describes my military conduct as 'exemplary'. On the back there is a Testimonial: 'A keen hard-working N.C.O. Honest, sober and reliable. A/n was employed as a Sergt./Inst. in Army Educational Corps from 16 March 1946, teaching German and English and running discussions in "Current Affairs". Knowledgeable and painstaking, he proved himself to be capable and efficient. He has a pleasant personality and is easy in his contact with both staff and students. He achieved his results by the sincerity of his approach and not by virtue of military rank or bearing. Completely loyal, he showed himself prepared to give of his best at all times. Discharged on appointment to an Emergency Commission.' My final discharge took place exactly one year later.

The document makes no mention of my years as a foot-slogger in the poor bloody infantry, or my near-suicide by drink, or of any of the peculiarities that made my military conduct far from exemplary during the greater part of my service. The Army, it seems, has a memory even more defective than mine. This is borne out, too, by the testimonial written for me by Col. Impson, Commandant of the Army College, Central Mediterranean, after my final release. Almost as over-generously as the other, it commends my work as 'Second Master at the Children's School', yet omits all reference to my Headmastership there, the most taxing responsibility ever thrust upon me not only in the course of my army years but at any time of my life — by none other than that same Colonel. The half-year elapsed since the leave that had terminated it was enough, apparently, to erase it from the record. If ever I 'gave of my best' — and there were long periods in my army service when I didn't and couldn't because no one wanted it — that headmastership was what I gave it to, holding so little of myself in reserve that the giving had to stop. Perhaps it was a good thing, after all, that among the books carried around with my kit I had studied the Bhagavad Gita, with its doctrine of work done for the work's sake; and writing poetry, that 'mug's game', was a discipline of the same order. Incidentally, I never made use of either testimonial in civilian life. The one thing I have never wanted is a career.

If I try to sum up what I owe to my four years in the British Army other than trench coat and riding boots — I should be defeated by the impossibility of knowing how I should have developed if I had spent the same years as a civilian. What I do know is that this highly authoritarian institution cured me of a whole complex of attitudes and prejudices bearing on authority, on social, moral and intellectual gradations, and on the rock bottom basis of communal life. I doubt that any other institution would have tested me in so many different ways, or imposed such contrasting conditions — from the barest servitude, with needs and expectations confined to little more than the minimal means of physical survival, to relative luxury, and responsibility for the welfare of a fair number of people, including some sixty children. The Army taught me that one can sleep on cold wet earth in the open air, suffering from a fever, on hard floorboards or a sack of straw, sitting on a bench in a railway station and even standing on one's feet in the corridor of a train, if only one is tired enough — or in the most expensive hotels in Europe; and that the difference isn't worth talking about. It taught me that I could live with the roughest, most ignorant of men, and find the company of more polished, well-educated men insufferable. It taught me to delight in sheer movement, without caring about the destination. It taught me more than I can begin to outline.

Above all, it rubbed in the ironies of outward experience, ironies inherent in the whole course of my life that have made me doubt nothing so much as the meaningfulness of given identity. That the Army found a use for me at all, after being wary of accepting a former enemy alien, is hardly less extraordinary than the use I was able to make of the Army, not only by setting up a 'progressive' boarding school under its authoritarian nose — and, in essence, getting away with it. Almost every condition and code the Army imposed on me could be turned into its very opposite, if the lesson drawn from it was the lesson I needed to learn. Admittedly, this would have been harder, or impossible, if I had found myself obliged to kill my fellow men rather than learn to live with them; but the fact, the irony, was that the Army spared me that obligation. I did much more fighting at my various schools than ever I did in the Army; and I ran an Army school in which boys felt no need to fight among themselves. I fell into the habit of swearing like a trooper — no sentence was complete or effective in a barrack-room if it didn't contain at least one of the obligatory boosters — only to find myself back among 'gentlemen' and among children. While serving as a soldier I wrote poems in the person of a tramp who was also one of the displaced persons of Europe. I was devoutly religious amidst profanities, and turned agnostic when it was incumbent on me to organize religious instruction and perfunctory devotions. Nothing was what it seemed or what it was meant to be; and later life confirmed that state of affairs, involving me in a long sequence of contradictions between what I did and what I thought I was doing, what I wanted to do and what I achieved in doing.

It is not the Army's fault that in those four years I didn't overcome my emotional inhibitions and inadequacies. To expect the most spartan of male institutions to undo the harm done to me by the other male institutions I had been 'privileged' to attend, would be asking too much of those ironies. Yet in the course of those four years I did get rid of the moral inhibitions, if not the emotional and psychic ones, that kept me in a state that makes me sorry in retrospect for every woman unlucky enough to get entangled with me. Another twenty years and more had to pass before I could write a love poem that wasn't 'impersonal' or metaphysical, and by then I was middle-aged, with children old enough to come up against erotic difficulties I couldn't even admit to myself at their age.

As for my writing, the Army provided me not only with spells of leisure for it but the material enough for novels, epics, plays or what have you. Again I wasn't ready; and the Army wouldn't have stopped me if I had been. Those disgusting Army diaries of mine, with their half-baked literary glosses and almost total lack of response to what was going on around me, are the proof — or were before I burned them. When I had outgrown that phase, by the time I went abroad, I ceased to keep diaries and preferred to ride my horse. So once more the material is missing. What I saw and heard and felt in Italy and Austria has been overlaid by the impressions of too many later travels. My first collection of poems — circulated in typescript by my friend until withdrawn at my request was called *Itinerary.* A book of my poems published more than twenty years later is called *Travelling*. This points to an obsession with travelling itself — every conceivable form of travelling, literal and symbolic — that has remained with me since my Army years, that tramp sequence and other, even earlier, poems in my first published collection.

So, in the end, I don't know what the Army did to my writing. Even the books I glossed in barrack-rooms did something to me, though I've forgotten what most of them were about. Everything I saw and heard and felt did something to me, though I've forgotten most of the details. That's one reason why one writes: sooner or later almost everything about a life is forgotten, by the person who lived it and by the others. The great mystery of the written word and its justification in the teeth of everything that people say about the 'media' — instant communication and instant blankness — lies in its power to oppose biological time, to create its own time dimension, the dimension that distinguishes human being from animals. A novelist may deal in biological time, or try to, and so may an autobiographer, but by doing so he inevitably shifts his material into the other dimension. If that shifting fails, the work will be neither here nor there. A poet knows that biological time can be nothing more than his complaint. If the things in his poems aren't at home in the other dimension, he's wasted his time putting them there. His material is what he doesn't know, what the other dimension demands. If anybody ever feels like taking the trouble to look at my poems in the light of the little I remember of my life — that is, if they're worth the effort — he or she will find superficial traces in them of my army experience; but the real sources, connections and developments are underground. My guess about them would be no better than his or hers.

Six

When I returned to England in July 1947, I moved back into my mother's house before going up to Oxford in October. My mother had kept my room intact all those years, jealously guarding my books and papers from potential borrowers and browsers. She had also had shelves put up all round the walls of what was my bedroom, library and workroom, knowing my inability to work in public libraries and my need for a personal library already growing awkwardly large and forever growing. If not the fatted calf, at least one lone survivor of her war-time hens awaited me on my return, if my memory hasn't jumbled up the dates. Soon the chicken wire made room for a greenhouse.

I was not very keen to return to Oxford. When the possibility of a special early release for students had arisen soon after the end of the war, and my sister Eva made an application on my behalf to Christ Church, I decided that I would rather do my full term of military service. My friend John Pettavel, who was in the Air Force, wrote to me in October, 1945: 'I think you are quite right about Oxford. It is in a sense a dangerous place insomuch as one is likely to sink into a rather jejune form of intellectualism; discuss a lot and do nothing. The danger comes to a great extent from the social side of the life on account of the people one meets there. On the other hand it is in a sense excellent if one is willing to stand a little aloof and avail oneself of the facilities & beauties it offers.'

The root of the reluctance was a kind of restlessness on which John Pettavel had also commented in an earlier letter: 'One develops a wandering spirit in wartime, and I think this is the cause of all our unrest. I am desperately attracted by the idea of finding some permanent place where to lay my head, and at the same time afraid of it, afraid of becoming bookish and stale there: most of all afraid of becoming attached to it, as I believe that perfect freedom can only be attained irrespective of place or person (the general idea being to write a masterpiece on a park bench, which is quite impractical), a sort of feeling like Browning's

Curse
Whoever loves above his liberty
House, land or life.'

John Pettavel, too, was half relieved when he was posted to India after the war instead of resuming his studies at Oxford. 'In any case intelligence is a grossly overrated quality,' he wrote in the same letter; and part of my difficulty over Oxford was that I was in an anti-intellectual and anti-bookish phase, precipitated by a variety of immediate experiences which I hadn't wholly assimilated. The more I had seen of post-war Europe, the more restless I had become; and even after my return I continued to write my tramp sequence, from a point of view more powerfully rendered by Yeats in his late poem 'Meru',

> Civilisation is hooped together, brought
> Under a rule, under the semblance of peace
> By manifold illusion ...

though even the illusion had been thoroughly shattered in post-war Europe. That was not a recognition or a frame of mind conducive to the academic study of literature.

The same restlessness made it difficult for me to settle down either at my mother's house or at Oxford. That very autumn I was off again on my travels, going to Paris, which I had missed out, though I had passed through France more than once on my journeys to and from Austria. These travels were to continue over the years. Even marriage, children and the one home which I came to love almost above my liberty, couldn't cure me of the recurrent itch to be on the move again. For another decade or so my poetry was pervaded by a conflict between the need to settle and the feeling that every kind of stability was a sort of betrayal of my true vocation. This conflict became acute in 1952 when I ceased to be a free-lance writer and odd-job man to become a regular university lecturer.

In London, meanwhile, I picked up most of the threads of my earlier life, including the Soho nexus, though Dylan Thomas was no longer at its centre, and my visits became rarer before fizzling out in the early 'fifties. Part of the Soho crowd had moved to Cornwall. I hitch-hiked and walked there with an army friend, John Boothby a continuation of our military way of life. We had next to no money, and we went fishing at Mousehole with a primitive line and hook to supplement our diet of bread and butter and tea. To our astonishment we caught a great many 'horse mackerel', a fish usually spurned because of its spiky exterior, and found they were perfectly edible when the skin and fins were removed; and we caught a large pollock, too. At Mousehole we met Kit Barker, the painter, and were invited to spend the night in a fishermen's loft which he used as a studio. We had just settled down there for the night — the loft was much like a barrack-room, with beds all over the place, but no electric light — when a torch or paraffin lamp was turned on us and we were commanded in no uncertain terms to get out. Dead tired though we were after our walking, we didn't feel like arguing about it, and didn't know, in any case, who was throwing us out. It was George Barker, Kit's brother, it transpired, and he apologized for it when we met again in later years. John and I had no choice but to sleep out in a field, to wake towards dawn drenched to the skin with dew, and shivering. In the army we had been better equipped — with ground sheets that could be made into bivouacs, and greatcoats. Yet by moving on at once we got warm again and suffered no damage. In Penzance I looked up another army friend, Graham Durrant, and stayed at his house.

The return to Oxford did prove something of an anti-climax. For a term or two I was given rooms again in Peckwater Quad — a whole suite, with two bedrooms, though the College was overcrowded. The easy sociability of my earlier residence was beyond me now, though I was also less studious than before. Very few of my earlier friends had returned at the same time. The intervening five years had changed the whole structure and spirit of the university, just as they had changed me. It was characteristic of the post-war period that what I wanted now was to finish with it all as soon as possible, so as to get on with my own life, whatever that might be. I was poor enough to feel at once parasitical and misplaced at Christ Church. During my first period of residence I had availed myself of the 'facilities and beauties' of Oxford, as John Pettavel put it, for my own personal needs. Now I stood even more aloof, but was too conscious of the economic basis of my residence — a government grant that supplemented my Exhibition — to work on my own literary projects without a bad conscience.

German now became my main subject, with French as a subsidiary. This reversal may have accorded with the more practical considerations of this period, but it also marked a genuine shift of interest. If my studies were to connect in some essential way with my recent experiences and concerns, they had to touch on the practice of poetry on the one hand, the peculiarities of German literature and their bearing on the breakdown of European civilization on the other. For the former I needed only leisure to read, write and reflect. The latter ought to have linked up with my academic work proper, but the latest period covered by the syllabus — and this only for a special paper — was the 'modern' lyric of George, Hofmannsthal and Rilke. My main interest as a student and critic of German literature had little to do either with philology or with the history of literature, as understood and taught at the university. These concerns, therefore, were soon to be diverted to my activities as a translator and as a journalist. My inability to concentrate on texts that didn't engage me — either as a poet or as a man who had been hammered into and out of shape by what was going on in his time — led to my not doing very well in my Finals, in which I obtained only Second Class Honours. Although the possibility of an academic appointment had been discussed with my German tutor, Dr. E. L. Stahl, I didn't wait for the results of the examination before deciding that I would try to make a living as a writer.

During the earlier period most of my social life at Oxford had taken place in private rooms, my own or my friends', where one dropped in or attended parties. Now it was more usual to meet in pubs, since earlier restrictions on drinking in town were rarely enforced by the Proctors. It was like Soho all over again, only not quite the real thing. The place where I tended to drink in the evenings was White's, near St. Aldates, the rather glossy haunt of Oxford's semi-bohemia. When Dylan Thomas appeared there one evening with Margaret Taylor, my post-war melancholia reached a climax of revulsion at the shoddiness of it all. Dylan, at least, was the real thing. He was drinking himself to death in earnest — unlike me and that Oxford crowd. When he left I rushed out after him into the street, but couldn't tell him what I needed to say to him, since I didn't understand it myself. So I mumbled something about seeing him again — somewhere else. We did meet again on various occasions, but there was nothing more to be said. Whether I liked it or not, I half-belonged to the post-war generation who, somehow or other, would get away with the disreputable profession of poetry. So, in his fashion, did Dylan, as a film-script writer, performer and 'character'; but he punished others for the duplicity of the role they demanded of him with his open contempt for them, and punished himself for playing it all the same, by methodical self-destruction.

There was much in Dylan Thomas's work that I couldn't accept in later years; but, because of that basic integrity, I could never forget him as a man, to the point of dreaming about him and even having a vision of him in broad daylight years after his death, in a Berkshire lane.

At White's I formed no lasting friendships. There would be an occasional visitor from an earlier period, like John Waller, who had edited the magazine *Kingdom Come*. The new generation was represented by Kingsley Amis, already married, unlike most of my coevals, but we never exchanged more than a few words at this period. At Christ Church and at the English Club, of which I had become President, I met Hilary Corke, who did become a close friend for several years; and through the English Club I got to know Kathleen Raine. Although she and I had been published by Tambimuttu during the war, we had never met at that time. Our meeting at the English Club was the beginning of a friendship that has outlasted many changes in our lives and literary practice. I could not share the later Neo-Platonism of her writings and prescriptions for writers; it struck me as too exclusive, when my own development was in the opposite direction, towards concrete particulars. But I preferred her insistence on absolutes to the characteristic post-war stance of making do with whatever was doled out to one in the way of everyday experience. Before the so-called 'Movement' — to which I didn't belong and didn't wish to belong — was launched by literary journalists, I reacted to the new spirit in a piece of deliberately limping doggerel called 'Poverty, 1949'. There I wrote of the poets of my generation that we

> gathered words like rags and dumped the bundle
> anywhere we were licensed to trundle
> the barrow that was a coach and four ...
> begged our keep, strummed and became
> conveniently feeble, blind or lame,
> stood at corners or queued for the dole ...

I should have avoided the sociological metaphors in this piece — which could be misunderstood as a disparagement of the Welfare State — if I had been more aware at the time of the hidden connections between literature and economics. It took me many years as a 'free-lance' writer to see through the freedom of that profession to the subliminal pressures that make it merely another kind of economic dependence —

much as a mercenary is merely another kind of soldier, serving political ends like any regular, even if those ends are not of his choosing.

While at Oxford I received my first 'commission' to write a poem, an invitation to write a tribute to T. S. Eliot for his sixtieth birthday, for inclusion in a symposium edited by Tambimuttu. This request plunged me into a dilemma. I revered Eliot and wanted to produce a tribute; but the thought of writing a poem to order, with a deadline attached, repelled and inhibited me. I procrastinated, half-accepted, half-refused, and was about to finalize my refusal when the poem was suddenly there. The penny had dropped, the 'commission' made its way through the machinery of resistance to the sub-conscious, which delivered the goods, a poem no worse than any I was writing at the time. Though I didn't know it, this was a foretaste of the way in which external pressures act upon that part of the psyche which seems least accessible to them. The resistance was due to romantic preconceptions of independence which became questionable when I realized that the need to publish poems in periodicals, and be paid for them, made me write more of them than I should otherwise have done; also, that a work I considered an incomparable masterpiece, Bach's *Musical Offering*, had been not only commissioned but based on a set theme. So, for that matter, were Beethoven's *Diabelli Variations*, another favourite of mine.

From my suite in Peckwater Quadrangle I moved to a room in a terrace house, now demolished, in Paradise Square, St. Ebbe's, with no Scout to wait on me — or be hoodwinked when my London girl friend came for a week-end — no bathroom and no running water. To walk to Christ Church for a bath or for meals was no great inconvenience after army life. Even in the College one had to walk quite a way for either. When I had been allocated a batman in Austria, a Ukrainian D.P. who stole my spirit ration but got away with it by a disarming mixture of childlike ingenuousness and peasant guile, I made as little use of his services as was compatible with my excessive load of work, which simply left me no time to clean my own shoes and boots. I was sorry that my landlady in Paradise Square had to fetch me jugs of water for shaving, but felt that those slum lodgings accorded better with my situation than the anachronistic amenities of the College. True, my girl friend couldn't stay there, and had to be accommodated in hotels as respectable as my own room; but I found I could work in that place, with no hankerings after the fuller social life I had led during my first stay at Oxford.

Christ Church Meadows, the river, the college buildings and gardens retained much of their early attraction, though now I tended to go farther afield, to Binsey and other places outside the city. I still made use of the Boat Club, but only for sculling. I played tennis when I could, and bowls with Hilary Corke, in the College garden. I attended more lectures than before, especially those given by my tutor E. L. Stahl, and dutifully made my way to North Oxford for tutorials in philology and mediaeval literature, though the literature was treated as philology and the philology belied its name. Such Middle High German as I picked up and retained came in useful later, for translations of a few lyrics by Walther von der Vogelweide. I imagine that it was my performance in mediaeval language and literature that produced poorer Finals results than were expected of me; and the impatience that made me sit for Finals after only another four terms' residence, the minimal requirement for ex-servicemen.

In the spring or early summer of 1948 I went to Cornwall again, staying with David Haughton, the painter, at Nancledra. There was quite a colony of artists and writers in those parts. Bryan Wynter lived nearby, and David Wright, an Oxford and Soho friend of the war years, was also on a visit from London. Around Nancledra I was fascinated by the disused clay pits, in which I swam and zoologized, for they had reverted to nature and were full of newts, frogs, and aquatic insects.

It is to restlessness and overwork that I attribute the failure of my memory to retain the texture of my day-to-day living at any one period, and my need to rely on documents here. It is clear to me now that since early childhood and almost to the end of my life I have simply done too much and too many disparate things, so that my continuities wind through a tangle I cannot unravel other than in moments of fusion or recognition. Such moments could sustain poems, but not a continuous narrative or chronicle. The return to Oxford is a case in point. Here I was in a place I had loved (and resisted) once: but at the wrong time for me, with my needs at odds with all the requirements, working for a degree that could qualify me only for a profession, the academic, I did not wish to take up at the time, and half engaged in a different profession which, I had already learnt, could never be relied upon for a living.

I was lucky enough to have a refuge, my mother's house, and a mother who made no demands on me, giving me every possible freedom to come and go in that house and pursue my own interests there, while she saw to my practical needs; but I had no home of my own, and no possible basis on which to establish one. Because such dependence, too, was the opposite of what I needed in my early and middle twenties, after years spent in institutions of one kind or another, travels became my escape over the next few years, both before and after my graduation at Oxford.

It must be about my first trip to Paris in 1947 that I wrote: 'Restless as I still was, I couldn't settle down on the seat assigned to me on the ferry, but was soon wandering all over the decks, before going to the bar. From this vantage point I observed my fellow passengers, playing the would-be novelist's guessing game. (I had started work on what I thought would become a novel, *The Vacation*, but was never to be more than a travel book with a few short stories woven in.) Yet I put away four cognacs with the English coast still in sight, and remember nothing at all of all the people in whom I believed myself to be so passionately interested. After the sixth brandy I had to look for my seat in the lounge. A few minutes later I was asleep.

Though the last stragglers were on the train and even the cars had been unloaded, no one seemed in a hurry to move on. I sat on a low quayside wall, listening to a strange hum that may have been mechanical but sounded like distant sea shanties; the little cafés told me that this was Dieppe, this was France, and here idleness was not a sin. Even the clouds and waves seemed to be taking their time.

I had several hours in which to think so, for suddenly the train had moved off without me.

By the time I was standing outside the Gare St. Lazare, I was cold sober, and no amount of drinking in Paris ever brought back that first euphoria. From the moment I picked up my cases with the idea of making for the Left Bank, for St. Germain or Montparnasse or the Latin Quarter, and with only the vaguest notion of how to get to any of those celebrated parts — to be in Paris as a tourist was to be faced with a void to be somehow filled each day with a wholly gratuitous choice. The rue St. Placide, it turned out, was neither a celebrated nor a pleasant part, but that is where I happened to find a suitably cheap hotel, a little cell of a room from which I could escape to the Dôme café or the Halles or to Versailles — anywhere, anywhere, out of that room. In the course of a week I not only 'did' the Louvre so thoroughly as to leave its content a jumble in my mind, but was driven to explore a variety of suburbs of which I recall one river bank, rural but for an intimation of factories not far away. Everything seen and heard and smelled, like the peculiar exhalation from the vents of the *Métro*, not to mention the open, street-level *pissoirs* — was pervaded by a sense of gratuitousness. Even tramps tend to keep to a circuit of sorts. Tourism alone creates the total outsider, totally alienated and isolated from the life around him without the excuse of being a rebel or an outcast.

Why did I do it? Why does anyone do it? There I was, sitting at café tables, cultivating disgust. I was acquiring experience, of course, but the experience was useless. Any involvements into which I might enter could only be fortuitously entered, fortuitously cut short. And why Paris, of all places? With its whistling policemen, its cars going nowhere that mattered to me as fast as they could. Without the excuse that I had a part to play in that megapolitan farce, or that I was enjoying my place on the fringe, where it all seemed a vast misunderstanding passed on from one generation to the next, with the interest added: bigger and better neuroses, a new line in dilemmas each week. There I was, watching the artists and writers, wondering when they found time to work. Most of them seemed too much aware of being one of the sights. I should hardly have been surprised to learn that the tourist agencies had paid for their drinks and elaborate fancy dress. The most crowded café at that time was one which Sartre had been known to frequent — before it was crowded. Now, I supposed, the *patron* employed a small retinue of mock celebrities to sit there correcting endless reams of dummy proofs, occasionally stopping to fake an autograph for a specially hired fan.'

There I sat, looking on and trying to record my impressions in a diary which I thought it necessary to keep while travelling. It is filled with the names of people, places, buildings and pictures about as useful to me now as a railway timetable of that year. Neither the pavement of a boulevard nor the dark and stuffy interior of a café proved conducive to the creativeness which I associated with Paris. As for my room in the hotel, it did contain a chair of sorts, but no table. If the electric light had any purpose at all, it was to make writing and reading an agony after ten minutes. There are no entries in my diary about the noise of people cleaning their teeth in the room next to mine, creaking beds or portable radios. After days mostly spent in the cafés, museums and galleries, sooner or later I had to face the hotel room, except when I walked all night from one end of Paris to the other. I remember seeing the dawn from Montmartre after a stroll that began at Montparnasse, the prostitutes on the bright boulevards of the Right Bank, the old women rummaging in dustbins after the last and unluckiest of the *poules* had gone home to sleep.

Never again, I said to myself, and did keep away from Paris for ten years. Yet I stuck it for a week or so, because I still had illusions to spend. Foreign travel in troopships and lorries and jeeps had whetted, not dulled, my craving for it. I must have thought the freedom of civilian travel would fill the many gaps left by all those involuntary journeys. What I didn't consider was the advantages of having a job to do, and of staying long enough in one place to become a little more than a tourist.

It was in the following year, 1948, that I moved on from Paris to Provence, partly for a meeting with my friend Tom Good, who was working at Aix-en-Provence as a teacher. Having destroyed my diary for that year, when I had cannibalized it for my would-be novel and the short story, 'Mlle Monet' that was part of it, I have to extract the facts of that trip from the fiction — an almost impossible task, because memory does not distinguish between fact and fiction, and would have made a fiction of my whole life, if I had let it, for the present book.

My decision to take a taxi to the Gare de Lyon was as arbitrary and sudden as any other; and it happened that a train was about to leave for Avignon. I made a dash for it, found an empty seat, and prepared to settle down for the night. I was awakened by a ticket inspector, fumbled drowsily for my ticket, and remembered that I'd never had time to buy one. My corner seat, it turned out, was in a second-class carriage and the train was packed. Rather than risk the discomfort of a night in the corridor, I decided to buy a second-class ticket and stay put, though a third class was recognized in those pre-welfare days. I was fast asleep once more when a middle-aged man on crutches was ushered in by his wife. The set expression of his large face was resolute and aggrieved. As though in concert, five accusing hands pointed at me — all but the hands of a dark girl of about eighteen, who had been weeping quietly when I first noticed her in Paris, and was still weeping now. Or were they pointing at something just above my head? Could it be my luggage on the rack? I looked up and saw the incriminating notice: *Place réservée aux Mutilés*. So that was it. There was one spare seat next to mine, but as I got up to make room for their luggage, the disabled man and his wife took possession of both seats. Now public opinion was on my side. There were murmurs of protest and disapproval. A fat peroxide blonde explained that *la femme du mutilé* had no share in her husband's prerogative. As though deaf and dumb, the two of them simply sat there, holding hands in token of matrimonial solidarity. I gave up the struggle, left my cases on the rack, and retreated to the corridor with my useless second-class ticket. Six pairs of eyes followed me out, expressing different blends of incomprehension, mockery, and pity.

Sleepy though I was, I saw the dawn unwrap a new day, peeling off layers of darkness, exposing dark green hills, pink houses and ochre soil. I saw slender cypresses emerge one by one, almost as black as the night that had enveloped them.

A small hotel was already serving glasses of coffee as sweet as liqueur when the train reached Avignon at about seven. I was able to wash and shave. A friendly barmaid told me the way to the Pope's Palace and the broken bridge of the song. I dumped my bags in the café and left. As soon as I was out in the streets, which were by no means deserted, though the shops were still closed, something like the Dieppe euphoria returned at last. The fragrance of trees and flowers was still pure, without the admixture of domestic and animal smells so characteristic of southern towns. As I walked up the main boulevard to the Palace, a cicada was grating away in the pines, slowly at first, then faster and faster, like a two-handled saw being set in motion. It was too early to see the sights. In the Palace forecourt a gardener was watering shrubs with a hose-pipe. He didn't seem to mind my wandering about, looking at the artificial grottoes with the swans that seemed artificial too, as though their function was purely decorative, the baroque statues, and the yellow and red canna, at once fleshy and formal — official plants, I thought, exactly right for a French public garden.

Down below, I could see the grey, shallow width of the Rhône, and remembered the secret tunnel which is said to have connected the Pope's Palace with the castle on the other bank. The famous bridge of the song had broken because its piles were not round but square, and had resisted the current. So, at least, an old man told me that morning, going on to tell me long stories about the Papal villa up in the hills and the nearby convent. Since my ear wasn't yet attuned to the dialect, I was never quite sure that I'd understand him correctly, but his great guffaws left little doubt as to the gist.

Very soon the tourist machine took over. To see the interior of the Palace I had to join a conducted tour through large empty halls furnished only with the guide's mechanical evocations, past enormous paintings and tapestries, and into the former kitchen. By the time we got to a room packed with local curios — coats of arms, busts and etched portraits of former curators, odd bits of furniture, manuscripts and official notices — my only wish was to escape into the contemporary world. The exit, of course, was locked. I had to sit down on a window sill and wait for my release.

Outside, a hot landscape lay hypnotized, older even than the bridge or palace. There were no mountains of any great height, no chasms, no dense and enticing forests like those I knew in the North, no meadows, no moors, no vast expanse of land or water. There was only the peculiar light of Provence and the stark intensity of every object seen in that light. Every mushroom-shaped pine was visible for miles. It seemed strange to me that any living thing could bear such isolation and such exposure: a rock, a house, a cart or a human being — each, like the pine-trees on the horizon, was only itself, stripped of sentimental accretions.

Later, as I walked through the narrow cobbled streets that lead down to the river, not even the garbage in the gutters, the smell of bad drains or the obvious inadequacy of these ancient hovels could damp my spirits. Even the old women in black and the mangy cross-eyed cats seemed to belong there in a way that would have made pity an impertinence. That, at least, is what I felt when a Parisian business man insisted on joining me with no other object than to tell me that the old South was *foutu*. I had noticed the same man among the guide's flock in the Palace. The same people who would travel miles to see some pile of mediaeval or pre-Christian rubble that looked no different to them from the ruins to be found in any bombed city could speak contemptuously of the lazy southerners, the squalor that was the continuation of whatever they had come to see. Why, I wondered, did this man trouble to climb up through these slums, sweating in his lounge suit, at the hottest time of the day? He had clicked his tongue with admiration at the gigantic proportions of the Papal kitchen. Yet these despised slums had supported the Palace, and it was the slums that were still alive.

Once again I decided to move on. After lunch at the café where I'd left my cases, I picked them up and waited for a coach to Arles. Independence was what made me happy. To move on when I felt like it, to be involved with no one, dependent on no one. I would avoid conducted tours and irritating conversations with fellow tourists.

At Salon I made use of the odd hour between buses to look at the town. Drawn like a pin to a magnet, or a maggot to a piece of carrion, I ended up in the oldest part, near the castle; a fort on a hill complete with crumbling walls and all the required appendages. I got as far as the courtyard, but hardly needed the excuse that I was pressed for time to resist the efforts of a garrulous caretaker to lure me into the building.

The coach to Arles broke down after twenty minutes, just in front of a small roadside café. At first I thought that the driver and conductor had merely stopped for a drink. Then, slowly, rumours of disaster spread among the passengers, and one by one they got off to inspect the damage. At last the conductor left his beer to explain the breakdown in technical terms and to tell us that a relief coach was on the way. After another half-hour or so, I decided to take a walk. I turned off the main road into a path bordered on one side by a field of tall plants which I took to be maize. Later I was told they were the cane used for making fishing-rods. On the other side there were shrubs, brambles and what I thought were some sort of damson or sloe. I was just about to taste one of these when someone yelled at me. It was the man who had sat next to me on the coach, and he came running up to gasp that I was on the point of poisoning myself. Though I didn't believe that anything so much like a plum could be poisonous, it would have been grossly discourteous to deprive the fellow of the satisfaction of having saved my life. Luckily a series of frantic hoots rang out at that moment. We all made a dash for the coach.

Like most of the cheaper hotels at Arles, the one I chose was in the old and gloomy quarter behind the Place de la République, near the gloomier ruin known as Constantine's Palace. After a night and a day of travelling, I felt more sleepy than hungry, but forced myself to wash, shave and unpack before going out for a meal. Sights and tourists' restaurants were to be avoided at all costs. Though the solid walls of the Palace were imposing, I was not going to look at it that night — or the following day for that matter. Otherwise I'd be sure to run into a student of French literature. One was always getting involved. If it wasn't with tourists, it was with tourist sights. What I wanted was to see the country and the people. Why couldn't I see Constantine's Palace as they saw it? To them it was simply part of the town, like the Gendarmerie, the Public Gardens, and the statue of Mistral in the little square.

I made a point of going to a workman's restaurant in one of the adjoining streets, for a meal of bread, soup, red and rubbery liver, broad beans, and a bunch of grapes. Entertainment was provided by an old peasant who addressed everyone in turn, changing from mock formality to melodramatic complaints or nagging criticism. He spoke slowly and clearly, like a foreigner or an actor, with the Provençal's accentuation of the final 'e'. No one paid much attention to him, except the *patron*, who was the butt of his most insulting wisecracks; at times it looked as though he was taking them seriously. The old man compared his own hard life with that of a *bourgeois* who lives by exploiting other people's hunger; there were sly digs at the *patron's* fatness, mock-idyllic descriptions of peasant life, and sententious observations on destiny. He ended by inviting everyone, including the proprietor, to share a bottle of wine with him. I was too sleepy, and excused myself.

The next morning, too, I refused to be diverted from my own quest. I sat on the bank of a small river — a tributary of the Rhône — which forms one of the city boundaries. I watched a fisherman pull out an occasional catfish. The water was too shallow and too muddy for other breeds, though on the high embankment of the Rhône itself more ambitious anglers caught pike and gudgeon. He was fishing for his three cats, he told me, and catfish were good enough for them. From time to time families of Spanish gypsies, who lived in shacks and sheds on the outskirts of the town, came down to wash in the little river. The man spoke of them with contempt, referring to them as 'ça', although they understood French and were close enough to hear all he said. At one point a skinny black-haired girl of about twelve looked at him with sad, reproachful eyes, so that he stopped and reverted to the subject of fish. Then he began to talk about museums, churches and Roman remains! Not as a polite concession to me, I couldn't help noticing, but just as naturally as he had talked about catfish.

I shouldn't have been at all surprised if he'd gone on to quote Mallarmé! And that, precisely, was how the French way of life differed from ours, with its artificial division between intellectuals and 'ordinary people'.

As I strolled back to town, past booths with clothes, shoes, food and picture frames, I decided that there must be a middle way somewhere between the beaten track and sheep-pen of tourism, and a stubborn avoidance of anything that qualified as a sight. If I were really as independent as I thought I was, or wanted to be, there would be no need to deprive myself of what might prove to be genuine experiences, merely because they were recommended by Baedeker. On my way out that morning I had caught sight of the beautiful portal of St. Trophime, without so much as stopping to take a good look; and here I was, mixing with the crowd that had collected around a monkey, the decoy of a man selling some patent metal polish! There was no need to choose between the ancient church and these café terraces packed with farmers who had come in for the day to buy and sell in the market. Others stood and chatted in little groups on the pavement, discussing prices and exchanging gossip. Posters in café windows advertised forthcoming bullfights, most of them in outlying villages. I bought a ticket for one that same night in Arles. After lunch I returned to St. Trophime — to find it empty and silent, with no one to distract me or detract from its rounded repose.

My next days were spent at the museum of Roman art at Arles, the Roman cemetery at Alyscamps, or walking along the banks of the Rhône as far as the plains of the Camargue. I had also remembered my ticket for the bullfight, though I think I had been warned that those in the South of France were not the real thing. I arrived at the arena long before the fight was due to begin. The enormous Roman amphitheatre was almost empty and only dimly lit. Apart from the arena itself, the place was grim. The stars twinkled malevolently above the cold stone of the galleries, unsoftened by any kind of cover or decoration. As the seats slowly filled, my excitement was affected by the strangeness of that setting, which promised a kind of drama different from any to be seen in modern theatres. Besides, I had a guilty conscience about being there at all. But what was the point of admiring Roman remains if one was too squeamish to watch a bullfight? It couldn't be half as cruel as some of the spectacles for which the theatre was built.

The audience, now complete, began to shout impatiently. There was a curious noise behind one of the two entrances to the ring, less like the snorting of a bull than the revving up of a motor. The entrance was opened. Instead of the expected procession of horses and toreros, a man in white flannels and a white peaked cap drove into the ring in a jeep, followed by two *banderilleros* in the traditional Spanish costume and carrying capes. These took up position at each end of the arena, behind wooden screens close to the barrier. I suddenly remembered my slight misgivings when reading the poster, on which the hero of that night had been called *le grand sportsman espagnol.* I should have known that outside the Anglo-Saxon countries that word has the most dubious connotations.

The great sportsman proceeded to show off his skill as a driver. His red jeep, padded on one side with a sort of mattress, skidded around the ring at some speed. The audience applauded half-heartedly. The great sportsman halted, got out of the jeep and bowed to the audience. The other entrance was opened, and a bull trotted in, peered myopically around the *muleta* of one of the minor sportsmen, who promptly vanished behind his screen. This performance was repeated several times. Then the driver began to draw circles around the bull, making a din loud enough to frighten the life out of a dragon, let alone a bull. With the greatest reluctance the bull charged not the man, but the mattress. There was a sickening thud, a crack, a bellow of pain. The bull had broken off one of his horns. Stunned and bleeding, he stood in the middle of the ring. Not content with this victory of steel over bone, the sportsman tried to provoke the bull to charge again. The bull refused to budge, the audience hissed and booed. There were cries of '*Remboursez!*' When a number of young men threatened to storm the ring, the sportsman left in a hurry.

That was only the first round. After that there was a longish interlude, with people from the audience getting into the ring with young bulls. What they had to do was to get hold of a rosette attached to the bull's horns. But the horns were padded. It was fun for the local boys. Most of them just ran past the bull and jumped over the barrier when he chased them. All the same, a few did manage to snatch the rosette. They were given prizes, and new bulls were sent into the ring. One boy even used a *muleta* and showed a lot more courage and skill than that professional charlatan. Once he had literally to take the bull by the horns. He got a lot more applause than the fellow in the jeep.

What I noticed was that those bulls stopped their snorting and pawing as soon as they were left alone. At one moment they were savage beasts, at the next they were as meek as cows. When it was all over a special bull with a bell round its neck was sent into the ring, trotted round it once, and went out again, followed obediently by the fighting bull.

After five or six of those bouts the great sportsman came in again still in white flannels, but without his jacket and cap. This time he was on foot, and his two stooges carried *banderillas*. The jeep had been his substitute for a horse. He'd done — or bungled the *picador's* job, now he was coming in as *matador*, though with a new bull. His job now was to strike the bull between the eyes, as if to kill it, though in France the bull must not be killed.

The sportsman was unnerved, and he didn't seem keen to begin. The new bull looked formidable enough with several *banderillas* planted in his neck. At last the man stepped forward and attracted the bull's attention. The bull charged, he side-stepped neatly, but got his *muleta* wrapped around one of the bull's horns. One of the stooges had to get it back for him. There were jeers and laughter; and one could see that the public's contempt was breaking the man's spirit. He looked weary and desperate. When he walked back to the barrier, wiping his face, someone offered him a drink, and he almost emptied the bottle. His next attempt was an even great fiasco. He fell flat on his face and would have been gored if the bull hadn't walked away. That was the funniest thing of all — the way that bull walked off, as though it couldn't be bothered to finish him off. I was beginning to feel sorry for that man. He'd been terribly punished for his performance in the jeep. When he picked himself up he knew that it was his last chance; and he actually brought it off that time. At least, that's how it looked. He got his applause. But later I heard that the bull had been struck in one eye, and had to be destroyed like the other one. So that must have been the end of the great sportsman's career, if only because fighting bulls are valuable.

In the coach to Aix I took care to sit next to an old Frenchman who looked as though he wouldn't open his mouth unless it were absolutely unavoidable. I didn't allow my eyes to leave the back of the seat in front of me, except for a glance or two at the landscape. In any case I had discovered that I was less interested in panoramic impressions, like those obtained in passing from the windows of trains and coaches, than in details. The more I saw of Provence, the more I concentrated on Pascal's *infini de petitesse*, even making notes in my diary about the plants, birds, lizards and snakes observed during my walks. What made the landscape real to me was the composite fragrance of soil, flowers and trees, the quality of the light at one particular moment, the way the feel of a place was affected by a breeze. Nothing of this could be photographed or described, nothing of it experienced if one moved faster than at a walking pace.

With the help of friendly Aixois, it didn't take me long to find a hotel. There seemed to be even fewer tourists than at Arles, apart from people driving through on their way to the Cote d'Azur. But my request for a room was answered with some rudeness. The *patronne* looked me up and down suspiciously. Because of the heat I had put on an open-neck shirt and a pair of rather baggy khaki drill trousers left over from my army days. If they'd been shorts, it struck me, I should have passed for a cyclist or hiker. As it was, she couldn't place me in any of the acceptable categories. So she gave me a room that looked as though it wasn't intended to be used at all, saying that it was the only one left. I rather liked its undisguised shabbiness and the excellent view over the rooftops of Aix.

When I'd washed, shaved, and changed into a suit, I decided to go out for a stroll. My descent caused extraordinary convolutions. The *patronne*, now joined by her husband, apologized profusely for the room, called a chambermaid, told her to clean it thoroughly, wished me a happy stay, promised me a better room that very afternoon, asked me whether I had any special requirements and said they would be glad to cook for me, though the hotel had no restaurant. I told them that the room was excellent. When they insisted that I exchange it for a better one, I firmly refused to move, adding that in any case I'd intended to ask for the cheapest room, since I was very short of money. As I made for the door I heard them argue about the unpredictable behaviour of Englishmen and the growing complexities of the social and economic structure. The chambermaid tittered, and the *patronne* roared at her to get on with the job.

I made for the Cours Mirabeau, the widest avenue in Aix. The cafés were almost deserted, and the whole town seemed wrapped in an air of quiet retrospection. It had once been the capital of a kingdom, and was now a university town; but most of the students were on vacation. On weekdays only a few habitual *flâneurs* — visitors, artists, and some of the wealthier inhabitants — hung about the cafés at all hours. On Saturdays, I discovered later, the town filled up with country people who brought a different sort of life into the rather melancholy sedateness of its old streets.

After a light lunch I must have explored the greater part of the town, coming out into the open countryside at several different points. Here I felt little of the blatant discrepancy between past and present that had disturbed me at Avignon and elsewhere. True, I found the façade of a ruined church, but it was tucked away among inhabited houses and didn't cry out that its body was missing. As for the Cathedral, it clearly served its purpose still, despite the scepticism of the *Midi*. Like St. Trophime at Arles its front concealed a little cloister that was a separate world of light and darkness, stone and greenery, full of contrasts that made me think of forest clearings. The Bishop's Palace, too, with its wrought iron gates, was not too grandiose for survival. Children played in its forecourt, just as they played in the streets and the public gardens on the outskirts. Most of the town, including the residential quarter south of the Cours Mirabeau and the other side, with its shops, market and workshops, wore its age without effort or pretence — though with a touch of resignation, I thought.

The residential quarter remained solidly bourgeois. There were whole streets and squares built in the seventeenth century, tall houses with tiled floors, stuccoed ceilings and narrow windows with shutters. Though most of them were now sub-divided into flats, their character had not changed.

After dinner I went for another stroll. The fountains seemed much louder now, as though all the incidental noises had been absorbed by their falling water. But I could hear a clarinet somewhere, monotonously plaintive in those quiet streets. When I listened more intently I made out a piano and castanets. So it was a dance band; but without the accompaniment those phrases played by the clarinet changed from a samba into some weird and questioning soliloquy. I walked on and found that the music came from the casino, though nobody was dancing. I turned back.

I slept late next morning, and was woken up by the bright chatter of the chamber-maid who came in with a breakfast tray. I hadn't ordered breakfast, and was all the more appreciative of this unexpected luxury. The chambermaid still seemed to find me extraordinarily funny. The mere expression on my face when she told me the time was nine o'clock was enough to give her the giggles.

I spent most of the afternoon at the swimming-pool of the Hotel Sextius, but decided that in future I should try to get to the sea. The baths looked like a shipwreck in a film, full of boys holding on to wooden boards and desperately flapping their feet. An older boy yelled instructions at them. After swimming a few lengths I collided with one of those wooden boards, and gave up. The steps leading up to the hotel garden were monopolised by the brown bodies of girls in bikinis. Here, too, an unwritten law imposed a kind of segregation, and it took me some time to find a neutral spot for my sun-bathing.

I was up in time to catch the 6 a.m. coach. I must have felt that there was something I should have missed by leaving at a more reasonable hour. But, so many years later, I can only speculate about the motives of the person alleged to be identical with myself. I can no more share his impatience than I can remember what it was like to have so much energy to waste on the mere catching of empty coaches. Yet there he was — 'I' was — travelling on an empty stomach, leaving the hills behind.

We drove through flat uncultivated land covered with patches of brown vegetation. The coach made a long detour through the Crau desert, through Istres and Point de Bouc, where I caught my first glimpse of the sea. Though the sky was cloudless, the water was less blue than I expected, tinged with grey, green and white. I saw tents and cars on the beach, and feared the worst. We passed factories, warehouses, cranes, and my heart sank. I might as well have gone to Marseilles, or stuck to my shallow river near Aix.

At Martigues I had to cross two bridges before finding any sort of accommodation. A Canadian merchant vessel had anchored in the Lac de Berre, and the little town was full of seamen on shore leave. All I could do was to book a room for the following day in a not too squalid hotel, and go out again to find what I could for that night. It turned out that I'd passed a small hotel on the way without even noticing it, though I'd been tempted to stop for a coffee at the little *bistro* attached to it. I lugged my cases all the way back again.

Did I want a *chambre de nuit*? I had no idea there was any other kind. For one person only? The *patronne*, a buxom blonde of about thirty, seemed to think it odd, but told the barmaid to show me the single room. I groped my way up the narrow dark staircase. Between the second and third floors the girl stopped, rested her arm against the wall and buried her face in it. I couldn't pass, and waited for her to move on. She was a tall girl, dark and sturdily built.

'*Trop de travail?*' I suggested.

The place smelled of fish, garlic and lavatories.

'*Non, ce n'est rien.*' She looked up and smiled at me.

We moved on to the fourth floor. The room was more like a cabin or a cell, its only furniture a bed, a tiny table and a chair.

'*Ça vous suffit?*' she asked.

It had to. I told her that I'd tried all the other hotels I could find.

'I shall look after you,' she said.

There was no room for my cases, though, and nowhere to put the contents.

'Shove them under the bed,' she said.

I did, also taking the precaution of looking at the sheets. They were clean at least, and that was something to be thankful for. In any case I shouldn't be using the room in the daytime.

'Are you really alone?' she asked.

'You can see I am. Is there anything extraordinary about that?'

She smiled again.

'Are you a sailor, then?'

'No, a tourist on holiday, from England.'

'We've never had anyone like that here. We get sailors mostly. But I'd better get back to work. *À bientôt.*'

I got out my bathing-trunks and a towel, and made my way downstairs.

The *patronne* told me I had to pay in advance and fill in the *affiche* before going out. I did so and asked her how to get to the beach. She sent her little daughter of six to show me the way.

I needn't have worried about tourists. No one was bathing, and hardly anyone was to be seen the whole length of the beach. The vast salt lake was almost repulsively smooth and still. A fisherman was going out in a small motor launch. In the distance two large cargo boats lay at anchor. I thanked the little girl and gave her some money to buy sweets. She waved goodbye and ran off.

I had got to the sea at last — or to something hardly distinguishable from the sea, and I had it almost to myself. There was nothing for me to do but spend the whole morning in and out of the water, soaking or drying in the sun with a white deposit of salt on my skin. It cost little effort to swim in that buoyant water, which recalled what I'd heard about the Dead Sea. A dead sea — that was what I didn't like about this salt lake, whatever its other advantages.

Soon after one o'clock boredom was getting the better of me. I decided to go back to the hotel to fetch a book and some notepaper. I could buy bread, cheese and grapes while I was about it, and picnic on the beach.

The *patronne* intercepted me, saying that she'd cooked some rabbit. Would I care to have lunch at the hotel? She took me to a gloomy room between the *bistro* and the kitchen. The little girl joined me. Her bright continuous chatter was unexpected after her silence before and during our walk to the beach. Were there a lot of sweets in England? Did I like dancing? She loved dancing, she told me, and promptly performed for me, improvising a grotesque ballet to a piece of light orchestral music on the wireless. By the time her mother came in with cheese and more bread, she was telling me that she wanted to marry me.

'Good,' I said, 'but we'll have to wait a little while. People aren't allowed to marry till they're grown up.'

Her mother didn't think this a joking matter. She told the little girl that under no circumstances was she to marry anyone but a Martégal.

The little girl began to sulk and wouldn't finish her meal. The woman got angry and slapped her face. I said that it was natural for little girls to indulge in fantasies of that kind, and I could see no harm in such patter. She ignored my objections and asked me whether I had ever eaten *bouillabaisse*. She'd make some for me in the evening. In the restaurants it would cost me at least a thousand francs, and she'd let me have it for eight hundred. Since I'd already glanced at a menu outside one of the restaurants, I knew that this wasn't true, and became a little suspicious of the whole establishment. I'd noticed that the price demanded for my room was out of all proportion to its size and quality, especially as it didn't contain so much as a wash-basin. I'd have to go down two floors and use the sink in the W.C. I thanked her for the offer, but said I was going out in the evening.

When I got back to the beach it was completely deserted, though from time to time a woman or girl would emerge from one of the houses that bordered it to pour slops and refuse into a ditch. When a man appeared with a spade and began to dig a drain from the ditch to the sea, I had to pick up my clothes and move away from the stench. Still I went on swimming and basking by turns, with a book to relieve the tedium.

When I left at about five my skin was burning. Sun and salt, I thought, but began to wonder whether I hadn't overdone it. Mad dogs and Englishmen! At the hotel I washed as best I could in the stinking lavatory, changed, and went down for a drink. My throat was parched, and I felt that I could drain a whole barrel of beer. The *patronne* immediately pounced on me again, saying that three compatriots of mine would like to speak to me, and pointing to a table in the *bistro*. Only one of them turned out to be English. The other two were Australian and Canadian, and all belonged to the crew of a Canadian ship. They were on their way to South America.

They seemed to be pleased to have got hold of me, and immediately asked me what I'd like to drink. The English sailor wondered whether I'd come off another ship. When I'd introduced myself and told him how I came to be here, he said it was unusual to find any tourists in a dump like Martigues. And was I really staying in this knocking-shop? I didn't know the word.

'Yes, it's a bit rough, I agree. But it's better than nothing. I once spent a night sleeping out without cover in Italy, when I was in the army, and got precious little sleep, what with the cold, the dew, and the insects.'

The sailor bellowed with laughter and nudged his Canadian friend. They shared some joke which I didn't catch. They'd been on shore leave all day, and had spent most of it drinking. I ordered another round —

cognacs for them, beer for me. All the female staff of the hotel were standing round our table, trying to make conversation and serving drinks in quick succession. There was the *patronne*, the tall barmaid, a rather pretty blonde, and an Italian girl whom I hadn't seen till then.

'Do you speak the lingo?' the English sailor asked me.

When I nodded my head, he said that might come in very useful.

'You could be our interpreter, like — if you don't mind.'

At that moment a fourth seaman came down from the hotel with a girl. Her hair was dyed red, her eyes shaded with purple, and she wore a dark blue jersey with slacks of the same colour. She carried no handbag but a number of little boxes that struck me as sinister. 'Her boxes of tricks,' I thought, without having any clear idea of what they might contain.

The Canadian, a tall burly fellow with blue eyes, began to tell the Italian girl how much he liked her and what he would like to do to her. She couldn't understand a word. He asked me to interpret. I gave her an expurgated version of what he had said. She clearly didn't want to get involved and disappeared in the kitchen. The Canadian showed no disappointment and no emotion of any kind.

After two more rounds the party broke up. The Australian asked me whether I'd like to take a walk with him. I said I was going out in any case. He arranged to meet the others in a different bar, and we went off together.

'I'm the third mate,' he told me, 'and I have to keep an eye on those men. They want to paint the town red. I don't drink much myself, and I don't pick up girls. Once bitten, twice shy.'

I asked him what he meant.

'I got married seven years ago because I had to. I haven't been back since and never want to go back. That's why I'm a sailor.'

'But what about your wife? Doesn't she want you back?'

'She's all right. She's got a good job in Australia. We don't get on together. I've never cared for women since. I like my job and I like getting around.'

He was worried about the others. So we separated, and I continued the walk by myself.

The little square of water, enclosed on two sides by old houses and filled with brightly painted boats, was no more like Venice than the part of London called Little Venice. It was pleasant and colourful, and I could understand why it attracted artists. The houses were brightly distempered, unlike the tall grey façades of Venetian palaces. And yet it did remind me of something in Italy a beautiful island village with fishing-boats, a little bridge at Murano, was it, or Torcello? Not far from Venice, anyway.

The rest of Martigues was hardly picturesque — a fishing village that had almost turned into an industrial town but avoided turning into a holiday resort. I walked up the main street, crossed three bridges, and continued along the road to Marseilles. On my right there was a steep rocky hill, which I left the road to climb, using shrubs and rock plants to get a better hold. I was not too steady, though I hadn't had much to drink. From the top I could see the whole town, the salt lake, and the canal which connects it with the sea. I went down the other side, intending to explore the countryside behind it, when all at once I felt extremely ill. My head ached, the landscape began to spin, and I was afraid that I should never get back to town.

I made an effort and started walking down the hill. I had to wait in front of the movable bridge, which was just swinging back into place. My whole body was shaking and felt as though it were on fire. I managed to get back to the hotel, picked up the key to my room, dragged myself up the stairs, and lay down.

Though it was a relief to lie down, all the strength seemed to be draining out of my body. Having no previous experience of sunstroke, I felt that I should never be able to get up again, but should simply lie there, with my body shivering and smarting, my teeth chattering. No one in that hotel would bother about me, once they had got hold of what was left of my money. What a fool I was to have gone up to my room without telling anyone I was ill! Perhaps that barmaid really would have looked after me. And I might never be able to get downstairs again now! The fever was eating into me, blurring my eyes, clouding my brain, sapping my will-power. And now I knew what the sailor had meant. This place was a brothel. And I had to fall ill, perhaps die, in a brothel — of all places! I closed my eyes.

It really was dark in the room. My shirt and trousers clung to my body, soaking wet, yet it couldn't be very late, for I heard voices and laughter down below. I felt much better, but very thirsty.

I changed into dry clothes and went down to the café. An American sailor and a Spaniard were drinking at the bar. The Spaniard looked at me and knew at once that I was ill. He advised me not to drink anything alcoholic. The *patronne* disagreed with him, maintaining that it all depended on what was wrong with me. Sunstroke, the Spaniard said, and I confirmed it, telling them about my day on the beach.

'May-be,' the *patronne* said, 'but it could be just a common cold.'

Perhaps that suited her better, I thought. I was less likely to sit up very long over soft drinks.

'Rum is the best remedy for colds,' she said.

I asked for orange juice and water. She shrugged her shoulders.

The American sailor was making advances to the Italian girl, who had taken over the bar. He had picked up French around Quebec, and had no difficulty in making himself understood. Yet she seemed to be weighing him up without relating his words to herself. She gazed at him with a kind of nonchalant candour quite free from mockery, as though he were a child with a craving for chocolate or ice-cream. Her self-possession goaded the American. His demands grew desperate and rhapsodic. At last she deigned to speak:

'Think for a minute. If you want someone to sleep with for an hour or two, that can be arranged. But not with me.'

'But it's you I want,' he said.

'*Tant pis*. I'm sorry. Let's talk of something else.'

The American gave up and turned to me.

'What are you doing here?' he asked.

Before I could begin to answer he went on to tell me about his love life, his jobs in the U.S.A. and in Canada, and his reasons for joining the Merchant Navy. I listened as sympathetically as I could, but found myself wondering whether there was something about me that invited confidences at the most inconvenient moments. At last I managed to get in a word and tell him that I was ill, that I'd just had a severe fever, and must get back to bed. He shook hands and wished me luck. I thanked the Spaniard for his advice, said goodnight to the *patronne*, and went back to my room. It must have been four o'clock in the morning before I could get to sleep.

From Martigues I moved to Fos-sur-Mer, with more difficulties over accommodation and an offer from a chambermaid to share her room. Despite my recent sunstroke I made my way to the beach; but it began to rain the moment I left the hotel. It was still cold and windy when I went swimming, but after the heat and calm of the 'dead sea' at Martigues it was good to be up against waves.

It was a mistake to go swimming. I felt feverish again and so lethargic that the only thing to do was to lie down. But for the barking of a dog outside my window I should probably have fallen into a deep sleep. As it was, my mind bobbed up and down between consciousness and dream.

I set my watch by the dining-room clock and went out, making for the fortress I had already gone to see that day. Leaning on the parapet I looked out over the village and to the sea. Very faintly, dance music drifted in from the beach, and the even fainter lapping of the waves. The night air held a remnant of the afternoon heat, only just perceptible under the cool sea breeze. In the old village streets boys were playing a last game of *boules* in the lamplight. The metal balls chinked against paving stones and caught the light as they rolled.

On my way to the beach a short man, unshaven and dirty, with curly black hair, stopped me to ask for a light. A Neapolitan, I knew by his accent almost before he told me. Why had he left Italy? A stupid question, asked only to make conversation. It provoked an outburst of fierce anger mingled with nostalgia. No work, no money, the selfishness of the rich, a life unfit for pigs, but the beautiful bay, the sound of his own language that sings without music, the Via Roma and the crowded piazza, alive at any time of the day or night! Here, in this dead provincial hole, he had worked in the salt marsh till they sacked him. Now he slept on the beach and no girl would look at him.

He walked back with me as far as the Casino. I gave him a little money, which he accepted gratefully and without embarrassment. I left him with his nose pressed against a window-pane, hungry for the mere light and noise in the place, the mere sight of beautiful girls.

On August 18th, I wrote to a friend from Aix-en-Provence: 'I have started to write a kind of novel (or travel book) in which I make use of what I have seen and heard in France but without committing myself to telling the literal truth ... Instead of telling a story, I am writing a series of brief episodes in the present tense and my hero is far from superhuman ... I mean that my hero's exploits are those of a man awake and inhibited.' I also admitted: 'As you see my approach to novel-writing is still rather naive.' The mere circumstance that I had begun the writing while getting material for it meant that this work must fall between two stools. The Mademoiselle Monet episode, which I published separately as a short story, was rewritten several times when the real events had become vague in my mind, letting the fiction impose its own demands.

From Provence I went to St. Malo, to be my grandmother's guest for the last time. At some junction near Vichy I had to wait a few hours between trains. I went out for a walk and found myself in a river valley that delighted me more than any landscape I had seen in Provence or was to see in Brittany. My stay at St. Malo was brief. Though I enjoyed talking to my grandmother about the state of the world — as she wrote in a letter of that period, she ought to have been a politician or a social worker, but devoted herself instead to looking after her moody, unoccupied and emotionally arrested son — I could no longer adapt to the life in a conventional seaside hotel, and I wanted to get on with the writing of my prose book before my return to Oxford and preparations for Finals.

A friend had put me in touch with an American lady, Mrs. Garrett, who edited a magazine called *Tomorrow.* Soon after my return to London she accepted two poems of mine — the first to appear in America — and invited me to a party at Claridge's in September. I duly put on my best suit for the occasion, but, in my preoccupation with the book I was writing, forgot to do up my fly buttons, an omission I discovered only when people began to stare at me in Mrs. Garrett's suite. I believe that her main interest was in extra-sensory perception, with poetry as a side-line, but the place was full of mundane people whose perceptions were sensory enough to cause me acute embarrassment in that state. I kept turning to the window to admire the view. No sooner had I done so when someone could come up to me to engage me in inane conversation. By the time I had become respectable the party was nearly over.

At Oxford, not long before I went down, I met a remarkable man, the poet and anthropologist Franz Baermann Steiner, a few of whose poems had appeared with English translations in Tambi's *Poetry London*, though most of them remained unpublished until after his early death. Born in Prague, Steiner had come to England in connection with his anthropological studies, and stayed on when Czechoslovakia was annexed. I had met learned poets before — John Heath-Stubbs was one of them — but never one at home in so many languages and cultures, including the Arabic, American Indian and Eskimo. The death of his parents and other close relatives in extermination camps was the theme of a poem of his I especially admired and translated, 'Prayer in the Garden'. It was also the blow from which he could not recover. His heart disease, thrombosis, seemed less like a physical condition than like an after-effect of that blow. He seemed to waver between its promptings and the desire to live, to marry, travel and work. When he came out of hospital after a crisis he told my wife and me that during his convalescence there his broken life-line had joined up again, and he was full of plans accordingly. Yet even his wish to see some of his poetry in book form was frustrated when his German publisher went bankrupt with a collection of Steiner's poems at proof stage. The same publisher had produced the first post-war edition of *Die Blendung* (*Auto-da-Fé*) by Elias Canetti, Steiner's friend, whom I also met at this period. When my first book of poems appeared in 1950 I felt ashamed to show it to Steiner, knowing how crude it was by his standards; but he asked for a copy, and read it with the minute attention he gave to everything to which he applied himself. He asked me how I had hit upon one line — 'The Congo ticks with our clocks' — and was astonished when I told him that it wasn't based on anything I had heard, seen or read. His positive response to that one line meant more to me than anything written about the book by reviewers.

One of my newer Oxford acquaintances wrote a play called *A King must die*, each act of which was set in a different historical period. Before the play was put on he organized a procession to advertise it. I agreed to take part in the procession as a mediaeval knight. A horse was hired for the occasion. I had never mounted a horse in a suit of plate mail and helmet, nor had the horse ever been so mounted. From the moment the procession set out from North Oxford the horse decided that it wasn't going to put up with the clanking nuisance on its back. For a while I was able to entertain passers-by with a free bucking bronco show, but the poor animal's terror grew inventive. When it couldn't throw me by rearing it tried to push me off by pressing up to a wall, and finally fell on top of me. The neck piece of the armour cut into the back of my neck, and I made no more attempts to mount the horse. The author of the play had to be content with a rather sullen-looking hack led by a bleeding knight.

I had another accident when I went riding with John Mortimer while staying at his parents' house near Henley. All went well on the way out, but as we cantered or galloped back I didn't notice that we were passing a path that led back to the stables. The horse knew better, and veered so suddenly that I was thrown. As in all my falls, I suffered no damage, but the horse ran home without me. That fall was also the end of my horse-riding, the recreation I had enjoyed more than any other. If horse-riding was not a skill that could be left in abeyance for long periods — and for me it was less a skill than a disposition — this had to do with the nature of horses. Unlike a bicycle or motor car, a horse is immediately sensitive to any lack of familiarity, practice, control or assurance in its rider. How it responds to such a lack depends on its individual character, training and function, not to mention its moods. Unless it has been so thoroughly broken as to have lost its mettle, it does not suffer fools gladly; not new and indifferent fools at any rate. My favourite Cossack mare in Carinthia had put up with all sorts of incompetence, carelessness and absent-mindedness on my part, only because we had established a *rapport*. Circumstances were never again to allow me another with a horse.

Altogether, my second stay at Oxford was a period when nothing went positively or seriously wrong, yet nothing was quite what it could have been. Somehow I wasn't all there — couldn't be all there. Part of me remained suspended between the larger world I had glimpsed, but only marginally experienced, in my army years, and the wholly adult life I was eager to begin, without being quite ready for it or having a very clear idea of how I fitted into it. The people I regard as true Oxford figures are people who have succumbed to Oxford's hermeticism, living as though Oxford were the world, world without end, amen. I was to write a few poems with a specific Oxford setting, but after I had left; as a visitor, not a resident. While I was there, in 1947 and 1948, what I worked on was my European Tramp sequence, poems about civilized countries reduced to a physical and moral rubbish dump. Till I had got those images out of my system I couldn't yield to the attractions of a place that had been left very nearly intact; and by that time I had 'gone down', as they say, down into the nether regions of dirty, battered London. It was the old sin of impatience all over again.

Seven

After going down from Oxford in December 1948 I continued to live at my mother's house for a year or so. Though writing was the only thing I wanted to do, I had made one dutiful attempt at Oxford to provide myself with a part-time job. When I went to the University Appointments Board I was told that they knew of no part-time job for literary men, but that a place in the Intelligence Corps could probably be obtained for me in the event of another war. I thanked them for that reassuring piece of advice and made no further use of their services.

The next step was to establish myself as a book reviewer. I had already published a few book reviews and longer critical pieces, and for another twenty years or so I reviewed pretty regularly — for the *Times Literary Supplement*, for the *New Statesman*, for *World Review*, while it lasted, then for *Encounter* and the *Spectator*, as well as little magazines in Britain, America and Germany. I think that I positively enjoyed this occupation until the mid-sixties, though often it clashed with my other writing and translating projects. I reviewed hundreds of books over the years. As long as I remained an avid reader of new and old works in several languages, it was a way of obtaining books I couldn't afford to buy. Destructive though it could be of long-term projects, the deadline attached to each piece was also stimulating. It made me do something when I might have moped or procrastinated. Yet it was a medium scarcely less ephemeral than broadcasting. If one ceased to review for some periodical to which one had contributed for a decade or more, hardly anyone so much as noticed the dropping-out. The columns were fed by someone else, just as radio or television transmitters are fed with one thing or another. In the end something in me revolted against that machinery. The instant judgements no longer presented themselves. The opening sentence, once thrown so readily across any dividing distance or depth, became an impassable barrier. Whatever skill I had acquired in long practice of writing to order simply fell away. I couldn't do it any more.

I remember feeling offended when a girl I knew said to me at a London party: 'Congratulations. I see you're writing for the *New*

Statesman now,' referring to a poem I had published there. The idea that one could write poems *for* periodicals was more than I could stomach. Probably she meant no more than that my poems were appearing there, as they did rather frequently under Janet Adam-Smith's literary editorship, but the little word 'for' implied that she regarded my verse as a form of journalism. I shouldn't have taken that to heart but for the grain of truth in her remark. Living as a 'free-lance' writer meant the need to be paid for one's publications; and the odd guineas paid for poems by periodicals like the *New Statesman* were part of my wretched economy. Since books of poems brought in no money to speak of, without those odd guineas I should have been unable to write poems at all — as long as I remained a 'free-lance'. It was a vicious circle — how vicious, I didn't know until my friend Philip Rawson pulled my second collection of poems to pieces, and I had to admit to myself that economic pressure had made me publish too many poems too soon, with at least a dash of the journalist's promptness. Instead of the two years between my first collection and the second, six years passed before my third; and I became as wary of the sort of 'success' on which that girl had congratulated me as I had once been eager for it, under the delusion that to publish poems in periodicals with a relatively wide circulation was to communicate with more readers more effectively.

Nearly ten years earlier I had asked John Heath-Stubbs in the Swiss pub, Old Compton Street, whether he had ever had a poem in an anthology, other than the Oxford one of which I knew, and told him I thought that to be anthologized would be a true breakthrough for a poet — as though anthologies were compiled by recording angels for all eternity, and one's admission into one an assumption to a higher world! If I had begun with ambitions, they were deluded ones of that order. The anthologies did follow in due course: some two hundred of them by now, most of them wholly commercial commodities purveyed to readers who cannot find their own way through the bewildering superabundance of poetry, new and old; many of them put together by editors too busy, lazy or diffident to do more than rifle earlier anthologies for their fortuitous pickings, perpetuating those anthology pieces that are the kiss of death to living poets. A true anthology of contemporary verse would have to reduce its plurality by a daring reliance on personal judgement or only personal taste — an arrogant undertaking at a time when literary reputations tend to rest on a consensus as ephemeral and labile as opinion polls in politics. The merely 'representative' and 'comprehensive' anthology of contemporary verse re-registers that consensus or brings it up to date. It does not get to grips with the trouble acknowledged by Yeats long ago: that there are always too many poets at work and in print. Anthologized or not, for a living poet there were no certainties, no arrivals; only comings and goings like my travels of those years, searches for nothing to which I could have given a name.

Looking back at the four years between my going down from Oxford and my first university appointment, I can only wonder how I managed to persuade myself that I was 'free', when I had to take on almost any job of work that happened to come my way. These jobs included evening lectures for the Worker's Educational Association and for the London County Council; acting as a guide to foreign visitors for the British Council; coaching private pupils for an agency; teaching elementary French to convicts in Pentonville Prison; and adapting the libretto of the opera *Leonarda* by Else Headlam-Morley, who had been a pupil of Liszt, for its first and only performance in England, at the Chelsea Town Hall, on March 30th 1950.*

Yet between such jobs, book reviews and broadcasts, I did get on with my own writing and translating, no matter whether this work would find a publisher or not. However hard I worked, I couldn't scrape together more than an average income of £5 a week — still enough, in those days, to pay the rent for my first one-room flatlet, my second two-room flat, or my third of three, cover overheads like heating and telephone bills, and keep me fed after a fashion. What was left of my army gratuity paid for holidays abroad.

On May 2nd 1949, I was in Paris again, meeting a number of writers and painters introduced to me by Jacques Calmy, who had lived in England before the war and become friendly with my friend X. The very next day I moved on to Milan, then to Florence, where I met John Pettavel, visited churches, art galleries, museums, and began a poem, never finished, about the cemetery at San Miniato, fascinated by the Italian custom of commemorating their dead by photographs fixed to grave-stones. As usual, my dutiful sight-seeing was unproductive. What really captivated me in Italy was the least palpable of phenomena — the mere smells on the banks of the Arno, the precise colour of olive trees, silver-white-green-

*The composer, unhappily, died a few weeks before the event, on February 25th, at the age of 84.

blue-grey, something about the landscape at Fiesole that I couldn't describe. 'Self-sufficiency of the landscape, architecture, people,' I noted. 'No need for transcendence. How the sun melts the written word.'

Soon I was saturated with works of art and monuments, and moved out of Florence to San Domenico di Fiesole. At Maiano I found a pool where I could swim in complete solitude, not counting the frogs and the water snakes. The two castles of Vincigliata and Poggio, together with the legend attached to them, the olive groves and the cypress wood of their settings, made me write a couple of sonnets later included in my first collection. Contrary to my usual practice, I set to work on them on the spot. 'Inaccessible and locked,' I wrote in my diary. 'Climbed over wall. Perfect isolation. Glimpse of courtyard: cypresses, urn. Wrote poem there.' From time to time I would come down from my retreat to see John Pettavel and his friends in Florence.

John Pettavel was a more devout sight-seer than I. His guide-book mentioned a picture by Perugino to be seen at the Hospital at Castiglione. When he drove me to Umbria, on a trip lasting several days, we stopped at Castiglione. Repeated enquiries brought us into the office of the Sindaco. His permission, we were told, was needed before anyone could be admitted to the convent hospital. We were cross-examined, submitted our passports, waited while he conferred with other officials. At last he granted permission. A guide showed us through ancient passages, unlocking ancient doors. At the hospital entrance we were received by a nun. She seemed astonished at our request to see the Perugino, but led us through more passages to a small white-washed room. 'Ecco il Perugino!' she said. We stared at the walls, blank but for a little crucifix above the bed that was the only furniture in the room. The bed was occupied by an old man, and he was obviously dying. His wide-open eyes were incapable of any response to our intrusion. He was the Perugino — a man from Perugia. There was nothing we could do to repair the blunder. We thanked the nun, who seemed utterly perplexed, and got out as fast as we could.

That lesson in the disparity of art and life wasn't lost on me. In any case I had long known that I needed nature more than I needed art, that what I wrote poems about was not the Raphael at Castiglione or any other masterpiece but the photographs the living used to preserve the image of their dead. This was where art and nature — human nature — linked up.

When we drove on to Perugia, where we had ample opportunity to make up for the missed picture, I wrote about the landscape between

Siena and Arezzo: 'Abstract. Very small hills, undulations with shadows forming patterns. This scenery isn't "natural".' A related formality made me more receptive to the *fondo d'oro* paintings in Siena and at San Gimignano, especially those by Taddeo di Bartolo and Simone Martini, than to most of the too many pictures seen on that trip. Music presented no such difficulties. In Florence I heard Mozart's *Don Giovanni*, *Requiem* and *Ave Verum*, went to a Beethoven recital by Rudolf Serkin, and attended a performance of Monteverdi's *Orfeo* — not long after discovering Monteverdi through the few gramophone recordings of his works available at the time.

On June 8th, I returned to Paris, on my way home. Again I tried to pin down the peculiar qualities that drew me to Italy, this time by comparison with Paris. About the courtyard of a house in the rue Nôtre Dame des Champs — a courtyard that was to appear in a poem I wrote more than ten years later — I remarked in my diary: 'Not beautiful as a Neapolitan courtyard can be beautiful, architecturally; but full of melancholy, as if it had absorbed the souls of all those who have lived there; full of something unrealized or lost. The misery of Paris, unlike that of Italy, is not one of poverty, but of frustrated ambition or aspiration. Paris is of the North, transcendent. Fragments of statues in the courtyard. (It doesn't matter whether they are or were good.) And the moss, the damp, the half-light.' I was to pass through Paris again in the next few years, but never spent more than a few hours there between 1950 and 1972. If I have no business in a large city, and no close friends, all I find there is ghosts — 'the soul of all those who have lived there', absorbed by walls. When, in September 1947, I walked in the park at Versailles, and the first person I saw in the almost deserted avenues was David Gascoyne, that encounter was like a meeting of ghosts. Each of us, in his own way, was trying to relate to the place, but the presence of neither of us could have filled it or been filled by it.

Such sensations may have been no more than projections of my own melancholy, strangely bound up, as it is, with large cities and the transitoriness they won't allow me to forget. Travelling, I was to find out, doesn't necessarily offer an escape from one's obsessions. It confronts them with new material, which will be taken up or rejected in a way one can neither predict nor control. Guidebooks never did me any good.

In February 1949 I had received a letter from a person I had never heard of at the time, D'Arcy Cresswell, who lived only a few streets away from my mother's house, in Abercorn Place, St. John's Wood. He wrote that he was making a study of Hölderlin's Greek affinities, mainly from my translations, and asked whether there was a complete translation into English of Hölderlin's long poem *Der Archipelagus*. I had not yet translated this poem, but sent Cresswell a translation of a short ode by Hölderlin I had recently done, the love poem 'Apology'. Cresswell replied: 'It's a Diotima verse, I suppose; but what then can "life's obscurer, more secret griefs" mean? It makes me suspect that he was homosexual, & that the whole of his breakdown was due to his inability to accept that. This is where the decadence of modern Europe is seen — moral terrorism, & artists who haven't the courage, or a strong enough instinct of self-preservation, to defy it. Hence unreal & neurotic marriages & romances & either disaster or no development after. Of course nothing can quite smother a genius like Hölderlin, but at what a price ...'

I should have been forewarned by this cranky and arbitrary interpretation of Hölderlin's 'case' and guessed that it sprang from D'Arcy Cresswell's own case. In the more than ten years of friendship that ensued from his first letters he never told me that he had been married in New Zealand, before settling in England, and fathered a son who was farming on the Welsh border. What did become clear almost at once was that he had turned not only into a homosexual but into an extreme misogynist. This obsession, and D'Arcy's equally extreme anti-modernism in the arts, was to set rigid limits to our association, though D'Arcy did seem to exclude my wife from his general loathing of women, whom he blamed for almost everything that was wrong with the world. He composed a gavotte for my wife to play on her flute, and brought her a Christmas cake sent to him from New Zealand.

In the 'twenties and 'thirties, D'Arcy Cresswell had been well received in England as a writer, being taken up by Lady Ottoline Morrell and powerful literary figures like Edward Marsh. His friends had included E. M. Forster, and T. S. Eliot had published his first autobiography, *The Poet's Progress*, written in a curious Ciceronian style which D'Arcy had evolved from his reading not of Latin but translations from the Latin. When I first got to know him he was living in a two-room cottage behind a terrace house, still producing his poems and satires as leaflets at his own expense, but no longer hopeful enough to hawk them, as he used to do. He had been totally forgotten as a writer, at least in Britain. In later years he worked as a night-watchman in a Ministry. He died in the same cottage in 1960, asleep with the gas on. Before leaving for New Zealand in 1949 he had made a will appointing me his literary executor, but I could not find the copy of it he had given me. Since our disagreements became more outspoken in later years, he may well have revoked this will in any case; and there was little I could have done for his work here, having failed in every attempt I made while he was alive. His literary remains went to New Zealand, where there is at least an historical interest in his work.

Since D'Arcy believed that English poetry had come to an end with Tennyson, and tried to write accordingly, there was more than a generation gap between us. Almost thirty years older than I, he had served in the First World War. This made him more interesting. What came between us in our literary exchanges was his total rejection of Yeats and Eliot, and his lampoons against my friends. I should have been forewarned, but could not resist such whole-hearted eccentricity as D'Arcy's, maintained to his own detriment. Nor did I care that he could have no more use for my verse than I had for his, though he did address some lines to me called 'Advice to a Modern Poet'. Even when I had moved out of London, and visits to his cottage were complicated by his need to sleep in the daytime, as well as by an alsatian bitch that slept on his bed and longed to get her teeth into any visitor, I would try to attend his tea-time levée from time to time. D'Arcy's wrong-headedness was a challenge to me. I wanted to understand it. If it had been an affectation it would have bored me after a time; but his silly views on women — central to the best of his later works, the verse play *The Forest*, which I tried in vain to get published in England — and on poetry were as sincere as the Hellenism that made him publish a pamphlet of poems in support of Greek nationalism in Cyprus. Nor was he self-righteous. What he believed in was not himself, or the importance of his opinions, but some compelling necessity that governed his work. Though I could quarrel with his opinions, and did, I respected what he called his 'Providence': 'I now see,' he wrote to me in 1955, 'that tho' my "satires" are ready for a publisher, I am by no means ready & fit for the publicity or success which might attend their appearance. And until I am, my wise Providence won't allow them to appear. Doubtless anger, bitterness, desperation were necessary to the composition, but I must rid myself of them before I can hope the verses themselves will be allowed to appear. And if I do this, they will appear soon enough without any unusual efforts by me. It has been so with each of my few books. There has been something providential in the way each found a publisher. So I had better look to my inner life & go quietly on with my work...'

In a later letter D'Arcy himself wrote of his 'outlandish ideas and viewpoint'. Much of his intolerance of what was going on in the arts may have been literally 'outlandish', due to his New Zealand background and a sense of outrage at the sophistication which to him was wicked and perniciously subversive. I had come across similar attitudes in Roy Campbell, whom I met from time to time in London, sharing a poetry reading with him on one occasion. What Roy Campbell liked in my early verse was the very roughness, directness and awkwardness which I was doing my best to outgrow. D'Arcy's advice to me was:

You'll nothing learn from those
Who labour to invent
And clamour to be heard.
Look to the modest rose
That fills the air with scent
And never says a word!

Well, yes. If only it had been as simply as that! But neither D'Arcy's sincerity nor his faith in a tutelary Providence saved him from falling into such triteness. His Satires at least had an edge to them. I tried to convince D'Arcy that none of the English poets he admired had written quite like any other, and that there were good reasons for that. His answer, in a letter written five weeks before his death, was a voluminous denial, with this conclusion: 'The poetical utterance, I say, has had an almost identical likeness for nearly 3,000 years, until suddenly, at the beginning of this century (earlier in France) we hear the cry: "A New Poetry! A New Art! Everything is to be changed. Everything different! — A complete reversal, in fact: for music, discord; for beauty, ugliness; for meaning, nonsense; for order & measure, confusion; for spirit, mere mind, etc. etc." It is, of course, the counterpart in art of the mad race for novelty and sensation which is apparent in everything now. And the only cure of it the rediscovery of divinity in Nature & its reflection in art ...'

I am glad that I got to know D'Arcy Cresswell and was able to give him a little companionship and encouragement in that lonely last decade of his life. Yet I could do nothing to change the course of the Providence that had forsaken him and his works. Since I could never give him what he really needed, enough affection, enough approval, enough support, it might have been better for him if we had never met.

When he offered a visit on February 16th 1960, and proposed calling on me at the University, I had to tell him that I could not see him there that day. Four days later he was dead.

Again and again we had come up against a barrier of sheer incompatibility, beginning in 1949, when I had introduced John Pettavel to him at his cottage, and he wrote on a postcard from Liverpool: 'I like your friend, more than I could wish you to like mine', simply assuming that other people shared his inclinations; or when he insisted on reading out his embarrassingly solemn elegy on the death of the first of his alsatian bitches, Kass, to us at our house, telling my wife to listen attentively and get on with her embroidery! The death of the same carnivorous animal turned D'Arcy into a vegetarian, though he wrote that his new diet made him ill. The mental and emotional processes that led to this resolution were as peculiar to D'Arcy as the motives behind everything else he did to damage himself; and it was useless to argue with him. For some twenty years after D'Arcy's death I corresponded sporadically with Helen Shaw, who edited two books of his letters in New Zealand. Not till after her death, when her husband sent me a book of her poems, did I know that she was a poet in her own right, and a true one, less opinionated and less quirky than D'Arcy, but the better for that. She had never drawn my attention to her own work, and it had not come my way.

D'Arcy Cresswell was mild and amenable compared to another poet I knew in those years. During one of my army leaves Fred Marnau had introduced me to the German poet Peter Höfler, who wrote under the pseudonym Jesse Thoor. Since Höfler had ceased to write letters at this period, just as he would not use the telephone, I lost touch with him until I returned to London and looked him up again in the one room he shared with his wife and used as a workshop for his gold and silver artefacts. D'Arcy was short, slight and birdlike, though wiry and athletic. Peter Höfler was even shorter, but broad-shouldered, with abnormal strength in his arms. His features, dominated by a domed forehead, were strangely reminiscent of William Blake. Like Blake, too, Höfler was a visionary, on intimate terms with spirits who might address him or appear to him when we were walking on Primrose Hill; and his invective, too, was as fierce and demotic as Blake's.

Peter Karl Höfler was born in Berlin in 1905, of Austrian parents who had settled there shortly before his birth, but returned to Austria briefly during Peter's childhood. His father was a carpenter. Peter Höfler decided to train as a dental technician, but broke off the training to work in a great variety of trades and crafts, always with intervals of tramping. He tramped to Bavaria and Austria, to Northern Italy and to Hungary. He tried to stow away on a ship, but was discovered in a coil of rope under a tarpaulin. Later, he was allowed to join the crew of another ship not as a sailor but as an entertainer — the German word 'Thoor' means 'fool', and one of Höfler's rôles, right up to his death, was that of the jester. He got as far as Spain, and lived for a time in Rotterdam with a prostitute. In a pub brawl there he received a serious stab wound in his chest. Earlier on he had been consumptive, but recovered his health and strength on his travels.

He returned to Berlin with no money, only a sack of coffee beans. There he fell in with a group of proletarian writers and artists, predominantly Communist or Anarchist. At this period he also began to model, becoming skilled enough as a portraitist to receive quite a few commissions in later years. There was hardly a manual skill — from the roughest to the most delicate — that Höfler did not master. He joined the Communist Party and was active in groups that resisted National Socialism. After several narrow escapes he had to leave Germany for Austria early in 1933. His mother had died in 1932. His father was often out of work and addicted to the bottle. An Austrian aunt sent him money saved from her wages as a maid-servant, and looked after him when he moved to Vienna, where he worked as a carpenter, portraitist and silversmith. He could also get odd jobs as a tailor or cobbler. He had begun to write poems and stories in Germany, but published no book. As soon as he had made a little money in one way or another, he would give up his job to write. In 1935 he was able to read some of his poems over the Austrian Radio. He had some success as a writer and reader of his works in Switzerland, where he visited Thomas Mann and Hermann Hesse in 1936 or 1937.

In March 1938 he was on the run again from the Gestapo, with money sewn into his shirt collar by his aunt, and managed to get to Czechoslovakia. His manuscripts and typewriter had to be left behind in Vienna, and he did not see his prose works again until after the war, when he had changed so much as to have no more use for them. He did a portrait bust of President Beneš, and was helped by a Czech lady, who put him up for a time when he was tired of sharing lodgings with fellow Communists and was beginning to be rejected by the Party as a deviationist.

Höfler had sent some of his poems to Prince Hubertus zu Löwenstein, General Secretary of the American Guild for Cultural Freedom. Recommendations by Thomas Mann, Franz Werfel and Alfred Neumann won him a grant that reached him just before the German invasion. He got out on one of the last planes to leave for London, with a permit obtained for him by the Prince.

Höfler had been brought up as a Catholic. In his London years he became a Christian again, though an unorthodox one. In spite of continued grants he wanted to earn his living as a craftsman, asking his aunt to send him the tools he had left in Vienna. 'And, besides,' he wrote to her, 'language is nothing more than a means of communication — but not a means of making money or getting on in the world. That's something one should do with a plane, with a plough, through material.' He could not get used to England and never learnt to speak the language with any fluency. He married a fellow refugee from Vienna in 1939. A number of his sonnets was published in a magazine edited by Thomas Mann, but Höfler was no longer interested in literary recognition. Towards the end of his life he refused on principle to publish any of his work in periodicals. He did a head of Chamberlain, describing it as a 'caricature'. At that period he lived in Chancery Lane, Parton Street and Great Ormond Street. Shortly before the war he wanted to emigrate again, to the South of France, to feel closer to his friends on the continent. As he wrote in letters at the time, he could not get over the events of 1938: 'What Czechoslovakia injected into me, I try and try, but can't get it out of my head ... The fact is, I'm completely confused now. This damnable mistrust, that eats deeper and deeper into one after such experiences!'

This mistrust became little less than paranoia after Höfler had been denounced by the Communists as a Nazi and interned in Devon immediately after the outbreak of war. Although freed after two months at the intervention of the Archbishop of Canterbury, he was interned again, on the Isle of Man, in 1940.

Attempts by his friends, after his release, to get him a regular job as a gold and silver smith were frustrated by Höfler's obstinate refusal to work for any employer. He did accept commissions from a London goldsmith, but would not work anywhere but at home, the two-roomed flat in Hampstead, of which one room had to be permanently sub-let. His wife had to work as a cook in a boarding-house, though her health was poor. They might have managed financially if Höfler had not insisted on giving away many of the artefacts he produced — silver chalices to churches, symbolic golden flowers to friends. When he was living on horse-meat in 1951, he made my wife's wedding ring and, far from allowing me to pay for the gold, bought us another present as well.

One difficulty in my relations with Peter Höfler was that he would not make appointments but would suddenly appear at my mother's house, until 1950, or at my flat, and expect to be welcome, regardless of what I was doing or of who else was there. What was more, he made no effort to relate conventionally to other people, whether it was my girl friend, Monica, or one of my literary friends, but responded vehemently to their aura, which was far more likely to be diabolic than angelic. For one thing, Höfler's conversion had by no means palliated his earlier prejudice against the bourgeoisie and bourgeois attitudes of mind. At a dinner party to which he was invited before the war, when the British literary establishment was making a few gestures of recognition towards him as a political refugee, Stephen Spender was a fellow guest. Whenever I mentioned Spender's name to Höfler, he would tell me that Spender was no poet but a bourgeois, because at that dinner party he had seen Spender absent-mindedly crumble up his bread. A man who despised and wasted matter — and in the sacred form of bread — was simply unmentionable, all the more so when everything material had assumed a symbolic significance for Höfler. If the aura of a person was evil or wrong, Höfler made no bones about saying so to his or her face. This made every call of Höfler's an ambiguous pleasure if I was not alone. Had I ever turned him away he would not have forgiven me, and I should have contributed to the terrible crises that followed every imagined rejection of him by other people.

Neither I nor our friend Alfred Marnau was exempt from his imprecations. I think it was at an early meeting, during the war, that he stopped dead in the street, when he and I were walking near Primrose Hill, to curse Fred Marnau for having stolen his thoughts and visions, using them for his own poems. As for me, I too was a bourgeois intellectual, living not by manual work but by my wits. When I gave Höfler my first book of poems in 1950 he placed his hands on the book, never opened it, and told me the poems were no good. Books too emitted vibrations by which they could be judged as surely and immediately as faces. When I asked Höfler why the poems were no good, he told me why they couldn't be: because I hadn't paid for them with experience like his own, hadn't earned the words I used. 'You're no flowering cactus,' he said taking the title of the book to be a characterization of myself, which it wasn't meant to be. The judgement didn't offend me. I knew that Höfler didn't read more than a few indispensable books, didn't need to, and certainly didn't need to read mine — quite apart from the language barrier. On another occasion Höfler wanted to see the family photographs I kept. He approved of my great-grandparents' faces, or some of them, but said that there had been a progressive deterioration in character after them — perhaps because my forebears had moved from villages or small towns to the larger cities and become more bourgeois.

His paranoia came out when some welfare organization for refugees sent a representative to his room with a name like Nieman, which he associated with the German word 'niemand', nobody. 'It's come to that,' he raged when I saw him soon after; 'They've sent me Nobody; Nobody has been visited upon me.' Such outbursts could end as suddenly as they began. Höfler would then fall back into the jester's role, smiling mischievously not so much at himself as at the demons his curses had exorcised before they could make a fool of him.

Höfler was well disposed towards my uncle Alfred, who couldn't be accused of being a bourgeois and was earning his living by a manual skill, but he had no use for most of my friends. Once I got him an invitation to a dinner party in Kensington, at the house of a German painter married to an Englishwoman. Over dinner the painter began to criticize England and the English in a way that Höfler felt to be insulting to the painter's wife and to the country that had given hospitality to both the painter and himself. Höfler objected so violently that everyone was reduced to silence. After dinner he did a quick round of the painter's pictures on the walls and said they were wretchedly bad. Then he walked out, and would never have anything more to do with that painter.

The worst of the crises I witnessed occurred when Höfler had gone to Russell Square to present T. S. Eliot with a golden flower he had made for him and ask Eliot to buy him a ship, so that he could spend the rest of his life sailing the seas and never settle again on land. His rudimentary English must have been an obstacle on this occasion. In any case, he was turned away by a secretary and never saw Eliot. This incident shattered Höfler for days. A symbolic offering had been refused, by one who called himself a Christian poet. This mattered more than the frustration of Höfler's project. The forces of evil had triumphed again, another seemingly great man revealed himself to be a fraud. Eliot, needless to say, was unmentionable after that.

Höfler's only book to be published in his lifetime, a collection of sonnets, appeared in Germany in 1948. In the previous year he had sent some of them to Prince Hubertus, and was invited to return to Germany. Three brief visits to various parts of Germany could not induce him to settle there again. From a fourth visit, unannounced as usual, to the Prince's Bavarian home when he happened to be away, and the symbolic offering could not be delivered, Höfler returned in a state of mind similar to that after the call on Eliot. He never revisited Berlin or his father and brother, and ignored or rejected every literary opening that presented itself after the publication of his book. In 1951 he left again for Switzerland, intending to go on to Austria, but returned after a brief absence. In the summer of 1952 he suffered a serious coronary thrombosis. His condition improved in hospital, although he refused to stay in bed and entertained his fellow patients with gymnastic feats and mimes. When he was sent home, with strict instructions to rest and avoid every sort of physical exertion, he bought a single ticket to Lienz in Austria, where he was to stay with friends and meet his aunt Josefine from Vienna. Shortly after his arrival at Matrei, near Lienz, he went on a mountain walk with his friends, and collapsed on his way to the bus stop to meet his aunt. She nursed him for another four days. Then he was taken to hospital at Lienz, where he died two hours after his admission, on August 15th, at the age of forty-seven.

My association with Peter Höfler was something other than a friendship. I could not relax with him or talk with him about trivial things. To associate with him was a favour and an ordeal. At first, not knowing what he might say to anyone he found in my company, I was nervous about his unexpected calls, and that nervousness provoked him, since he disliked the sensitive bourgeois ego's need for protective fences and walls. Later, as I began to demolish those fences and walls, I was conscious only of the uniqueness of a man who had learnt long ago to be totally disinterested, totally exposed. 'He lived a metaphor', I wrote in the sonnet sequence 'A Wreath of Thistles' — the last sonnets I was to write — about an absoluteness in him that made his life seem different from anyone else's, a quality that obsessed me when his visits had ceased and I remembered little of what he had said to me. A decade after his death I began to edit his works and collect material for a biographical introduction, a quest that took me from Höfler's grave in Lienz to his aunt in Vienna, and led her to make the first air journey in her life, at the age of eighty-six, to stay with us in England. That association, too, interwove with the legend, since Josefine Matschl had much in common with her nephew. She died a day or two before her ninetieth birthday, killed by the gas heater — also the first in her life — which friends had installed in the same room she had once shared with Höfler. Like him, she had roughed it, learning to live without heating through Austrian winters. Unlike him, she remained unembittered, undivided and unconfused, as strong and generous as he had been before 1938.

Early in 1950 I moved into a one-room flatlet at the White House, on the corner of Randolph Crescent and Randolph Avenue. The latter had had to be re-named, because it was the refuge of prostitutes who had passed their prime and could no longer afford the West End. More than one of them had been murdered there, and I often heard screams and yells reminiscent of my first home in Berlin. Those elderly prostitutes solicited in the street. When they got to know me not as a customer but a neighbour, conventional greetings were the rule — extended to my wife, too, when she came to live there. The house itself was respectable, shared with a painter and a photographer, among others. An even more respectable maiden lady with whom I shared a bathroom was the only source of conflict. She didn't like sharing a bath-tub with a man, and bombarded me with notes telling me to scrub it.

If I had to live in London — and I did, at the time, to scrape the barest of livings — the fallen gentility of Maida Vale suited me well enough. Little Venice might be a euphemism, but the Canal was water of a sort, with a reflecting surface that made me write a poem, as did the elderly prostitutes in the street. A good many friends lived within easy walking distance, in St. John's Wood and Hampstead, and on my walks I could explore the many bombed sites in those parts, with their interesting vegetation and bird life. In the slum area on the Paddington side of the Canal, soon to be 're-developed', Lucian Freud had a studio. D'Arcy Cresswell lived in Abercorn Place, both John Pettavel and John Minton in Hamilton Terrace. Family gatherings continued at my mother's house, only a few streets away. My grandmother had died in Bedfordshire while I was abroad, but my uncle Alfred — who had forbidden me to insult him by calling him 'Uncle' — became a friend until his death.

My girl friend Monica, a former art student whom I had met soon after my return to civilian life at the Chelsea house of my army friend Geoffrey Wickham, had returned to London after teaching in Nottingham. We had met there, at Oxford, or in London as often as we could, but in 1950 the relationship became strained, mainly because I was still too unsettled for the kind of domesticity she envisaged. The relationship hadn't been easy from the start, if only because we never lived together, and there were hesitations on both sides. We made love where and when we could, with the same distance to be covered again and again, after every separation, the same obstructions to be overcome or evaded.

In the Spring of 1950 I made my way to Sicily. Through my mother's social work for the Quakers I had met the Austrian poet Felix Braun, who lived with his sister and very old stepmother off Maida Vale. Felix Braun, who had once been a professor at the University of Palermo, recommended me as a possible successor, and, though I was by no means sure that I wanted such a job, the possibility of it gave me a good pretext for another trip. Felix Braun had been associated with Hofmannsthal and Rilke. He introduced me to a great variety of people, including Countess Nora Wydenbruck — a niece of Rilke's patron, Princess Marie, and translator both of Rilke into English and Eliot into German — and her husband Alfons Purtscher, to Ellen Delp, another correspondent of Rilke's, and Erica Marx, who was to publish my first two collections of poems in her small press at Aldington, Kent. For the trip, Felix Braun also provided a recommendation to the Baronessa Burgio in Palermo, who gave me hospitality there and forwarded the letters that followed me around from Paris to Taormina.

I must have got to know Felix Braun and his family on one of my army leaves, for he first wrote to me when I was serving in Austria, the country with which he remained identified and to which he was to return as soon as he could, that very year, to spend his old age as very nearly the last representative of an Austrian traditionalism that had become questionable long before the *Anschluss* and his emigration. Born in 1885, he belonged to the generation of the innovators, Kafka and the Expressionists, but was not one of them. As a devout Roman Catholic, though of Jewish descent, he embraced the cultural conservatism of his mentor and model Hofmannsthal. On our last meeting in London before his resettlement — we were to meet again there when he returned to lecture on Grillparzer — he took me to the National Gallery and made religious paintings the pretext for a gentle catechising. A demon of mischief induced me to shock him by pretending that I thought that the Trinity consisted of the Father, Son and Virgin Mary — which happened to be what many of those Italian paintings could have led a heathen to infer, for reasons that have less to do with doctrine than with the limitations of representational art.

Lovable though he was, I could not help hurting or shocking Felix Braun repeatedly in the course of a friendship that lasted up to his death some twenty-five years later. Because he believed that art is timeless, and that poetry is a gift of grace, he approved and praised my early verse, but grieved when I had fallen into what to him was the heresy of modernism. His anti-modernism, though, was not cranky or militant, as D'Arcy Cresswell's was. Religiously, gently, magnanimously and immovably, he assumed that he could and must write historical blank verse tragedies in the manner less of Hofmannsthal than Grillparzer, who was born in 1791, and lyrics in a diction uncontaminated by allusions to temporal experience. Unlike Cresswell, too, he did his best to appreciate the work of T. S. Eliot and Auden, both of whom he knew and respected, but could give whole-hearted assent only to the choruses in *Murder in the Cathedral* and a few of Auden's more derivative lyrics, also shocked once more by the ravages he read in Auden's cracked and corrugated face.

Uncharacteristically, too, Felix Braun was deeply hurt when he found no poem of his in the anthology *Modern German Poetry* which I co-edited with Christopher Middleton in the early 'sixties. The word 'modern' in the title alone explained the omission, as did that of Hofmannsthal's poems in the same anthology. Felix Braun knew that in those very years I was translating and editing Hofmannsthal, since my Hofmannsthal researches had taken me to Vienna; and he must have known in his heart that personal affections and loyalties were one thing, artistic criteria another. He was hurt because, for that anthology, we had made modernity or innovation our touchstone, confirming that I was now of the devil's party.

Neither could his own generous responses to persons be consistent with his artistic criteria. That is how through him I first came across the work of Paul Celan, a poet still more alien to his canon from the start than mine became. On one of my visits to Greville Place, Felix Braun showed me a bundle of typescripts received from a young poet who had just escaped from Romania to Vienna, wondering whether I could make anything of those bizarre poems, including the 'Todesfuge', which had not yet appeared in book form. Impressed though I was by that first glimpse, I did not take the scripts away or ask for the poet's address. I was to meet Celan a year or so later when he read from his work at the London house of Erich Fried.

At his Grillparzer lecture, in English, Felix Braun perpetrated a memorable mistranslation that inflicted agonies of suppressed laughter not only on me, but on the doyen of German studies in Britain, Professor L. A. Willoughby, who had to kick me when he saw my contorted efforts to contain it. With high pathos — heart-felt, because it was his own — Felix Braun spoke of the Viennese public's rejection of one of Grillparzer's later plays, his bitter old age and resolve not to offer his last plays for performance. These, Felix Braun concluded, were discovered only after his death 'in the drawers of his secretary'. (In German, the 'Sekretär' that is a writing-desk is masculine in gender, at least; but it is the innocence of the man that made the double ambiguity possible, and the natural response to it a coarse and cruel one, to be avoided at all costs.)

In later years, when, in his eighties, Felix Braun was a lonely survivor in Vienna, he reported visits from Ernst Jandl and Friederike Mayröcker, puzzled once more by their outrageous ways with words, but delighted with their company. For their part, they were drawn to him by his incorruptible innocence and constancy, qualities that have become rarer still than literary distinction; and qualities that did amount to literary distinction in him, just because they made so much of Felix Braun's writings utterly anachronistic, and he knew that, too, but would not budge from what to him was the good, the true and the beautiful, in art as in life.

It was by the prompting and under the aegis of this man that I set out on another journey, though it would not and could not take me to the destination he had in mind for me, only on another search for the unknown one that might eventually prove to be mine. I don't know what induced me even to consider a professorship at that stage, in a region that attracted me but would have left me bewildered and displaced once more. I suspect that it was never more than an excuse for more adventures, and for putting off the decisions and commitments I was not ready for, when my danger had long been to make duties out of inclinations and impulses, turning them into compulsions or routines which I then had to break. Aimless travelling was my therapy at that stage in my life.

This time I didn't stop in Paris, but took the Rome Express from Calais. 'How literature dogs me!' I noted even about that train journey. A lady from London insisted on hearing all about me and the purpose of my trip. This conversation, which took place in the corridor, where I had fled to avoid it, was overheard by a gentleman in the next compartment, who turned out to be Count Umberto Morra, soon to be Director of the Italian Institute in London, a friend of Princess Caetani, editor of the international literary magazine *Botteghe Oscure*, and of my friend Hermon Ould. In the compartment from which I had fled, a lady from South America was reading *The Cocktail Party.* Umberto Morra not only drew me out of conversation with the persistent Londoner into conversation with him, but invited me to stop in Rome on my way back from Sicily, introduced me to more literary personages there, and became a good friend for many years. It was not he, but the Portuguese poet Alberto de Lacerda who told me that Umberto Morra was an illegitimate son of the last king of Italy.

'Spent about two hours walking about in Rome. Then train to Taormina. After Rome the journey ceased to be lively. Conversations with Sicilians on train. The women at Villa San Giovanni: bright clothes, heavy sacks on their heads.'

I arrived at Taormina on May 5th. 'Weather still gloomy, cold and wet. Went to post office to post some letters. Next to me stood André Gide (pointed hat, plus-fours). Can't get away from literature. Found place: Pensione Villa Valverde. Only guest. Too tired to write more.' When I gaped at him incredulously, and he knew he had been recognized, André Gide invited me to call on him at his hotel, the 'Timeo'. I did call next morning and was taken to his rooms by his chauffeur. He received me graciously, inscribed a copy of his latest *Journal* (1942–1949) for me, and said he hoped we should meet again.

'Went to Giardino Pubblico and ruined church of San Domenico. Lunched at my pensione, was served "nespole" (new medlars) and the padrone's political views. Wishes that the Germans had won the war; at the same time hates Americans who, he says, planned the last war (here Communist propaganda has fused with Fascist). Went swimming at Isola Bella. Finished translating first scene of (Büchner's) *Leonce & Lena*. In the evening met a Sicilian waiter who had already acted as guide in the morning. I wanted to buy a bottle of wine. He took me to a place where it would be cheaper by a hundred lire — the usual approach. The wine cost 120 lire a litre. I paid 280 for it, because the Sicilian ordered about a litre and a half to be drunk all round at my expense. It was worth it. Anecdotes. Story of his affair with Viennese girl, a guest at the hotel he worked at, who found she was pregnant when he had gone to Verona. Story of overturned cart. A bit drunk when I left.'

May 7th: 'Can't sleep after dawn — a chorus of crowing cocks, accompanied by nightingales. One of these sang nearby & sounded strangely raucous, almost unpleasant; but can see the moon reflected in the sea by sitting up in bed — then the lovely moment when dawn merges in moonlight. Snow on the top of Etna.

'Yesterday heard girl sing Sicilian song. When she saw me, changed to Auld Lang Syne. Alas for tourism, which has quite corrupted this place, turning the whole population into parasites.

'Intoxicating scent of flowers in public garden and that of the "Timeo". Even in the streets, though there it mingles with that of sardines & other things not so savoury. Spent morning on beach (Mazzarò) & stayed too long; horribly sunburnt now.

'Evening: conversation with American. Incredible cult of success, in every possible shape. Money sanctifies vulgarity and greed. His sophistries; but when challenged said that in the ideal state some are bound to starve. God, he said, intended that it should be so. I envy him his intimate acquaintance with God, but suspect he's got him mixed up with Ford.

'This morning talked to Germans on beach. Never, I'm sure, has Europe been so deeply split or people so proud of being unable to see beyond the tips of their noses. Here one can see Europe in miniature. It doesn't look very promising.'

May 8th: 'Walked up to Castel Mola, a village full of atrocious hovels like rabbit hutches. In the only café they keep a register signed by everyone who's been in the area — the attraction of high & inaccessible places. A few stones scattered about there & on another hill are described as historic ruins. That draws them. And there's the view, of course, which transforms the countryside into a sort of contour map. What compensated me for the arduous climb in the heat was the incidentals — it's always the incidentals that are worthwhile. A very fat woman riding up on a donkey, her backside quite smothering the poor little animal. A slender black snake hunting lizards: its agility and grace. A little boy who gave me a bunch of wildflowers —

one of the few spontaneous acts of giving, rather than taking, I've come across in Italy. The lovely clover blossom — deep red and purple. The school at Mola — absolutely nothing was being taught.'

May 9th: 'Ran into André Gide again, at the bank. Shook hands & exchanged a few meaningless words about travellers' cheques. Looks much less than his age, but it shows in his weariness and distraction.

'Spent most of the morning working on *Leonce*. Finished Act I.

'Went swimming in afternoon — a rather idiotic pastime, especially when it consists in lying on the beach all day, as most of the addicts seem to do. They even stay at a hotel on the beach — which might be anywhere — & rarely go into the water. An American girl on the beach.' (I was to write the short story 'Genia' about her.) 'Can't imagine the Greeks — or Elizabethans for that matter — tanning their bodies all day.

'The difficulty of writing letters or only postcards here. So far away from everything. Anything I put down is a lie — because at the moment I'm a different person, perhaps not a person at all, since my usual preoccupations have simply fallen away. A person is what he wants to do — and here I don't want to do anything in particular.'

May 10th (more about the American girl). Then: 'Meanwhile André Gide was on the terrace (of the beach hotel to which he had moved meanwhile), lunched there & retired to a room after lunch. Later as I passed, he emerged, and after him a Sicilian boy of about thirteen.

'The countryside at Sant' Antonio (past the cemetery). Harmony of wild and cultivated vegetation. Then the woman coming up the steep track with a heavy basket on her head. But what's the use of describing scenery, or anything beautiful for that matter. There may be such a thing as beautiful words, but they have little connection with anything they pretend to describe.'

May 11th: (more about the American girl). 'How D. H. Lawrence would have hated his spiritual progeny! It's more numerous here than he could have dreamed.'

May 12th: 'Changed plot of the Don Juan play' (which I was writing at the time. Unpublished. Unperformed. Scrapped). 'Instead of the scene with Weatherston at the end, he must meet his feminine counterpart — who disgusts him so much, he's cured for good. In any case the play should be a comedy. Dialogue to be completely rewritten: less theorizing &, if possible, fewer commonplaces. No need for realism. More wit, more extravagance in the dialogue — perhaps even a little concealed poetry. Or shall I write the play in verse? Tragedy is done for, anyway: we no longer have the right to take ourselves seriously. Perhaps poetic comedy, or even poetic farce, is the answer. *On verra.*

> *Nichts ist schwerer zu ertragen*
> *Als eine Reihe von schönen Tagen.*
>
> (Nothing's more difficult to bear
> Than a succession of days all fair. — *Goethe.*)

Perhaps I should leave Taormina. I'm going to sleep, & the Muse hasn't stirred once. Probably she's basking on the beach or resting in the shade of an olive tree at Sant' Antonio. Unless she's chosen one of those tall cypresses in the cemetery. I shouldn't blame her.

'The damned familiarity of the Sicilians here. Either one has to keep them completely at a distance, treat them as "natives", or they call you "tu" before you know where you are, tell you about their love affairs, want to know about yours, pester you in various ways, try to sell you things, etc. Shall have to avoid talking to them, wrap myself up in a false "hauteur".'

May 13th: 'Went to Syracuse by coach to see Euripides: *Bacchantes* in Greek theatre. The thing was picturesque, but couldn't understand more than a few words. Spent most of the day in the coach. Saw a little of Catania & don't want to see any more. The gigantic church & the doves in the cloisters; a bird chirping somewhere in the building. The university. Ragged bunch of students. Catania very much like Naples or any large town in the South.

'In Syracuse, liked the cord-makers' cave, part of the Greek quarries. It has a fairy-tale charm — green & damp & quite unreal. Lovely setting for a romantic play or a film. The same is true of Dionysius's Ear, though it's much more sinister. Then there's the Latonia del Paradiso, really like Eden, especially as the man who showed us round (the Wilsons & myself) picked all the best flowers & presented them to Mrs. W. — also invited us to eat *nespole* off the tree. Didn't see the serpent though, & without it Eden is incomplete. Passed some fine baroque buildings in a town on the way. Saw a little of Syracuse, where I wanted to stop a few days but couldn't. All the hotels are full because of the plays, which are the equivalent of a race meeting or Cup Final in England. Never seen so many cars & carriages lined up in one place in

Italy. The theatre was packed — & it must hold several thousand people. Got back at 1 a.m. feeling sick.'

May 14th: 'How difficult to find a silent & solitary place in Italy out of doors, I mean. Even here, at Taormina, I was about to write that I'd found one — at Sant' Antonio — when there was a hell of a noise behind me and a man leading a donkey came down the track. Now it's begun to rain, just as I was about to fall into a poetic reverie. The donkey's gone, & I've found a pretty sheltered place. At night I'm tormented by mosquitoes, in the mornings by flies, when I've already been woken up by a wireless set, a screaming child, a shouting man & woman ... at this moment the man is yelling at his donkey, and the rain has penetrated the almond tree I'm sitting under. There's something about the air in Italy that carries sounds and smells much farther than the air elsewhere. Of course the Italians are more productive of noise as well, they love the sound of their own voices (literally), and the theatrical gesture.

'Talked to Werner in the evening. An extraordinary situation to be in — no profession, no income & no country of one's own. Says that when his money runs out (when he's sold the last of his possessions) he'll kill himself. Can't imagine how anyone could choose to spend his whole life at Taormina, unless he belonged there. Must find out what the attachment is. Does the beauty of the place sustain him? Or is it a habit now?'

May 15th: 'Worked on last act of *Leonce*, then went swimming at Mazzarò. Lunched there with the Wilsons, who've been most kind to me (brought me cold turkey yesterday). After lunch sat down to write letters, when Gide's daughter — who arrived with her husband, Jean Lambert, two days ago — asked me to join them for a drive to Etna, at Gide's suggestion. Went off at once. Weather was bad, rainy, but that went well with the scenery around Etna, the black lava beds, the woods & rocky mountains. A volcano, after all isn't a pretty thing, whatever the picture postcards make out. The strange birds there, grey and white; the flowers, wild pansies & asphodel. Gide's interest in the things we passed on the way, especially flowers, & his knowledge of them. Our conversation about Hölderlin. My rudeness in contradicting him when he made mistakes — "daisy" for "pansy", Hölderlin's references to Sicily in *Hyperion*, etc. But what's the point of conversation in which one agrees with the other man's mistakes? Too many conversations are like that. The Sicilian carts & their legends: Othello, Geneviève de Brabant, St. George and the dragon. Gide telling the driver to stop, & looking at them; wanting us to pick flowers he hadn't seen (bushy, yellow, sweet-scented). His delightful animation & good humour.

'Tea at the hotel. Then the view from there & the Sicilian songs we heard in the valley below — quite Arabic. The rising temperature as we came down, & the cold above. Jean Lambert silent, reserved, perhaps out of respect for Gide. Translates from the German. His wife, her quick response to everything (like Gide's), her candour.'

May 16th: 'Rain, rain, rain. & how it splashes. At Mazzarò for a short time this morning, but didn't swim. Talked to Wilsons. Gave proof of poem (*A Poet's Progress*, received this morning from *Penguin New Writing*) to Gide's daughter, who wanted to see something I've written. Reading Gide's *Journal*.

'Low clouds; on the rooftops even — or so it seems from the window.

'*Leonce & Lena* nearly finished. Realized it'll never be performed in England, because there are too many characters. Still, the great thing is to work, if only at a translation.

'Had tea with Werner. Listened to his gramophone records, which he's had for about 25 years. Richard Strauss's *Morgen*, which he says was composed here, fascinates me. Like most of Strauss it's emotionally shoddy — but a *tour de force*. What interests me is that the song manages to convey exactly the opposite of what the words say: the words say "tomorrow", the music says "never again". This isn't really a contradiction, because the moment when beauty is perceived is also the moment when it's lost — & nothing is ever the same again. That's why "tomorrow" is nonsense & "never again" is true. The music is right.

'Went to San Domenico garden after the rain. Quite drunk with the scent — there were roses, arum lilies, forget-me-nots, various sorts of begonia (but they don't smell), geraniums of many kinds (with a harsh, almost bitter smell) & those enormous white hanging flowers which Gide calls "trumpets of Jericho" (datura). They're poisonous, he says, but their scent is exquisite. Many unfamiliar plants, especially creepers; one kind is deep purple, a bit sinister but attractive (bougainvillea).'

May 17th: 'The solitary white pheasant (white, red & black) in the public gardens; very old, they say, & quite apathetic. It stands on one leg, & looks. If you put your fingers through the meshes it pecks viciously. No wonder. (So should I, if I'd been locked up alone for years.) Next to it, two fine peacocks — no hen either. Typical of the Italians' unthinking cruelty to animals. Heard one scream today. A horrible sound. But they have two cries, a low-pitched, mournful one, & a scream.

'Saw a creature like a chameleon today. Saw it only for a second but it seemed quite different from lizards. My first impression was, a dragon in miniature. Exactly the colour of the wall it sat on (near Mazzarò), but it flicked into a hole before I could see it well.

'Tonight there's a performance of Sicilian songs & dances in the Greek theatre. The singers & dancers are using my *pensione* as a changing room. Have already heard one magnificent dance played on a Sicilian pipe, guitar & tambourine. It made one dance inwardly.

'Chatted with Lamberts at Mazzarò. Apparently both they & Gide like my poem, Gide being reminded of Rilke; but of course one can't tell what they really thought of it.

'I was right about those little reptiles. Tonight — coming home after the show at the Greek theatre, which was nearly as good as the informal rehearsal here — I nearly trod on one on the stairs. It's certainly not an ordinary lizard — more like a chameleon. It changes colour. I caught it & tried it out. It's a baby one, & has large black eyes, quite different from a lizard's; a shorter, broader body.

'The Greek theatre is much larger than it seemed when I first saw it. Not till it's used does one get an idea of its capacity.'

May 18th: 'My "chameleon" turns out to be a gecko — so Mme. Lambert tells me. Gide was delighted with it. It's quite tame now, & I took it down to Mazzarò this morning on my hand. Now I've brought it back, & it's sitting on a saucer in my room. It's eyes have turned white, with a black pin-point in the middle.

'Ate sea-urchins today on the beach, to supplement my daily diet of bread, olives & wine — all I can afford if my stay is not to be cut short. Really it was their roe — at least that's what the interior looks like once it's been cleared of waste. Stomach & reproductive organs — that's all they are, like many human urchins I've met.

'Started a poem at last.

'Showed the Lamberts the public garden & San Domenico garden.

'The Wilsons are leaving tomorrow. Extraordinary how possessive people can become in next to no time: they want to give me things, & are quite jealous of anyone else I see. They're very kind. But there's no defence against kindness. It's the most effective of tyrannies — at least with people like me, so terrified of hurting anyone.

'The deaf-mute I met drinking in the wine store followed me as I went home tonight at about 11.20. He stood at the bottom of the steps leading up to the pensione & produced a ghastly sort of sound. I didn't stop. When I opened the window of my room he was standing outside. Went down & made him write down what he wanted. It was to go drinking with him again.

'Met an American novelist called Windham, who was with Gide today at lunch-time. Have seen him around before with Truman Capote, who's also living here.'

May 19th: 'An uneventful day. Said goodbye to Wilsons, who invited me to stay with them in Staffordshire. G. W. tells me that I "get through my friends like ..." gloves, I suppose he said. But that's because they took me to be a waif who needs to be adopted; & that's the last thing I want.

'Nothing seems to have happened. A bad day, one of those on which I don't quite wake up. Stayed too long in the sun, as usual, & felt rather ill. Poem hasn't progressed much — trickled painfully, like an espresso, drop by drop, line by line. Seem to have lost ability to concentrate — or only facility? A loss, due to book reviewing, journalism, which violate the faculties? Other forms of corruption too — the dismembering process in general, adaptation to "reality" as though one knew what reality is. Or will the product be more concentrated, because the resistance is greater?'

May 20th: 'At Sant' Antonio. Saw a large glossy black snake. Shot away as I came down the path.

'A strange sound in the shrubs. Like twigs burning, a gentle crackling. Could it be locusts feeding? But I didn't see any.

'Spending the morning in Taormina & surroundings. Sick of Mazzarò, oiling, salting, roasting the body, with no other result than raw red skin & sickness. Also, the sun hates thought & burns it up.

'Talked to Donald Windham & two local boys tonight. Telling us stories about Taormina — scandal. A good many strange things go on here, though one would never think so. No moral code here — for men. They can do whatever they like, as long as they don't "dishonour" a girl & get caught, in which case relatives will be after them. The local adolescents go off regularly to Giardini or Giarre to visit brothels. Talk about this loudly in the street, like going to the dentist. Don't know whether the difference is entirely one between Catholicism & Protestantism. Northern Italians & French are more like people in

Protestant countries, with inhibitions about such things. Sicilians seem to be inhibited only by authority, not by conscience.'

May 21st: 'Done nothing, seen nothing, thought nothing. Spent most of the day at Mazzarò with Lamberts. Talked, played draughts, lunched off bread, olives, oranges. Sun getting too much for my skin & head.

'Poem doesn't progress.

'Gide is not well. Spends a great deal of time doing nothing — a bad sign, his daughter says. Hardly makes use of his car now, feels no wish to do anything, go anywhere. Nor, for that matter, do I. My state of mind, anywhere but here, could be described as one of the utmost boredom; but boredom, in Taormina, is so delicious a poison — like the datura's — that one hopes it will last for ever. That must be why Werner stays here, dying, dying, while that sickly song says tomorrow.'

May 22nd: 'Beginning to think of departure, which I can't very well put off. "Look your last ..."; but I can't raise that much sentiment. Instead, I've bought a litre of the most potent Sicilian white wine which is proving most effective.'

May 24th: 'A bad day yesterday. Woken up by flies after being kept awake by mosquitoes at night. Sleepy & bad-tempered all day; unable to do anything. Poem in a bad way: nothing but the opening lines remain. Getting expert at crossing out. Went to bed at nine ... Fireworks, because today is a fiesta.

'Letter from X. A literary crisis in England. 4 or 5 magazines have ceased publication.

'Went out in a boat with Lamberts. The sea was rough, though it's very hot & there's no wind. Strange.

'A man has come to see Gide about the mise-en-scène of *Les Caves du Vatican*, which G. is dramatizing. (How, I wonder.)

'Tea with Werner, listened to records of Brahms: 1st Symphony. During second movement his Sicilian girl friend (who works in a dressmaker's shop) walked in, embarrassed to find a stranger there. Called him "Signor Werner". He called her "tu". Gave her a collection of photographs taken during the German occupation, topmost a swastika flying over Taormina, the rest German officers & soldiers. Has always claimed to be a victim of the Nazis. Is he, was he? She couldn't stay long. When she'd gone, he said: "She's very fond of Germans." What's interesting about all this is the survival of the Nazi myth, after so much destruction in Germany. But a myth can't be killed, except by another myth. The Russians are supplying that. We (& the Americans) are not, & that keeps the old alive.

'Procession tonight. Little boys, little girls in white, the choristers, priests, image of Madonna with flowers: a little girl dressed as a cherub, with wings(!), sitting under the wax image. Old woman in black, singing. The brass band, various odd bodies, Boy Scouts, etc. All the girls & women carried candles in blue lanterns. Meanwhile those atrocious bombs are let off. Fireworks on the main piazza.'

May 25th: 'Sirocco — cloudy, little sunshine, but a moist oppressive heat. Almost regret my decision to stay a day or two longer, if this weather continues.

'Went up to Donald Windham's rooms in a disused hotel ("Belvedere"), which really does have a fine view. He has a large room, a bathroom & a terrace — the best thing about it. Wish I'd known of that place. A tree with orange coloured blossoms in the garden.

'After a horrible day, moonlit night with a cool wind blowing, the lights of the fishing boats on the water, and the harbour lights all around the coast. Can just see Etna in a haze.

'The family opposite. The woman yelling all day at the children. Then the man takes off his belt & beats them. A small boy leaves the house, sulking, & walks down the road. The woman follows & coaxes him back. More yelling, tears, protestations.'

May 26th: 'Swam out to the grotto. Detached some coral but lost it on the way back. Went out in a boat with Catherine Lambert, to a little creek. The sea was blue-green & quite transparent. Saw extraordinary fish, crabs, squids &, in a rock-pool, a soft creature like a giant slug. Prodded it, but it withdrew & we couldn't see it again. A splendid day, bright but not too hot. Don't want to leave now, but shall. Saw my third snake on the way down to Mazzarò.

'Said goodbye to Gide. May send him the poem later, if it ever gets finished. Said goodbye to all my acquaintances here.

'A strange night — hot and moonlit, with a few isolated clouds becalmed in the sky. Then, suddenly, a strong, cool breeze that sends everything flying, blows life into the town. Went to the Palmara with Windham. Strange place, American, without character; prices of drinks about five times what they are elsewhere.

'Don't feel like going to bed tonight. Last visit to Greek Theatre.'

From Taormina I made my way to Palermo, stopping briefly in Messina, a city that seemed robustly drab after Taormina, and resisting the temptation to stop in another imposing and alluring town, Cefalù, where Aleister Crowley had once established his Abbey of Thelema. In Palermo I had the usual trouble with accommodation, being 'taken for a ride' by the driver of a horse cab, only to end up in the station square from which we had set out, in a room 'like a cell'. When I opened the window I could almost touch an old couple living opposite and looked straight into their living-room. They were obviously used to it, never bothering to look up, but it embarrassed me. I had to move out next day, after trying in vain to do some writing by the dim, flickering lamplight in that room.

That day I called on Baronessa Burgio and her old mother. The Baroness made an appointment for me to see Professor Lavagnini about the professorship that had been my pretext for going to Sicily, though I had almost forgotten all about it by this time. He suggested a job in Catania but warned me that professors in Italy need a private income. Though I didn't think I should need one, the way I was used to living, and I was touched by his eagerness to help me, the whole idea of becoming a professor anywhere in Sicily seemed more and more fortuitous and absurd. That was the end of the matter, as far as I was concerned.

At the British Institute in Palermo I attended a lecture by Edwin Muir, was introduced to him and his wife Willa, and arranged to see them again in Rome, on my way back. Most of my days were divided between explorations of the city as such, including its slums, and visits to Monreale, the Capella Palatina, the Martorana, and my favourite place of refuge from the otherwise inescapable din of the city, the little church or mosque of San Giovanni degli Eremiti. On one occasion I went all the way out to Mondello, but found the flat coastline disappointing after Taormina. When I tried to swim there, all I could do was wade through seemingly endless stretches of shallow water.

One evening Giovanna Morello, Baroness Burgio's niece, took me to a puppet show, in a slum hovel full of little boys in rags. A man with a long stick tapped them on the head when they got too uproarious. 'Stories of the Paladins,' I noted, 'mixed up with magicians and devils. Beautiful knights in armour, an occasional Saracen or Moor. When one of them gets killed in a fight his body breaks in half. Puppets very expressive. A barrel-organ provides incidental music; & it's extraordinary how much variety of mood it can render, according to the speed at which the handle is turned. Best of all, the voices of the operators: the squeaks required of evil characters, the operatic sing-song, sobbing & heroic harangues of the good ones. The voices went right through one, even if one didn't understand the words.'

Walking through the city on my last day there, June 2nd, I tried once again to sum up what it was that made me return to Italy despite the discomforts I had to put up with there, the squalor and the noise; but in my diary it remains 'something difficult to define. Even the naked children in the slums and the beggars at street corners partake of it. They have an openness, an abandonment, a fatalism peculiar to the South. It's as though they didn't take themselves as seriously as people in the North, as though personal identity were somehow less important than it seems to us. That doesn't mean they're unselfish. Far from it. They're out for what they can get, by fair means or foul. But they have a communal soul, stronger than their individual souls. Fathers and mothers pick up their children more roughly than one would a puppy in England — by one arm or by the hair — but it doesn't seem to matter. The "cruelty" is part of their condition, everyone's.'

Since I travelled 3rd class to Naples, I got next to no sleep on the boat, especially when the bunk above mine was occupied by a man who couldn't afford the price of a bunk, so that he had to make do without a mattress and bedding. Then someone switched off the ventilator. I gave up, and left the dormitory, just when the sun was rising over Capri, at 4 a.m. Thinking that Naples would be little more than a repetition of Palermo, I decided to move straight on to Positano, with three and a half hours to kill at Sorrento, on the little pier I remembered from my army days, where boats leave for Capri.

At Positano I took up swimming again, preferably around midnight, when there was no competition, and phosphorescent bubbles slipped through one's fingers. In between dips I drank wine at the Buca di Bacco, where tourists and foreign residents gathered for drinking and dancing. 'Talked with various Americans,' I noted in my diary. 'A writer, homosexual; has sold a novel he hasn't written for 1000 dollars. Educated at Oxford and in Germany ... His girl cousin, he said, wanted to meet me; but he wouldn't let her talk to me, & she left in tears. Also a widowed opera singer who plays patience with shaking fingers or paddles a canoe. Talks to anyone and everyone, when he's not singing to himself with what little remains of his voice.'

Positano is the only place in Italy that I found too silent, oppressively so. My room seemed to be suspended over the sea, with the town or village above and behind, straggling round the hillside. The place had a starkness and aridity that drove me out into the countryside. I walked to Praiano and back, delighted to find some organic life in the oasis-like vegetation of the ravines. Though walking in the heat was not an unadulterated pleasure, that expedition was followed by another, to Monte Pertuso, a village up in the hills that had been recommended to me by a German woman painter I had met on the beach. By the time I got there my shirt stuck to my skin. Yet it was good to see a genuine village, to smell cow dung and hay, rather than the frying oil from the restaurants in Positano. Part of the way I walked along a dried-up riverbed. 'Invisible water everywhere, feeding the rich vegetation.'

Four days in Positano were enough for me. In Rome I announced my arrival to Count Umberto Morra, who had written to me in Sicily since our chance encounter on the train. He had arranged all sorts of social engagements for me, beginning with an invitation to lunch at the Palazzo Caetani. There I committed three gaffes — over sherry, when I absent-mindedly put peanuts in my sherry glass; over coffee, which I spilled on to an elegant arm chair; and in my conversation, over a matter of literary politics. Princess Caetani overlooked all three on that occasion, though years later I fell from grace over something I wrote to her about the difficulty of translating René Char's work, pointing out that certain near-surrealist effects became faintly comic in English, when in French they were exquisitely solemn. She took this as a stricture on the poet she admired most, did not publish my translations of Char, which she had previously praised, and ceased to publish my work in her magazine, *Botteghe Oscure*. I translated two books by Char for her, but one of the translations has been lost ever since, because I gave my only other copy to the guest editor of a little magazine, and he vanished or died. Another regret is that the only poem of mine she published in her magazine is one which I came to loathe; and since she had been generous to me, even giving us a wedding present, I was sorry to have offended her.

Throughout my stay in Rome I was tormented by an unquenchable and unaccountable thirst that made me consume any liquid, preferably alcoholic, that came my way. Such sight-seeing as I did was further complicated by the vast crowds of pilgrims who had gathered for the Holy Year. Luckily for me, Umberto Morra provided respite from my thirsty pilgrimages by getting me invited to dinner at the home of Ian Greenless, who worked for the British Council and occupied a luxurious apartment in the Palazzo Massimo. Concealed behind the Spanish leather of the dining-room walls there was a little chapel dedicated to St. Philip of Neri, who miraculously healed a Massimo child in the 17th century. The guests included John Lehmann, an old acquaintance from London. After dinner I went on to the home of Professor Gabrieli, where I met Mario Praz. That meeting, too, had been arranged by Umberto Morra, who was there. The conversation was less about literature than about people, and I was astonished by some of Praz's remarks about people I knew.

Umberto Morra's office was in the Palazetto di Venezia, once the apartment of Mussolini's chauffeur. Count Morra told me that a man I talked to on the train was Edda Ciano's lover, just returned from England, where he saw signs of 'recovery', as he told me. Morra also introduced me to Alberto Moravia, at Babington's, and to von Hassel's son-in-law, Pirzio Bironi, who had fought in the Resistance and whose children had been taken away by the Germans, imprisoned, and given a new name — so that he had to search every orphanage and children's home in Austria and South Germany before finding them after the war.

On my last day I went to lunch with Edwin and Willa Muir. He was unwell, depressed by his imminent departure from Italy, and said little. Willa was lively and humorous. Edwin Muir took me up to a roof terrace to show me the swifts of Rome that had a special significance for him. He asked me to keep in touch with them and meet again if possible.

The brief stay in Rome had contrasted a bit too violently with the style of my previous travels in Italy. At the dinner party in the Palazzo Massimo John Lehmann had defended privilege, after all the left-wing publications he had edited, and that made me feel as uncomfortable as I'd felt in the Buca di Bacco. Yet I welcomed a little social life, after a glut of solitude in dingy hotel or boarding-house rooms; and my second meeting with Edwin Muir had confirmed a sympathy between us that made it something other than a social occasion. I was to see more of Umberto Morra, too, over the next ten years, and of Marguerite Caetani, when she came to London.

In Paris I ran into David Gascoyne again, at *Les Deux Magots*, on his way to Provence, where I was to visit him with my wife and children more than ten years later. In the course of two days I also ran into three people from Taormina, including 'Genia's' girl friend. Jacques Calmy lent me an amusing novel by an Egyptian, Albert Cossery. It reminded me that Calmy, too, was born in North Africa. Like the hero of the book he was a true *fainéant*, an Oblomov, always putting off the decisive moment when he'd get down to the writing of his long-delayed books. I couldn't imagine myself ever living comfortably, as he did, with artistic friends and a well-paid job in journalism. I always had to be doing something; and was always dissatisfied with what I had done.

In Paris, though, I wasted many hours in the St. Germain and Montparnasse cafés, pleasantly surprised when I managed to do a little reading or writing between drinks. In one of those cafés one was sometimes entertained by an eccentric called Loppe, who made half-witted speeches and thought he was going to be President of the Republic. He was always surrounded by a claque, mainly of students, who encouraged him with shouts of *Vive le Maître!* Everyone enjoyed the joke as a caricature of 'serious' politics. 'If only politics were ever serious,' I commented at the time, 'in any way but their effects on the governed.'

I went out to the suburb of Puteau to see my painter friend Françoise and meet her family — a real French family, for once. Her young brother found fault with the way I was dressed, especially with my shirt, saying it wasn't 'sportif' enough. I wondered whether Françoise had a chance as an artist, with no influential friends, a lower middle-class background, no contacts in the cafés or galleries.

After all the walking I had done in Italy the soles of my shoes were worn through, and when it began to rain, I couldn't keep my feet dry. That made me take more walks, between the Luxembourg Gardens and the Bois, so that the moisture was evenly distributed.

On June 14th, I went to Gide's flat in the rue Vaneau, at his daughter's invitation. Gide and Jean Lambert were still in Italy, at Sorrento. It was an enormous flat that could accommodate all his family, down to his brother-in-law and sister-in-law. I looked at his library and pictures, particularly the Sickerts and Bussys, and his two grand pianos, thinking that nothing could be more solidly bourgeois than the old Immoralist's home. Catherine Lambert drove me to her house near Le Mesnil St. Denis, a seventeenth-century mansion with a large garden. Before my return to Paris by train we drove to Port-Royal des Champs, or what was left of it after its destruction in 1709 — a small chapel, now a museum, with holographs of Racine, Arnault and others, the old font, ruins of the dovecot and barn.

In some of the hours spent in cafés I scribbled away at what I called a 'nasty' poem, though it wasn't nasty or incisive enough to render my growing disenchantment with the *vie de bohême* — nor the misery of some of its survivors and hangers-on, exemplified for me by a meeting with Loulou Albert-Lazard, Rilke's friend, and her daughter. In the café Loulou was trying to win a little attention or recognition by reading out poems addressed or given to her by Rilke — 'about all she has now', I felt, looking at her walking-stick, dyed hair, and splotched dress. I never reprinted those verses after their first appearance in Charles Wrey Gardiner's *Poetry Quarterly.* They may serve here to mark the end of my early wanderings, even though their purpose, if they had any purpose, was not to exchange the literary life of London for that of Paris, Rome or any other place, but to get away from it altogether. Travel impressions less casual than those recorded in *Left Bank, Paris* would reappear in poems written years, or decades, later. This, at best, was a snapshot, taken for lack of anything better to do:

Is it not a superfluous accumulation of individuality
That bubbles and bursts on the flooded boulevards
Of this hectic hysterical terrible city
Amidst the hurry, hooting and screeching of cars?

Can it be Art they're after, these bearded boys,
These girls in dungarees at their café tables?
Can craft or vision feed upon such noise,
Their minds grow sensuous by exchanging labels?

A circus for the bourgeoisie that gives them bread,
They live in imagined exile near,
Too near their homes, self-disinherited,
And, dressed in banners, challenge their own fear.

Their ancient enemy loves them without passion,
Asks only to be amused while, all defiant, they
Bombard him with his needs: a change of fashion.
Something to stare at, talk about and put away.

Eight

That was the longest and fullest of those wanderings abroad which I thought interesting enough to record in diaries, while I kept no record of my working life at home; very much as I'd kept army diaries about my reading, thoughts and feelings, but not about the details of daily life that might have been of use to me in retrospect. The few days at Positano gave me the setting of another fiction incorporated in my would-be novel, *The Vacation* — about a woman again, Jean, married to an alcoholic expatriate 'writer' from America who had ceased to write. I still don't understand why travelling meant so much to me in those years; or why I needed chance encounters in foreign places for my only attempts at prose fiction, never taken up again in later years. Poems needed no stimulus of that kind. On the contrary: I wrote very few passable ones anywhere but at home. One reason, I think, is that I never took short-story writing quite seriously as an activity for me, treating it as a sort of vacation from verse; another, related to the first, is that my few stories were attempts to get outside myself, whereas poetry always brings one back to one's home ground, to the 'foul rag and bone shop of the heart.'

The meeting with André Gide led to my being invited to act as tutor to the Lambert children just before or just after his death in the following year. I procrastinated, then got married instead. My wife, baby daughter and I did join the Lamberts for a holiday on the Île de Ré, where they had a villa, in 1954; and I was to meet Jean Lambert again some twelve years later, in Massachusetts. Clashing life styles — we were still miserably poor — put severe strains on our relations with the Lamberts on the Île de Ré. What I shall never forget about our stay there is another 'accident' very nearly fatal. Ignoring a storm warning and prohibition to bathe in those treacherous Bay of Biscay waters, I swam out too far, then found that every inch of the return had to be wrested from a powerful undertow, much more daunting than the breakers. My wife and child were sitting on the beach, and there were moments when I thought I was making no progress at all and could never get back to them. This time, though, no death-wish had entered into the matter. It was sheer folly and arrogance that made me feel I knew better than the official warning; and I got away with it, just, as I've done again and again in the accidents to which I was prone, with as many lives as a cat's — the one animal with which I have shared those lives whenever I had a home for one.

My London life continued much as before, with literary work, odd jobs, and very little money. (Travels abroad, in that era, had to keep within the statutory travel allowance of £50, though the length of my stay in Italy and Sicily may mean that for once I was compelled to augment it with the sale of some bit of personal property like a watch or watch chain. A sale of that sort occurs in my short story 'Genia', set in Sicily and based on an involvement with an American girl I met there. Since the fiction has wholly overlaid the facts of that casual involvement, which was not a love affair, but in which I acted as a sort of involuntary father confessor, I have cut it out of my account.)

One of my odd jobs in London, French lessons in Pentonville prison, gave me trouble. When I started my teaching there — compulsory lessons probably instituted in the hope that some of the convicts would emigrate to the French-speaking part of Canada after their release — my pupils were marched into the classroom by a prison officer. I expected him to leave once the class was seated. He stayed, to watch them or protect me. Needless to say, I got no response at all from my pupils. I asked to be left alone with them on future occasions. The request was granted, and from then on I got all kinds of responses, few of which had anything to do with the work I was being paid to do. There was one old lag out to sabotage the whole operation. He came into the class equipped with some antiquated textbook. If I was teaching conjugations he would read out some rule about verbs and nouns, shouting out: ''Ow about that, Guvnor?' I would then have to explain the difference between verbs and nouns, getting nowhere, until he threw in the next red herring. Another, older, man was more interested in ethics than grammar — only too understandably, in his situation. He had read a novel by Somerset Maugham and found a quotation from Pascal: 'The heart has its reasons, which reason knows nothing of.' That did have something to do with French — and with one of my favourite French authors, as it happened; but he brought it up because he had been thinking about his crime and punishment, and wanted me to confirm that a man can do things under a compulsion that absolves him from guilt. I, too, was more interested in the implications of his question than in teaching grammar to people who had no wish or reason to learn it. After a month or two I had to conclude that my assignment was a hopeless one. The more I came to care about those men and their needs, the less I could teach them elementary French. So I gave up.

My visits to Soho had almost ceased. One of the last friends I made there was Thomas Blackburn, of whom I saw a great deal over the following years, also going to Cornwall and North Wales with him more than once, to climb Snowdon again, reluctantly balance on ridges and even scale rock faces with a rope, but no passion like his for rock-climbing. He loved danger, and looked for it not only on mountains but in personal relations and humdrum things like driving a car. One night, when he was drunk after a party, he zigzagged from one side of the road to the other on our way through London to Putney. When I pointed out that sooner or later he would be colliding with another car, he said: 'You're my friend, aren't you? You don't mind dying with me, do you?' It was hard to answer those two rhetorical questions, except by telling him that at the moment I was not keen to die with anyone at all. Even in North Wales he would park his car with the back wheels just touching a ledge. Every personal relationship, too, had to be pushed to the verge of crisis, if not over the verge, so as to release the energies that went into his poems. In some ways this accorded with the Soho ethos, though few of my Soho acquaintances pushed dangerous living quite so far, so consistently; and Tom Blackburn was more than a Soho acquaintance to me, because I knew him in day-time also, and knew a good deal about his day-time work as a Grammar School teacher, then as a college lecturer, and his difficult family life, even before his family and mine shared a holiday cottage at Tintagel, where he worked a farmer and his wife into a state of psychic exposure and extremity they can never have thought themselves capable of. He had complained bitterly that nothing of the same order had occurred between my wife and me, no high tension, breakthrough or breakdown or conflict of the kind he needed to release his own demons and get down to the archetypes. That is why the farmer and his wife, from whom we had rented the cottage, had to step in as media. Wholly unprepared, as they were, for what he wanted of them, they proved far more amenable than we were to his requirement. We could keep up that friendship only by being on our guard; and in later years, when Tom was destroying himself with a mixture of barbiturates and alcohol, it proved too much for my wife, who had grown up in fear of her father's drunken fits, and we saw less and less of Thomas. His second wife, Rosalie de Meric, and his daughter Julia have remained our friends.

Another of the late Soho acquaintances was Brian Higgins, whom I saw only rarely outside Soho but corresponded with, mainly about the 'loans' he asked for and I came to refuse on principle, having discovered that the people who regarded me mainly as a source of 'loans' ended by hating or despising either me or themselves for the gift. When Brian Higgins's need turned out to be genuine and acute for once, just before his early death, I hated and despised myself for having allowed those experiences to harden into a principle. Patrick Kavanagh was another poet I met in Soho when he was in London. I very much liked his poems and his novel *Tarry Flynn* — and was able to help towards the publication in England of a book of his poems — but had little communication with him beyond his requests for another whiskey.

The war-time Soho circle had disintegrated. Some of its members now went to the Anglo-French Club in St. John's Wood, where I spent evenings when I had nothing better to do. Many of the same people went to the annual Christmas party at the Phillips's house in Hampstead, an all-night festivity to which I had been introduced by John Mortimer. Though never invited to it — as one was meant to be — I became a repeated gate-crasher there, and was never turned away. It was a bohemian event in a style that proved what I had come to feel, that every bohemia is sustained by its dependence on the class it thinks it is in revolt against. When that class lost its privileges and wealth, the bohemia I had known had nothing to batten on and withered away. Its residual members were those who had been wholly formed by it, had no other resources or resorts, and no way of making other lives for themselves. Some of those continued to haunt Soho, more and more like ghosts, long after Soho had become a playground for very different sets.

One of the first things I had done after returning to London was to prepare a reading of selected poems by Edwin Muir, with introductory comments, for broadcasting, since Muir was still a neglected writer, better known for the criticism he wrote for a living and for his translations than for his poetry. On September 22nd 1950 he wrote to me from Newbattle Abbey, Dalkeith, the college that was to educate and sustain a great many younger Scottish writers whose prospects otherwise might have been as bleak as his own had been when he was young: 'I'm delighted you're thinking of getting together some of my poems for broadcasting. I like your selection very much, and have no criticism to make of it. You ask about my earlier work. Much of it I do not like very much, with an exception here and there. I think you yourself (for private reasons) might like a poem, "Hölderlin's Journey", from a small volume *Journeys and Places*, published by Dent at 2/6, I think.* But then you may not like it, for the same reasons. And if you don't please forget all about it, for it is your selection, not mine, and should follow your taste. "Merlin", I think, appeared in the one book I don't have a copy of, else I would have sent it. And probably (though I hope not) it may be out of print. I have written some poems recently which I like better than any of the others: but it would be inexpedient to touch them.

'I wish I had known earlier that you were in Italy, for I would have seen more of you. If you are in Scotland any time do come and see us and spend a night or two. This is a curious place, with lots of passages in which I got lost for the first week, and historical objects like Bruce's saddle and Mary Stuart's font (if genuine). I hope you're writing poetry.'

Edwin Muir, who developed late as a poet, was writing his best poems at the time — the best, I thought, that were being produced by a British poet. His 'delight' at an attention he should have been able to take for granted is characteristic both of his situation and of his response to decades of neglect.

In November he wrote again, apologizing for not writing sooner about my book of poems: 'I've been terribly busy, not only with starting the College (it's been going just for a month now) but with countless things which have turned up, indirectly connected with it. These will not recur (at least I hope so) and I should be having much more leisure in a short time. But I've really been having far too much to do during these last four weeks.

'I got the script of the poems and your commentary two days ago, and I should like to thank you very much indeed, and to say how much I like what you say about me. I'm very glad indeed to be introduced to the Third Programme audience in a way I like so much.'

Muir was sixty-three years old. His first book had appeared in 1918, since which time he had produced increasingly distinguished work in prose and verse, not to mention his early concern with writers almost unknown in England, such as Hölderlin and Kafka. Yet he could write without irony about being 'introduced to the Third Programme' by a man almost forty years his junior. A postscript to the letter refers to a review of my book of poems: 'Who is Mr. P. who was so supercilious to

*This volume turned out to be still available in 1950, 13 years after publication. The price was now 3/-.

you and the other poets? And what right has he to be so lordly? What nonsense reviewing is.' Almost up to his death Edwin Muir had to turn out book reviews, since his own books provided no income to speak of. 'I do hope that the vein of poetry is running again with you,' he wrote in 1955; 'with me it turns itself off and on in the most disconcerting way, and generally when it comes on I have no leisure to deal with it. I have a few poems in my mind just now, but whether they will come to anything I do not know. I may find leisure in Harvard.'

I met Edwin Muir again in 1952, when he attended a small gathering at our London flat, meeting Kathleen Raine, G. S. Fraser and J. C. Hall there. 'I was pleased to meet some writing people again,' he commented: 'they really are the pleasantest people one can meet, I'm convinced, though others deny it.' In 1955 I attended a reading he gave in London, and in his last years I visited him more than once at Swaffham Prior, near Cambridge. After his death Willa Muir remained a loyal friend.

Almost better than anyone else I knew, Edwin Muir understood the conflict in my early verse between preoccupations mainly ethical or 'philosophical' and the aesthetic demands of the medium. This had been his own problem, when metaphysical concerns tended to impoverish the sensuous and linguistic fabric of his poems. Though he was too gentle and considerate to censure the same shortcoming in my work, I drew my own conclusions from his remarks in a letter of 1952. 'Sincerity is a matter of degrees, and I feel sure a necessary quality of poetry, and it is in that sense (not the equivocal sense in which it is so often used by smart reviewers) that I'm speaking about it. Sincerity becomes grace (and not, again, a mere surface grace) when it is effortless, and not willed; and I think your poetry has that quality at its best. It's something that you have by nature, or have achieved: I find it difficult to tell which. In any case, if you are in doubt about your poetry (and who is not in doubt about his poetry?), it is a quality which you should respect and cherish. I am no good at discussing the technical points of verse; the word technique always gives me a slightly bewildered feeling; if I can translate it as skill I am more at home with it, for skill is always a quality of the thing that is being said or done, not a general thing at all. A thing asks to be said, but the only test is whether it is said well. You certainly have things to say of your own; and, from the enquiring, accepting spirit of these poems, I feel that there are many more things, of which just now you are probably not aware, which you still have to say: I go on my own experience ...'

The comments on specific poems that followed — including one negative comment on a poem later picked out by a prominent actress for public readings and broadcasts that became an excruciating embarrassment to me — were helpful too; but it was the crux about sincerity that I really took to heart, knowing that mine had not yet become effortless, had not become 'grace'. Between the lines of Edwin Muir's approval I found an indication of the route I must take — towards 'negative capability'; and that indication was far more valuable to me than praise. It could have come only from a poet who had known related conflicts and perplexities.

In October 1950, I started a diary, with misgivings about the usefulness of keeping one when I had more than enough writing to do as it was. 'There's so much one can't put into one's poetry,' I noted — as if those things could be pinned down and preserved by the magic of the written word. Even poetry couldn't catch what, in a poem of that period, I called 'the wasted substance of our daily acts'. All a diary could do was to record a few of those acts. It was in the nature of their 'substance' to be partly absorbed, partly wasted.

'This morning, for instance,' I wrote on October 21st. 'Answered a notice from my tutorial agency. Left here at 9.30, went to Celtic Hotel (Guildford Street) to be interviewed by a Welshman who needs a tutor for his son. The man organizes tours ("The Shakespeare Country", Windsor, etc.). The hotel lounge, covered with murals of North Wales mountain scenery. Dim isn't the word. A true Celtic twilight. Then the man arrived. I was shown into an office. During interview, interminable chatter of hotel staff going in and out. The first thing he said was: "I won't take a chain-smoker", meaning anyone who smokes. Then asked about my qualifications. What was the subject of my M. A. thesis? Then: "You'll be given a room of your own and will stay there for an hour, no one will disturb you, you'll go on teaching till the hour is up" — as though tutors normally taught in corridors. Wears boots and bow tie. Very sure of himself, of his Welsh morality and his London success. Owns the hotel, I suppose, as well as the motor coach business. Don't think he'll want me. Told him I was a heavy smoker.'

I didn't get the job. Next day I had dinner with X and tried to assuage his doubts over a biography he was writing, the first non-fiction book he had attempted.

Next morning — I was just getting dressed — Peter Höfler suddenly arrived. 'Apocalyptic diatribe against the spirit of the age. Comparison with the Destruction of the Temple. — Told me that two friends of his had read a poem of mine in the *New Statesman* and disliked it; and why he agreed with them, though he hadn't read the poem.' While he was there, Käthe Braun-Prager (Felix Braun's sister, a visionary, too, in her fashion, both as a poet and as a portraitist) rang up to tell me how wonderful she thought my last poem ('In October'), and asking for permission to translate it into German. 'It was all a bit confusing, first thing in the morning,' I commented.

Then my uncle Fritz turned up to repair my electric light switch — the kind of job he was glad to do, for lack of any other employment or occupation — driving out Peter Höfler, who couldn't relate to him. Soon after my uncle had gone, my sister Maria telephoned, in despair because she couldn't get into my mother's house. She had forgotten that the clock had been put back one hour, so that my mother was still at her Quaker meeting. The best thing for her was to come to my flat and stay till it was time for the family lunch.

The diary resumes on the 28th: 'Midnight. Don't really remember what I've done all week. Oh yes, written a review for the N.S., at the rate of about 200 words a day. Changed two words in a poem. Read the life of Pericles in Plutarch; and some sayings of Buddha. Given 2 French lessons (2 hours each) to the Chinese girl from Singapore. Gone to 2 bad exhibitions with John Pettavel. Had dinner with Simon John, who wants me to take her to a party so that she can wear a shawl her mother has given her. Louis Adeane came to supper and looked at my diary; was shocked by its "cruelty". But it wasn't meant to be read by my friends. (What was it meant for? What are diaries for?) Yet he's right, in a way. My feelings go into poems. The diary is heartless.'

October 31st: 'Cocktail party at Miss Lockyer's — the Purtscher-Wydenbrucks, Harold Rutland and others. Miss Lockyer less nervous than usual, very charming. Went with John Pettavel. On Monday, lunched with him, Erica Marx, Neville Braybrooke. Then tea with Noel Welch, who showed me her poems & gave me a novel to read. Writing "Interrupted Nocturne" — with too many interruptions. Not happy about it.' (This was the dialogue poem on which Edwin Muir commented adversely. The better parts of it were written at a retreat from London, Bosham Manor in Sussex, in August. I had got to know the Wornum family, whose home it was, through John Pettavel.)

'Monica came to see me at 7. Yet another reconciliation. No remedy but to break it off, and I can't.

'Letter from N. S. asking for poems. Could send only epigram and three translations, as the rest went to Princess Caetani. Phone call from Newby about the Muir reading, asking me to make it longer. Shall have to do it tomorrow, and the "Interrupted Nocturne" will be interrupted yet again. Gave Phyllis Young a French lesson. Improving.'

Nov. 6th: 'Finished re-writing — mainly cutting — "I. N." Read more Buddha, D. H. Lawrence: *The Rainbow*, Ezra Pound's *Cantos*. Phyllis Young cancelled her last lesson, either because she was ill, as she said, or because I'd been a bit impatient with her. Saw Chaplin's *City Lights* with John P. Visited Felix Braun on his birthday & had to recite a poem from memory. Ellen Delp there. Was so embarrassed that I sweated in his cold room.

'Hurried back home because I was expecting M., but her sister telephoned to say she was ill. Sick with disappointment, as usual. Went to Anglo-French Club, talked inanely with a great many people & drank too much draught cider.

'Poor Fritz is going away on Friday. Plans to spend a year on the Continent and in Tunis, but really hates the idea of leaving. Complete emotional vacuum since his mother's death. No one to love or badger. Unemployed in every possible way.

'Saw X last night. Advised me not to get married, except to an "independent & academic woman". On the way home, while pondering his advice, ran into Dannie Abse, who's having a play put on.'

Nov. 7th: 'Met Erica Marx after lunch & discussed her publishing projects. Then went to see M. at Purley. She really does have a cold. A day that seemed dead, sodden with moisture, inert. M. wants us to marry. I'm deterred by the example of so many of my friends, who've capitulated after marriage, taking comfortable jobs. That's an excuse, of course, for a deeper hesitation. M., after all would work. But then I'd be sponging on her, writing poems at her expense. And it can't go on like this.

'Today, Tuesday, did nothing but worry. Also, French lesson in afternoon. Nearly went to sleep, because of coal fire; but P. Y. brighter than usual.'

Nov. 9th: 'Terrible scene today, when Fritz drove off, on his way to France. In tears most of the time, when other people would envy him his trip, his leisure, money, etc. Helped to strap his cases on the car, & tried to console him by saying he could come back, after all, whenever he likes. But back to what? At that point reason breaks down. Can't bear his solitude, & can't enter into any adult relationship.

'Continued translating Heinz Priebatsch's novel — about 5 pages today. Wrote an epigram — poor. Gave my lesson. Received another letter from Stephen Spender, who wants me to help him translate Hofmannsthal.

'Yesterday, had lunch with Heinz, who had just been looking for a new job in the timber trade and had an interview, unsatisfactory. Gave me two recent poems. In the evening, went to see Louis Adeane, about to leave for Cornwall, selling his furniture. Intent on an objective, I'm glad to say. Letter from W. S. Graham, recovering from an accident in Cornwall.

'Still wondering whether to go to France as private tutor. Salary would be 6000 fr. a month. Would regular income, however small, put an end to the compromises by which I live here?'

Nov. 10th: 'Still unable to write, but got on with translating. Caught M.'s cold at Purley; began yesterday, as she predicted. She came here last night, & we discussed the future, as far as the future can be discussed. Still undecided about France, but certain that I don't want to commit myself for any length of time.

'Letter from Tom Good, who's returning to France. After much resistance went to a Kensington party at Diana Johns's, which didn't take place, because she'd got food poisoning at lunch. Met David Wright there. Rain didn't do my fever any good. Glad to get home. Listened to Beethoven: *Grosse Fuge* & Chopin: *24 Preludes* on wireless.'

Nov. 12th: 'Full of plans, but unable to start anything. The importance of waiting for things to happen — in poetry, at least. They do happen in the end, if one knows how to wait — attentively, not impatiently.

'Wrote to Catherine Lambert yesterday, saying yes and no: I'd go to France, but stay only for a few months. Clumsy, as usual, but no more indecisive than I feel.

'Went to Stephen Spender's this afternoon. Looks older, but the better for it. Saw his son Matthew, about five, I think, and baby girl. Natasha seems more nervy than 8 years ago, when I last saw her, I think. She burst into tears while practising a difficult new sonata by Samuel Barber. Matthew has put a stick through a painting by Cecil Collins. While he was there he splashed ink over Stephen's suit and the couch. Helped Stephen with his translation of poems & short plays by Hofmannsthal. Corrected one of his bizarre howlers, due to mixing up a German adjective with a French noun. Stephen seems more capable than he used to be of taking in another person's presence. Asks questions at least, though one still feels his attention slipping away as one answers them.'

Nov. 13th: 'Tom Good called on his way to France. Wonder whether he really felt as cheerful as he made out to be — about going away again, leaving his family and friends, even if he is convinced that he can't live in England. Can't help feeling that he's always running away — from himself, from his past, from his commitments. Can anyone be as independent, as free from attachments, as he claims to be?'

Nov. 18th: 'On Tuesday, after a lesson in the morning, went to Oxford to give a talk on Edwin Muir's poetry. Before the talk went to John Donne's rooms to drink, then to a pub with him, Watt and Martin Seymour-Smith. Dined at the Taj. Was a bit drunk by the time the talk began, didn't look at my notes, must have talked nonsense. Slept in Oriel guest room, began to write poem. Can't get away from obsession with time, change. Do I have any other theme? It's what one has to come to terms with in order to survive, to develop. Yet one's growth isn't natural, like a tree's. Mind & memory insist that what's gone is as real as what's there, going, too, passing. The moment a poem tries to capture is past by the time the poem is written.

'After breakfast went to Elinor's barge, talked, went out to her Department. Quarrelled over her fellow anthropologists. Went to see Franz Baermann Steiner. He's much better than when I last saw him, but frail, vulnerable still. Back to the barge for lunch. Soon after lunch, E.'s mother turned up; more talk, tea, then rowed over to Salter's. Had supper at Kemp's & caught 7.35 train back. Strange effect Oxford has on me since I went down. Tried to render this in poem, but it hasn't come off — so far.

'Strange dreams about Russia. There as a soldier, fighting, but without firearms. A sort of intellectual war, fought with words and, on their side, truncheons!'

Nov. 22nd: 'With John Heath-Stubbs to see Keats's *Otho the Great*. But we got the date wrong. So we wandered about in Soho, drinking mildly in pubs and at the Mandrake Club.

'Monday, letter from Thames & Hudson, offering me another book to translate. May accept this time, if I have a free hand over selection of material — from Beethoven's letters, diaries, conversations. Anything to do with Beethoven will be fascinating. Went to their offices to discuss the book. Louis Adeane called in the evening. Told me how he saw the Devil in Cornwall.

'Tuesday: read Pound's *Cantos* in the morning. Gave lesson at 3. Supper with X, who's already started a new novel, after handing in the typescript of his biography. Never allows himself to be unable to write. Doesn't wait for the mood, like poets; induces it, by working.

'Today, Wednesday, re-wrote poem I jotted down at Oxford. Rather weird. May not come to anything.

'In the evening heard Schönberg's Chamber Symphony, No. 1. New to me, & exciting.'

On November 25th, W. S. Graham wrote me a long letter. I had written to him when I heard that he was in hospital after falling off a roof and breaking his knee-cap. He wrote from Perranporth: 'The whole unreal world of hospital with all its strange new values which one must live among is strange. It can be maddening but it is interesting. Almost all the time there is light I work — working at verse, trying out new verse patterns, reading prose and verse and making "copious" notes (Cook's Voyages, Nietzsche in translation, the Wild West mag., Joyce, the Ballads, Lowell, Pericles), over-revising my long poem *The Night Fishing*, taking other poetry to pieces to see how its mechanism works, planning a project which will be my next book — and it is in that that I work and keep reasonably sane. I just can't imagine how other men here stand it with no "centre" in them to live in, lying there thinking what they will do or how something will be or thinking of what they did or should have done. The children are so good — patient and courageous — accusing examples to complaints I have harboured...'

Sydney went on to comment on our differences as poets. They could hardly have been more extreme, since his starting-point was 'verse patterns' and sound effects, a peculiarity about which I wrote to him too sweepingly in a later letter. He then analysed a poem I had sent him, 'In October'. Not till many years later, when the poem had been published and anthologized, did I try to act on his strictures, only to find that I couldn't re-write it so long after the event. As with many other poems, all I could do was to lop off the offending parts, when nothing less than a transplant could have given new life to the poem. That was one of the drawbacks of my way of writing. I can no more emend a poem, once it has set, than I can will myself to write a new one. This has meant that much of my earlier work is irredeemably flawed.

A casual remark at the end of W. S. Graham's letter impressed me more than his objection to two lines in the poem: 'A curious fact (which doesn't mean anything re subject or technique) the number of negative words — "passionless", "unshed", "nameless", "unborn", "unbroken".' This addiction to negatives, and their interplay with positive counterparts, was something of which I had been quite unaware. I became increasingly interested in the resort of other poets to negations and negatives. Nearly twenty years later I touched on the matter in my critical book, *The Truth of Poetry.*

It may well be that negatives and negations have remained conspicuous in my prose, if decreasingly in my poems. Most of my positives could be maintained only by protecting them constantly against the negatives, which pressed in on me in every activity, almost every personal relationship in which I was involved. Other positives had to be arrived at by a process of elimination, rather like the attributes of God in the *Summa* of St. Thomas Aquinas; or by a process of sloughing off habits and needs, a process traced in my sequence of poems 'Travelling', the very writing of which took me nine years in my middle age, because each part had to be lived before it was written.

As a corrective to the negations, perhaps I should mention that the alacrity with which I was born set a pattern for every day in my life, for the moment when I was born again to the light of each morning, if only that morning was to be my own, to be filled with the work of my choosing. I could not wait to be up and at my writing table. Had that been otherwise, I could not have done the work I have done, for half a century now, when much of that work was done only for the work's sake. Most of the letters from which I have drawn to document my youth had to be written in the evening or at night, though, after days filled with work not of my choosing. That alone goes far to explain the preponderance in them of negatives and negations. Most of the writers I have known — and I have known far more than there was room for in this book — could be divided into day and night workers. Almost from the start, I was a diurnal, if not a matutinal one. Early mornings, from the moment of dawn, were my favourite time of day and my most productive. If the morning could not be my own, for one reason or another, the whole day was lost to me for all but writing merely dutiful — or darkened and overcast by the past day's cares.

For another year or two the diary continued to chronicle the events and non-events of my London life, but never in enough detail or depth to tell me which were the events, which the non-events. Its laconic entries were a sort of shorthand. The assumption must have been that memory would know how to read it, using fragments to reconstitute the whole. Memory does no such thing. It rejects those fragments of fact and circumstance. If I let it have its way, it would insist on its own version of the story, and that version would not be a reconstitution but a reconstruction. Memory was the Mother of the Muses because she is the identical twin of Imagination; and what both of them mother is fictions.

The diary continued to chronicle what poems I was writing, when, what friends I was seeing, where, what jobs I was doing, thinking of doing, refusing to do. For November 26th it records: 'Thick fog yesterday. Voice heard in the fog, small boy's: "Look at that wall! You can't see nothing there!"' Those random words emerge from the fog more vividly than the odds and ends of my own daily life.

In late November, too, I went to Kathleen Raine's for tea, then to a poetry reading by her and Roy Campbell in Bayswater, at Margaret Crosland's home. Since Kathleen Raine was preoccupied with a survey of the year's poetry she was writing, we could not talk as freely as usual. 'Literature got between us — that soul-destroying activity in which our writing involves us. It was: "What do you think of so & so?", a kind of small-talk that corresponds to other people's talk about the weather — except that I prefer the weather.' At the reading Roy Campbell was spinning some of his inimitable but repetitive yarns.

Meanwhile half a million Chinese soldiers were being mobilized to fight in Korea. I was undergoing dental treatment, and theorizing about pain: 'Based on fear — an alarm signal; and it can be made more bearable by a mental adjustment. But this doesn't apply to pain that's either sporadic or hard to localize. In those cases one can't forestall the mechanism of fear. Nor, of course, does it apply to any but physical pain.' I might have added that it didn't apply to those fighting the war in Korea.

After a party at *World Review* I was taken off to Soho by Francis Bacon and Tony Curtis, whom I'd known since my prep school days. At the Colony in Dean Street we met John Minton, Lucian and Kitty Freud, and a variety of club members. Francis Bacon ordered champagne and expounded why 'artists have to become crooks'. In spite of many martinis I had drunk at the party, my immediate response was to freeze up. From that moment I was a wet blanket, and I wasn't surprised when Bacon, Minton and the Freuds decided to move on to another haunt, leaving me to reflect on the tedium of the setting — 'the elderly barmaids with whom the guests exchanged endearments and insults, the jazz being strummed in the background by a Negro, the young artists trying to be younger than they are.' A few nights earlier, at the Anglo-French, someone had said: 'I wish all these girls didn't remind me of the poultry yard.' It was the sort of remark I had failed to be amused by nine years earlier, at Oxford. 'One says that people are "profoundly stupid"', I noted that month, 'but not that people are "profoundly clever". Common usage is right about that.'

On December 29th, I was to give a poetry reading at Dulwich, but still couldn't face reading out my own verse in public. Bernard Bergonzi came to tea and relieved me of that burden by offering to read the poems for me.

This little cross-section of my life in 1950 has been left as raw material, unprocessed by memory or invention. If I had continued the diary beyond 1954 — when I became too busy to keep it — I should be able to drop hundreds of names of writers famous or forgotten, record hundreds of literary or social occasions, introduce more characters than any reader could wish to know within the covers of one book or I could wish to introduce to him or her, retrace the itinerary of countless trips around the British Isles and beyond them.

Of the characters already mentioned without any introduction, I will say only that Louis Adeane was a poet, totally forgotten now, though as good as many who are remembered only because they survived longer and kept their names in print more assiduously than he did in his lifetime. As a friend, he excelled in drawing me out to tell him stories about my life that made him roar and writhe with laughter. He was an anarcho-syndicalist, close to Herbert Read, on whom he was writing a book, and did appear in print as long as anarcho-syndicalism was taken seriously by a minority of British intellectuals as an alternative to centralized Socialism, up to the late nineteen-forties and the emigration to Canada of George Woodcock, one of his associates. As a poet he was a perfectionist, working for years on a single short poem, and caring little whether he published it or not. In later years he lived in Cornwall, where we were his guests at least once, and he would visit us when we were in London.

Heinz Priebatsch was a refugee from Germany who had got in touch with me when my first book appeared in 1943. I spent years translating a novel of his that was never published either in Germany or in England, only to please him and save him from utter despondency, since I have never felt inclined to translate a novel-length prose work, however distinguished. Nor was I moved to translate his poems, but I placed a book of them with the same Fortune Press whose owner, Caton, makes an appearance in an earlier chapter of this book. This collection of German poems published in England and a long story published in

Switzerland were the only books that Heinz was able to publish. The Fortune Press book could not have appeared either if Heinz had not had a job at a timber merchant's in Mitcham, Surrey, as a foreman, if not as a manager. Caton did not pay his authors, but required guarantees in the form of copies bought by them, otherwise he would not have published a book of German poems. In Germany Heinz Priebatsch had been a friend of the sculptor and writer Ernst Barlach. Because even the novel he wrote in England was rooted in his German regional allegiances, I must have known from the start that my translation would never find a publisher in England. The same regional fixations and a manner old-fashioned by then made the novel unpublishable in Germany after the war, when German writers of fiction were looking to foreign models, mainly American, for liberation from the literature of 'blood and soil'. Ironically, therefore, Heinz Priebatsch's novel was too essentially and conservatively German to be publishable in Germany in the immediate post-war years. I never knew whether Heinz and his wife had left Germany on political or on racial grounds; but whether or not he was of Jewish or partly Jewish descent, as a writer he had more in common with non-Nazi writers who had remained in Germany than with what was to be known as *Exil-Literatur*, the literature of exile; and his status as an expatriate made him ineligible for either category. He remained a misfit everywhere, because of the tendency, widespread among German historians of literature, and among journalist critics everywhere, to classify and judge writers by their outward circumstances rather than by what, as writers, they are.

A real event occurred just before Christmas. X took me to a house in South London to meet the three File sisters and their parents. At that meeting or the next the youngest of the three girls, Anne, played the Elysian Fields piece from Gluck's *Orpheus* on her flute. On another visit, in February, I left my bunch of keys behind. Anne returned them to me on the very day, February 19th, of my final break with Monica, adding a tiny gilt key to the ring. The Orpheus legend was to become as significant for our relationship as the key.

On Boxing Day, Monica and I decided once again to part. We were to have met on December 20th, but she telephoned one hour before she was due for supper, saying that she was too tired to go out. I wrote her a furious letter, then tore it up, and wrapped up her Christmas present instead. At 8, I telephoned to apologize for my anger on the telephone.

She was out. Even after our new resolutions to break if off she asked me not to lock the door to my flat, in case she were to 'act on impulse'. I'd once given her the key, but she had 'forgotten' to put it in her bag. Even that resolution was not the last, though we stuck to it for about a month.

After Christmas Philip O'Connor arrived from Suffolk, spent the afternoon at my flat, and dragged me off once more to the Soho pubs, to meet his friend Edith Young. Like George Barker, whom I'd seen at a New Year's Eve party, she told me off for living the wrong sort of life, not letting myself go, not suffering enough or allowing myself to get hurt. She spoke of Rimbaud. Perhaps because of that prodding, I did go on to Little Venice with one of my old Soho acquaintances, to a studio where a party was in progress. My friend immediately started beating a drum to jazz records that were being played, falling into a trance-like frenzy. Far from letting myself go, I became the cold observer: 'Meat safe on one wall, wash basin and pails in one corner, table with beer dripping from it, making a small puddle on the floor, a large divan bed and a couch. Two portraits on easels, both of women, one of a large girl who was there, with a bottle of brandy between her knees, promising all the men in turn that she'd make passionate love with them that night. Another woman was trying to persuade her to stop drinking. A third woman, small and blonde, sitting on the floor with three men. And an incongruous group, perhaps the landlord's family, trying in vain to enter into the spirit of the thing — much as I did, before creeping out.' If I'd ever felt that a bohemian way of life had anything to do with art, that was a thing of the past.

Out of all my years of pub and club crawling I got only one poem and that, when they were far behind me, in 1956, and I had settled into a way of life far more congenial to the introverted outdoor man I have always been. The poem, 'An Unnecessary Visit', could have been a belated answer to the banter of Edith Young and George Barker — if I had still been quarrelling with them, rather than with myself. The 'I' of that poem, too, is a cold observer, an academic and anthropologist, astray in a hell of self-induced torment, and emerging from it — into a hell not of his own choosing. I never found it necessary to look for trouble or 'suffering'. Nor to inflict it deliberately on others, so as to set up an extreme situation conducive to the writing of poetry — a procedure to which at least one of my ex-Soho friends was patently addicted.

Early in the new year I got down to work on the Beethoven book. At the same time Stephen Spender telephoned, suggesting that he and I collaborate over the Hofmannsthal translations he was doing for the Bollingen Foundation. A line-by-line collaboration proved impossible. Each of us translated different works. After complications of various kinds, and the lapse of nearly a decade, the editorship was offered to me. Since that was a way of breaking the deadlock, I accepted, with Stephen's generous consent. Though the attempted partnership had strained our relations at times, we remained friends; and Stephen Spender contributed translations to one of the Hofmannsthal volumes that finally materialized under my editorship. Edwin Muir was to have been another contributor; but it was Willa Muir who translated the play he had wanted to translate before he became too ill.

'It's extraordinary how much work one can get done when one is driven to it by some necessity, real or imagined', I noted in the diary. Also: 'Even here I don't tell the whole truth — nothing like it. The whole truth is too gruelling to be put down, even for one's own use. Recently I've made some discoveries about myself that horrify me.' I was using work as an 'anaesthetic', as the diary puts it, as an escape from the muddles and tensions of my personal life. It was my task-master, the super-ego, that made me break with Monica on the grounds of our 'incompatibility', but also nagged and punished me for deserting her. Whenever either of us 'acted on impulse' we were together again, 'incompatible', and drawn to each other, as we had been from the start.

At the Phillips's annual Christmas party I met a girl painter. We talked a good deal that night, and saw more of each other for a month or so. She came back to my flat one evening from the Anglo-French Club, and stayed the night, sharing my one narrow bed but placing an invisible sword between us. We continued to meet, curious about each other, up to the point where she became evasive. I had now developed an allergy to alcohol, so that another, easier 'anaesthetic' than work was denied to me. A single drink could make me ill for days. After a drink or two at the Institute of Contemporary Arts I felt so faint and sick that a friend offered to drive me home. The girl painter saw me back to the flat and read Chinese poems to me, though I could hardly keep my eyes open.

Much later, when I had stopped seeing this girl, a casual acquaintance laughed at me for not knowing what 'everyone' knew, that she was a lesbian. Yet she was feminine enough to attract men, to flirt with them, and to choose to share a bed with me when she could easily have gone home. We had had no difficulty in establishing an immediate rapport, of the kind I had never been able to establish with Monica.

But Monica, I noted, was 'three-quarters unconscious, often inarticulate and immersed in some aquatic depth which words could only skim like those long-legged flies on ponds'. The other girl could give much more of herself away, just because her coquetry was all surface, and her depth not accessible to a man.

In the midst of this brief entanglement I came home from a film I'd been to see with John Pettavel and found a note from Monica, who'd called and left a bunch of grapes. I telephoned her at once, despite our latest resolution. She said she needed to see me. We met again, up against the same barrier. About ten days later she sent me two photographs of herself, one going back to the time when we first met, and I knew that this was the end. On February 19th she telephoned to tell me she was getting married in May.

That day, too, I signed the contract for the Beethoven book, long after I'd started work on the selection and translation. The death of André Gide that month didn't release me from my undertaking to go to France, even though Gide had initiated the arrangement; but in the course of March I saw more and more of Anne, besides being fully employed and committed over literary projects. At the same time I was trying to raise money for Peter Höfler, this time with Stephen Spender's help, since earlier efforts on my own had failed. My uncle Alfred was in financial straits again, and I helped him out. Philip O'Connor, too, needed a loan and testimonial for a job.

During one of his unexpected calls at this period Peter Höfler expatiated on the figure of the Wandering Jew, perhaps in connection with his own wish to spend the remainder of his life as a perpetual voyager — a Flying Dutchman if not an Ahasuerus. This almost turned me into another of his 'plagiarists', for I found myself jotting down bits of a poem on the same theme. The poem came to nothing, as it happened; not, I think, because I'd been forewarned of Höfler's vehement reaction to friends who 'stole' his ideas and visions.

'Anne was here every day last week', I noted on March 17th. Since Anne had been trained as an actress, with a special liking for reading out poems, we attended quite a few readings at this time.

On March 20th, Anne and I left for Cornwall, to stay at Gorran Haven with Louis Adeane. 'In the evening walked with Louis and Pat along the beach, then along and over the rocks to Vault Beach. Dull, rainy and very windy (East wind). Primroses, out on the bleak hillside just above the sea; a few violets, gorse. Collected driftwood and took it back to their house. Seagulls and mews — the most elemental of birds — their crying not different in character to the sounds of the wind and the sea. Great accumulation of spume (like dirty lather) at that place — blown about by the wind in flakes torn from the huge mass. Extraordinary effect of this walk on us all. Pat running along the beach in a sort of ecstasy. I too felt like running, singing, dancing. Yet the sea, more than ever, was like a great hungry monster trying to get at us. Our exaltation was a sort of defiance.'

On the following day, my 27th birthday, we walked over the cliffs to Mevagissey. It was very wet. 'The two men and two dogs trying to get a flock of sheep through a gap: seizing the wether and dragging him through — but in vain. Dogs no good, compared to the little Welsh sheepdogs. Bracken and gorse. An early skylark — no, not early, I heard one at Richmond several weeks ago. — Visit to the Savage family at Mevagissey; but D.S. wasn't in. His wife and three boys. Very cramped in a small cottage, but the hospitality and composure of Mrs. S. were admirable.

'Still reading Jefferies: *The Story of my Heart*, at the rate of a few pages a day.

'Found a hermit crab, but killed it either by feeding it on cheese or by adding tap water to the salt water. Collected shells with A.'

On the 23rd, Good Friday, we walked to Dodman and Penare with Louis and a friend of his, Geoffrey Gibeon, then back to Gorran Haven along cliffs and beaches. 'Pheasants on the cliffs (overgrown with furze, brambles and gorse). Fine view from Dodman: a large stretch of sea and the brown cliffs of the coastline.'

That evening we walked to Helligan Mill and the woods. 'The sky had cleared, for the first time since our arrival. Walked back at night, by moonlight, via Mevagissey and Port Mellan. Very calm night.'

March 26th: 'Yesterday, walked to Caerheyes and Port Holland. Fine most of the time. Lunched on the beach at St. Michael Caerheyes. The woods of the Castle grounds come right down to the sea. Intended to go on to Port Low, but turned back with A., whose feet were sore.'

It was raining again. 'Have been down to the sea, but no long walks today. Began to write the Beethoven introduction. Reading Shakespeare's *King John*. Food shortage here (especially bread), so that Mary has had to bake twice today. Her two girl friends left today.

'Predominance of yellow in early spring flowers (primrose, daffodil, celandine, gorse, forsythia, crocus) — but exceptions, of course.'

March 27th: 'Walked to Helligan Mill, in fine weather, to have dinner with the Kittos. Looked at gardens at Helligan House, especially the sub-tropical garden planted below ground level — enormous rhododendrons, palm trees, lily ponds, exotic trees & shrubs. A strange air of decay. Walked back to Gorran Haven at midnight. Very dark at first, only starlight, then a red moon rose over the sea, growing paler & brighter as it rose higher.

'The introduction progresses slowly. As so often, first ideas on the subject recede when it comes to the writing. Someone will have to invent a machine that records pre-verbalized thoughts, instantly. (As I write the weather has turned: it's hailing.)

'Incredible conversations about the weather each morning in front of my bedroom window — an elaborate ritual in the village street. All the mental resources of those people must go into variations on the weather theme.'

March 29th: 'Lunched with D. S. Savage and his family. Dinner with him the previous night. His generosity: gave me seven books by W. J. Turner. Has difficulties with his four children. Uses long words and sarcasms when talking to them. Doesn't listen to what they say, then paraphrases what they've said, reproachfully — so with Romer, his daughter. His bitter insistence on the need for poverty. I agree with the insistence — there's no decent alternative to it for a writer — but am disturbed by the bitterness.'

As soon as we returned to London, early in April, there was too much work and social life for more than the most cursory and irregular diary entries. No sooner had I finished the Beethoven introduction than I began a review of Pound's *ABC of Reading*. 'Not a single poem this year,' I noted on April 9th, 'other than two small songs. Must try not to be distracted.' For once I had to turn away Peter when he called, because Anne was there, and I had to prepare her for Höfler's impact. Philip O'Connor needed clothes. D'Arcy Cresswell needed encouragement — more than I could give him when I was out of sympathy with the work he was doing or planning. I wanted him to get on with the third part of his autobiography, but he considered prose writing an activity for which he ought to be subsidized by a publisher — not unreasonably, except that I thought his prose superior to most of his verse. For twenty years that sequel to the two published autobiographies was taken up and dropped, to be left largely unwritten when he died.

X lost his job in journalism, but seemed almost relieved, if not elated. Year after year he had done his writing after a strenuous day at the office, putting on his 'thinking cap', a magical accessory that served to switch him over to the wavelength of imagination. Now freedom had been thrust on him, and he was going to make the most of it.

On April 14th my Austrian friend Felix Braun returned to Vienna with his family. A few days earlier we had gone to Bumpus's bookshop in Oxford Street and run into Vernon Watkins, on one of his rare visits to London. I introduced the two poets, and Felix Braun was delighted to meet a British poet who cared about German poetry.

When Vernon Watkins and I first met, in 1942, he was in the Air Force and had come to the Swiss pub in Old Compton Street to see Dylan Thomas, whose haunt it was at the time. Dylan Thomas introduced us, knowing that the interests we had in common included a special one in French and German poetry. Vernon's first book of poems had recently appeared, but at the age of 18 I did not keep up with new publications. Living poets were idols or nothing; and my idolatry was divided between T. S. Eliot and Dylan Thomas, disparate deities whom Vernon also acknowledged, together with W. B. Yeats, whose work I was still in the process of discovering. That first meeting was cordial, and I promptly bought *The Ballad of the Mari Lwyd*. Though I have a vague recollection of another meeting in London at that period, when I introduced Vernon to a London friend, I am almost sure that Vernon never returned to the nightly gathering of poets, painters and aspirants to the arts, or artiness, in the Swiss; and I too was waiting to join up.

Vernon and I must have lost touch during my four years in the Army and subsequent four terms at Oxford, unless Vernon came to Oxford in 1947 or 1948 to read his poems. The earliest letter from Vernon I can find, dated November 12th 1949, refers to our just missing each other at a London exhibition where we must have made an appointment to meet. 'I well remember meeting you in 1942,' he wrote. 'I hope you didn't have too bad a time in the Army. I was over here through the war, demobbed early in 1946, and lucky to have a pleasant environment during the last 3 years of it.' I must have offered to send him my first book of poems, due in 1950. His reply to this continued:

'What I look for first in a poet is intensity, and you have this. A poem must, for me, contain intensity in a unique form, impossible to paraphrase without loss. It is found in Hölderlin constantly. But large tracts of contemporary verse derive from a speculation situation allied to lucidity of thought; and there is everything there except the soul.'

Most probably I had sent Vernon — or got Tambimuttu to send him — a copy of my first book of Hölderlin translations. Vernon too, was to translate a good many poems of Hölderlin, and I can only hope that the friendship between us that developed in the next few years had nothing to do with his reluctance to collect these translations in book form. I certainly urged him to do so.

Having a memory at once selective — like a sieve — and telescopic, with a total incapacity for dates or chronological sequence, I can't remember when I first availed myself of Vernon's invitation, in the same letter, to visit him at Pennard, though I should think it must have been in the early 'fifties. I do remember being put up in his study on at least one occasion, before several longer stays in a shack that belonged to Vernon until he had to sell that part of the garden to his neighbour. In 1955 and 1958 — his letters tell me — I stayed there with my wife and children, and remember a night when a horse suddenly poked its head through the window. That must have been after the shack was sold, when we rented it from the neighbour, who owned a riding-school. By that time Vernon's family had grown too large to leave room in his bungalow for summer guests, and it was difficult enough for Gwen to cope with her normal chores. In June of 1962 we stayed at a small Swansea hotel, driving out to Gower each day. When Thomas Blackburn and I stopped at Pennard to see Vernon and Gwen in the spring of 1958, the accommodation problem was acute. Tom and I had to share a bed in the only room to be had in Southgate Village.

During that visit Vernon took us for a walk to Pwlldu and the Bishopston valley. Tom is an expert rock-climber, as I had been able to see for myself on the same trip, scrambling after him in the Snowdon area or waiting at the foot of rock-faces; but we were both amazed by the speed with which Vernon led us down almost invisible tracks on the steep cliff-side in failing light, agile and sure-footed as a chamois. That instinct was supported by familiarity; and altogether the Gower landscape is as inseparable from my recollections of Vernon as his poetry and person are inseparable from the place in which he chose to spend all his mature years, despite practical hardships and inconveniences aggravated by the recurrent bronchitis that weakened his heart. I also met Vernon in a London bookshop, at Kathleen Raine's house in Chelsea and at the ICA in London, where Vernon and I shared a poetry reading, in Swansea

— where I saw him behind the counter of the Lloyds Bank branch in which he worked until two years or so before his death — and in our house near Reading; but my image of him will always be out of doors, on walks above or below the cliffs, working in the garden, playing games, or on the rocks at low tide, out for lobsters, crabs and prawns, quick and efficient and somehow absent-mindedly absorbed in whatever he was doing. Nor did that image change in the twenty-five years of our acquaintance. I have the feeling that Vernon's hair was grey or white when I first met him; and when I saw him last, less than two months before his death, his face and movements were as youthful as ever. Though he knew about his heart, and his doctor had warned him years before to give up tennis, he could no more abstain from physical activity than from mental activity. On my last visit to him he was busy packing up and sorting books and papers that he would be needing in America, yet he found time to play cricket with his sons, to play croquet in the garden of the house which my sister had rented in the village, and to take me down once more on the rocks, insisting that I have the whole of our catch, though it was he who knew every rock-pool, prawn ledge and lobster or crab hole. Since the tides were unfavourable, that must have been Vernon's last prawning expedition.

As far as poetry is concerned, our relations were closest in the early and middle 'fifties, when I sent many poems to Vernon for criticism, dedicated a poem to him and received his *Epithalamion* for our marriage in 1951. Vernon became godfather to our second child Richard, born in 1955. His severe financial strains never prevented him from sending presents to Richard, any more than shortage of time prevented him from writing letters to him or typing his poem 'Parable Winkle' for Richard in 1964, though Vernon had five children of his own. What Vernon and Gower meant to me as a poet at that period becomes clear to me when I re-read my poem 'The Dual Site', not dedicated to Vernon, yet dominated by his image and by the wild life of Gower, including the ravens he had shown me on one of our walks, though their nest had been destroyed by the time I sent the poem to Vernon, as he told me in a letter. Vernon's image is fused with one of the two conflicting selves of that poem, though Vernon's other self — that of the bank teller who took the bus to Swansea morning after morning, year after year — also lent certain features to the first person of the poem. It was Vernon's single-mindedness, his utter refusal to make concessions in either sphere — by accepting promotion in the bank or by writing anything that he did not wish and need to write — that made his image exemplary. Yet Vernon accepted the division that tormented me. I did not want those spheres to be wholly separate; and I wanted my poems to draw on both of them, even if it meant sacrificing intensity to a wider awareness of heterogeneous, recalcitrant realities. These differences never became explicit between us, and our friendship continued, although the divergence increased in later years: but we ceased to comment on each other's work.

One reason why we could remain friends is that Vernon's single-mindedness and severity towards himself did not make him in the least intolerant. He could respect and even admire poets quite different from himself — W. H. Auden, for instance, or Heinrich Heine, whom he translated. It was I who quarrelled with Heine's impurity of feeling, Vernon who defended it in a letter referring to my review of his translations of Heine's 'The North Sea': 'Of course I feel more for the poems of Heine than you, but that is because the irony seems to me a mask which Heine had to wear because of his sensitivity. The nature of his genius is elusive, and so many readers treat the mask as absolute, whereas I think Heine really believed only in love, and rarely found it.' The mere fact that I wrote book reviews and critical essays might have been held against me if Vernon had been less generous, since he would not write criticism himself and was deeply distrustful of analytical, as distinct from intuitive, processes of any kind. Here are a few extracts from letters in which Vernon expressed his feelings about poetry and criticism.

'In poetry of the soul what is fragmentary is completed by love, and the work of art is made fragmentary by love; both revolve around the same centre, and both create themselves continually in relation to their artist who was only a medium.' (23/6/51)

'I've seen excellent numbers of the *New Statesman*; it is just that their attitude to poetry often seems false to me, just as I think Connolly's attitude to it is false, though he has often printed fine things. The weakness of that attitude is that aesthetic ideas are applied to metaphysical truth whereas in true poetry metaphysical truth transfigures the aesthetic ideas. I hope Connolly has changed in this, and enlarged his horizon.' (13/8/51)

Both these statements arose from an almost mystical creed, a creed that enabled Vernon to reconcile his religion of art with his Christian faith, an aesthetic dedication with an ethical and metaphysical commitment. In later years I could not accept that creed or Vernon's romantic cult of poets, as in the poems of homage collected in his book *Affinities*. Yet I had begun with a similar creed, and in my twenties I profited greatly not only by Vernon's detailed criticism of my poems, but by the convictions from which it proceeded;

'I like the new poem, but "promoted to madness" strikes me as too Rilke-like a phrase; it is also a little Audenesque. It is the "promoted" that I don't like, which has something of the macabre Rilke and the prep-school Auden; both are unworthy of its serious context.

'I'm no good at criticizing anyway. I can sympathize with your not wanting to do reviewing and that sort of thing. I saw a review on Saturday which filled me with disgust and made me feel that any poet passing judgement on a living contemporary is damned.' (28/10/51)

The word 'damned' was a strong word for Vernon to use, since he was as charitable as he was tolerant. His use of it in this connection, like the word 'disgust', shows that his religion of art made him peculiarly vulnerable, as well as giving him an integrity and a steadfastness that I never ceased to admire. Despite his charity towards individuals his rejections could be sweeping and categorical:

'Poetic criticism without quotation seems to me valueless. And general criticism such as I have seen in articles in English periodicals — ("Why is it that the output of poetry in post-war Germany is, on the whole, so disappointing?", etc.) — seems equally valueless. The answer is obvious: "Sorry: the poetry factory has closed".' (19/2/52)

Yet when I expressed my misgivings about being a free-lance writer and odd-job man (as I ceased to be in 1952, taking an academic job instead), Vernon wrote as follows:

'I hope you'll manage to get a job that you'll find congenial. I can quite understand your wish to extricate yourself from journalism. I imagine, though, that the critical work you write is irregular in character and that you have freedom of choice. In that case I don't feel that there is anything wrong with it. What is to be avoided is the weekly or monthly dissertation on a set of books the regular, commissioned review. But surely voluntary enthusiasm for writers of one's own choice must deepen one's understanding of them, just as translation in its laborious way brings to light so much that was hidden or marginal in a poem. The critic I despise is the pontifical evaluator of contemporaries, the speculator on the poetic stock exchange, the soulless monster who has never seen or heard of a widow's mite. I only despise him *as critic*.

'My own choice of a career was made for me, but you mustn't think that it would be the right choice for everybody. I would, in any case, be a hopeless journalist, especially as I am a slow reader and can hardly even follow a plot without Gwen's assistance.' (20/3/52)

'Don't worry about your poems. Poems do take a hell of a time when they want to, and then it's just better to leave them alone and turn back to them later. I saw (I think) a very stupid review of your book with one-line quotations whose potential depended so much on the context that the critic's comments were meaningless. I think I've missed few reviews of contemporary poetry in the *Listener* for several years, but I haven't seen one that was worth printing except for its quotations. The little "summing-up" is just not good enough; it turns sour in the ear.' (22/8/52)

'Don't be anxious or upset about your poems, or about the difficulties which lie between your writing and your lecturing. The creative impulse is generally impatient but the creative process is often slow, and what a poet sometimes mistakes for barrenness is the necessity of lying fallow. You know what I think generally about critics in this country, with perhaps two or three exceptions. I also believe that there can be no great criticism without love, and that the very nature and habit of most critics makes them incapable of an act of love. Their reputations are at stake, and they do not know what an excellent thing it would be to lose them.' (25/11/52)

That kind of encouragement, badly needed at a time when I was dissatisfied with the poems I had been writing and unable to make any progress, because of anxiety about my new academic duties, was one of the many things that I owe to Vernon's friendship. I still agree with what he says in those letters about poetry journalism, and I gave up reviewing the work of contemporary English poets with whom I was not in special sympathy. Yet what had hurt me in the reviews of my work to which Vernon alluded was that they confirmed my own dissatisfaction with it; and I think that even negative criticism, whatever its motive, proved useful to me in the end, once I had got over the distress of having my own doubts confirmed. Vernon helped me to become more patient and detached, though I had more use for criticism than he did. This came out once more when Vernon had read my critical book *Reason and Energy*, which he liked on the whole, apart from these disagreements:

(About Heine): 'In the short poems which many despise I find the expression of great genius. The key to the apparent triteness of some poems is in the cadence, which is the reverse of trite. Heine's protest seems to me absolute, and closely related to a profound belief, because he is near the beginning, near the act of creation at its simplest and purest. "Perhaps not", you will say. Perhaps not, indeed; but it takes more than logic to prove it.

'My only criticism, so far, of your book is that you pass relative judgement on poems. I suppose I represent the minority of one which believes that no critic does any service as to good and bad in anticipating the judgement of his readers. To present in terms of praise, which may be quantitative, or of censure, which may also be quantitative, is a different matter. Something inimitable has something secret about it. To compare productions in terms of "goodness", "merit", involves a comparison of the problems set in different works, and if that comparison is not exact and searching the other comparison will be futile. Nearly all great critics do it, of course, but it still seems to me unjustified, and I always feel uneasy when it happens, as though I ought to clap, perhaps at the wrong time.' (23/4/57)

Vernon's own criticism was consistent with those principles, as Dylan Thomas's letters to him also show. Commenting on my 'Spring Song in Winter', which I had sent him, he wrote:

'I don't, though, like the inversion at the end, and the structure of the final sentence seems to me too complex for the ending of a song ... I agree, of course, that you must keep your irregular stresses if you want them. For every lyric poet the rule must be: "Let the ear find its own true music." Still, I do feel that the sixth line is unsatisfactory: perhaps it is because the word "thing" is not strong enough to carry the emphasis of so long an epithet ... In a song where language is economical the salient points are terribly important. You must know that all the criticism of poetry that matters rests upon detail and upon fine points.' (16/2/53)

I did know it, and find that I must have acted on at least one of Vernon's strictures in this case, since the printed version of that poem does not contain the word 'thing'. In the same letter Vernon wrote:

'I'm glad you met Heller. He's a very nice person. I haven't seen him for months, but I heard his talk, or most of it, on the Third. It failed, I think, as all eloquence must which tries to displace reality, but it was stimulating enough. Wisdom consists of crumbs, I think. I distrust the wide open spaces of competence.'

That love of particulars, in literature and elsewhere, was common ground between us at all times, as in the years from 1959 to 1962, when I was editing two volumes of translations from Hofmannsthal and had to act as Vernon's critic. After much correspondence about points of detail arising over Vernon's contributions, he proved as willing to adopt my suggestions, or most of them, as I had been to adopt his, or most of his; and Vernon was my senior by almost twenty years. If our meetings became rarer in the next few years, and our letters shorter, confined to news of what we were doing, it was not only because my work was moving in a direction which was alien to Vernon, but also because both of us were subject to external pressures that made meetings and correspondence more difficult. Pressure, haste, and perhaps a certain self-entrenchment, due to Vernon's more and more isolated position among the poets of the 'fifties and 'sixties are evident in his handwriting, which changed at this period, becoming much more difficult to read. Vernon's teaching post at Swansea, after his retirement from the bank, and his visiting professorships in America only strengthened his opposition to critical methods based on general theories or on a rational positivism. A few months before his second visit to Seattle he wrote about his appointment at Swansea:

'I am rather independent in my "teaching" of poetry and ask my students not to read any criticism until they have received direct the poems they want to receive. Even good criticism can be so narrowing and misleading.' (14/6/67)

That was Vernon's last letter to me. Yet after our stay at Pennard in August, he wrote again to my son to comment on a poem which Richard had sent him, though Vernon had already left Wales with Gwen and his younger children, and was waiting to embark for America. The next news was the news of his death at Seattle, where another friend, Theodore Roethke, had died in a way all too similar.

Our last conversations at Pennard were overshadowed not by forebodings of his death — Vernon was as vigorous and keen-edged as ever — but by an event in my life of which he knew. For once the Gower coast left me cold, and nothing that I saw and heard could quite penetrate my painful preoccupation. Vernon showed me new poems and told me about the new book he had recently put together. He too was preoccupied, with practical arrangements and preparations, but dealt with these as cheerfully and energetically as he had dealt with all the practical hardships of his life, always finding time for other people, if not for his own work. Had I had any reason to fear that those meetings would be our last, I should never have written to him about my troubles, though he would surely have sensed them; and I should have made a greater effort to be a more responsive companion than I was.

As for the differences in our work and outlook, these were inevitable, and not to be regretted. Though Vernon was the one who remained immovably centred — even physically, in a place and house that did not change substantially in all those years, while I must have moved house at least six times since my return to England in 1947 — both of us did what we had to do. Vernon purified and intensified his vision, perhaps at the cost of certain potentialities that strike me in the shorter poems collected in his first book. All his allegiances remained constant, even that to his public school. (I had paid tribute to mine in a poem written at the age of twenty — a poem I cannot recall, let alone re-read, without the most acute embarrassment.) The variety of his work lies in its extraordinary range of forms and metres, by no means always traditional, yet always mastered and made his own by an infallible ear. His range of themes and imagery was circumscribed by the constancy of his allegiances, as his musical range was not; and this has to do with anti-realistic, anti-rational premises hardly reconcilable with many phenomena of the modern world. Yet, until poetry itself becomes obsolete, or this earth uninhabitable, Vernon's natural and human archetypes will be accessible to a few readers at the least.

I can no more pass judgement on Vernon's work than I can on my own, since I cannot separate his work from his person, or his person from my life and my work. I shall never be able to read his poems without hearing his voice and seeing him as he was — one of the most admirable and lovable men it has been my good fortune to know.

Another of my brief visits to Oxford in April produced a poem, 'Islands'. I stayed with my childhood friend Elinor McHatton on her barge, only barely avoiding one of the quarrels to which we were prone — about politics, about religion, about her fellow anthropologists at Oxford, about almost anything. Bryan Wynter was also there and acted as a buffer between us.

With the help of Anne, soon to be my wife, I gave a poetry reading at Goldsmiths' College. There I read a few poems myself. I hadn't yet learnt to detach myself from my work, and to read any of it in pubic was an agony of self-exposure. Nor had poetry readings become the sort of institution and routine that they tend to be now. For one thing, most of them were unpaid, so there was no extrinsic pressure to harden oneself to the ordeal, as to any professional function.

Thanks to a cheque from the Bollingen Foundation, my income shot up to an unprecedented £500 odd that year, only to revert to a miserable £210 in 1952 — the year in which I capitulated, taking an academic job. 'Perhaps it's time I permitted myself the luxury of destitution,' I'd written in March, 'and let others help me for a change. It would be refreshing.' But that was before my marriage: and a combination of pride and anxiety ruled out that pleasant alternative in any case.

Vernon and Gwen Watkins came to tea at my flat in April. Vernon read some of the poems I had been writing and made useful suggestions for improvements of weak lines. As usual, I was dissatisfied with my work in a more general way, noticing that London life — and literary life in particular — elicited nothing but 'gloom and visions of dissolution, while I come back refreshed and stimulated from almost every excursion.' John Pettavel had drawn my attention to a quotation from a Zen Buddhist in a book by Suzuki. I asked for a copy of this apothegm, which I thought the last word on art: 'Draw bamboos for ten years, become a bamboo, then forget all about bamboos when you're drawing. In possession of an infallible technique, the individual places himself at the mercy of inspiration.' I must have recognized the relevance of those 'ten years' to my dissatisfaction with the poems I was writing. It was one thing to be aware of their inadequacies, quite another to overcome them, except by constant practice and repeated failure. After more than ten years of writing I hadn't reached the stage of 'becoming a bamboo'; but I had begun to understand why I might have to wait much longer. I was still trying to make simple lyrics out of complicated experiences and perceptions. At that time it was a sequence called 'The Pagan Dream', which wouldn't cohere as a sequence, so that most of the parts had to be discarded. Too late, I concluded that the whole thing should have been written as one continuous poem, for which I never had leisure enough; and that I must 'cultivate patience', letting poems grow in their own good time.

I took Anne to Mitcham to meet Heinz Priebatsch, and to Hampstead to meet the Höflers. Peter Höfler delivered a jeremiad about the Festival of Britain and the new concert hall, whose acoustics were reported to be bad. He also told me to give up trying to be a poet, as I had more aptitude for criticism and essay-writing, like Herbert Read, whom he said I should 'replace'. Knowing what Höfler thought of critics, essayists, and Herbert Read in particular, I was in no danger of feeling flattered by his advice; but the substance of it wasn't new to me, and I'd got used to Höfler's intuitive judgements. He had taken to Anne — who was rehearsing her part in a production of *Everyman* put on in connection with the Festival — and that was the main thing. Early in May, Anne and I decided to get married. Kathleen Raine, to whom I had announced the news, wrote on May 22nd from Ross-shire: 'I am delighted to hear that you are thinking of getting married, and I'm sure that you will be happy, and make an infinitely better husband and father of a family than quite any poet I can think of ... I wish you could find some kind of regular job — part-time even — when you come back, because marriage on a free-lance income is difficult. But I'm sure it will all work itself out. I came here to work in peace, but there are so many more distractions (for me) in a remote Highland glen, and little chain of islets on to which you can walk at low tide, than even in London, that so far I have done little beyond reading. However, if the weather breaks, I may work, for then there would be no distracting alternative of cloudless skies and seas.'

Later that month I went to France again — briefly to Paris, loathing it, then to Vézelay and Avallon. I was worn out with hack work and needed to recuperate. Since I kept no record of the trip, all that remains of it is the greenness of the Yonne countryside, and the richness of the birdsong to which I woke in the mornings. These came back to me in a poem about Berkshire mornings some ten years later. Otherwise they, too, might well have been merged in other impressions and memories, like the buildings I admired at Vézelay. A letter from Anne, posted on May 24th to the Hotel Pas de Calais in the rue des Saints-Pères but forwarded to Vézelay, tells me what drove me out of Paris almost as soon as I got there. It was the bohemia of the cafés, and an exhibitionism which I contrasted with the unpretentiousness of my painter friend Françoise, a genuine and gifted artist who didn't have a chance of being recognized. Anne suggested that I take some of her work back to England and try to sell it, but I had left Paris by that time, and shouldn't have known in any case how to be an effective agent for a painter.

Before our marriage I met Dylan Thomas again, at a reading he gave in Bayswater. I also had an appointment with T. S. Eliot at his office in

Russell Square. I had seen him once or twice since our first meeting, but had little conversation with him at a dinner-party given by his friend Miss Lockyer at her club. Our formal meeting at Faber's was disappointing. He seemed tired and bored. He asked me what I was doing, and I mentioned the forthcoming marriage. His response was something like: 'Well, yes, I suppose we all have to get married once in our lives.' I never made another appointment with Eliot. The only meeting with him at which he talked freely occurred by chance, after his second marriage, when I caught up with him walking in Kensington Gardens. It was a hot day. He was formally dressed, as usual. I saw him hesitate, then disappear behind a tree — to take off his waistcoat, making sure that this indecent operation was conducted as inconspicuously as possible. I didn't want him to know that I had spied on him at that point, but did go up to him later, when he had difficulty in lowering himself into a deck-chair, and I was able to help him. For the next hour or so we talked about anything and everything, from the ducks on the pond to the difference between Catholic and Anglican priests, and Eliot's relations with Hugo von Hofmannsthal.

Anne and I were married at the Paddington Registry Office on July 28th. Our wedding reception, at my mother's house, was a slightly precarious affair, since I had invited quite a few of my literary and bohemian friends, some of whom didn't mix too well with people invited by my mother and parents-in-law. Philip O'Connor arrived drunk, ground biscuits into the carpet with his heel, slapped elderly ladies on the bottom and asked them: 'Are you a bloody bourgeois or a Communist?' My father-in-law wanted him thrown out. I resisted; and in fact Philip was there, fast asleep, when all the other guests had left.

Philip O'Connor is too complex a character and writer to be summarized here in the cursory fashion of this book. Much as I saw of him over the decades ever since our first meetings in Soho during the war — staying with him at Clare, Suffolk, and at Croesor in Wales, seeing him in London and on his unexpected calls on us at Tilehurst, near Reading, when he was tramping — I did not begin to understand him until a recent meeting in London, after a party for the re-publication of his best-known book, *Memoirs of a Public Baby.* The reason why I did not understand him, only liked him despite all the differences and difficulties between us, is that I had taken his paradoxes and provocations too literally — much as I had some of the utterances of Francis Bacon and Lucian Freud — instead of responding to them as the gestures they were.

Because I remained so shockable, he felt compelled to shock me whenever possible, quite especially when we were not alone but in company he felt to be inimical or only indifferent to him. Very often I refused to be amused by the more outrageous acts or utterances of the *persona* he had assumed since childhood, that of the 'public baby' and *enfant terrible*, quite forgetting that beneath all his performances there was a seriousness and an innocence even more consistent than the *persona* which he could drop at times in writings like his book on tramps and tramping, *Vagrancy*, just as he could drop it when he merely talked in private. The correspondence we kept up all those decades, sporadically, did not help much, as long as I could not translate his paradoxes and provocations into gestures that had another meaning, often diametrically opposed to the surface one. This was to happen only after a flash of insight at our late meeting and in subsequent letters from France, where Philip has been living for the past fifteen years; letters in which Philip himself dropped the verbal mask. Amongst other things, he is a brilliant comedian, as on a tape I still have but cannot play back — because it was made for a machine long anachronistic — of an interview with himself. As long as I have known him, for more than 45 years, Philip has been engaged in a dialectic of extremes, very often unintelligible to anyone but himself, and only rarely carried to a synthesis that would be intelligible to others. He himself has recorded that dialectic in his autobiographical books and in an unpublished journal.

For our honeymoon we went to Austria, first to the Tyrol, then to Carinthia. Felix Braun had suggested that we meet him at Alpbach, where there was an annual gathering of artists and intellectuals. When we got to Brixlegg, near Innsbruck, we found that there was no suitable accommodation to be had at Alpbach, but we did find a farmhouse about half-way up the mountain. We preferred that house, with its smell of timber and hay, to any hotel. Frau Bradl cooked us extraordinary meals. When quite a succession of these had consisted only of 'Mehlspeisen' — various sorts of pastry, always sweet — I couldn't help asking her whether this was their usual fare. She took it as a complaint, and promptly went out into the garden to kill one of her indispensable hens. The whole of this was served for the next meal, though Anne was a vegetarian at the time, and I couldn't possible eat it all. After that I made a point of praising her 'Mehlspeisen', which were delicious, but not what we were used to as a main or only course.

At Alpbach I gave a reading, and we attended others, by Friedrich Dürrenmatt — an almost unknown young writer at the time — and by Ilse Aichinger, whom I had already met in London and whose twin sister, Helga, was an old friend. On one of our Alpine walks we met the physicist Erwin Schrödinger, another participant in the Alpbach gathering, though in a capacity beyond our ken. Ignorant as I was at the time of his books and their relevance to my very different specialization, it was his personality alone that impressed us when we walked back with him to Alpbach; and his extraordinarily warm response to a couple of young people met on a mountain.

In Carinthia I showed Anne the places associated with my years in the Occupation, including Manya's shack and the D.P. camp — or what remained of it — into which Manya and her family had moved after vacating the shack. Tourism was just beginning to encroach on the lakes and villages, but the mountainside paths were as unfrequented as they had been four years earlier. On August 17th I wrote to Elinor McHatton from Seeboden: 'Thank you for writing at last. I wondered what had become of you, but could get no information. The only common friend of ours I've seen since you left for the Sudan is Steiner, and he hasn't heard from you. He is now in Spain, is much better and hopes to go out on field-work next year ...

'Yes, I'm now married, have been since last month. So, apart from writing "sad poems" (I wasn't aware that they're sad) we (Anne and I) have been looking for a flat — no easy matter in London these days, if one hasn't a lot of money. We seem to have found one the day before we left for Austria; so I expect we shall be moving some time in September, though the place is in a filthy state ...

'Have decided to write a little more, though I'm rather weak after an attack of dysentery (or something very much like it) which made me run out into the fields last night, as we live in a small annexe and there is no lavatory, except in the main building, which they lock at night. We can't cope with Austrian food generally, for it's full of fat and garlic, neither of which I can stomach. I forgot to say that I'm doing one other thing — revising my Hölderlin book and translating more of his poems. He is such a fine poet that I shall be sorry when I've translated all the poems I like; and he makes me feel a mere poetaster. There's some hope of a new edition of the H. book, but this won't be decided till September, as it depends on an American publisher, who must buy 2000 copies of the book before the English publisher (Routledge) will venture to publish it ...'

While we were in Austria I corrected the proofs of the Beethoven book — not very well, in those circumstances, as I discovered when a musicologist listed my errors in a review. One unforeseen consequence of the book was that I was mistaken for a musicologist, as well as being confused with Paul Hamburger, the pianist and music critic. I was invited to take part in a discussion of a Beethoven quartet on the Third Programme, and did so. Much later, and in a different connection, I even recorded a bit of impromptu piano playing for the BBC — in a radio play based on Hölderlin's life that I wrote with Anne's help. When it came to Hölderlin's strumming on the piano in his madness, there was no one available in the studio to produce the right sort of noise; so I volunteered for the job.

For a time we lived in my one-room flatlet in Randolph Crescent, then moved into a two-room flat in Alexandra Road, Hampstead — the ground floor of a semi-detached house that had come down in the world, like the whole street. Anne was content to share my poverty and put up with the compulsive working habits that kept me at my desk every morning of the week, whatever else was going on, whether there was a poem demanding to be written, a slack line to be replaced, or only some journalistic deadline to be met. Our way of life was still free compared to that of people with regular jobs and she had been one of these for a while — or compared with the restrictions imposed on her private life before marriage by a somewhat Victorian father. As for me, I should have been cured of my chronic melancholy at last but for a succession of deaths among my friends in the first year or so of our marriage.

Hermon Ould's stomach trouble turned out to be cancer, of which he died that autumn. In March, Andrew Ciolcosz, a gifted Polish refugee whom I had first met at Oxford, killed himself. Peter Höfler, Heinz Priebatsch and Franz Baermann Steiner died in the course of 1952 — all of cardiac thrombosis, all three in their forties. Each in his way had been not only a good friend but a component of my own awareness, a link with concerns and experiences from which I could easily have been cut off by my early transplantation. And there was the sheer pity of those deaths — brought home to us almost physically in the case of Heinz Priebatsch, since Anne and I were with him when he died; the pity, too, of work left undone and of work left homeless. Peter Höfler's apparitions proved as sudden and demanding after his death as before it. I tried to lay his ghost in a sonnet sequence, my last, called 'A Wreath of Thistles', but was still preoccupied with him ten years later. Franz Baermann Steiner died very suddenly in November 1952, at the time of the Stalinist purges in Czechoslovakia, only a few hours after feeling well enough to receive students in his rooms.

Peter Höfler, for one, undoubtedly thought that I had adapted too well to my British upbringing; and there was a time, in my late teens and early twenties, when I may have 'over-compensated' for my foreign origin, as naturalized subjects — not excluding my idol of that period, T. S. Eliot — are apt to do. (Relations with step-mothers, notoriously, tend to be more complicated and more intense than relations with natural mothers, if only because the incest taboo becomes a matter less of instinct than of mere propriety.) Yet some instinct always warned me off the more extreme forms of mimesis, such as changing my name; and, from the same early period, I had also felt the need to be in touch with refugees less assimilated than myself. Alfred Marnau and Peter Höfler were among the earliest of my refugee acquaintances who wrote in their first language, German. At Oxford I was put in touch with a young poet from Breslau, Silesia, Hans Werner Cohn, who was working as a hospital orderly, and became interested in his work. Not much later I got to know his friend Erich Fried, who was to become prominent and prolific as a post-war German poet. His early poems were published by the Austrian P.E.N. Club during the war, in London and Zürich. At the time I met him he applied much of his prodigious energy to helping other refugee poets, circulating their work in typescript, arranging poetry readings for them, and generally acting as a catalyst. Through F.B. Steiner I got to know H. G. Adler, who had spent the war years in German concentration camps, yet was capable of enough detachment from his ordeals to write scrupulously documented studies of their structure and organization — in between poems, novels and short stories. At Erich Fried's, I first met Paul Celan, on one of his rare visits to London from Paris, and began to follow his work, which became increasingly important to me.

Since I had begun to write in English, and the true home of a writer, *qua* writer, is the language he writes in, my problems could not be the same as theirs. When much later, in the 'sixties, I tried for a while to write in both languages, far from mending the rift between two areas of experience or giving me the freedom of dual nationality, the attempt left me feeling stateless in a no-man's land, though the German prose pieces I produced were not ambitious in manner or range. Translation, I had to conclude was the right bridge for me; and even that was for one-way traffic only, into the language in which I felt at home. It wasn't a question of what I chose to do or chose to be, of identification with this or that, loyalty to this or that. The turning-point had come before I was old enough to choose. Now I had to make the most of my anomalous situation, regardless of whether the language I had adopted would wholly adopt me. It was one more risk to be added to those inherent in the mug's game.

At the same time, a language is always more than a language. To use it is to be involved in ways of thinking and feeling that have shaped it. The first stage in acquiring a language not one's first demands an almost passive acceptance of its peculiar conventions, and this process is conducive to the overcompensation I have mentioned — the exaggerated correctness that betrays foreignness. For the next stage, a more critical engagement with the idioms and sinews of the language, I had to be at once inside it and outside it. A second turning-point occurred when I recognized and accepted that paradox.

In 1952 I published my second collection of poems, as a pamphlet in a series which I didn't much like; and the very much revised and enlarged edition of my Hölderlin translations. I was still a fairly regular contributor to periodicals. Yet it became clear to me in the course of that year that I was turning out too much, without any prospect of earning enough money to keep more than one person alive. The lukewarm or hostile reception given to my pamphlet of poems in the press discouraged me less than the response of friends whose judgement I knew to be free from the professional envy and malice of the poetry cliques. At least one friend, Philip Rawson who wrote poems, but was mainly a draughtsman, sculptor and orientalist — damned that collection more thoroughly than any reviewer had done. True, I also received positive responses from poets whose judgement I valued. Kathleen Raine, writing from her lighthouse retreat in Ross-shire, praised many of the poems in the pamphlet and, what mattered more, out of real understanding of the tensions I was grappling with: 'You certainly write beautifully about London. It is easy to be a peasant-philosopher in the country where "nothing, once made, is wasted, No web undone", but harder to see it as still true in the world of the Interrupted Nocturne. In the Highlands that natural economy survives, but is dying out. It is the old women of seventy to a hundred (of whom there seems to be a good number) who dye the wool from their own sheep with bogmyrtle and heather-shoots, spin it, weave it, and wear it. Life of that simplicity is hard, but free from anxiety, because our survival is in our own hands, a matter between ourselves and the earth ... No, it requires great courage to be a poet now, to affirm the good against the triumphing evil. You do so, and so does Edwin Muir, and Vernon Watkins, and Dylan Thomas, and a few other poets and painters, but many are on the side of the evil, mere mouth-pieces of the time ... It is all the more important because you are affirming in the City — Muir and Watkins, and Dylan Thomas, and myself all affirm it from our peasant roots, but yours is the harder task, and the more necessary.' Yet I knew it was high time I ceased to be dependent on prompt publication. When Professor L. A. Willoughby proposed the possibility of an assistant lectureship at University College, London — where he had been head of the German Department before retiring — I took up the proposal and applied for the appointment.

Meanwhile we made the best of the mobility I was soon to give up. In April we left for Spain, stopping at Carcassonne. The night train journey from Paris was exasperating and funny. The third-class compartment was packed. Two mothers, with three children between them, believed that ventilation of any kind was deadly. A mute war began almost at once. I would open the compartment door, one of the ladies would shut it. We had the tacit support of a man in a beret. The remaining occupant, a dark-haired girl who kept re-reading a black-rimmed letter and contemplating a photograph, was not interested enough in survival to take sides. Not a word was spoken; but the middle-aged man in the beret kept us amused by miming his discomfort or poking the fat lady next to him with his pencil when her snoring became too obtrusive.

Despite a sleepless night we spent the morning walking around Carcassonne, looking at the cathedral, St. Vincent, and the ruins of the old town, with its basilica. After lunch we had to go to sleep. Over lunch we made friends with one of those small-headed, under-fed French cats, touched by the timidity and gentleness with which it begged for food, standing on its hind legs and lightly touching me on the elbow. At the cathedral we had been harangued in dialect by an old woman, half-comedian, half-Cassandra, who ended by giving us her blessing, in exchange for alms. On the train to Barcelona, next day, I talked with Spanish fellow-passengers in a mixture of French and Italian. They warned us of the expense of staying in Barcelona, where foreigners were over-charged in every restaurant and bar. One of them, the owner of a hotel in Le Havre, not only recommended a hotel in Barcelona but took us there. We had really intended to go straight on to Mallorca, but decided to stop for a few days and see a bullfight — with very mixed feelings. After my disappointment and disgust with the bullfight I had seen in Provence I wanted to see the real thing.

We liked the Public Gardens, though the zoo and aquarium were poorly stocked and badly kept. In the half-light of the cathedral, an interplay of candle-light with daylight filtered through stained glass, there was enough activity to keep us fascinated for hours. It seemed strange to us that geese were kept in the cloisters. Unlike the goldfish in the pool they could hardly be considered ornamental. There was no clear division between the sacred and the profane, the spiritual and the material, as in Protestantism. A cathedral was as much a place to be lived in as a house or a street. From the window of our hotel room we looked on to a small roof garden, of the kind I had seen in Italy. On this one no hens were kept, but there was an alsatian dog and various plants in pots. Four children played there. Once we threw them a bar of chocolate, to their uproarious delight.

On our way to buy tickets for the Sunday bullfight we admired the flowers and caged birds on sale along the Ramblas. That same day we took a longer walk to Montjuich, and got our first idea of the city's full extent. We had seen only a fraction of it. Trees and shrubs were in full flower on the hillside. Yet it was a different smell that overpowered us on our way back, when we found ourselves in a colony of hovels above the harbour. The children who ran about there were either naked or in rags. A woman was roasting sunflower seeds. There were no drains or bathrooms, though the interiors of some of the hovels looked quite clean. Anne was frightened; but most of these paupers — we assumed that they'd been removed from the city and forced to live here — didn't so much as look up when we walked by. One man did speak to us, in English, and complained bitterly about the government. Even he retained his Spanish pride, and didn't beg. We had given some money to a woman from the same settlement when we met her on the road; and more to a gypsy girl from another settlement nearby that was even more primitive, with no houses at all, only tarpaulins for shelter. These Gypsies seemed to spend their time squatting on the ground in their filthy alley.

The bullfight was a harrowing experience. We saw five of the six scheduled fights before Anne had to leave, feeling sick. I should have taken her away sooner, since the very first fight reduced her to tears, and she could hardly bear to see more. I didn't feel too well either, but I couldn't drag myself away. I tried to explain to myself at the time what had transfixed me there: 'The confrontation with death is at the root of the game: the bull's death is the crudest form in which this confrontation is realized. Ceremony overcomes the fear of death. The animal dies so that men may know their humanity. That is why the spectators are merciless: the actors must act out their parts. To stumble or misjudge becomes a crime, because it distorts the meaning of the play. A bad performance is disgusting: ritual slaughter becomes plain butchery. One can't apologize for the cruelty of the thing by saying that the antagonists are well matched. The bull doesn't choose to fight and doesn't know how to take advantage of his opponent. (Tonight, for instance, two men would have been gored on the ground if the bulls hadn't turned away.) If one can't face the cruelty, the whole performance is revolting and painful, as it was to Anne; but there is a good reason, difficult to formulate, why the cruelty should be faced, as it is in tragedy. The bull, too, is both victim and hero. The bull is always cheered at the end, but more enthusiastically if it put up a good fight.' The experience went deep enough to bring about a change in my poetry. 'Pity and terror in the raw', is how I summed it up in the poem 'Palinode' that was to serve as a sort of introduction to the harder verse in my next collection.

Before leaving Barcelona we attended a service, Benediction, in Santa Maria del Mar, the church nearest to our hotel. The boys' choir was almost inaudible at times, like the rest of the service, because of workmen hammering away — no one seemed to mind or even notice the noise. Every member of the congregation was handed a lighted taper, walked to the altar in procession, kissed the cross, extinguished the taper, and left.

It was still rather cold when we took our last walk through the town, along the Via Layetana, across the Ramblas and narrow side streets to Ronda San Pablo and the Plaza Real. Despite the cold sea breeze the air was full of dust and grime, not to mention the rubbish thrown into the streets out of windows. We crossed to Mallorca overnight, leaving on April 28th.

At Palma we found a note from Robert Graves, to whom we had been introduced in writing by Kathleen Raine. We moved into a *pensione* near the harbour. After lunch we called on Robert and Beryl

Graves at their Palma flat, also seeing Martin and Janet Seymour-Smith. Martin, whom I had met at my Oxford lecture on Edwin Muir, was acting as tutor to the Graves children, Jan was helping Robert Graves with classical research. We joined Robert Graves and Martin on a shopping expedition, and went back there after dinner to play pontoon.

On the way home I began to feel ill. Though I had drunk some brandy at the Graves's, this time it wasn't the alcohol but one of the sudden fevers I had had before in Italy. I spent the night shaking on my bed. In the early morning, on my way to the lavatory, I had a blackout and collapsed. Poor Anne, who'd had no more sleep than I, had to drag me back to bed. She tried to get a doctor, though I told her I didn't need one.

Robert Graves and Martin called next evening, bringing books and magazines. Robert prescribed lemon juice for what he diagnosed to be a sort of food-poisoning, and I was up again by the morning. After some desultory sight-seeing, we walked with Robert Graves and Martin to San Roca, a village near Palma, then to the woods beyond. I was mainly interested in the flora, asphodels and some sort of wild iris, and in the local snails, conical and pointed like a species of watersnail I had kept.

After lunch with Martin and Janet we saw Robert Graves's work-room and read a poem he had just finished. He had been kind enough to read my new collection in proof, but would not comment on it beyond saying that he had read them with pleasure and liked a particular poem. Later, on one of our walks to the beach at Deya, he made some general observations which may or may not have been directed at what he knew of my work. I remember his warning about the use of adjectives and present participles, also of sibilants. For a time I tried to write poems with no adjectives in them at all, before realizing that some adjectives are functional and essential. The slurring heaviness of present participles, too, proved indispensable in the right place. Rightness, in the end, depended on what effects were needed in any one instance. Yet I did make a principle of avoiding the kind of epithet that produces fuzziness.

After dinner we joined the Graves's for coffee and literary gossip. Then we went with them to see some Spanish dancing. On the way Robert Graves talked to me about his forthcoming book on Christ, but I could say nothing intelligent about his thesis. The only scrap of dialogue I remembered long enough to write it down was this:

R.G.: 'Do you mind if I change over? For some reason I always have to walk on the left side of people.'

M.H.: 'They say the left side is the side of intuition.'

R.G.: 'Yes. It's also the side of destruction and cursing.'

I tried to sum up my impressions of Robert Graves at this stage, but was sure they were superficial. 'He has something of the satyr about him, even in the set of his features, the curve of his mouth and the very striking blue eyes, which are wide, almost staring, without being dreamy or in any way expressive of feeling. He is very proud. His conversation is witty and erudite. I have the feeling that he avoids certain depths & prefers details to generalities, especially the more disturbing ones. He adopts a casual and hearty manner, the ex-officer's, and is probably capable of a certain ruthlessness in personal relations. (To us he has been consistently kind.) But I don't pretend that I understand his complex character after only a few days. What strikes me most about him is his subtlety. He's a master of the indirect approach — which means, of course, that he know exactly where he wants to go. I've probably mistaken the mask for the face. For he wears a mask, and rightly so. It becomes more and more clear to me that a poet can't do without one. It protects his face from all sorts of indignities and afflictions. Above all, it keeps it intact. R.G. has enormous energy. Without it he would never have been able to live by his writing. At the moment he's writing two long works (one on Greek mythology, one on Christ), and translating two or three others.'

Robert Graves talked both to Anne and me about our future. He almost persuaded me to continue as a professional writer and withdraw the application for a lectureship. Yet I had to allow for the differences between us, knowing that I should never be able to subsidize my poetry from the proceeds of historical novels, as he had done. Nor were conditions what they had been when he was a young writer. Fees and royalties had not risen in proportion to the inflation of prices, and the 'general reading public' that had sustained him was in the process of dwindling away. As for universities, Robert Graves's one experience of a teaching appointment, in Egypt, was too exceptional to be applicable to my situation, though I could understand his anti-academicism, and shared it to some extent after my second period at Oxford. What I couldn't explain to him was how unacknowledged pressures had caused me to publish too much, too soon; and that I could see no remedy for this but a regular job of some kind. Perhaps

Robert Graves was right in principle, nevertheless. After twelve years in universities I did cut myself loose again; but that's another story, not to be told here.

We stayed in Palma over the week-end, seeing a great deal of Martin and Janet, while the Graves's were at Deya. Janet, Martin and I went to another bullfight. The first thrill and horror had been modified by a cooler interest in the finer points, to which Martin was able to draw my attention. One of the matadors, Lozano, fought three times instead of the scheduled two, because the first two bulls were not good enough, and too easily dispatched. One novelty of the occasion was a woman picador, whose horse slipped and fell almost at once. Since the matador also proved incompetent, the whole performance fell flat. An important factor I had scarcely noticed until Martin pointed it out to me was the short-sightedness of bulls. I learned that I should never become an 'aficionado'. The first impact had been enough for me.

On May 8th we moved to Deya by coach, passing through Valdemosa and over mountain roads. We went straight down to the bay and swam, though the deep blue water was still cold. We stayed at the little village inn, the Fonda, exceptionally well looked after, perhaps because Señor Graves, the local squire, had recommended us. Robert Graves had also given us the key to his house by the church, *La Posada*, and the use of it for work. We picked up the key from his secretary, Karl. When we got to the house I found that for once, I could do no work. So I read *Goodbye to all that* while Anne did some flute practice.

On our walk up one of the mountains around Deya I concentrated on the flora, as usual, also picking wild flowers for Anne. There were holm oaks, a few pines, and twisted olive trees so stunted that I wondered how they could still bear fruit. (Robert Graves gave us a bottle of local olive oil to take home, and it was the best we ever tasted.) I found the same wild iris or gladioli I had seen near Palma and a wild garlic, also asphodel and broom. Three black piglets suddenly appeared and followed us. All but the highest parts of the mountains were terraced, with olive groves and plantations of locust trees. On the slopes we met woodcutters with mules and carts. Some of the terraces were being ploughed.

Our habit of reading and flute practice in the mornings continued, thanks to the use of La Posada. In the afternoons we walked or swam, taking either the steep path over the rocks (favoured by Robert Graves) or the lower and longer path. Occasional clouds and rain did not change the colour of the sea or its translucency. We took a moonlight walk to the little churchyard. 'The weather cleared shortly before dusk,' I noted on the 8th; 'the mountains were golden, pink and mauve at sunset. Night sounds: frogs, nightingales, crickets, the bird (nightjar?) that emits a single unvaried note; sheeps' bells. The lemon trees, now in blossom, seemed to smell more strongly in the dark, perhaps only because it had rained most of the day.'

On the 9th we set out on a long walk, hoping to get as far as Soller; but the sky had now cleared, and about half-way to Soller we turned back, taking the coast road in search of shade. The scenery was wilder than at Deya, with wild honeysuckle on the roadside, and a profusion of lizards and geckos. We stopped for tea at the Costa d'Or.

In the evening we had tea with Karl, from whom I borrowed a number of books. The Graves were due at Deya the following day. We met their bus, had tea with them at Canellun, and went swimming with Robert and his son William, not from the beach this time, but diving from the rocks. On the way down I nearly tripped when Robert Graves said that Yeats was a sham and a bad poet. The recent poets he praised were Doughty, de la Mare, W. H. Davies and Charles Sorley, whom he thought the most promising of the First World War poets. I didn't yet know the story of Graves's quarrel with Yeats over *The Oxford Book of Modern Verse* and Yeats's rejection of poems by James Reeves, or his hostility to almost every contemporary poet who had not been a personal friend or disciple. 'His views were disconcerting' I noted, 'but only as far as other poets are concerned. Everything he said about the writing of poetry was most interesting and useful. He told me that the only thing a poet learns as he grows older is to grow aware of the point of boredom, to eliminate the superfluous and the tedious. He also talked about what words are admissible in poetry & which are unpoetic, saying that certain modernisms are admissible only for the purpose of satire' — an anti-modernist, classical standpoint which I couldn't quite accept even at that time, when my work kept well within the bounds of convention.

We went back to Canellun for sherry, ate at the Fonda, and returned at 9. We missed Martin and Janet, who had stayed behind in Palma because Martin was ill with malaria. Quite a number of British and American residents at Deya turned up at the Graves's house that night, and there was no opportunity for further conversation on poetry. We spent more time with Robert next day, when he showed us round the

Fonda with three of his children, took us to the houses of friends, went swimming with us again, and invited us to Canellun for the evening. Swollen glands and a sore throat didn't damp his animation. (One of the friends we met in Robert Graves's circle was the American painter James Metcalf, whom I was to see again quite unexpectedly on visits to Mexico in 1981 and 1986. James Metcalf had established a centre for traditional arts and crafts in Michoacan, helping to preserve them from obsolescence when all the economic pressures favour the production of internationally saleable junk, of the kind I saw displayed at Tijuana for the tourist market; and when plastic dishes have largely displaced the indigenous pottery for home use by all but the very rich.)

On May 11th Robert and Beryl left for Palma. We took a long walk to San Marroig and La Foradada, down steep paths through pine woods. Around La Foradada the sea boomed uncannily, probably because there are caves in the rocks. Robert Graves had told us the story of the Archduke Ludwig who kept a mistress at San Marroig, which was guarded by bloodhounds. He thought she had leprosy, but according to Robert Graves it was syphilis. Now the place was a museum. When we passed it on our way back, eight coachloads of tourists had arrived. We looked at the museum and were struck by the contrast between what Robert had told us about the Archduke and the official presentation of him and of his anonymous books on Mallorca. There was something sinister about the place nonetheless; and a sense of utter wilderness at La Foradada, where I swam from the rocks. I went swimming again that afternoon at the Cala at Deya. This time the sea was rough, the water dirty and full of drifting seaweed.

Before leaving Deya we called on our various acquaintances there. I also collected rock plants, ferns and cactuses. We were sorry to be going, but our time was up. We caught an early bus to Palma, where Robert had invited us to breakfast and was waiting at the bus stop, though he was still unwell, taking penicillin against his throat infection. After breakfast we went out to buy our boat tickets and do some shopping, spending the afternoon and evening with Martin and Janet — whom we were to see much of after their return to England.

Robert Graves's generosity and kindness towards us did not lead to a lasting association, though we corresponded with him sporadically, met him again a number of times in England, and became friendly with one of his close associates, James Reeves. My sense of being bound to Graves by gratitude and loyalty conflicted with a growing need to be independent. Rightly or wrongly, I felt that Robert Graves demanded a sort of allegiance I was no longer able to give to any writer whatever, much as I liked him personally and valued his advice. I had depended too much on mentors, living and dead, throughout my apprentice years; and the last, most tenacious of those mentors, W. B. Yeats, could hardly be reconciled with another who dismissed him as a 'sham'. Friendships between poets — even between coevals with certain assumptions in common — tend to be precarious, or else to turn into alliances that have more to do with the struggle for survival than with the writing of poetry. Though I could not know at the time how few of my friendships with fellow poets would continue into middle age, I had already come up against differences of temperament, outlook and practice that could not be bridged, only evaded by forbearance, silence or equivocation. In the end it seemed more honest to go one's own way, with friendly encounters now and then that didn't amount to commitments or alliances, let alone allegiances. One thing I was determined to avoid, and did avoid over the next twenty years, was membership of any group or movement in poetry. When the so-called Movement was launched in the 'fifties, I agreed to contribute to an anthology of work by non-Movement poets — only to find myself branded as a 'Maverick', the member of an anti-Movement group. That absurdity taught me a lesson, and confirmed my resolve to write what I must, how I must, and let the work take care of itself.

The boat to Barcelona was held up because a well-connected lady — the wife or mistress of some important official — arrived late. In fact the boat had already left the quayside when she did finally appear, and was turned back to pick her up. This incident, our glimpse of the paupers' settlements and the political prisoners we had seen being marched away by the Police, gave us some second thoughts about the attractions of Mallorca and the cheap villas available there to foreign residents. We also remembered the brutality with which a policeman had chased away a Gypsy girl who had come to beg from us on a café terrace. The one morning left to us in Barcelona on our way home was enough to make us tourists again, suddenly aware that we hadn't seen the Roman City or the exhibits in the National Palace, as we promptly did — so hurriedly that we might just as well have sat in the railway station.

Soon after our return, in June, I wrote 'Palinode', my only poem that contains allusions to things seen and heard in Catalonia and Mallorca.

'After us, the Savage God', Yeats had written. For several years to come, that Savage God's presence was what I tried to capture in poems less obtrusively Yeatsian than many I had been producing. Two poems also written that summer, 'London Idyll' and 'River Song', picked up threads from the earlier period, but the idyll of the former poem is a broken one set in the bombed sites I continued to explore. In July we stayed with James and Mary Reeves in Weymouth, also visiting other parts of Dorset and meeting James and Tania Stern. In August we went to Devon to stay with Noel Welch. Even there, in the woods around Chagford, I met the Savage God, too explicitly named in a poem begun there, 'Respite' — a formal reversion to the Yeatsian mode. Of the two *persona* poems I was working on in the autumn, 'Philoctetes' and 'Guatemeotzin's Prayer for Montezuma', only the first was finished, and this only after a re-working in August 1953. Both were confrontations with the Savage God.

In October 1952 I began to teach at University College. Anne was expecting our first child, Mary Anne, born in July 1953. In 1954 we moved again, to a slightly larger flat in Campden Hill Gardens, our last London home before our removal to Berkshire in 1955. Anne's pregnancy was a difficult one. For days on end she couldn't eat at all without vomiting. My academic duties set up new tensions that affected us both, since she had no part in them, and felt less related to them than to the literary work which I couldn't bring myself to give up, only postpone when necessary. Poems presented themselves at the worst moments — 'Spring Song in Winter' on my way to work in a rush-hour tube train, so that I couldn't even jot down the first words.

I ought to have remembered the old soldier's soothing words when I had found it hard to adapt to military life. Certainly, the first two or three years of academic life proved to be the hardest, because they set up anxieties that had more to do with my disposition than with the work as such. It was understood that I should write a thesis during my three years' appointment as an Assistant Lecturer, but I found that I had no inclination for scholarly research that wasn't intimately bound up with my preoccupations as a writer and translator. Years of writing at home made it impossible for me to concentrate in a public library, least of all in the British Museum Reading Room, where my colleagues pursued their researches. It was a place full of characters far too interesting to be ignored as part of the fixtures. The thesis was never written, or even begun. Instead, I worked on a collection of more or less critical essays that appeared long after my three years' probation had expired. To work at home, where those essays were written, was to stay on one's own terrain, doing one's own thing; but, with a wife and child at home, it was also to place oneself in another field of conflict, between the work one was doing and their claims on one's attention.

My state of mind was such that Kathleen Raine advised me to see a psychiatrist: 'You are extremely fortunate,' she wrote that winter, 'in being able to command a university teaching job at all — most poets cannot — and to be free from the strains of the worst financial anxiety, in an honourable way. Scholarship is, after all, infinitely to be preferred to journalism or the BBC, and teaching is one of the least useless things one can do. I feel, therefore, greater anxiety than if there *were* any reason, outwardly ... These inner burdens are the hardest to carry, I know. Don't think that I am unsympathetic, but I cannot feel sorry for your *outward* situation, only for the inner one that makes a very favourable outer one seem as hard to carry as a real burden of adversity...'

Kathleen Raine's letter was as perceptive as it was kind. There could be nothing wrong or dishonourable in communicating one's interests and enthusiasms to other people; but the emphasis, in universities, was not on interests or enthusiasms — or insights, for that matter — but on knowledge, and the systematization of knowledge. I should never have been able to tell any psychiatrist what it was in me that resisted the pursuit of knowledge as an end in itself — and knowledge of literature, at that, when it was the practice of literature that taught me how little I knew even about my most intimate and intense concerns. Nor could I have told him about the complex of assumptions and obsessions behind that resistance, if only because I couldn't see it myself, until the poems I wrote brought it to light. I hadn't yet begun to understand what Keats meant by 'negative capability', or Thomas Hardy by the 'nescience' to which poets cling more stubbornly than to whatever knowledge, subtlety or even erudition they may also have needed to acquire; but in every poet, living or dead, who mattered to me I recognized a core of commitment not necessarily to the 'ceremony of innocence' but to innocence itself. (*One Foot in Eden* is the title of Edwin Muir's last book of poems; the other foot can be anywhere, but preferably in a place unmistakably human and not too tidy.) If that commitment was lacking in a poet, he could be as knowing, subtle or erudite as he pleased, and his work would leave me cold. There would be no room in the poetry for the unexpected knowledge that comes in a flash, and comes only where 'nescience' has left a gap to be filled.

All this was something I couldn't have explained to my closest friends, let alone a psychiatrist or psychologist — who, in any case, would have translated it into very different terms; and the last thing I wanted was to expose a 'heart mystery' to the kind of analysis I sometimes avoided applying to literary texts in my teaching, by deviating into an old-fashioned historical approach. The sense of betrayal, of capitulation and compromise that afflicted me in those first years as a university lecturer was undeniably absurd, in relation to anything but my secret commitment; but there was no getting away from it, no getting over it, except in my own absurd way.

On Christmas Day I noted: 'No time to keep this diary. My vacation began on Dec. 17th, but have been working harder than in term-time, preparing lectures, choosing passages for translation, typing them out, etc. Can't even think of translating.' After Christmas we were to have gone to Oxford, but I had to cancel the trip. 'Can now understand why X hates going away,' I jotted down in my increasingly scrappy diary. 'There comes a point where travelling can be nothing but a disturbance. Changes of environment used to be jolts that started a poetic crystallization. Now I need no physical jolt. It could be that imagination is beginning to draw on the resources of memory. In the past a poem began with something seen or heard. Now it begins inside. No need of a midwife. The poem grows and, in due course, makes its own way out. But it does need a long period of undisturbed gestation, and a good deal of attention after birth.' That was one of the troubles. Something had gone wrong with the way my energy was distributed and directed. It wasn't a matter of time. It was a matter of not being able to afford, or feeling that I wasn't able to afford, the blank and passive process of gestation. There was always something on my mind, something that had to be done or thought about. For reasons difficult to understand, Anne, too, had been happier when we lived from hand to mouth.

In February, I was still working on the tiny 'Spring Song in Winter' that had announced itself between Notting Hill Gate and Tottenham Court Road on December 3rd. Leisure both for writing and for general reading had become very scarce. I did read Paddy Kavanagh's novel *Tarry Flynn* in January, noting: 'The Irish still have a sense of grass roots — the advantage of being a "backward" nation.' And at that most impossible of junctures I felt a sudden urge to write a verse tragedy, of all things. 'The difficulty is the disconnected life one leads: a few salient moments and a great flat desert of indifferent work.' In March I was finishing a poem begun in the spring of the previous year, before our departure for Mallorca. It hadn't yet occurred to me that obstacles were the very thing I needed to curb my facility and my impatience.

In February, too, Martin Seymour-Smith offered to publish another pamphlet of my poems in a small press he had started in Mallorca, but I knew I wasn't ready, and declined the offer. Erich Heller wanted me to write a monograph for a series he was editing for Bowes & Bowes. This, too, couldn't be done. The difficult adaptation to academic work, and the enforced specialization in German Literature it entailed, had made me react against critical and analytical processes in general. I did arrange a meeting between Erich Heller and David Gascoyne, who had reached a stage where he needed an external incentive to work. Early in February he had turned up unexpectedly at our flat, staying to dinner. I had invited him after Christmas, but he neither came nor got in touch with us. 'He still seems to suffer from his old dread of appointments,' I noted. 'His conversation was coherent enough, but always on the verge of some personal abyss ... Went on to Dannie Abse's whom he said he wanted to meet. On the way there he disappeared for about an hour, to go to his lodgings, perhaps to rest from the strain of conversation ... Hadn't visited me for about eight years, I think.' On the 14th he and I had lunch with Erich Heller. David agreed to write a monograph on Rimbaud for the series. He talked about Heidegger, Fondane and philosophy, mainly existentialist. Like many of his projects at this time, including an essay on Heidegger he had begun to write, the Rimbaud monograph did not materialize.

A dream I'd had in December about Robert Graves told me why I was wary of entering his sphere of influence. In the dream 'I visited him in a vast derelict palace, where a room or two had been lent him by the owner. The palace was otherwise uninhabited. The dream seemed to hinge on the possibility of being admitted to his presence, as I was in the end. He was there to "work", though in fact he wasn't working at all.' I recognized the dangerous and ambiguous attraction of father figures, the hero-worship to which I'd been prone since my father's early death. Now, rather belatedly, I'd come of age, and that kind of dependence had to be left behind. Many of my literary friends and mentors had been a good deal older than myself; but from now on such relationships could last only if some kind of reciprocity could be maintained.

This was one of many dreams that helped me to discover truths about myself which I could not face up to consciously. In later years I also wrote a number of dream poems, very faithful transcriptions of the sequence of events in specific dreams, and at least one of these not only told me something I didn't dare to know but predicted a situation that was to occur several years later.

Anne felt better during the later stages of her pregnancy. Early in March we were able to get out of London for a day, to visit James Reeves and his family at Chalfont St. Giles. On the 19th we went to Germany, taking up an invitation by Curt and Eva Cassirer to stay at the Odenwaldschule, a progressive boarding-school with which they had been connected since before the war. Eva Cassirer, a correspondent and admirer of Rilke's, had got in touch with me by letter and visited me in London that year.

We arrived at Heppenheim at one o'clock in the morning, after missing our connection at the Hook of Holland because the boat was delayed by fog. The journey was such that Anne became despondent and had to spend a day in bed to recover. We stayed at a villa above the school buildings, at Oberhambach, with beech woods on the hills and a few scattered farm houses, most of them old. We were warned not to venture far into the woods, since one could walk in them for eight hours without meeting anyone.

Though a specialist in German literature now, I hardly knew Germany. I wanted to see more of the country, but my first conversation with a German, a railway official at Heppenheim, made me wonder whether it had been a good idea to come. At one o'clock in the morning, while we were waiting for a car to pick us up, he proclaimed himself a Nazi, told us that America had started the war, and asserted that the British secret service had persuaded Hitler to attack Russia. He was at once hysterical and pig-headed, falling into mawkish self-pity when telling us about the plight of his colleague, a Sudeten German. I had to point out the connection between the expulsion of Germans from Czechoslovakia and pre-war events. He immediately inferred that I was a Communist, refuted nothing I had said, but told me that he, too, didn't believe the bad things he had heard and read about the Russians. The arrival of our car saved me the effort of explaining why I wasn't able to share his disbelief.

'Woke up in a foul temper,' I noted next day, my birthday, 'feeling we were stuck in this little place when I should like to see different parts of Germany.' This frustration continued for a day or two. 'We are near three great rivers — Rhine, Main and Neckar and have seen none of them. Should probably feel happier if we hadn't travelled here in the dark.' Meanwhile we walked in the woods, hoping to see deer and wild boars, which had multiplied since the end of the war. The first day we saw only woodpeckers and chaffinches, and four birds of prey that 'sounded like buzzards'; also butterflies, peacocks and brimstones, out earlier than in England. Soon the woods became monotonous 'at this time of the year, when the sun penetrates evenly'. We found more variety in the landscape in the valley, around Heppenheim, where there were vineyards and orchards. On our way to Kirschhausen, the next village, we did see a couple of deer.

On the 24th we 'walked down through the woods to a village called Scheuerbach, unspoilt, the houses and farm buildings timbered and white-washed. Stopped at the inn to drink local wine. Arranged to lunch there, after going to the next village, Mittershausen. At the inn they sell coca-cola. The village set in a beautiful valley. The walls in the inn distempered and covered with murals of birds and flowers. Can't understand the local dialect.'

The following day we walked to Gornau, a larger village. 'Took the wrong path and made a long detour through the most beautiful valley we have yet seen. Saw buzzards mating or fighting in a tree.'

On the 26th I left for Tübingen and Bebenhausen, separating from Anne, who still needed to rest. I stopped briefly in Stuttgart, then took a coach to Bebenhausen, a tiny village dominated by the monastery that had become a palace and now housed the Hölderlin Archives. When I became engrossed in the Hölderlin material collected there, I tried to find accommodation in one of the two inns, but was offered only a noisy room overlooking the main road. I looked at the Romanesque and Gothic chapel and the monastery buildings; also the fishponds, already used by the Cistercian monks to breed carp, and still in use.

Alfred Kelletat, the keeper of the Archives, recommended the Christian Hostel in Tübingen, and I put up there. It was pleasant enough, but the lights fused that night, just when I wanted to read and write. Next morning I set out on a tour of Hölderlin's sites, the 'Stift' (Protestant Seminary) where he studied and the tower where he spent the second half of his life, and was astonished to find how close one was to the other. His room in the tower had been gutted by fire, but a room downstairs he occasionally used had been filled with relics. I went on to look at the Town

Hall and Cotta's house, where Goethe had stayed. I liked the market, too, with women in black shawls selling fruit, vegetables and flowers.

I had left Bebenhausen on foot, but had been given a lift by a boy from Berlin on his motor-cycle. That morning I walked back to Bebenhausen with Alfred Kelletat, an intelligent and sensitive East Prussian to whom I had taken immediately. I did some reading at the Archives and met two eminent Hölderlin scholars, Professor Beissner and Professor Beck. In the afternoon I visited Hölderlin's grave in Tübingen.

On the 29th I returned to Oberhambach, walking up from Heppenheim. Anne had been unwell, nearly fainting at the school play she had attended. Our hostess at the villa had looked after her.

The woods were now coming into leaf, and there were more wild flowers than before. At Heppenheim, on the 31st, Anne saw her first stork, the female in her nest on the chimney of our hotel, the male in flight over the nest. That day we moved on to Heidelberg.

We found a room at once, in a private house behind the main street. Our landlady, a button-maker, was an East German. She was friendly and talkative. Since she had no licence to let rooms she pretended that we were relatives, and would yell out some name like Karl when visitors came for us. We also depended on her for hot water, since there was no bathroom or basin in the 'Gartenhaus'. Anne learned to ask for hot water in German.

The Cassirers had introduced us to Paul Obermüller, a bookseller, publisher and collector, mainly of Rilke books and letters, and we had arranged to have lunch at his house that day. At a travel agent's we had difficulties over train and boat reservations for our return. After a rather hectic day Anne felt exhausted, and I had to take her back to our room before going to a lecture at the American Cultural Institute. There I met two German poets to whom I had already been introduced that morning, Ernst Meister and Paul Becker, the translator of Dylan Thomas's *Deaths and Entrances*.

Next day we saw the Riemenschneider Altar at the Museum, but didn't feel in the mood to see much besides, except a collection of old glassware. Ernst Meister called at our lodgings at 12.30 and showed me two of his poems. He had begun to write and publish before 1933, then suffered a breakdown and stopped writing until after the war. Now, belatedly, he was writing a doctorate thesis for the university.

In the afternoon we called on Richard Benz, a specialist in Romantic literature and music, some of whose books I had read. We stayed for tea. Benz, too, was unhappy, though for reasons quite different from Ernst Meister's. He complained of losing his savings through the currency reform, and was generally opposed to what he felt to be the 'Americanization' of Heidelberg, even refusing to use a wireless set. We knew what he meant, having been kept awake at night by the din from a dance-hall, yet worse things had happened in Germany while Heidelberg was intact and Benz's savings were secure.

Over dinner at the Museum restaurant we saw Ilse Aichinger at another table and arranged to see her next morning. That was to be our last full day in Heidelberg, since I could get no berth for Anne on a later day, and she was not well enough to travel without one. Ilse Aichinger called at our lodgings with her future husband Günter Eich, some of whose poems and radio plays I was to translate, and she was struck by the coincidence that we were staying at a button-maker's just when she was writing a radio play called *Buttons*. After lunch we went to the Castle, after rain; there was a pervasive fragrance of buds, earth and leaves. Not up to a conducted tour, we made do with the exterior and the view over the river valley. In the evening we took a walk along the Neckar bank. It was Good Friday. In our courtyard there had been no shouting, for once, and no noise of an electric saw.

On our last day we went to the Heiliggeist Church, impressed by its Lutheran austerity, which accorded well with the Gothic buttresses and decorated ceiling. We especially liked the stained glass windows, with non-figurative designs but rich colours. We went on to Neckargemund, walking along the Philosophenweg, on to the Neuburg Monastery, crossing the Neckar by ferry, and taking a train from there. Almond, cherry and pear blossom was out in the gardens. When we sat on a landing-stage after lunch on the right bank of the river it was as hot as on a summer day in England.

Immediately after our return to London, on Easter Sunday, I was able to take up a poem sequence I had begun before leaving, *Early Love*, but did not finish it until May. There was endless reading to be done — for lectures, for the essays I was preparing, for the thesis which I registered that term, after being warned that my appointment could not become permanent without one. I got as far as acquiring a new reader's ticket for the British Museum Library, but not as far as using it.

Kathleen Raine was undergoing a crisis that made her give up writing poetry for many years. As so often before, I found myself unable to help — or even to write an adequate reply to the letter she had written me in her distress. Busy though I was, it was not my occupations that got in the way, but a hardly conscious preparation for the birth of our child. In April I dreamed that I was a ghost. I could see and hear, but was invisible to all but a few close relatives. My feelings, in that state, were of lightness, power and the relief of knowing that I was out of it all. In May I wrote a poem *A Child Accepts*, quite unaware of any connection it might have with the expected birth. When I had taken Anne to the Middlesex Hospital by ambulance, and was waiting at home from 3 a.m. on July 3rd to 11 p.m. — with instructions not to telephone in the course of the day — I understood why fathers are supposed to pace an ante-room on these occasions. Without so much as an ante-room to pace, I could do nothing but wait. At some point I cooked some sort of meal and swallowed it, suddenly reminded of the meal I had swallowed thirteen years earlier while waiting for my father to die. It wasn't that I believed Anne or the baby to be in danger; but birth and death were the two ends of a passage, and at both ends there was pain.

The birth had been a difficult one, and called for an operation; but both Anne and the baby were well when I was allowed to see them at seven. More than three weeks later complications began, because the forceps' cuts on Mary Anne's head went septic, and daily treatment was needed.

Early in July, before Anne's return from hospital on the 12th, Louis Adeane brought D. S. Savage to our flat. Savage was drawing up a list of 'uncommitted critics', potential contributors to a projected English edition of *Life*! I wondered how Savage's purism, which I respected, could possibly accord with such a project. 'He's recruiting nuns for a brothel,' I noted. As far as I know, nothing ever came of it. I lost touch with D. S. Savage, and missed his trenchantly polemical contributions to periodicals in later years. 'England hath need of thee', I felt about him in the 'sixties, and feel even more strongly now.

The American poet Peter Viereck arrived in London. We had lunch, and I spent the afternoon accompanying him on various errands. We had been corresponding for several years, after an earlier meeting in London, and I had read most of his books. He amazed and confounded the assistants in a large West End store by insisting that he must try on a pair of pyjamas he wanted to buy, then asking for an additional hole to be punched into a leather belt that fitted him well enough, but might cease to fit him if he put on or lost weight. I left him engaged in a long conversation with another assistant about a cashmere coat which I was pretty sure he had no intention of buying. I was to see more of this highly gifted, eccentric and ill-fated writer — a descendant, by an illegitimate line, of the Hohenzollerns — over the years, both in England and America. At this time he was at the height of his reputation, a winner of the Pulitzer Prize for poetry, and the widely discussed originator of that 'New Conservatism' which was to discredit him when the phrase was taken up by reactionary extremists, and his opposition to them was ignored. His mistake, I think, was to believe that a somewhat idealized European traditionalism could be transferred to America, where it didn't apply and was almost certain to be misunderstood.

I saw Edwin and Willa Muir again at one of G. S. Fraser's literary evenings, where he read some of his poems. I, too, was asked to read, but still hadn't got over my shyness. As I attended several of those literary evenings — virtually an open house for poets and literary men, kept going and held together by George Fraser's wife Paddy with admirable efficiency and patience — I can't be sure who else was there that night, except that I took Elizabeth Jennings. The Frasers' Chelsea flat is the one place I knew in London where writers and critics of every kind and persuasion were apt to mix. At times there were fights, and I seem to remember a formidable one involving John Davenport, a man who enjoyed using his fists, and Peter Redgrove; but, considering the notorious paranoia, insecurity and competitiveness of poets, the surprising thing was that the Frasers made a success of those gatherings, and continued them for years.

Early in August I spent three days with Philip and Barbara Rawson at their old farm house at Shabbington, near Thame, one of my favourite places at this period. The house was said to be haunted and had a history of violent deaths, but Philip and Barbara were among the least haunted people I knew. Old Joe White, the cowman there, contributed certain features to a poem I wrote about ten years later, *Old Poacher.* That summer he was seventy-nine. When I saw him again in January he was carrying a log as tall as himself. A widower for the past fifteen years, he lived alone and cooked for himself, but preferred fish and chips. He was still an expert ditch-maker. When he was short of money and couldn't afford fish and chips from a shop, he would kill a rabbit by stalking it and hitting it on the head with a stick.

For Philip and Barbara, and their home, I wrote a poem called *Bread and Butter Letter.* I liked everything about the place, even the ruined barns, with their skeletal timber, and the barn-owl that lived there and once attacked one of their many cats. The nearest I came to feeling haunted there was when I left the house one night to make my way back to London, lost the path and my sense of direction in a pitch-black field, stumbled around for half an hour or so in a circle, snorted at by invisible bullocks and colliding with them, then found myself back at the house.

'London has come to mean as much to me as it might to an oyster,' I wrote in January 1954. 'That's one reason why I can't write. All closed up, withdrawn. Antennae not working. Even the bombed site, which I'd ceased to visit, has been fenced off. They're building everywhere. St. John's Wood Park being demolished at last. No more walks through the lovely wilderness of gardens with creepers let loose & the shrubs fighting for space.' For about half a year I could write no poems. I wanted to move out of London, but couldn't take the risk of giving up my job. Our two-room flat was now too small yet I didn't apply myself to finding a larger one, though we obtained one by chance in August of that year. Since I hadn't produced a thesis, my London Appointment ended in 1955, the year in which our second child, Richard, was born. I applied for a lectureship at Oxford.

The Oxford application was turned down, without my being short-listed. Later I was told that only Enid Starkie had supported it. We moved into a flat in Campden Hill Gardens that summer. We had two rooms on the ground floor, a conservatory which I converted into a study, and a separate room on a half-landing which we had to sub-let. The letting went well enough except for one tenant, an old Etonian who turned out to be schizophrenic. Not only did he fail to pay his rent, leave us to pay his milk bills and make compulsive appointments to settle with us at the most extraordinary hours, only to be out at the time and then excuse himself with fantastic stories, but when we finally asked him to leave he smashed the furniture, slashed the mattress with a razor, covered the mirror with pink paint, forced and rifled the gas meter. Another disaster at the flat was a virulent outbreak of dry-rot, which looked anything but dry, since it produced giant fungi that ate into my books. One distinct advantage of the flat for me was a study separated from the living room by a small staircase, another the little backyard with one flower bed — the first 'garden' I had owned. Though we had no room for guests, in September 1955, W. S. Graham spent a night there, also borrowing a 'wee pound' from Anne when I had gone to work, and going off with the latch-key, which he returned by post with a characteristically charming verse-note:

> 'Dear Michael herewith the key of the door
> And please forgive me for being a bore
> And phoning up too late at night.
> Surely somehow some time we might
> Talk together about what's woven
> Round the fact of the great Beethoven.
>   So tune the tuning fork of light
>   Thanks to you both. Goodnight, Goodnight.
>   Love, Suddenly Graham'

Whenever I was free and the weather permitted I took Mary Anne to Holland Park. One afternoon I was puzzled because she seemed to have grown extraordinarily heavy overnight, before it occurred to me that I was pushing her pram with the brake on. Though a doting father, I was a pretty useless one, so that far too much of the burden of care for the children fell on Anne. Mainly because of my old-fashioned upbringing, I could not relate myself to indoor chores, whereas I was ready to take on almost any kind of outdoor labour, such as clearing our out-of-date (and illegal) land drain when we lived in the country.

Of our friends and acquaintances in that part of London, Cecil Day Lewis and Jill Balcon lived just round the corner from us, and we spent several pleasant evenings at their house. There was also the former Expressionist poet and doctor Bluth, whose patients included at least one poet we knew. Bluth prescribed 'psychedelic' drugs for nervous complaints before these had become fashionable. Piano playing was another of his accomplishments.

In the autumn of 1955 we moved to Tilehurst, near Reading into one half of what had been a Victorian manor, Westwood House, with nearly two acres of land to ourselves — flower garden, vegetable garden, orchard and paddock. This gave more than ample scope to my peasant needs, never previously satisfied. Reading University suited me much better than University College, a sprawling and intricate complex of buildings and departments in which I never felt at home. As though the reclaiming of my long-neglected land had not been enough, I also went to and from work on an old policeman's bicycle, losing so much weight in my eagerness to get home, up a steep hill, that I was finally advised to learn to drive a car.

Anne was not happy at Westwood Lodge, and hadn't liked the last of our London flats, while the nearness of Holland Park had almost reconciled me to London. For the next nine years I found a balance congenial to me between indoor and outdoor life — with no absence, needless to say, of tilting or rocking scales. The balance was a precarious one. We occupied the servants' wing of what had been a house for country gentry. My study had been the butler's pantry. The land I cultivated after a fashion — scything, digging, planting new trees, pruning old ones — had been looked after by a whole team of gardeners. In one way we were parasites on the past, in another its victims, trying to preserve a place beyond our means. Even the situation of the house, up on a hill overlooking the river valley and farms that were disappearing one by one, was ambiguous. The entrance to the drive was in a suburban street. The four-barred gate at the bottom of our sloping paddock opened into a country lane. After two or three years a large estate of skimped houses sprang up where cows had grazed (and stampeded when I set fire to the tall dry grass that smothered the old vegetable and soft fruit garden, without the precaution of digging a ditch). Soon the countryside was littered with old bedsteads, armchairs and the wrecks of motor cars.

At Tilehurst, Claire, the third and last of our children was born, in 1957. When we moved out, in 1964, the house was demolished, the land built up. Nothing remains of the one place I thought of as a 'permanent' home. Even the two old elm trees on the hill — a landmark for miles away — were felled.

Whether I liked it or not, in middle age I became a traveller again. Stability proved as much an illusion as freedom. If one tried to stay in one place it was the scenery that did the moving, as in some old film. If one tried to hold on to a person or a thing, it was the person or the thing that changed and fell away. 'Old men ought to be explorers', a middle-aged poet wrote. The story of my later travels and explorations, the mobility of middle age, cannot be told yet, and may never need to be told.

In middle age a liberation takes place. What the German novelist Arno Schmidt has called the 'fourth factor' appears beside the ego, super-ego and id, smiling or unashamedly laughing at their silly little squabbles. The taskmaster who ruled my early years was a pedant, a literalist, a stickler for facts. Even the bits of fiction I produced under the shadow of his rule allowed only a limited freedom to sift and transpose the data on which they were based. The fourth factor is a relativist and a joker, with little use or respect for any truth but the truth of fiction. If I'd let him have his way he would have played word games with the material of my life, character games with the people in it, not excluding myself. He would have cocked a snook at the taskmaster, jumbled up his documents, chronological sequence and functional syntax. The very idea of an autobiography strikes him as absurd, since he doesn't recognize such a thing as a 'self' or any literary genre other than what he calls 'writing'. As for 'life', the remaining component in the word, he looks for it in epiphanies, moments of revelation or fusion, when the 'self' is least itself. He would have cut out all the dead matter of experience, the record of my negative responses.

As for the mug's game of poetry, its pursuit has become harder and easier. Harder, because ambition, like every external incentive, has fallen away. Easier, because that loss is another liberation. I can be no more sure than I was thirty years ago that my poems are good enough to be worth the price paid for them, by which I mean not the time and work that have gone into them but the specialization they demanded, the concentration claimed at the cost of other pursuits and commitments. What I am sure of now is that, whether good or bad, durable or negligible, the poems I write are those I have to write. The profession of authorship has no bearing on that. The opinions and judgements of critics have no bearing on that. Nor have the anxieties that used to beset me when I couldn't write. There are more than enough good poems, real poems, in print than any reader can exhaust in a lifetime. Ours is the first recorded age in which it has become almost a crime to reproduce the species. Much the same is true of the writing of poems, now that our world is over-populated with them; and, unlike even the best people, the best poems obstinately refuse to die and make way for others. I would much rather write no more poems than poems I do not need to write.

Though as susceptible as anyone to the doubts that must nag any specialist not indifferent to what goes on in the world beyond his specialization, I have no regrets about my specialization — one that is open at all ends. Its risks are part of the game. A premature drying up is only one of those risks, and I face it with equanimity. 'Premature' in any case is a misleading word in that context. Ripeness may be all, but no one can be all ripeness. My experience tells me that a certain immaturity — a partial immaturity — is a pre-condition of productivity in the arts; perhaps of productivity in all fields, though it is the failure of poets to 'grow up emotionally', to accommodate their feelings and demands to given realities, that has struck me again and again. Yeats's rejuvenating operation in old age is the classic instance; and it seems to have worked, if only by convincing him that he was young at heart. If human beings live by illusions, as I'm sure they do, they need a residual stock of illusions in order to live, far more to live as intensely as the writing of poems requires; and to have illusions is to be immature. Until now I have been in no danger of attaining a maturity that would put an end to the game — a premature end, from my point of view, if I were to survive it. From the point of view of the world at large, in so far as it takes any notice of poetry, and cares about it, the closing down of one 'poetry factory' makes no difference to speak of. Another will take over, producing slightly different goods from raw material much the same.

There's no getting away from it: the fourth factor has taken over, and had taken over by the time of writing. Yet I defied his taunts and sarcasms, just as in the past I had to defy the taskmaster's perpetual nagging. 'Keep out of this,' I said. 'Those formative years are none of your business, for the simple reason that you weren't there. The person it's about may have been a bore, trying so hard to be real, to define and locate himself, when he could have been connecting himself to the flux. But if that's what he was like, that's how I will present him. Posthumously, if you like.'

— Of course. If a man must write his 'autobiography' he should write it posthumously.

— Publish it posthumously, you mean.

— No, you commonsensical idiot. It's high time you understood that I always say what I mean. Write it posthumously. So that he can draw the necessary conclusions.

— You may say what you mean, but you don't mean what you say. So your flippancies are unhelpful. You know better than I do that there are no conclusions to be drawn. Just because I've grown away from the person I wrote about, that doesn't put me in a position to judge him or to sum him up; and wouldn't if I'd written his story at the age of ninety. I've seen a man of ninety more securely caged in his delusions than I was at the age of twenty.

— Because you were a displaced person, perhaps? But don't indulge yourself by thinking it's enough to be displaced. The next, and harder, step is to misplace your person. Mislay it. Lose it. Forget about it. And begin to move. That's the point where autobiography becomes truly posthumous — and not worth the trouble of writing. Least of all when the future of the species is in doubt, because of the damage done to this earth by the positive capability of persons, corporations, states intent on defining and locating themselves by what they've grabbed, manipulated and wasted.

— That's too much. I'm not going to be lectured by you about the state of the world. You stick to your fictions. And preserve your innocence by playing — all you were ever good for. Who are you, anyway? Some sort of relative of the id, I suspect. An id that has emerged into consciousness.

— I don't care who I am. I don't care who you are. I care about the current we conduct. That's what my games are good for — unlike your processed happenings.

— Minimally processed. Dredged up and exhibited, for what they're worth. In case they should come in useful to someone. In case...

— Stop. Stop. Or you'll fall into premature conclusions. And think up more uses for your uncalled-for exhibition. Anything but that, when uselessness is its only justification.

— Not quite. What's more, it was you who taught me the usefulness of indiscretion. So what are we arguing about? Here's a bit of doggerel I wrote on the very matter of persons and impersonality. It's more conclusive than anything you allow me to say in prose. And it isn't only about 'me' — any more than my story is only about 'me'.

Vehicles

But you preferred my 'one' and 'he' and 'we'?
My reticence? Humility? Liked me more
When wrapped in myth and mask and metaphor
I kept the beast heraldic, men heroic,
Rhythm and stanza tidy, bearing stoic?
Before, a blabber, I loosed 'the odious me'?

Humble? I cared for it, I made a fuss
Of that indifferent, second-hand machine,
(It looked as good as new), for ever busy
Maintaining, patching up my poor tin lizzy,
So anxious then to keep the panels clean
And spare the engine, I would go by bus.

And now? I like it more and less
All scraped and dented, in a mess,
My boneshaker that still keeps going,
Beyond re-chroming now, re-spraying,
Past washing too. And so I let
The garage, park it in the street.
I cannot sell it, cannot lose it,
Can neither spoil it nor misuse it
Though far I drive it, drive it hard,
Knowing that in the breaker's yard
Something will last, perhaps to move
What singular and plural cove -
But not the paintwork, not the chrome:
No car of mine will drive me home.

Postscript, 1990

A Poet's Progress

Like snooker balls thrown on the table's faded green,
Rare ivory and weighted with his best ambitions,
At first his words are launched: not certain what they mean,
He loves to see them roll, rebound, assume positions
Which — since not he — some power beyond him has assigned.
But now the game begins: dead players, living critics
Are watching him — and suddenly one eye goes blind,
The hand that holds the cue shakes like a paralytic's,
Till every thudding, every clinking sound portends
New failure, new defeat. Amazed, he finds that still
It is not he who guides his missiles to their ends
But an unkind geometry that mocks his will.

If he persists, for years he'll practise patiently,
Lock all the doors, learn all the tricks, keep noises out,
Though he may pick a ghost or two for company
Or pierce the room's inhuman silence with a shout.
More often silence wins; then soon the green felt seems
An evil playground, lawless, lost to time, forsaken,
And he a fool caught in the water weeds of dreams
Whom only death or frantic effort can awaken.

At last, a master player, he can face applause,
Looks for a fit opponent, former friends, emerges;
But no one knows him now. He questions his own cause,
And has forgotten why he yielded to those urges,
Took up a wooden cue to strike a coloured ball.
Wise now, he goes on playing; both his house and heart
Unguarded solitudes, hospitable to all
Who can endure the cold intensity of art.

(1949)

During part of the period chronicled in these memoirs, self-questioning and self-analysis came easily to me: they were essential to the process of growing up. By the time I wrote the first version, published in 1973 as *A Mug's Game*, my juvenile agonizings about my verse-writing — how to do it, how to make it better than it was, how to keep it going — were behind me. Had it not been for a crisis in my personal life that made it necessary for me to discover as much as I could about my formative years, so as to break the pattern they had set up, I was past wishing to write about myself at all. What I did feel the need to write was something other than biography, which is supposed to be written as near the end of one's life as possible out of an awareness, if not understanding, of the totality of a life and a judgement of what mattered in it, what did not; on the assumption, too, that one's selfhood is constant from birth to death, like one's name (though even names can be changed.) Yet the older I have grown, the harder it has become for me to be sure what in my life was mine, what was anyone's, what I made of my life and what life made of me.

It had also become clear to me that recollection is inseparable from imagination — and so from invention. Whether one likes it or not, autobiography — as distinct from the documentary patchwork I produced — is a form of fiction. As in fiction, too, the protagonist becomes a hero or heroine only by virtue of a sort of magical transference, due to nothing more than the inordinate attention focused on him or her by the writer. The more imaginative the writing, the more this transference will approximate to self-identification on the reader's part: imaginative writing carries the reader away. Because I did not wish to write fiction about myself, nor to write an apology for my life, I chose the same approach I should have adopted in writing about anyone to discover such truths as documents convey. Where there were gaps in my documentation, as well as in my memory, they were left as gaps, though I have been able to fill some of them in this second version, with documents not available to me for the first. By selection and quotation, rather than evocation and reconstruction, I retraced the stages, presenting the fragments as they were experienced at the time, with only explanatory or linking comments. This meant denying myself the satisfaction of hindsight and the greater satisfaction of the fluent and seamless narrative which imagination might have produced.

To some extent this procedure may have been imposed on me by a purism that has inhibited me for most of my life. If so, it belongs to the substance of my book as much as to the presentation. Strict truthfulness was one of the demands my father made on himself and on his children. I remember inquisitions at the dinner table about some peccadillo committed by one of us, and blushing not because I was the perpetrator but only because I was under suspicion. (So much for the reliability of lie detectors!) I should never have tried to write poems, of course, if imaginative truth were not something other than literal truth; but for the purpose of this book the literalism I inherited from my father had to prevail. So the writing could not be 'poetic', even where it was about the hammering into shape of a vessel for poetry.

Needless to say, I could not tell the whole truth, whatever my approach, if only because one doesn't know the whole truth about oneself, let alone about others. What I did know, or discovered in documents I had forgotten, involved other people whose private lives I had no business to make public. Despite the reticence imposed by that restriction alone, I had to conceal the names of several persons in the book and omit all reference to events and relationships that were part of my early life. Yet the writing of the first version precipitated a break with my oldest and closest friend, whose memory or imagination contradicted my account of our earliest meetings and his circumstances at the time.

Almost as soon as I had finished the first version, I planned a complement to it; not a chronological sequel on the same documentary lines, but a text altogether different, as free to range over my various concerns and epiphanies as the other could not be — a book mainly about what I had left out of the first. This second book was not wanted, and I put off the writing again and again in favour of other work. My growing distaste for self-searchings of any kind makes it unlikely that I shall ever write it now. Some of its material went into poems, some into brief essays or prose pieces. The story, in any case, will have no sequel. Later experience has set up too many misgivings about the decency and usefulness of chronicling one's own life.

I took my title and epigraph for the first version from this remark by T. S. Eliot: 'As things are, and as fundamentally they must always be, poetry is not a career but a mug's game. No honest poet can feel quite sure of the permanent value of what he has written: he may have wasted his time and messed up his life for nothing.' When he wrote these candid words, Eliot had received ample confirmation from others that what he had written was of 'permanent value'; but because an honest poet can place no reliance at all on how other people judge his work at any one moment — even if their judgements amount to a consensus, as they rarely do — this remark struck me less as a personal confession of Eliot's, or a gesture of humility on his part, than as a general and incontrovertible truth about being a poet.

If I tell the story of my early life, though, without wishing to write fiction, I assume that either my life was typical enough for others to recognize my experiences as their own, or that my life was so exceptional as to be of interest to others for that reason. The second assumption, for a poet, would rest on the belief that his or her work is of 'permanent value'. If mine is not — and I have no means of knowing whether it is or not — that would leave only the career I never wanted and succeeded very well in warding or breaking off before it could take me where I did not wish to go. Any sequel to the story told here would have to deal with the ups and downs of this career and non-career; but I cannot attach enough importance to the occasional gratifications and recurrent setbacks of my professional life to write about them.

There is nothing glamorous about the life of the kind of full-time writer I became again in 1964, after dropping out of regular university teaching. What was adventurous about it was due to the impossibility of making a living out of the work I chose to do. It was this impossibility that took me all over the United States of America, from South Carolina to Montana, from Buffalo to Taos, New Mexico, and has kept me travelling in Europe, Canada and Mexico. When my home life was not disrupted by travel and engagements — as it was, utterly and messily after my first visiting professorship in America in 1966/7 — it was an attempt to maintain stability in the teeth of improvization, a routine unlike most professional routines, but a routine nonetheless.

At the age of ten or eleven, in South London, my son Richard wrote a verse caricature called 'Michael Hamburger at Home' — with special emphasis on my grumblings and irritations first thing in the morning, when the post brought in the daily vexations and before I could defy them at my writing table:

> I sit by the fire,
> watching it wash itself
> in front of the cat.
>
> I sit at the breakfast table
> reading my mail.
> Oh, bills, bills, nothing but bills.

There's a ring at the door.
It's the undertakers.
'You've come to the wrong house.'

I come back to breakfast.
The telephone rings -
that blasted Hölderlin!

I open my letters.
Oh, Frederick is dead!
Poor old Fred, I knew
it would happen some time.

I go to my study with my mail
and light a fag.
Damn, the price has gone up again.

....

I start work
and waste the morning
writing to Hölderlin...

Where shall I go
for my afternoon walk?
I wish I lived in the country.
I'm fed up with parks...

The surrealism in that sketch captures part of the reality. Friedrich Hölderlin, who lived from 1770 to 1843, worries me on the telephone, but is also the Fred who has died and the friend to whom I write my letter. Involvement with the dead, almost as much as with the living, was indeed a peculiarity of mine, not only as a writer and translator, and connected with the gloom for which I was notorious. As soon as possible, too, we moved out of London again, away from those parks; and eventually all our three grown-up children were to follow us to Suffolk with their families. What my son's caricature leaves out is that on those same walks in South London I would often drop in on my friend Ron Kitaj, the painter, who was living a few streets away from us in those years, for the most engrossing conversation about shared and clashing concerns. To exchange those decaying South London parks and the slums of Brixton and Camberwell for the wide East Anglian skies was also to forgo such company, to become a recluse most of the time.

In some ways my life has been very much like other people's of my generation, in that I had to undergo an education, serve as a soldier in a war, earn my living in various ways, worry about those I loved, work very hard to keep up the vocation or hobby of writing — a seven-day week almost without exception, and only one brief vacation since 1964. It was exceptional or freakish in at least one regard, that I was born in Germany into a German-speaking family, uprooted at the age of nine and pretty thoroughly transplanted, so that by the age of fifteen I could begin my long apprenticeship as a British poet. This oddity must have been one incentive to write a book of memoirs: so as to explain it to myself in the first place, but in the hope that the story might be of interest or use to others.

Anyway, that work was done, and has now been corrected, patched up and filled in, possibly improved. The two bits of fiction I did include in the first version have been taken out, for the sake of consistency, so that the second version is even more rigorously factual than the first.

One reason why the facts and events of my early life are receding from my memory — which has always been 'like a sieve' — is that I care less and less about what I have done or failed to do, more and more about the conditions in which those things were done or not done. Drastic changes in the world at large — and in the country I persist in calling mine because I have continued to live in it — have called in question the ambition of 'permanent value' that has always underlain the poetic mug's game, where it wasn't played only out of self-deceived vanity. In the present state of affairs 'permanent' has become too big a word. I prefer the word 'durable'; but even durability, in products of any kind other than those made for the very rich to remind them that they are different, is no longer a value in the societies I know. Built-in obsolescence and instant consumption have replaced it. If that seems inapplicable to the arts, every sort of 'pop' or 'camp' art proves that it isn't. So do the personality cult and the cult of instant success, with their built-in obsolescence. These are exact counterparts and concomitants of the ethos of salesmanship that has replaced the value of durability. Now that even government and what used to be called statesmanship have been taken over by the salesmen, the arts, including literature, have been affected less blatantly than other activities only because their production cannot be controlled by any political or economic system, as their reception and distribution can be and are.

In our over-populated, over-exploited and over-manipulated world, the careers that were open to me have come to look like a luxury and self-indulgence, when the most I can wish those I care about is employment of any kind in an environment that still supports life. In the years that have passed since the first writing of my memoirs these have become the realities that confront my children and await my grandchildren, if they are allowed to grow up.

If anything seems predictable at the time of writing, after the upheavals of December 1989, it is that the liberal and individualistic culture which I learned to take for granted in my youth is not likely to last much longer. Its basis in Britain was a class structure that has been more thoroughly undermined by the populist monetarism of the New Right than it ever was by governments that called themselves 'Labour' or 'Socialist'. As long as that class structure held, it was pluralistic, layered like the classes themselves, though with mobility between the layers, and a civility that held them together precariously. I have no knowledge of any past civilization or culture bound together by self-interest and expediency alone, with lip service, for public and festive purposes, to religion, patriotism or 'Liberty'. This, in Europe, is something new; and it calls itself 'Conservative', at the very moment when it has become obvious that the only true conservatives are the minority intent on conserving and protecting our planet itself from the damage done to it by exploitation for private or national profit. Paradoxically, therefore — and all political ideologies tend to become paradoxical — true conservatism is now revolutionary. Conservation may be less than a religion in the theocratic sense of the Psalmist: 'Except the Lord build the house, they labour in vain that build it: except the Lord keep the city, the watchman waketh but in vain.' Yet it rests on the *pietàs* and reverence without which even pagan or thoroughly secularized societies could not and cannot cohere. In that sense, if in no other, it is *religio* — bonding; and the only one that is universal, because it holds good for all sects and tribes.

In that state of affairs it hardly matters whether I messed up my life for the sake of the poems that may or may not be durable. I did that, too, inevitably, though not in the spectacular way that would make me an interesting subject for the biography-reading public, either in my lifetime or posthumously. Even my close escapes from sudden death — and there were more in later years — were private and unsensational. No, the messing-up was due to the monomania one needs to keep up the writing of poems for better or for worse — at the expense of everyone and everything that gets in the way — when for the world in general this occupation is a harmless hobby at best, a 'career' only when all the prices have been paid and the messed-up life is over. Not that, for myself, I regret the price paid, or the things I might have done instead. That was my choice from the start, and I have been able to stick to it for half a century now. The trouble is that one cannot mess up one's life without messing up other people's, especially those with whom one is most closely involved; but printed confessions are the last thing that could absolve from regrets about that.

A second oddity — of which reviewers of my books remind me with tedious regularity — is that I am 'better known as a translator' than as a poet. The first book I published was a translation, and one I have repeatedly enlarged and revised ever since. Ever since, too, translation has been so much part of my work that for long stretches it displaced my own writing, and I have translated far more poems than I have written poems of my own. Because most translations have a very limited life-span, not even the possibility of 'permanent value' can be entertained for them, so that their main value must lie in being useful; and being useful, of service, is the only good reason I know for having a career. Translating, therefore, like the critical writing that was also a form of mediation, made up for the career the writing of poetry could not be.

Yet, unlike the jobs most poets have to do to subsidize the writing of poems, these secondary occupations of mine were hardly more remunerative than the other. So they, too, had to be subsidized — by teaching, lecture and reading tours, literary journalism and, for some twelve years, by visiting professorships in America. Translating was the next best thing to writing poems of my own, since it involves a grappling with the same medium, language, a related search for the right word, the right cadence and rhythm, the right verbal gesture in the right place. Because a translation called for all my attention, once I was immersed in it, I made a principle of not accepting commissions to translate book-length works, except in a few instances, if the commissions served as subsidies for work I was eager to do in any case.

Though it is easier to keep up a flow of translations than a flow of poems of one's own, my translating did not amount to a profession, if a profession is something by which one makes a living.

Any palpable conflicts between the two activities were simply a matter of timing, as when, not long ago, I spent a whole year's daily work on translations of poems and verse plays by Goethe. The writing of even the shortest poem of one's own takes much more time than most people think it does; not so much because that poem may have to go through many drafts before it is finished — I recall as many as thirty in some cases — as because a poem cannot get through at all in the first place if the writer's mind is cluttered with matters that compete with it, as it has to be when translating difficult texts.

By late middle age it had also been brought home to me that the 'man of letters' I was sometimes supposed to have become was as socially anachronistic and redundant now as the statesman in politics. When my son remarked, 'you've become a man of letters', he meant that I spent more and more of my working time writing the daily letters connected with it in one way or another, often very tenuously or vicariously. Increasingly, too, letter-writing became my substitute for a social life, for the kind of live communication I had sought out at an earlier stage, in Soho and elsewhere; but even to be a man of letters in that sense grew anachronistic when engagements came to be offered by telephone or not at all, because letter-writing had ceased to be a 'productive', that is, profitable occupation for important or merely busy people. (I don't count the 'personalized', but wholly impersonal, commercial mail with which one is afflicted instead.) As for the other sort of 'man of letters', he became dispensable for related reasons — a foreshortening of time-spans and awareness of them, in an age of short-term transactions, short-term expediency and the long-term, irreversible damage done by them.

My early poems had come out of reading, thinking, feeling not fed by immediate experience, and a state of excitement that needed no external co-ordinate. In later life my poems came out of living, above all, and recollected experience which, for me, did not exclude dreams. The harder I worked, the less I could live with the openness needed for the generation of poems, though at times they could break through any preoccupation whatever; the less, too, I could apply myself practically to causes, such as the ecological, to which I had been committed ever since I began to write. My commitment to such causes may have been implicit in many of my poems and even explicit in a few; but it does not take a poet long to learn that poems are not a practical or effective contribution to a cause. For a poet, therefore, busy-ness is the arch-enemy, not only of essential work but of needs and affections outside it.

An openness which, in a competitive society, looks like idleness, was a prerequisite for the sustained writing of my poems, especially the longer sequences. Outdoor labour, on the other hand, was not only congenial to me in its own right but became the sustenance of many of my later poems. Though written indoors, as often as not they were conceived and in part composed while I was walking, digging, scything, sawing or chopping wood, planting or clearing up a plot.

Cultivating my garden, in fact, has taken up so much of my time in later years that, for all I know, it may have been as essential an occupation for me as anything I did as a writer, while also falling short of being a career or a profession. On one occasion a photographer did arrive at our Suffolk home to take many pictures for a magazine feature on 'wild gardens', but the visit was all that came of it, and I was never told whether the garden was found too wild or not wild enough for inclusion in the series. That gardens are as much a matter of taste and convention as poems was brought home to me much earlier, when I showed Count Umberto Morra round our two acres or so at Tilehurst. At the end of the tour he said that he had enjoyed our walk, then added: 'But where is your garden?' Conditioned, as he was, to formal Italian gardens, he could not even see the peculiar balance between nature and art, wildness and amenity, I had put so much labour into establishing or maintaining there. It would have been fatuous to draw his attention to the wildflowers that coexisted there with the exotic evergreen magnolia, *grandiflora*, or the white alpine strawberries I had introduced and propagated with as much care as I gave to the fruit trees that owed their presence there to centuries of selection and experiment. Nor would it have helped to explain that, unlike the gardens he knew and recognized as gardens, its upkeep was my own handiwork, though it had been laid down originally to be enjoyed by 'gentry', but maintained by full-time, trained and specialized labourers. At a reading I gave at a public school — I think it was Eton — the presiding English teacher's comment was that I had read only one poem. The rest was prose, because it did not rhyme or scan. There I was able to answer back, pointing out that rhyme was only one of many modes and conventions of verse, and metre only the easiest, often the crudest, way of organizing its rhythms and sounds. This, clearly, was not what he taught his pupils; and most probably he could not hear my 'free' verse any more than Umberto Morra could see my informal garden. The gardening I did was another mug's game, played for its own sake and for the conservation of what I felt to be worth conserving in the way of foliage, flower or fruit; and, like the snooker table of my early poem 'A Poet's Progress', each garden of mine also became an 'unguarded solitude, hospitable to all'. What the visitors could make of it was up to them.

Not being a gardener yet, for that early poem I drew on an indoor game I had played once or twice in my adolescence — at a private house in blacked-out war-time London — as a simile for the mug's game of poetry. It was this snooker simile, sustained throughout the poem, that made the verse look new or modern at the time, and has made it partly historical now: snooker balls are no longer made of 'rare ivory', which has become so rare as to threaten the African elephant with extinction; and in Britain the game itself has been brought into any home that can endure or enjoy it, by television, becoming highly lucrative 'show biz', as poetry has not. So it is only the lone practising of the poem that remains actual as analogy; and the prediction, as far as I am concerned, because I did have to withdraw from the London-based literary scene so important to me in youth and early middle age, shedding even the 'best ambitions' of the poem. These have been driven out by concern about all the other games being played outside, on a playground far more 'evil' and 'lawless' than the snooker table. To do my own thing to the best of my ability is still the unquestioned requirement; but I now know how lucky I was to have a thing of my own to do, and that my mug's game could turn out to have been a waste of time not because I wasn't good enough at it, but because there will be no one left to invite into my 'unguarded solitude', house, garden or book, even if it is not obliterated physically like our house and garden at Tilehurst or my childhood home in St. John's Wood Park. An age of post-literacy and post-civility may be the least threatening of the prospects now to be faced.

For British writers the post-literacy would be less of a blow than for those in other countries, where writers constitute a clerisy or intelligentsia, with a claim to influence, if not power, though as individuals they may be solitary, eccentric or egregious. The prevalent (if often unacknowledged) function of British writers is to be not legislators but entertainers. This applies to poets, too, ever since Chaucer and not excluding Shakespeare, as a jobbing playwright. True, there are others, from Milton to Blake, Wordsworth and D. H. Lawrence, with claims to a vatic or visionary exemplariness which they may even have exercised at times, in places, without being acknowledged as national institutions. In so far as British writers remain entertainers, their performance is more dependent on the requirements and standards, the state of culture, of those whom they serve than the performance of their counterparts in countries where the acknowledged function of writers is an exemplary one. (As I write this, a Czech playwright has been elected President of his country, a Russian poet has been debating with the President of his country, and East German intellectuals are in the forefront of a political revolution in that State. Latin America provides many other instances.) Here the post-civility becomes critical. If those requirements and standards decline very steeply, as they are doing now in Britain, acute problems arise for the arts and for literature, as for sciences that fall no less short of being immediately useful as some artistic pursuits do of being immediately entertaining.

There may be no measurable difference between works of art that keep us entertained by merely catching and holding our attention and those that entertain us by enriching or transforming our awareness; but the difference is no less real for that. In Latin, Italian and Spanish it is a compliment to call someone 'egregious'. It means 'distinguished' or 'eminent', because to be 'gregious' is to be sheep-like, to run with the herd or flock. Despite a long tradition of English eccentricity and independence of mind, English writers are now expected to wear brand marks that make them easily identifiable as products of a breed, class or region. 'Egregious' is not only pejorative, but as damning as the word 'élitist', where people have become incapable of distinguishing between the requirements of a skill and those of social systems and attitudes. Democracy is the name given to a great variety of political systems, none of which has functioned without élites of one sort or another, whether elected or imposed by other means. I could never understand why it should be thought undemocratic to prefer the best to the second-rate or worse; but that may be an incurable blind spot of mine.

At the one dinner I ever attended at my old school, Westminster, for the retirement of its Head Master, J. D. Carleton, I met his predecessor J. T. Christie, who had been my Head Master some thirty years before the event. 'Ah, Hamburger,' he said, 'you've published a good many books, I gather, made quite a reputation for yourself as an intellectual. Well done. But we mustn't be priggish, must we?' No, indeed we must not, if it's our need or wish to fit in, to be acceptable. Those few words were enough to erase the thirty years as though they had never been, by putting me and my endeavours in their place. I could only smile at the neat reproof or caution. To J. T. Christie I was still the boy who, honourably and priggishly, had owned up to his part in the letter that told the truth, unpolitically, about the catering at our host college, Lancing, a letter that had made him smile in spite of his function; and the boy to whom he had awarded a 'digniora' in one of his divinity lessons — for taking it more seriously than it was meant to be taken, for priggishness. Quite truthfully, I think, J. T. Christie used to say, 'It hurts me more than it hurts you' to boys he had to cane. I should have liked to ask him what he thought of a fellow pupil of mine at the school, Tony Benn — much more notorious than I for an obstinate disregard of what was good for him; but I'd had my turn, and was never to meet J. T. Christie again. Besides, it would have been impertinent of me to ask that question. Compared with politics, literature was a marginal pursuit, and one in which priggishness harmed only oneself.

Morally, there is much to be said for the British attitude to artists and intellectuals, which does not encourage them to think themselves important, exemplary or indispensable; but neither does it encourage them to excel, if excellence is equated with arrogance, 'élitism' or 'egregiousness'. One can be unassuming about one's status yet uncompromising about one's values and commitments; and there is the false humility of those who run with the flock or herd because it is safer, more comfortable and more expedient — as long as that flock or herd is not running to its destruction, like the Gadarine swine. It is the humility of those who don't presume to have principles or only judgements of their own, who never stick their necks out, unless it is at the feeding-trough.

Among contemporary poets I was placed under the rubric 'Influences from Abroad' by one anthologist, who added in a note: 'Curiously enough, his own poetry remains more 'English' in flavour than that of some of his collaborators, such as Christopher Middleton.' (To set the record straight, Christopher Middleton and I collaborated only in a single short piece of writing, our Introduction to a bilingual anthology we co-edited in the 'sixties, *Modern German Poetry*. Beyond that, for a time we put together translations done quite independently of each other within the covers of a few books; and I can only wonder who any other collaborator of mine might be.) If it seemed curious to the anthologist that my poems should be 'more "English" in flavour' than that of other poets in his pigeon-hole, it is either because I was born in Germany or because I am 'better known as a translator'. It happens, though, that my earliest poems were influenced more by French models than by German ones; and that later it was American poets, above all, that shook me out of my rhymed stanzaic forms. If my poems did remain 'English' in flavour, despite those jolts, it is because they have remained firmly anchored in places, persons and things, representational even where the experience drawn on was dreams, with the 'literal imagination' that Christopher Middleton once ascribed to me, by no means as a compliment. Edward Lucie-Smith's anthology appeared in 1970. In later years the obligatory pigeon-holing or branding became so problematic in my case that most anthologists and critics found it easier to exclude my work.

Simile of the kind that ran through my early poem 'A Poet's Progress' is one of the poetic tricks I have learnt to do without. Metaphor, though, is inherent in language itself, not least in its most idiomatic, colloquial strata. Even the plainest diction cannot avoid it. Where no single word in a poem is deliberately and overtly metaphorical, it is the whole poem that becomes a metaphor, if it becomes a poem at all. Except for the kind of verse I have called 'owls' pellets' — 'poetry of the left hand', Robert Graves called it — which regurgitates the verbiage and jargon of our suicidal world for satirical or polemical purposes, I have come to prefer the plainest words. 'Poems of the right hand' are love poems, though mine may be about landscapes, townscapes, animals or plants as often as about human beings. All poetry that is not satirical is love poetry, poetry of celebration, no matter what it is about or whether it is in a major or minor key.

So it makes no difference to me whether I am classified as this or that, as a 'nature poet', for instance, or as an urban one. City, suburb, countryside, and their interactions, have been my concern from the start. It was only in middle life that I experienced true wilderness, in America, finding a fourth order and paradigm. All four have met and clashed in my poems. I have tried not to falsify the hardships and cruelties of any of these orders, whatever my personal preferences. In inter-human affairs, both experience and faith convince me, gentleness is stronger than assertiveness, mercy and magnanimity are stronger than retribution. Yet when the long-suffering, exploited and oppressed are exasperated into violence, I am on their side.

Whatever I may have done or known in my life, my poetry came out of a kind of wonderment whose other side — the left hand — is a sense of outrage. In general, too, this capacity to wonder, and to feel outrage, strikes me as a distinguishing attribute of poets, and a condition of their persistence in the mug's game. This core of naivety can go with a good deal of sophistication and worldly wisdom, but not, I think, with a smug or cynical accommodation to things as they are. If the wonderment and the outrage dry up, so does — or should — the poet. To many, therefore, poets are freaks who would become formidable monsters if they were taken seriously, because a core of naivety, even of childishness, lies hidden in most people, however mature they thing themselves or are taken to be — very much as an old cat, grown staid and dignified, will revert to kittenish play from time to time. That could be the main reason why poetry, a game played for no calculable public in a world engaged in other pursuits, is not as obsolete as, sociologically, it was judged to have become long ago.

Ultimately, though, it is not my business to ask why or how I go on, how or why my work appeals or does not appeal to those who read such work — a tiny minority at the best of times — nor even whether it will prove durable enough to have been worth the price paid for doing it. What matters to me now is the durability of that for which it was a receptacle and conductor. My business is to remain true to the wonderment and outrage as long as they recur, always unexpectedly, always a little differently, always in a way I can neither plan nor choose; and to keep quiet when there is nothing that wants to use me to make itself heard.

Index